ALL·IN·ONE

AWS Certified Solutions Architect Associate

EXAM GUIDE

(Exam SAA-C01)

W0010426

ABOUT THE AUTHOR

Joyjeet Banerjee works as an enterprise solutions architect with Amazon Web Services where he crafts highly scalable, flexible, and resilient cloud architectures that address customer business needs. Joyjeet helps organizations understand best practices around advanced cloud-based solutions and how to migrate existing workloads to the cloud.

Before joining AWS, Joyjeet worked as an enterprise architect with Oracle's Engineered System team based at Oracle Headquarters in California. Before joining the Oracle Engineered System team, Joyjeet was with Oracle Consulting where he assisted customers implement Oracle products. During his tenure at Oracle, he wrote several books on Oracle Database, Oracle Applications, and Exadata.

Joyjeet is a regular guest speaker at AWS reInvent, AWS Summit, AWS Popup LOFT, AWS Webinars, OAUG, Collaborate, and Oracle OpenWorld. He was on the panel of Oracle University that reviewed the course content and set up questions for the OCP for the Oracle Database, RAC, and Oracle Applications tracks.

Joyjeet earned an MBA in systems and operations management and was recently honored as an "Oracle Innovator" (www.oracle.com/us/products/applications/ebusiness/conversations-with-innovators-070240.html).

About the Technical Editor

Dhanraj Pondicherry manages a Solution Architect team at Amazon Web Services. His passion is to help customers, partners, or just anyone who's curious about understanding AWS to the level required for their specific use-case. With an education in computer science, and having worked with databases and database applications, he is especially passionate about all things data. He enjoys enabling customers on their journey with different data stores for applications, building analytics platforms, and beyond.

ALL · IN · ONE

AWS Certified Solutions Architect Associate

EXAM GUIDE

(Exam SAA-C01)

Joyjeet Banerjee

New York   Chicago   San Francisco
Athens   London   Madrid   Mexico City
Milan   New Delhi   Singapore   Sydney   Toronto

Library of Congress Cataloging-in-Publication Data

Names: Banerjee, Joyjeet, author.
Title: AWS certified solutions architect associate all-in-one exam guide
    (Exam SAA-C01) / Joyjeet Banerjee.
Description: First edition. | New York : McGraw-Hill Education, [2019] |
    Includes index.
Identifiers: LCCN 2018031625 | ISBN 9781260108279 (set/package : alk. paper)
Subjects: LCSH: Web services—Examinations—Study guides. | Cloud
    computing—Examinations—Study guides. | Amazon Web Services
    (Firm)—Examinations—Study guides.
Classification: LCC TK5105.88813 .B338 2019 | DDC 004.67/82076—dc23
LC record available at https://lccn.loc.gov/2018031625

McGraw-Hill Education books are available at special quantity discounts to use as premiums and sales promotions, or for use in corporate training programs. To contact a representative, please visit the Contact Us pages at www.mhprofessional.com.

AWS Certified Solutions Architect Associate All-in-One Exam Guide (Exam SAA-C01)

1 2 3 4 5 6 7 8 9 LCR 21 20 19 18

ISBN: Book p/n 978-1-260-10824-8 and CD p/n 978-1-260-10825-5
of set 978-1-260-10827-9

MHID: Book p/n 1-260-10824-4 and CD p/n 1-260-10825-2
of set 1-260-10827-9

Sponsoring Editor Lisa McClain	**Technical Editor** Dhanraj Pondicherry	**Production Supervisor** Lynn M. Messina
Editorial Supervisor Patty Mon	**Copy Editor** Kim Wimpsett	**Composition** Cenveo Publisher Services
Project Manager Jyotsna Ojha, Cenveo® Publisher Services	**Proofreader** Paul Tyler **Indexer** Jack Lewis	**Illustration** Cenveo Publisher Services **Art Director, Cover** Jeff Weeks
Acquisitions Coordinator Claire Yee		

This book is dedicated to my guru, Paramahansa Yogananda,
for his wisdom; my mom; my dad; my sisters,
Joyeeta and Tiya; my brothers-in-law, Sagar and Riju;
my little sweet niece, Saanjh; and my lovely nephew, Manav.

CONTENTS AT A GLANCE

5

4

7 SQS/SNS
Lambda
Step function

6

CONTENTS

ACKNOWLEDGMENTS

Many people have contributed a lot to the successful completion of this book. I would like to use this opportunity to thank all of you. Without your help, it would have been difficult for me to finish this book.

I would like to thank Lisa McClain, senior editor at McGraw-Hill Education, for her enthusiastic support and motivation throughout the book, for making adjustments to the schedule whenever there was a fire drill at my job, and for helping me in every possible way to make this book a reality; Claire Yee, editorial coordinator at McGraw-Hill Education, for managing this project and always staying on top of things to make this happen; Jyotsna Ojha of Cenveo Publisher Services for helping me in all phases of the production of this book; Patty Mon, editorial supervisor; and Kim Wimpsett for helping me in editing this book; and Paul Tyler for proofreading.

I would like to thank Dhanraj Pondicherry, senior manager of Amazon Web Services, for the technical review of this book and for providing his valuable feedback and advice at every step. I would also like to thank Francessca Vasquez, director of Amazon Web Services; Matthew Menz, director of Amazon Web Services; and the Amazon legal and PR teams for providing all the necessary approvals.

Last, but not least, I would like to thank to all my friends and colleagues who, without fail, motivated and encouraged me to make this happen.

INTRODUCTION

Congratulations! You have made the right move by deciding to pursue AWS certification. AWS Solutions Architect certification is one of the hottest certifications in the industry right now, and you are just a step away from being certified. Each year, Global Knowledge, an industry-leading training company, publishes its IT Skills and Training Report. This is a well-respected tool for assessing the trends and skills in high demand in the market. A summary of the 2018 data is available online in the article "15 Top-Paying IT Certifications for 2018" written by Global Knowledge instructor John Hales. As the article indicates, the AWS Certified Solutions Architect – Associate exam ranks second among the top-paying certifications, with a yearly salary of $121,292 (https://www.globalknowledge.com/us-en/content/articles/top-paying-certifications/#2). Given the continued dominance of AWS in the public cloud market, the demand for AWS professionals—especially those with a certification—is expected to continue to grow for the foreseeable future. The goal of this resource is to provide you with practical, hands-on knowledge in addition to preparing you for the certification exam.

About the Exam

Amazon has recently introduced the new version of the exam AWS Certified Solutions Architect–Associate (released in February 2018). This version of the exam introduces a lot of new topics and service offerings. The new exam reflects changes in the solutions architect role since the original exam was launched four years ago. The examination contains 65 questions, and you have 130 minutes to finish the examination. This exam validates an examinee's ability to effectively demonstrate knowledge of how to architect and deploy secure and robust applications on AWS technologies. The examination contains multiple-choice questions; sometimes one option is a correct one, and other times two or even three options will be correct. The examination will tell how you many options to choose.

It validates an examinee's ability to

- Define a solution using architectural design principles based on customer requirements
- Provide implementation guidance based on best practices to the organization throughout the life cycle of the project

As per the AWS Certification web site (https://aws.amazon.com/certification/certified-solutions-architect-associate/), the AWS Certified Solutions Architect–Associate exam is intended for individuals with experience designing distributed applications and systems on the AWS platform. Exam concepts you should understand for this exam include

- Designing and deploying scalable, highly available, and fault-tolerant systems on AWS
- Lifting and shifting an existing on-premises application to AWS
- Ingressing and egressing data to and from AWS
- Selecting the appropriate AWS service based on data, compute, database, or security requirements
- Identifying appropriate use of AWS architectural best practices
- Estimating AWS costs and identifying cost-control mechanisms
- Hands-on experience using compute, networking, storage, and database AWS services
- Hands-on experience with AWS deployment and management services
- Identifying and defining the technical requirements for an AWS-based application
- Identifying which AWS services meet a given technical requirement
- Understanding recommended best practices for building secure and reliable applications on the AWS platform
- Understanding the basic architectural principles of building on the AWS cloud
- Understanding the AWS global infrastructure
- Understanding network technologies as they relate to AWS
- Understanding security features and tools that AWS provides and how they relate to traditional services

The examination is divided into five domains. The following are the main content domains and their weightings:

Domain	% of Examination
Domain 1: Design Resilient Architectures	34%
Domain 2: Define Performant Architectures	24%
Domain 3: Specify Secure Applications and Architectures	26%
Domain 4: Design Cost-Optimized Architectures	10%
Domain 5: Define Operationally Excellent Architectures	6%
Total	100%

Objective Map

The following table of official exam objectives includes the objectives and where you will find them in the book:

Official Objective	Exam Guide Coverage
Domain 1: Design Resilient Architectures	
1.1 Choose reliable/resilient storage.	2
1.2 Determine how to design decoupling mechanisms using AWS services.	4, 5, 7, 8
1.3 Determine how to design a multi-tier architecture solution.	2, 3, 4, 5, 6
1.4 Determine how to design high availability and/or fault tolerant architectures.	3, 4, 6, 8, 9
Domain 2: Define Performant Architectures	
2.1 Choose performant storage and databases.	2, 8
2.2 Apply caching to improve performance.	8
2.3 Design solutions for elasticity and scalability.	2
Domain 3: Specify Secure Applications and Architectures	
3.1 Determine how to secure application tiers.	3, 5, 7
3.2 Determine how to secure data.	5, 8, 9
3.3 Define the networking infrastructure for a single VPC application.	3
Domain 4: Design Cost-Optimized Architectures	
4.1 Determine how to design cost-optimized storage.	2, 9
4.2 Determine how to design cost-optimized compute.	4, 9
Domain 5: Define Operationally Excellent Architectures	
5.1 Choose design features in solutions that enable operational excellence.	9

About the Book

This book was written with the February 2018 exam in mind. This book covers all the topics required to pass this version of the exam. When you study the chapters, you will find that AWS has a shared responsibility model; this means AWS is responsible for the security *of* the cloud, and the customer is responsible for the security *in* the cloud. To pass the exam, you also have to follow the *shared study model,* in which the book is going to give you the theoretical knowledge, and the AWS console is going to provide you with the practical knowledge. You need to have both theoretical and practical knowledge to pass this examination.

While studying for the examination, the AWS console is going to be your best friend. You need to create an account with the AWS console if you don't have one already.

You can create one by going to https://aws.amazon.com/console/. AWS offers free cloud service for one year under the free tier, so most of the services you will be using should fall into this category. It is important that you do all the labs in this book to get practical, hands-on experience on each subject. In addition to doing the labs, you should browse all the options in the console for a particular service. The more you explore the various options, the quicker you learn.

Amazon has 14 principles that every Amazonian uses on a daily basis. You can learn about them on the internet. To pass the examination, you need to pay careful attention to two of them: "Learn and Be Curious" and "Deep Dive." For every service you learn about in this book, go to the console and browse every possible option. Try to understand what an option does, why it is of use, and so on. Once you do this for all the services, nothing can stop you from passing the examination.

Currently AWS has 90+ different services, and as an SA, it is difficult to go deep into each one of them. There are some core services of AWS that are needed no matter what you want to do with AWS. These core services are also called *foundational services*. Examples include regions, AZs, Amazon Virtual Private Cloud (VPC), Amazon EC2 servers, ELB, AWS Auto Scaling, storage, networking, databases, AWS IAM, and security. You should have in-depth knowledge about the core services. Besides the core services, there are various other services of AWS such as analytics, machine learning, application services, and so on. For the other services, you don't need to have in-depth knowledge, but you should be able to articulate what that service does, what the common use cases are for that service, when to choose one service over another, and so on.

This book is divided into nine chapters. Chapter 1, "Overview of Cloud Computing and Amazon Web Services," gives an overview of Amazon Web Services. It teaches you the concepts of cloud computing, the advantages of cloud computing and AWS, and the building blocks of AWS. It also introduces you to the various offerings of AWS.

Chapter 2, "Storage on AWS," talks about all the storage offerings and includes Amazon Simple Shared Storage, Glacier, Elastic Block Store, Elastic File System, and various ways of migrating data to AWS. After reading this chapter, you should have deep knowledge of all the storage offerings.

Chapter 3, "Virtual Private Cloud," is focused on networking. It introduces the concept of Amazon Virtual Private Cloud. It covers how to create a network in the cloud, what some of the network offerings are, and so on. This chapter is also part of the core services.

Chapter 4, "Introduction to Amazon Elastic Compute Cloud," introduces Amazon Elastic Compute Cloud (EC2). In this chapter, you will learn the various instance types that AWS supports, how to create an instance, and how to add storage to an instance. EC2 is one of the core services of AWS.

Chapter 5, "Identity and Access Management and Security on AWS," focuses on the security of the cloud. You will learn about the shared responsibility model and how to secure a cloud environment. You will also learn about identity management, how to create a user and group, and how to integrate your existing users to AWS using federation. IAM is also part of the core services.

Chapter 6, "Auto Scaling," focuses on Elastic Load Balancer and Auto Scaling. It talks about all the different types of load balancers AWS has, including application, network, and classic load balancers. You will also learn about a service that makes the cloud very scalable, which is Auto Scaling. Auto Scaling is one of the reasons why customers are seamlessly able to scale up and scale down instantly as per their demand. This is also one of the core services.

Chapter 7, "Deploying and Monitoring Applications on AWS," focuses on deploying and monitoring applications on AWS. This chapter introduces lots of services that you need to know to build, deploy, and monitor your application in AWS. While reading this chapter, you will find that there are multiple ways of deploying an application. For example, you can use a combination of EC2, RDS, EBS servers, and VPC and deploy your application in a classic way. Another way is to use Elastic Beanstalk and deploy your application, or you can build a totally serverless application. You should be able to tell the pros and cons of choosing one architecture over the other in terms of built-in resiliency, easy manageability, performance, security, and cost. This chapter also focuses on monitoring the applications you are going to deploy in AWS. You need to know which monitoring tool to use for monitoring a specific aspect. You are not required to go very deep into all these services; however, you should know what a particular services does, what the use cases are, when to choose one over the other, and so on. In this chapter, there are no labs since the examination does not cover all these services in details; that does not mean you should not explore these services via the AWS console. For all these services, check out their options in the AWS console. For example, let's take in detail Amazon Kinesis Firehose. Go to the console and create a delivery stream, explore all the data input sources, and look at all the destination sources (you will realize that there are four destinations: Amazon S3, Amazon Redshift, Amazon Elasticsearch Service, and Splunk). Bingo! That's an examination question. At the end you don't have to create the firehose delivery stream; you can click the Cancel button at the last step. By doing this, you will have enough practical knowledge to pass the examination.

Chapter 8, "Databases on AWS," covers Amazon RDS, which is one of the core services of AWS. You should be able to tell when to host a database on EC2 servers and when to host a database on RDS. You should also know about Amazon's other database, which is Amazon Aurora. In addition, you should know about Amazon Redshift (the data warehouse offering), Amazon DynamoDB (the NoSQL database), and Amazon ElastiCache (the in-memory data store offering). All the topics included in this chapter are core services.

Chapter 9, "AWS Well-Architected Framework and Best Practices," covers architecture best practices. This chapter is divided into five domains, the same domains on which this examination focuses. After going through this chapter, you should be able to design with the five core tenets. As a solution architect, when you design architecture, you should design the architecture across these five pillars.

About the Digital Content

This book provides access to the Total Tester exam software, a customizable test engine that allows you to generate a complete practice exam in either exam or practice mode, which provides in-depth explanations, and to generate quizzes by chapter or by exam domain. You will have the option of accessing this test engine via CD-ROM or online. See the appendix, "About the Digital Content," for more information.

Overview of Cloud Computing and Amazon Web Services

In this chapter, you will

- Get an overview of cloud computing
- Learn the advantages of running cloud computing on AWS
- Look at three models of cloud computing
- Look at three cloud computing deployment models
- Explore the history of AWS
- Be introduced to AWS regions and availability zones
- Learn about AWS security and compliance
- Review AWS products and services

Overview of Cloud Computing

The National Institute of Standards and Technology (NIST) defines *cloud computing* as "Ubiquitous, convenient, on-demand access to shared computing resources that can be rapidly provisioned and released with minimal management effort." In other words, cloud computing is the on-demand delivery of IT resources available from the Internet with a pay-as-you-go model. Thus, the following are the three basic characteristics of the cloud:

- **On demand**   Cloud computing enables you to use IT infrastructure as a resource that is always available on demand per your needs. For example, when you go home and switch on a light, you don't care from where the power is coming. You don't generate power in your home. You know that power is always readily available for you irrespective of your needs, and you will be billed according to your usage. In the same way, cloud computing allows you to provision any IT resource on demand.

- **Accessible from the Internet**   All the resources that you deploy in the cloud are accessible from the Internet, which means you can spin up resources from anywhere in the globe and have your users work on those resources instantly from anywhere. If you want the resources to be available only from your corporate network and not the

Internet, you have the option to do that too. You can also connect to a cloud vendor such as Amazon Web Services (AWS) directly so that you can bypass the public Internet. You will explore this in subsequent chapters of the book.

- **Pay-as-you-go model**   When you use power in your home, you pay only for what you actually use. In the same way, when you use cloud computing, you pay per your usage. For example, if you need a server to run a job for two hours, you pay for the server usage for two hours and no more. Most cloud resources are billed on an hourly basis, but some cloud resource may be billed on a separate metric.

With cloud computing you don't have to own or manage your own data center or buy your own servers. You just provision the provider's resources—compute (server), storage, network, database, and any other service—as per your needs. You can scale up and scale down seamlessly without worrying about where the resources are. AWS manages and maintains the technology and infrastructure in a secure environment, and businesses access the resources via the Internet or via private connections. There are many reasons for using the cloud. For example, as an enterprise, you can run all your applications that support the business in the cloud, you can shift existing applications to the cloud, you can build all your new applications for the cloud, and so on. If you are a startup, you can just focus on the next big idea and forget about purchasing and managing the hardware. Thus, cloud computing caters to everyone's need regardless of whether you work as an individual, in a startup, or in an established enterprise.

You must be wondering, how exactly are the resources provisioned in the cloud almost instantly? Well, cloud service providers such as AWS own and maintain the hardware and keep it ready so that whenever you request some resource, it is available. In fact, AWS keeps network-connected hardware in multiple data centers and in multiple geographies so that you can provision the resource in the location nearest to you to get the best user experience. You will see this in more detail when you study regions and availability zones later in this chapter.

Advantages of Running Cloud Computing on AWS

The following are the advantages of running cloud computing on AWS:

- **Gaining agility**   Say you wanted to start a new project; the first thing you would do is provision hardware for the project. In a traditional IT model, it can take months to provision the resources before you can actually start the project. With the cloud, you can provision all the resources you need almost instantly, saving months of time procuring them. In some organizations, the procurement process is so complex that it can take up to three to four months just to get the hardware. By provisioning the resources in the cloud, you can eliminate this time and start your project early. In a similar fashion, if you want to scale up your infrastructure, you don't have to wait; you can do it instantly.

- **Avoiding guessing about capacity**   In a traditional enterprise, whenever you procure the infrastructure for any workload, the first thing you do is to size it. You take various metrics into consideration such as the number of users, the volume of transactions, the desired response time, the expected growth, service level agreements (SLAs), and so on, and come up with the hardware sizing. In some enterprises, it takes months to size the hardware correctly. When you purchase hardware, it sits in your data center for a minimum of three years. In the meantime, if the application requirement changes, it is difficult to refresh the hardware. If you oversize the hardware, you will have unused capacity for which you have already paid but are not using, but if you undersize, you are going to have business and performance impacts. Say you are designing the infrastructure for a portal where customers place orders. On Black Friday you anticipate 20 times more orders than the whole rest of the year. What do you do? Do you provision 20 times more hardware? If you do, you have 20 times unused capacity for the entire year, and if you don't, you won't be able to meet the demand on Black Friday. With the cloud, you don't have to worry about guessing capacity. Since the cloud is *elastic,* which means you can scale up and scale down based on your requirements at any time, you can provision only the resources that you need at any point of time. When you need more resources, you can quickly scale up, and when you don't need them, you can just scale down. For the Black Friday example, if you have to design the architecture in the cloud, you just spin up all the resources one day before Black Friday, and once the big day is over, you can scale down. This way you don't overpay for the unused resources and also never run under capacity if your application demands additional resources.

- **Moving from capital expenses to variable/flexible expenses** Cloud computing allows you to trade all your capital expenses for variable expenses. Whenever you purchase hardware, it always has an up-front capital expense associated with it. The capital expense model does not promote innovation in a company. Say you want to experiment with something, and for that you need to procure hardware. So, you make a huge up-front capital investment, but after three months you realize that the project does not make any sense and you need to stop experimenting. You just lost your huge investment. In addition, if you want to experiment with something else, it might require a different kind of hardware. It becomes difficult to get approval for new hardware each time you want to start a project. With an operational expense model, you have *zero* up-front costs. As a result, you don't have to think much before you start a new project. Even if it does not go well, you can get rid of all the resources just by paying the usage cost of them. The variable expense model facilitates innovation since you can experiment as many times as you want.

- **Benefiting from massive economics of scale** You might have noticed when you go to Costco that most of the products are often 10 to 15 percent cheaper than market price. This is because Costco buys in bulk and sells in bulk, and therefore massive economies of scale come into the picture. In the same way, a user of cloud computing benefits from the massive economics of scale since hundreds of thousands of customers are aggregated in the cloud. This in turns translates to low pay-as-you-go prices.

- **Avoiding spending money on data centers** The cloud computing model allows you to stop paying for your own data center. Whenever you manage a data center, you need to manage the heavy lifting, racking, and powering of servers, and you have to pay for space, staff, physical security, planning, and so on. With cloud computing you don't have any overhead to manage the data center, and you can focus more on what the business needs.

- **Benefiting from the pace of innovation**   AWS is innovating at a startling pace. Customers can use all the new product and features instantly, whenever they are released. There is no need to upgrade or do anything in order to use the new features. The moment a new feature is available, it is automatically available to you.

- **Going global in minutes**   Say you are running all your operations from one data center and are creating a business continuity plan and want to set up a disaster recovery site in a different part of the country. Or let's say because of how well your business is doing you have to open an additional data center in a different part of the world. How much time do you think either of these examples is going to take? Three months? Six months? In a traditional model, it takes a minimum of three to six months to start operating from a different region. With cloud computing, you don't have to wait for months or even days to operate from a different region. With just a few mouse clicks and a few minutes, you can be ready to operate from a different region. So, if you want to deploy or host your application from a different part of the globe or if you want to have a disaster recovery system on a different continent, you can do it almost instantly.

Three Models of Cloud Computing

There are three models of cloud computing; when you choose to use cloud computing, you can choose any one of them or all three of these models depending on your business needs, how much control you want to have, how much you want to manage, and so on. The models are Infrastructure as a Service (IaaS), Platform as a Service (PaaS), and Software as a Service (SaaS).

- **IaaS**   IaaS provides the foundation for a cloud IT environment that includes compute (server), networking, storage, and space in a data center. IaaS lets you manage the IT resources just like the way you manage them in your own data center. It provides you with complete flexibility, and you have total control over all the resources you spin off. You can visualize IaaS as your own data center in your cloud.

- **PaaS**   With the IaaS model, you manage the overall infrastructure. If you don't want the overhead of managing the infrastructure but just want to focus on deploying and managing the applications, then PaaS is the model you need. PaaS eliminates the job of managing the entire infrastructure layer. With the PaaS model, a cloud service provider such as AWS manages the entire infrastructure for you. As a result, you can be even more efficient and focus on the business needs without worrying about infrastructure, capacity planning, patching cycles, upgrades, and so on.

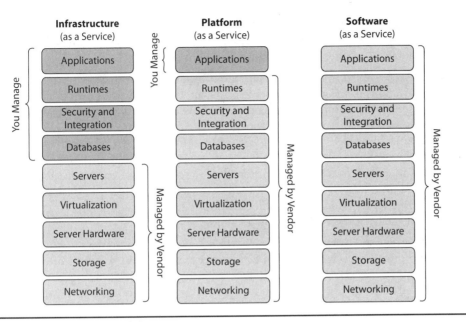

Figure 1-1   Three cloud models

- **SaaS**   The SaaS model is even simpler than PaaS. SaaS is a way of delivering applications over the Internet. If you choose the SaaS model, the SaaS provider offers a complete product that is hosted and managed by the product vendor. With the SaaS model, you just need to think about how you are going to use the product. You don't have to think about where and how the software is hosted, how to manage the software behind the scenes, what the patching or upgrading cycle is, what the maintenance window is, and so on. One of the most popular examples of SaaS software today is Salesforce.

Figure 1-1 depicts the three models of cloud computing, showing your responsibility versus the responsibility of the cloud vendor.

Three Cloud Computing Deployment Models

The following are three deployment models when working in the cloud:

- **All-in cloud**   When you design and deploy an application in a public cloud using a cloud service provider such as AWS, this kind of deployment is called an *all-in cloud*. There are two ways you can opt for an all-in cloud. First, you can create all your new applications in the cloud, or second, you can migrate existing applications to the cloud to take advantage of all the features of the cloud. Cloud-based applications either can be built on low-level infrastructure pieces or can use higher-level services that abstract the management, architecting, and scaling requirements of the core infrastructure. You might have seen in the news recently that Netflix has opted for an all-in cloud strategy, closing all its data centers and hosting all the streaming content in AWS.

- **Hybrid**   With the hybrid deployment model, you host some of the applications in the cloud and some of the applications at your own premises. By seamlessly connecting them together, the cloud acts as an extension of your own data center. This is the quickest way to embrace the cloud. Most organizations have already made huge investments in data centers running legacy applications, and it is not easy to move to the cloud instantly. With a hybrid cloud strategy, you can start deploying all your new applications to the cloud immediately and create a road map to migrate legacy IT systems to the cloud over a period of time. Cloud vendors such as AWS help their customers with the hybrid cloud deployment model.

- **On-premise or private cloud**   When you deploy the resources in your own data center using virtualization or resource management tools, it is often called an *on-premise cloud* or a *private cloud*. With a private cloud, you get some of the advantages of a public cloud but not all of them since it is impossible to mimic all the services the public cloud vendor provides at your own data center. Using a private cloud strategy, you can segregate your resources and can meter them and charge back to respective business units depending on their usage. Most customers started their migration journey from on-premise data centers with an implementation of a private cloud; this was about going from nonvirtualized servers to virtualization with automated consumption and chargeback capabilities. With virtualization, instead of assigning a full physical server to a project, a "compute node" gets assigned. This capability been around for decades in various forms, such as zones/containers in Solaris, IBM's server partitioning, and VMware ESX. Private clouds are basically the virtualization technology with self-service capabilities such as provisioning, start/stop/resize, and chargebacks.

History of AWS

Amazon is famous for innovation. The pace at which Amazon innovates amazes me sometimes. Even as a solutions architect I sometimes find it difficult to keep up with the latest products and services because the pace at which AWS releases them is unbelievable. The best part of Amazon's culture is it experiments with lots of things; of course, not all of them are successful, but those that are successful are wonders. AWS is one example of a successful experiment that has made history in cloud computing technology.

Amazon.com has been around for decades now. While operating and provisioning resources for Amazon.com, Amazon realized it had developed a core competency in operating massive-scale technologies and data centers. So, Amazon began offering this excess capacity to developers and businesses to build sophisticated, modern, and scalable applications, and that is how AWS started. AWS was officially launched in 2006. AWS has more than 50 products and has been named a leader in the IaaS space by Gartner's Magic Quadrant for the sixth consecutive year (as of August 2016).

AWS Regions and Availability Zones

AWS has more than a million customers in 190 countries around the world. To serve these customers, AWS maintains 18 regions and one local region spanning five continents in the world, with four additional regions being planned. A *region* is a physical location in the world that comprises clusters of highly redundant data centers. The regions are separated geographically, which provides data sovereignty. You can think of a region as a distinct geographical location where AWS services are made available.

 NOTE By default, data residing in a region never leaves a region unless explicitly moved by AWS customers.

When you use an AWS service, you choose the region where you want to host the services. You can also choose multiple regions depending on where you want to store the data.

AWS also offers the GovCloud region in the United States, which is designed for government agencies to run their workloads in the cloud. Though it is designed for government agencies, other customers can also use this region.

Within each region there are *availability zones* (AZs). An AZ consists of one to six data centers, with redundant power supplies and networking connectivity. As of this writing, there are 53 AZs. A single data center can be part of only one AZ. Each AZ is located in a different floodplain; power grids are designed in such a way that a natural calamity or disaster does not impact multiple AZs. The AZs have redundant power supplies that come via different power utility companies, plus backup generators to handle an extreme power failure. The AZs are engineered to be insulated from failures in other AZs. The networking among the AZs in a particular region is designed in such a way that it offers inexpensive, low-latency, private, fiber-optic network connectivity to another AZ in the same region. The latency between the AZs within a region is less than a single digit. As a result, you can synchronously replicate the data across the AZs. The biggest advantage of this is that you can design an application in such a way that it can run on multiple AZs, and since the data can be synchronously replicated within the AZs, in the case of a disaster taking one of the AZs down, there is no impact on your application. You can even architect an application in such a way that it automatically fails over between different AZs without any service interruption. You can choose which AZs you want to host your applications.

All the AWS data centers are always *hot,* which means they always have some customer using the data center. Each data center may host thousands of servers. They use custom network equipment and servers to cater to their customers.

In addition to regions and AZs, AWS offers edge locations, or *points of presence* (POPs), to provide a better user experience to customers. These edge locations are in most of the major cities across the globe. At the time of this writing, there are 70 edge locations. The edge locations are mainly used by content delivery networks to distribute content to nearby end users to reduce latency and provide fast performance. For example, when

Figure 1-2 AWS regions and AZs

you watch a video from Amazon Video, the video will be cached in an edge location so that when another customer watches the same video, it will be served from an edge location for a quick turnaround time and better user experience. In AWS, the edge location is used to serve Amazon CloudFront and Amazon Route 53 (which you will learn about in a little bit).

 EXAM TIP AWS has 18 regions and 53 AZs as of this writing. Since AWS keeps adding regions and AZs, please check the web site to get the latest numbers.

Figure 1-2 shows the regions and AZs. Circles indicate a unique region, and the numbers within the circles indicate the number of AZs in that region. A circle without any number is a proposed region in the future.

AWS Security and Compliance

AWS follows the model of *shared security,* which means AWS is responsible for the security *of* the cloud, and customers are responsible for the security *in* the cloud. In other words, AWS is responsible for the physical security of the data centers, video surveillance, hardware, compute, storage, virtualization, networking (including cabling, router, switches, load balancers, and firewall), and so on, whereas customers are responsible for securing the application, the data being hosted, and so on.

In the case of a managed service (for example, Amazon RDS, Amazon Redshift, Amazon DynamoDB, and so on), AWS is also responsible for the security configuration of it. Figure 1-3 depicts the shared security model. This shared security model allows customers to choose the level of security they need for their application, thereby giving customers more flexibility to protect their applications and data. With the shared

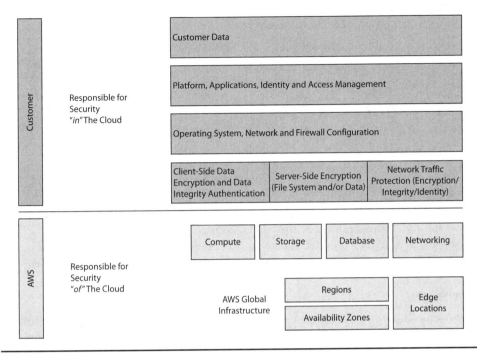

Figure 1-3 AWS shared security model

security model, the customer can secure the data and applications in the same way as they would do in a data center. You will learn more about this in Chapter 5.

AWS has earned several industries' recognized certifications, which provides complete peace of mind to customers since they know their data is secured and protected in the cloud. The key ones are as follows:

- SOC 1/SSAE 16/ISAE 3402 (formerly SAS 70)
- SOC 2
- SOC 3
- FISMA, DIACAP, and FedRAMP
- DOD CSM Levels 1-5
- PCI DSS Level 1
- ISO 9001 / ISO 27001
- ITAR
- FIPS 140-2
- MTCS Level 3
- Cloud Security Alliance (CSA)
- Family Educational Rights and Privacy Act (FERPA)

- Criminal Justice Information Services (CJIS)
- Health Insurance Portability and Accountability Act (HIPAA)
- Motion Picture Association of America (MPAA)

AWS Products and Services

AWS is continually expanding its services to support virtually every cloud workload and now has more than 70 services that include compute, storage, networking, database, analytics, application services, deployment, management, and mobile services. In this section, you will get an overview of the products and services, and in subsequent chapters you will learn more about them.

Figure 1-4 summarizes the services of AWS visually. If you look at the bottom, it shows the AWS global infrastructure, which consists of regions, AZs, and POPs.

Above that are core services. The core services are at the heart of the AWS offerings, and almost every customer uses the core services. The core services consist of the following.

Compute

The AWS compute services include a variety of products and services that provide scalable computing capacity in the cloud. The compute services include both servers and server-less configuration. The compute services also include the tools required for automatically scaling the resources and quickly deploying your applications on AWS. Let's explore the products in the compute area.

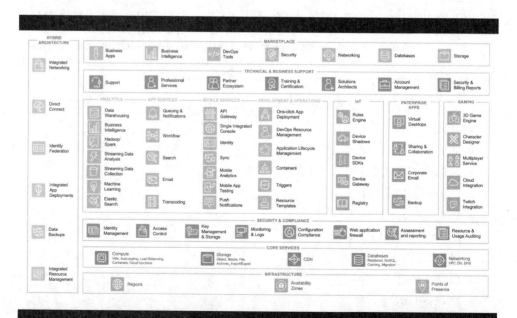

Figure 1-4   AWS product and services

Amazon Elastic Compute Cloud

Amazon Elastic Compute Cloud (EC2) includes the virtual servers, called *instances,* in the cloud. A customer can choose from more than 30 varieties of instances. Some of them are CPU intensive, some of them are memory intensive, some of them are accelerated computing optimized as in GPU optimized, some of them are storage optimized, some of them are input/output (I/O) instances, and some of them are general-purpose instances. Depending on the use case, the customer can choose from a variety of instance types. For example, if you are running a database workload that needs lots of memory, you can choose a memory-intensive instance, and if you are planning to run machine learning, you can choose an accelerated computing instance.

Amazon EC2 Auto Scaling

Amazon EC2 Auto Scaling helps in automatically scaling the Amazon EC2 instances up and down as per the policies you define. Combining Amazon EC2 and Auto Scaling, you can create a high availability architecture. Amazon EC2 Auto Scaling also ensures that you are always running with the desired number of instances. If for some reason an instance goes down, Amazon EC2 Auto Scaling quickly spins up a new instance. You can define Amazon EC2 Auto Scaling policies for various metrics and health checks. For example, you can set the CPU utilization metric to, say, 70 percent in Amazon EC2 Auto Scaling to add more servers to handle a load that exceeds that amount. Similarly, if a server is not healthy, you can use the health check metric of Amazon EC2 Auto Scaling to remove a server. There is no additional charge for using Amazon EC2 Auto Scaling. Amazon EC2 Auto Scaling integrates with Elastic Load Balancer.

AWS Lambda

AWS Lambda enables you to run code without provisioning or managing any servers or infrastructure. You can run any code for any kind of application or back-end service. You can also run code in response to event triggers such as Amazon S3 uploads, Amazon DynamoDB updates, Amazon Kinesis streams, Amazon API Gateway requests, and so on. The pricing for using AWS Lambda is simple. You pay only for the compute time when the code is getting executed; there is no charge when the code is not running. AWS Lambda scales automatically. Whenever you upload your code, AWS Lambda take cares of scaling the code automatically. When code is executed, the high availability is also taken care of automatically; in other words, the code is scaled with high availability as well.

Amazon EC2 Container Service

Amazon EC2 Container Service (ECS) allows you to run Docker containers on Amazon EC2 instances. Amazon ECS is scalable and is a performance container management service. With Amazon ECS you don't have to install, scale, and operate your own cluster management infrastructure. You can launch and manage Docker-enabled applications using application programming interface (API) calls. You can use the built-in scheduler, write your own scheduler, or use a third-party scheduler to meet business- or application-specific requirements. Amazon ECS integrates with other services such as ELB and Amazon EBS. There are no separate charges for Amazon ECS; you pay only for the AWS resources used such as Amazon EC2 instances, Amazon Elastic Block Storage (EBS) volumes, and so on.

AWS Elastic Beanstalk

AWS Elastic Beanstalk lets you run and manage web applications without worrying about the underlying infrastructure. You can use Amazon ECS to deploy web applications with Java, .NET PHP, Node.js, Python, Ruby, Go, and Docker on servers such as Apache, Nginx, and so on. You just need to upload your code, and AWS Elastic Beanstalk automatically handles deployment, load balancing, autoscaling, and application health monitoring. At the same time, you have full control over the AWS resource; you can access the underlying resources at any time using the console. There is no additional charge for AWS Elastic Beanstalk; you pay only for the AWS resources needed to run your applications.

Amazon Lightsail

Amazon Lightsail is the simplest way to get started with AWS for small businesses, developers, students, and other users who need a simple virtual private server (VPS) solution. Amazon Lightsail provides storage, networking capacity, and compute capabilities to manage and deploy web sites and web applications in the cloud. Lightsail includes a virtualized compute server, DNS management, SSD-based storage, data transfer capabilities, and a static IP address for a low, predictable monthly price. It's a one-stop shop to launch your project instantly.

AWS Batch

AWS Batch enables users to efficiently run hundreds of thousands of batch computing jobs on AWS. AWS Batch dynamically provisions the optimal type and quantity of compute resources such as memory-optimized instances, CPU-intensive instances, or storage-optimized instances based on the storage, capacity, throughput, and specific resource requirements of the batch jobs submitted. There is no need to install, deploy, and manage batch computing software or server clusters to run your jobs, enabling you to concentrate on solving problems and analyzing results.

Networking

Networking is part of the AWS core services. AWS networking helps you to isolate your cloud infrastructure. AWS provides you with lots of options for networking, which helps you to architect your application in the most optimized way. If you want an application to be Internet-facing or if you want an application to be non-Internet-facing, you can design this using the AWS networking tools. The following are the AWS networking products.

Amazon Virtual Private Cloud

Using an Amazon Virtual Private Cloud (VPC) you can isolate cloud resources within your own private virtual network. You can say that an Amazon VPC is your own data center in the cloud. You have complete control over the networking in an Amazon VPC. You can bring your own IP addresses, you can define the subnets as you want, and you have full control over the route table and network gateways. You can connect an Amazon VPC with your existing data center using Direct Connect or a virtual private network, making it an extension of your data center in the cloud. If you have multiple Amazon VPCs, you can connect them as well using Amazon VPC peering.

Amazon Route 53

Amazon Route 53 is a Domain Name System (DNS) web service. It is highly available and scalable, and its SLA is 100 percent uptime. Amazon Route 53 is IPv4 as well as IPv6 compliant. Amazon Route 53 answers DNS queries with low latency by using a global network of DNS servers. Amazon Route 53 translates names like www.amazon.com into numeric IP addresses like 192.0.1.1. Amazon Route 53 can be integrated with other AWS services such as Amazon EC2 instances, Amazon S3 buckets, Elastic Load Balancing, and Amazon CloudFront; it also can be used to route users to infrastructure outside of AWS. Amazon Route 53 can also be configured for DNS health checks, and thus traffic can be routed to a healthy endpoint. It is often used to manage failover from primary to secondary hosted applications. Amazon Route 53 can also be used to register domain names.

Elastic Load Balancing

Elastic Load Balancing (ELB) allows you to automatically distribute the load across multiple Amazon EC2 instances. It supports load balancing of HTTP, HTTPS, and TCP traffic to Amazon EC2 instances. It can be integrated with Auto Scaling; as a result, you can automatically scale up and down your Amazon EC2 instance and dynamically grow and shrink your operation depending on the traffic. ELB can also do health checks so you can remove the unhealthy/failing instances. ELB helps you to achieve fault tolerance for your applications. An ELB can support Amazon EC2 instances across different AZs within a region.

AWS Direct Connect

Using AWS Direct Connect, you can establish private, dedicated network connectivity from your data center to AWS. AWS Direct Connect can be used from either your data center or your office or colocation. By setting up AWS Direct Connect, you can reduce bandwidth costs for high-volume data transfers and get consistent network performance. AWS Direct Connect is compatible with all the AWS services. AWS Direct Connect provides 1Gbps and 10Gbps connections, and you can easily provision multiple connections if you need more capacity.

Security and Compliance

The security of the cloud is the highest priority for AWS. There are lots of safeguards at every layer in the AWS infrastructure to keep the data safe and help protect customer privacy. In addition, AWS provides lots of compliance programs in its infrastructure. In this section, you will learn about the products and services related to security and compliance.

AWS Identity and Access Management

AWS Identity and Access Management (IAM) is used to create users, groups, and roles. It is also used to manage and control access to AWS services and resources. AWS IAM can be federated with other systems, thereby allowing existing identities (user, groups, and roles) of your enterprise to access AWS resources.

Amazon Inspector

Amazon Inspector is an automated security assessment service that helps you to identify the security vulneraries in your application when it is being deployed as well as when it is running in a production system. Amazon Inspector also assesses applications for deviations from best practices, which helps the overall security of the applications deployed. Amazon Inspector has hundreds of predefined rules that it checks against. To use Amazon Inspector, you need to install the AWS agent on each Amazon EC2 instance. The agent then monitors the Amazon EC2 instance, collects all the data, and passes it on to the Amazon instance service.

AWS Certificate Manager

AWS Certificate Manager (ACM) is used to manage Secure Sockets Layer (SSL) certificates for use with AWS services. Using ACM, you can provision, manage, and deploy SSL/Transport Layer Security (TLS) certificates. You can protect and secure web sites as well. You can also use ACM to obtain, renew, and import certificates. You can use certificates stored in ACM with Elastic Load Balancer and Amazon CloudFront. The best part is there is no charge for the SSL/TLS certificates you manage with AWS Certificate Manager. You only pay for the AWS resource you use for the hosted application or web site.

AWS Directory Service

AWS Directory Service is an AWS managed directory service built on Microsoft Active Directory. It can be used to manage directories in the cloud. It enables single sign-on and policy management for Amazon EC2 instances and applications. It can be implemented stand-alone or integrated with existing directories.

AWS Web Application Firewall

AWS Web Application Firewall (WAF) is a web application firewall that detects malicious traffic targeted at the web applications. Using WAF, you can create various rules with which you can protect against common attacks such as SQL injection and scripting. Using these rules, you can block the web traffic from certain IP addresses, filter certain traffic from certain geographical locations, and so on, thus safeguarding your application.

AWS Shield

AWS Shield is a managed service that protects against distributed denial-of-service (DDoS) attacks targeted at the web applications. There are two tiers of AWS Shield: Standard and Advanced. AWS Shield Standard is free and protects against most commonly occurring DDoS attacks against web applications. With AWS Shield Advanced, you get higher levels of protection targeting not only against web applications but also Elastic Load Balancer, Amazon CloudFront, and Amazon Route 53.

Storage and Content Delivery

AWS provides a broad set of products for storing data. You can pick a storage solution on AWS based on your business needs. In this section, you will explore all the options available to customers for storage and content delivery.

Amazon Simple Shared Storage

Amazon Simple Shared Storage (S3) was one of the first services launched by AWS in 2006. Amazon S3 is the backbone of AWS. Many AWS services use Amazon S3 or rely on Amazon S3. It is the storage for the Internet, which is also used as an object store. Amazon S3 lets you store and retrieve any amount of data, at any time, from anywhere on the Web. Amazon S3 is highly scalable, reliable, and secure. It is designed to deliver 99.999999999 percent durability. Amazon S3 supports encryption, so you can store your objects in an encrypted manner. You can store unlimited amount of data but each file size can't exceed 5TB. With Amazon S3, you pay only for what you use. There is no minimum fee.

Amazon Glacier

Amazon Glacier is a low-cost cloud storage that is mainly used for data archiving and long-term backup purposes. Like Amazon S3, Amazon Glacier is secure and durable, and there is no limit to the amount of data to be stored. Amazon Glacier is cheaper than Amazon S3, and you pay only for what you use. There is no minimum fee. Amazon Glacier is integrated with Amazon S3. Through Amazon S3 lifecycle policies, you can optimize your storage costs by moving infrequently accessed objects from Amazon S3 to Amazon Glacier, or vice versa.

Amazon Elastic Block Storage

As the name suggests, Amazon Elastic Block Storage (EBS) provides persistent block storage for EC2 instances. You can choose from either magnetic or solid-state drive (SSD) disks for Amazon EBS volumes. Amazon EBS volumes are automatically replicated within their AZ to provide fault tolerance and high availability. Amazon EBS supports encryption for data in rest as well as data in transit between Amazon EC2 instances and Amazon EBS volumes. You can also create snapshots of Amazon EBS volumes in Amazon S3 at any point in time. Amazon EBS supports provisioned input/output operations per second (IOPS), which helps you to preprovision the IOPS based on your application needs.

Amazon Elastic File System

Amazon Elastic File System (Amazon EFS) is a fully managed service that provides easy, scalable, shared file storage with Amazon EC2 instances in the AWS cloud. It provides a simple file system interface and can be accessed concurrently for up to thousands of Amazon EC2 instances.

AWS Storage Gateway

AWS Storage Gateway is a service that helps to seamlessly integrate on-premise storage with AWS cloud storage. It is delivered as a virtual machine installed in an on-premise data center. You can connect it as a file server, or you can connect it as a local disk. You can also connect it as a virtual tape library. AWS Storage Gateway can be easily integrated with Amazon S3, Amazon EBS, and Amazon Glacier. The transfers are optimized since compression, encryption, and bandwidth management are built in.

Import/Export Options

AWS Import/Export is a service that helps to transfer a large amount of data into AWS using a physical storage appliance. By doing that, you can bypass the data transfer over the Internet. Using this option, you mail a storage device with your data on it. AWS loads the data into the cloud and returns your device. You can also use AWS Snowball in which case AWS ships a physical device to your premises; you can load the data and ship it back to AWS. This physical device is called AWS Snowball. Snowball comes in two sizes: 80TB and 50TB. Other options to transfer data to AWS are to use AWS Direct Connect, which is a dedicated virtual network from your location to the AWS data center, or to use Amazon Kinesis Firehose, which can capture and automatically load streaming data into Amazon S3.

Amazon CloudFront

Amazon CloudFront is the global content delivery network (CDN) service of AWS. Amazon CloudFront helps to accelerate the delivery of the static content of your web sites including photos, videos, or any other web assets. Amazon CloudFront can also be used to deliver all the content of your web site including the dynamic content. Amazon CloudFront provides advanced CDN features such as SSL support, geographic restriction, and private content. It can be easily integrated with other AWS products thereby providing businesses with an easy way to accelerate content. As of this writing, AWS has 100 plus Amazon CloudFront locations.

Database

AWS provides fully managed relational and nonrelational (NoSQL) database services plus fully managed data warehousing services and in-memory caching as a service. In this section, you will learn about all the database offerings AWS has.

Amazon Relational Database Service

Amazon Relational Database Service (RDS) is a fully managed relational database service. With this service, you can host a variety of relational database management system (RDBMS) engines in the cloud. Amazon RDS supports MySQL, Oracle, SQL Server, PostgreSQL, and Maria DB. In addition, Amazon RDS supports Amazon's own database, Aurora. AWS provides resizable capacity, so at any time you can scale up or down depending on your business needs. Since this is a managed database service, AWS takes care of database management and administration tasks including patching, upgrading, and backups. AWS also offers a high availability option for Amazon RDS for fault tolerance and durability.

Amazon DynamoDB

Amazon DynamoDB is a fully managed NoSQL database service of AWS. It is highly scalable, durable, and highly available and is capable of handling any data volume. It delivers consistent, single-digit millisecond latency at any scale. It consists of SSD storage. Since this is also a managed service, you don't have to deal with database administration. The data is replicated automatically in three ways, providing the high availability of data. It supports both document and key-value models. It is a great fit for mobile, web, gaming, Internet of Things (IoT), and many other applications.

Amazon Redshift

Amazon Redshift is a fully managed petabyte-scale data warehouse service. It stores the data in columnar format thereby providing better I/O efficiency. You should be able to spin up a Amazon Redshift cluster in minutes. The data is continuously backed up in Amazon S3. As a result, you don't have to worry about backing it up. You can choose either a magnetic or SSD-based drive to store the data. You can scale up or down a Amazon Redshift cluster depending on your business and processing needs and thus can process parallel operations. You can access the Amazon Redshift cluster via ODBC or JDBC.

Amazon ElastiCache

Amazon ElastiCache is a service that helps in deploying an in-memory cache or data store in the cloud. Amazon ElastiCache supports two open source in-memory engines: Redis and Memcached. Using Amazon ElastiCache, you can greatly improve the performance of your web application. Since it is a managed service, AWS takes care of patching, monitoring, failure recovery, and backups. Amazon ElasticCache can be integrated with Amazon CloudWatch and Amazon SNS, which you will learn about later in this chapter.

Amazon Aurora

Amazon Aurora is Amazon's relational database built for the cloud. It supports two open source RDBMS engines: MySQL and PostgreSQL. It supports databases up to 64TB in size. It is highly available, durable, and scalable. By default, the data is mirrored across three AZs, and six copies of the data are kept. You can create up to 15 read replicas in an Amazon Aurora database. It is a fully managed database service, so database administration is taken care of by AWS. The database is constantly backed up to Amazon S3, enabling granular point-in-time recovery.

Analytics

AWS provides a variety of ways in by which companies can analyze a vast amount of data quickly and efficiently. AWS provides analytics tools that can scale to very large data stores efficiently and cost effectively. In this section, you will get an overview of these tools.

Amazon Athena

Amazon Athena is a serverless, interactive query service that enables users to easily analyze data in Amazon S3 using standard SQL. There is no infrastructure setup or management required for end users, and you can start analyzing data in Amazon S3 immediately. Amazon Athena uses Presto with full standard SQL support that works with a variety of standard data formats, including JSON, ORC, CSV, Arvo, and Apache Parquet.

Amazon EMR

Amazon EMR is a web service that enables users, businesses, enterprises, data analysts, researchers, and developers to easily and cost effectively process enormous amounts of data. It utilizes a hosted Hadoop framework running on the web-scale infrastructure of Amazon S3 and Amazon EC2.

Amazon Elasticsearch Service

Amazon Elasticsearch Service is a fully managed web service that makes it easy to create, operate, deploy, and scale Elasticsearch clusters in the AWS cloud.

Amazon CloudSearch

Amazon CloudSearch is a fully managed web service in the AWS cloud that offers a simple, cost-effective, easy-to-use way to manage and scale a search solution for your application or web site. The Amazon CloudSearch service supports 34 languages and popular search features such as autocomplete, highlighting, and geospatial search.

AWS Data Pipeline

AWS Data Pipeline enables users to process, transform, and move data between different AWS compute and storage services as well as on-premise data sources, at specified intervals reliably and efficiently.

Amazon Kinesis

Amazon Kinesis is a fully managed service that makes it easy to collect, analyze, and process real-time, streaming data. This enables users to get timely insights and react quickly to new information. Amazon Kinesis offers capabilities to cost-effectively process streaming data at any scale, along with the option to choose tools that best suit the requirements of your application. With Amazon Kinesis, you can ingest real-time data such as web site clickstreams, application logs, IoT data, and more into your databases, data warehouses, and data lake or you can build your own real-time applications using this data.

Amazon QuickSight

Amazon QuickSight is an easy, fast, cloud-powered, fully managed business analytics service that makes it easy to build visualizations, perform ad hoc analysis, and quickly get meaningful insights from your data.

Application Services

AWS provides many options for running applications in the cloud. It provides you with the infrastructure for running the APIs, coordinating work across distributed application components, running microservices, and so on. In this section, you will look at the application services.

Amazon API Gateway

Amazon API Gateway is a fully managed service that provides developers with an easy, simple, scalable, flexible, pay-as-you-go service that handles all aspects of building, deploying, and operating robust APIs for application back-end services such as code running on AWS Lambda, applications running on Amazon EC2, or any web application. Amazon API Gateway handles several tasks involved in processing and accepting up to hundreds of thousands of concurrent API calls, including traffic management, access control, authorization, monitoring events, and API version management.

AWS Step Functions

AWS Step Functions is a fully managed service that enables users to efficiently and securely coordinate various components of distributed applications and microservices using visual workflows. This service provides a graphical interface for users to visualize and arrange the components of their applications, making it easy to run and build multiple layered step applications.

Amazon Simple Workflow Service

Amazon Simple Workflow Service (SWF) is a web-based cloud service that makes it easy to coordinate work across distributed application components. Amazon SWF enables applications for a range of use cases, including web application back ends, media processing, business process workflows, and data analytics pipelines, to be designed as a coordination of jobs and tasks.

Amazon Elastic Transcoder

Amazon Elastic Transcoder is an easy-to-use, highly scalable, and cost-effective way for users and businesses to convert (or *transcode*) video and audio files from their source format into the output format of their choice that they can play back on various devices such as smartphones, desktops, television, tablets, and PCs.

Developer Tools

AWS empowers you with lots of developer tools so that you can quickly build and deploy your code without having to manage the infrastructure running beneath. It helps you to continuously develop during the software development life cycle. With AWS tools you don't have to wait on anything for deploying your code. In this section, you will learn about the developer tools.

AWS CodeCommit

AWS CodeCommit is a fully managed source control service that makes it easy to host highly scalable private Git repositories securely. Users no longer need to operate their own source control system or worry about scaling their infrastructure.

AWS CodePipeline

AWS CodePipeline is a fully managed continuous integration and continuous delivery service for quick, reliable application and infrastructure updates. AWS CodePipeline builds, tests, and deploys code every time the code is modified, updated, and checked in based on the release process models you define.

AWS CodeBuild

AWS CodeBuild is a fully managed build service that builds and compiles source code, runs tests, and produces software packages that are ready to deploy, eliminating the need to provision, manage, and scale build servers.

AWS CodeDeploy

AWS CodeDeploy is a fully managed service that automates code deployments to any instance or servers, including Amazon EC2 instances and servers running on-premises. AWS CodeDeploy makes releasing new features quick and easy, helping you avoid downtime during application deployment.

Management Tools

AWS provides a broad set of services that help system administrators, IT administrators, and developers more easily manage and monitor their hybrid and cloud infrastructure resources. These fully managed services help to automatically provision, operate, configure, and manage AWS or on-premises resources at scale. They also provide capabilities to monitor infrastructure logs and metrics using real-time dashboards and alarms and to enforce compliance and security. In this section, you will look at the management tools at a very high level.

AWS CloudFormation

AWS CloudFormation helps automate resource provisioning using declarative templates and deploying resource stacks. It gives developers and systems administrators an easy way to create and manage a collection of related AWS resources, provisioning and updating them in an orderly and predictable fashion. You can use AWS's sample CloudFormation templates, or you can create your own template to describe AWS resources. AWS CloudFormation helps to keep the infrastructure as code, and you can spin them off wherever needed. You can even use AWS CloudFormation templates to deploy resources in a different AZ or region.

AWS Service Catalog

AWS Service Catalog allows IT administrators to create, manage, and distribute catalogs of approved products to end users, who can then access the products they need in a personalized portal. Administrators can control which users have access to each product to enforce compliance with organizational business policies. Administrators can also set up adopted roles so that end users only require IAM access to AWS Service Catalog to deploy approved resources. AWS Service Catalog allows your organization to benefit from increased agility and reduced costs because end users can find and launch only the products they need from a catalog that you control.

AWS OpsWorks

AWS OpsWorks for Chef Automate provides a fully managed Chef server and suite of automation tools that gives you workflow automation for continuous deployment, automated testing for compliance and security, and a user interface that gives you visibility into your nodes and their status. The Chef server gives you full stack automation by handling operational tasks such as software and operating system configurations, package installations, database setups, and more. The Chef server centrally stores your configuration tasks and provides them to each node in your compute environment at any scale, from a few nodes to thousands of nodes. AWS OpsWorks for Chef Automate is completely compatible with tooling and cookbooks from the Chef community and automatically registers new nodes with your Chef server.

AWS OpsWorks Stacks lets you manage applications and servers on AWS and on-premises. With AWS OpsWorks Stacks, you can model your application as a stack containing different layers, such as load balancing, database, and application server layers. You can deploy and configure Amazon EC2 instances in each layer or connect other resources such as an Amazon RDS database.

Amazon CloudWatch

Amazon CloudWatch is a monitoring service for AWS cloud resources and the applications you run on AWS. You can use Amazon CloudWatch to collect and track metrics, collect and monitor log files, and set alarms. Amazon CloudWatch can monitor AWS resources such as Amazon EC2 instances, Amazon DynamoDB tables, and Amazon RDS DB instances, as well as custom metrics generated by your applications and services and any log files your applications generate. You can use Amazon CloudWatch to gain systemwide visibility into resource utilization, application performance, and operational health. You can use these insights to react and keep your application running smoothly.

AWS Config

AWS Config is a fully managed service that provides you with an AWS resource inventory, configuration history, and configuration change notifications to enable security and governance. With AWS Config, you can discover existing AWS resources, export a complete inventory of your AWS resources with all configuration details, and determine how a resource was configured at any point in time. These capabilities enable compliance auditing, security analysis, resource change tracking, and troubleshooting.

AWS CloudTrail

AWS CloudTrail is a managed web service that records AWS API calls and user activity in your account and delivers log files to you via Amazon S3. AWS CloudTrail provides visibility into user activity by recording API calls made on your account. AWS CloudTrail records important information about each API call, including the name of the API, the identity of the caller, the time of the API call, the request parameters, and the response elements returned by the AWS service.

Messaging

AWS has offerings that help you receive notifications from the cloud, publish messages from applications and deliver them to subscribers, and manage the message queues to store messages to be processed. In this section, you will look at these offerings from a high level.

Amazon Simple Notification Service

Amazon Simple Notification Service (SNS) is a highly scalable, flexible, and cost-effective web service that makes it easy to configure, operate, and send notifications from the cloud. It provides developers with a highly scalable, flexible, and cost-effective capability to publish messages from an application and immediately deliver them to subscribers or other applications.

Amazon Simple Email Service

Amazon Simple Email Service (SES) provides developers with a highly scalable, flexible, and cost-effective capability to publish messages from an application and immediately deliver them to subscribers or other applications. Amazon SES is an e-mail platform that provides an efficient and reliable platform to send and receive e-mail using your own e-mail addresses and domains.

Amazon Simple Queue Service

Amazon Simple Queue Service (SQS) is a managed web service that gives you access to message queues to store messages waiting to be processed. Amazon SQS enables you to quickly build message queuing applications that can run on any computer. Amazon SQS offers a reliable, scalable, messaging queue service for storing messages in transit between computers.

Migration

AWS provides a variety of ways in which you can migrate your existing applications, databases, workloads, and data into AWS. In this section, you will learn all the migration services provided by AWS.

AWS Application Discovery Service

AWS Application Discovery Service enables you to quickly and reliably plan application migration projects by automatically identifying applications running in on-premise data centers and mapping their associated dependencies and their performance profiles.

AWS Database Migration Service

AWS Database Migration Service helps you to migrate databases to AWS reliably and securely. The source database remains fully operational during the migration, minimizing downtime. AWS Database Migration Service can migrate your data homogenously or heterogeneously to and from most widely used enterprise and open source databases.

AWS Snowball

AWS Snowball helps you transport a petabyte-scale amount of data into and out of the AWS cloud. AWS Snowball eliminates common challenges with large-scale data transfer such as high network costs, security concerns, and long transfer time. Transferring data with AWS Snowball is easy, efficient, fast, and secure, and it can cost as little as one-fifth of high-speed Internet.

AWS Server Migration Service

AWS Server Migration Service (SMS) is an agentless service that helps coordinate, automate, schedule, and track large-scale server migrations. It makes it easier and faster for you to migrate thousands of on-premise workloads to AWS.

Artificial Intelligence

Amazon provides four services for artificial intelligence. As of now, the examination does not cover these services, but it is good to know the offerings from AWS for artificial intelligence.

Amazon Lex

Amazon Lex is a fully managed service for building conversational chatbot interfaces using voice and text. Amazon Lex provides high-quality language-understanding capabilities and speech recognition.

Amazon Polly

Amazon Polly is a fully managed service that converts text into lifelike speech. Amazon Polly enables existing applications to speak and creates the opportunity for entirely new categories of speech-enabled products, including chatbots, cars, mobile apps, devices, and web appliances.

Amazon Rekognition

Amazon Rekognition is a fully managed, easy-to-use, reliable, and efficient image recognition service powered by deep learning. Amazon Rekognition has been built by Amazon's Computer Vision teams over several years and analyzes billions of images every day. Amazon Rekognition's API detects thousands of scenes and objects, analyzes faces, compares faces to measure similarity, and identifies faces in a collection of faces.

Amazon Machine Learning

Amazon Machine Learning is a fully managed machine service that allows you to efficiently build predictive applications, including demand forecasting, fraud detection, and click prediction.

Internet of Things

The Internet of Things (IoT) is a term coined by Kevin Ashton, a British technology pioneer working on radio-frequency identification (RFID) who conceived a system of ubiquitous sensors connecting the physical world to the Internet. Although things, Internet, and connectivity are the three core components of IoT, the value is in closing the gap between the physical and digital worlds in self-reinforcing and self-improving systems. The following is the overview of AWS's offerings in IoT. This topic is not required from an examination perspective.

AWS IoT Platform

The AWS IoT platform is a fully managed cloud platform that lets connected devices interact with cloud applications and other devices securely and efficiently. AWS IoT can support trillions of messages and billions of devices and can process and route those messages to AWS endpoints and to other devices reliably and securely.

AWS Greengrass

AWS Greengrass is a software solution that lets you run local compute, messaging, and data caching for connected IoT devices in an efficient and secure way. AWS Greengrass enables devices to run AWS Lambda functions, keep data in sync, and communicate with other devices securely, even when Internet connectivity is not possible.

AWS IoT Button

AWS IoT Button is a programmable button based on the Amazon Dash Button hardware. This simple Wi-Fi device is easy to configure and designed for developers to get started with AWS IoT, AWS Lambda, Amazon DynamoDB, Amazon SNS, and many other Amazon web services without writing device-specific code.

You can code the button's logic in the cloud to configure button clicks to count or track items, call or alert someone, start or stop something, order services, or even provide feedback. For example, you can use this button to do a variety of stuff such as control the temperature of your room, open the garage door, order food, remotely control all the electrical appliances at your home, and so on.

Mobile Services

AWS has offerings in the mobile space as well. In this section, you will learn about the services at a very high level. The examination does not cover these services.

Amazon Cognito

The Amazon Cognito web service lets you add users to sign up and sign in to your mobile and web apps fast and reliably. Amazon Cognito lets you authenticate users through social identity providers such as Twitter, Facebook, or Amazon, along with other SAML identity solutions, or by using a custom identity system. Amazon Cognito also allows your applications to work when the devices are offline, as it lets you save data locally on users' devices.

AWS Mobile Hub

AWS Mobile Hub is a web service that provides an integrated experience for configuring, discovering, and accessing AWS cloud services for creating, testing, deploying, and monitoring usage of mobile applications. In AWS Mobile Hub, you can select and configure features to add to your mobile app. AWS Mobile Hub features help integrate various AWS services, client SDKs, and client integration code to quickly and easily add new features and capabilities to your mobile app.

AWS Device Farm

AWS Device Farm lets you test mobile apps on real mobile devices and tablets. It is an app testing web service where users can interact and test their iOS, web, and Android apps on several device platforms at once.

Amazon Mobile Analytics

Amazon Mobile Analytics is a web service that enables you to measure the app usage and revenue. It helps to track key trends and patterns such as new users versus returning users, user retention, app revenue, and custom in-app behavior events.

Chapter Review

In this chapter, you learned that cloud computing is the on-demand delivery of IT resources available from the Internet with a pay-as-you-go model.

You also learned that the following are advantages of running cloud computing on AWS:

- Gaining agility
- Avoiding guessing about capacity
- Moving from capital expenses to variable/flexible expenses
- Benefiting from massive economics of scale
- Avoiding spending money on data centers
- Benefiting from the pace of innovation
- Going global in minutes

You learned about the three models of cloud computing.

- Infrastructure as a Service
- Platform as a Service
- Software as a Service

There are three ways in which you can deploy on the cloud.

- "All-in" cloud
- Hybrid cloud
- On-premises or private cloud

AWS has more than a million customers in 190 countries across the globe. To serve these customers, AWS maintains 18 regions spanning five continents. Within each region there are availability zones. An AZ consists of one to six data centers, with redundant power supplies and networking connectivity.

AWS follows the model of shared security, which means AWS is responsible for the security of the cloud and customers are responsible for security in the cloud.

AWS has been continually expanding its services to support virtually any cloud workload and now has more than 70 services that include compute, storage, networking, database, analytics, application services, deployment, management, and mobile services.

Questions

1. If you want to run your relational database in the AWS cloud, which service would you choose?

    A. Amazon DynamoDB

    B. Amazon Redshift

    C. Amazon RDS

    D. Amazon ElastiCache

2. If you want to speed up the distribution of your static and dynamic web content such as HTML, CSS, image, and PHP files, which service would you consider?

   A. Amazon S3

   B. Amazon EC2

   C. Amazon Glacier

   D. Amazon CloudFront

3. What is a way of connecting your data center with AWS?

   A. AWS Direct Connect

   B. Optical fiber

   C. Using an Infiniband cable

   D. Using a popular Internet service from a vendor such as Comcast or AT&T

4. What is each unique location in the world where AWS has a cluster of data centers called?

   A. Region

   B. Availability zone

   C. Point of presence

   D. Content delivery network

5. You want to deploy your applications in AWS, but you don't want to host them on any servers. Which service would you choose for doing this? (Choose two.)

   A. Amazon ElastiCache

   B. AWS Lambda

   C. Amazon API Gateway

   D. Amazon EC2

6. You want to be notified for any failure happening in the cloud. Which service would you leverage for receiving the notifications?

   A. Amazon SNS

   B. Amazon SQS

   C. Amazon CloudWatch

   D. AWS Config

7. How can you get visibility of user activity by recording the API calls made to your account?

   A. By using Amazon API Gateway

   B. By using Amazon CloudWatch

   C. By using AWS CloudTrail

   D. By using Amazon Inspector

8. You have been tasked with moving petabytes of data to the AWS cloud. What is the most efficient way of doing this?

   A. Upload them to Amazon S3

   B. Use AWS Snowball

   C. Use AWS Server Migration Service

   D. Use AWS Database Migration Service

9. How do you integrate AWS with the directories running on-premise in your organization?

   A. By using AWS Direct Connect

   B. By using a VPN

   C. By using AWS Directory Service

   D. Directly via the Internet

10. How can you have a shared file system across multiple Amazon EC2 instances?

   A. By using Amazon S3

   B. By mounting Elastic Block Storage across multiple Amazon EC2 servers

   C. By using Amazon EFS

   D. By using Amazon Glacier

Answers

   1. C. Amazon DynamoDB is a NoSQL offering, Amazon Redshift is a data warehouse offering, and Amazon ElastiCache is used to deploy Redis or Memcached protocol–compliant server nodes in the cloud.

   2. D. Amazon S3 can be used to store objects; it can't speed up the operations. Amazon EC2 provides the compute. Amazon Glacier is the archive storage.

   3. A. Your colocation or MPLS provider may use an optical fiber or Infiniband cable behind the scenes. If you want to connect over the Internet, then you need a VPN.

   4. A. AZs are inside a region, so they are not unique. POP and content delivery both serve the purpose of speeding up distribution.

   5. B, C. Amazon ElastiCache is use to deploy Redis or Memcached protocol–compliant server nodes in the cloud, and Amazon EC2 is a server.

   6. A. Amazon SQS is the queue service; Amazon CloudWatch is used to monitor cloud resources; and AWS Config is used to assess, audit, and evaluate the configurations of your AWS resources.

   7. C. Amazon API Gateway is a fully managed service that makes it easy for developers to create, publish, maintain, monitor, and secure APIs at any scale. Amazon CloudWatch is used to monitor cloud resources. AWS Config is used to assess, audit, and evaluate the configurations of your AWS resources, and Amazon Inspector is an automated security assessment service that helps improve the security and compliance of applications deployed on AWS.

8. **B**. You can also upload data to Amazon S3, but if you have petabytes of data and want to upload it to Amazon S3, it is going to take a lot of time. The quickest way would be to leverage AWS Snowball. AWS Server Migration Service is an agentless service that helps coordinate, automate, schedule, and track large-scale server migrations, whereas AWS Database Migration Service is used to migrate the data of the relational database or data warehouse.

9. **C**. AWS Direct Connect and a VPN are used to connect your corporate data center with AWS. You cannot use the Internet directly to integrate directories; you need a service to integrate your on-premise directory to AWS.

10. **C**. Amazon S3 is an object store, Amazon EBS can't be mounted across multiple servers, and Amazon Glacier is an extension of Amazon S3.

Storage on AWS

In this chapter, you will

- Learn the storage offerings of AWS
- Learn to use Amazon S3
- Learn to use Amazon Glacier
- Learn to use Amazon Elastic Store
- Learn to use Amazon Elastic File System
- Learn how to move a large amount of data to AWS

The storage offerings of AWS can be divided into three major categories, as shown in Figure 2-1.

- **Object storage**   An object is a piece of data, like a document, image, or video that is stored with some metadata in a flat structure. It provides that data to applications via APIs over the Internet. It is simple to build anything on top of an object store. For example, you can easily develop a web application on top of Amazon S3 that delivers content to users by making API calls over the Internet.

- **Block storage**   In block storage, data is presented to your instance as a disk volume. It provides low, single-digit latency access to single Amazon EC2 instances. Elastic Block Store is popular, for example, for boot volumes and databases.

- **File storage**   In file storage, data is presented via a file system interface and with file system semantics to instances. When attached to an instance, it acts just like a local file system. Amazon Elastic File System (EFS) provides shared access to data via multiple Amazon EC2 instances, with low latencies.

Amazon Simple Storage Service (S3)

Amazon launched S3 in 2006. Amazon S3 is an object store and is the backbone for many other services used at Amazon. It has a nice web interface to store and retrieve any amount of data from anywhere around the world. The capacity of S3 is unlimited, which means there is no limit to the amount of data you can store in S3. It is highly durable and has 99.99999999999 percent of durability. According to Amazon, this durability level corresponds to an average annual expected loss of 0.000000001 percent of objects.

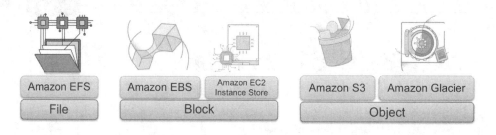

Figure 2-1 AWS storage platform

For example, if you store 10,000 objects with Amazon S3, you can on average expect to incur a loss of a single object once every 10,000,000 years. In addition, Amazon S3 is designed to sustain the concurrent loss of data in two facilities.

It is fundamentally different from other file repositories because it is does not have a file system. All objects are stored in a flat namespace organized by buckets. It is a regional service; that is, content is automatically replicated within a region for durability. It is one of the most popular object stores available on the Internet today. In this chapter, you'll first evaluate some of the advantages of Amazon S3, which makes it uniquely popular among customers.

Advantages of Amazon S3

The following are the advantages of using Amazon S3:

- **Simple**   Amazon S3 is really easy to use. It has an intuitive graphical web-based console in which the data can be uploaded, downloaded, and managed. S3 also has a mobile app in which it can be managed. For easy integration with third parties, S3 provides REST APIs and SDKs.

- **Scalable**   Amazon S3 is infinity scalable. You can store unlimited data in it without worrying about storage needs. You don't have to do any kind of capacity planning to store data in S3. If your business needs petabytes of data, you should be able to store that in S3 easily and quickly. You can scale up or scale down anytime as per your business requirements.

- **Durable**   Amazon S3 is the only service that provides 99.999999999 percent durability of the objects stored in it. The underlying infrastructure is designed in such a way that this durability is achieved. The data is stored across multiple data centers and in multiple devices in a redundant manner. Amazon S3 is designed to sustain concurrent data loss in two facilities.

- **Secured**   Amazon S3 supports encryption, and the data can be automatically encrypted once it is uploaded. S3 also supports data transfer over SSL. Using AWS Identity and Access Management (IAM), you should be able to manage granular permissions and access to an S3 bucket.

- **High performance** Amazon S3 supports multipart uploads to help maximize network throughput and resiliency and lets you choose the AWS region to store your data close to the end user and minimize network latency. Also, Amazon S3 is integrated with Amazon CloudFront, a content delivery web service that distributes content to end users with low latency, high data transfer speeds, and no minimum usage commitments.

- **Available** Amazon S3 is designed to provide 99.99 percent availability of the objects annually. The SLA level of 99.99 percent uptime/availability gives the following periods of potential downtime/unavailability:

  Daily: 8.6 seconds
  Weekly: 1 minute and 0.5 seconds
  Monthly: 4 minutes and 23.0 seconds
  Yearly: 52 minutes and 35.7 seconds

- **Low cost** Amazon S3 is very cost effective and allows you to store a large amount of data at a low cost. There is no minimum cost associated with S3, and you pay only for what you need. Also, there are no up-front costs associated with S3. With the volume discount, the more data you store, the cheaper it becomes. You can further lower the cost by storing the data in a different class of S3 such as infrequent access or reduced redundancy or by creating a lifecycle policy in which you can archive old files to Amazon Glacier to further reduce the cost.

- **Easy to manage** The Amazon S3 storage management feature allows you to take a data-driven approach to storage optimization data security and management efficiency. As a result, you have better intel about your data and can manage the data based on personalized metadata.

- **Easy integration** Amazon S3 can be easily integrated with third-party tools. As a result, it is easy to build an application on top of S3. S3 is also integrated with other AWS services. As a result, S3 can be used in conjunction with lots of AWS products.

Usage of Amazon S3 in Real Life

You can use S3 in the following ways:

- **Backup** Amazon S3 is popular for storing backup files among enterprises. Since the durability of S3 is 99.999999999 percent, losing data is rare. The data is distributed in three copies for each file between multiple Availability Zones (AZs) within an AWS region. As a result, the data cannot be destroyed by a disaster in one AZ. S3 also provides versioning capacity; as a result, you can further protect your against human error.

- **Tape replacement** Another popular use case of S3 these days is magnetic tape replacement. Many organizations have started replacing their tape drives or tape infrastructures with S3.

- **Static web site hosting**   If you need to host a static web site, you get everything just by using Amazon S3. There is no need to procure web servers or worry about storage. Since S3 is scalable, it can handle any amount of traffic, and you can store unlimited data.

- **Application hosting**   Since Amazon S3 provides highly available storage, many customers use it for hosting mobile and Internet-based apps. Since S3 is accessible from anywhere in the world, you can access and deploy your applications from anywhere.

- **Disaster recovery**   Amazon S3 is also used as a disaster recovery solution. Using cross-region replication, you can automatically replicate each S3 object to a different bucket in a different region.

- **Content distribution**   Amazon S3 is often used to distribute the content over the Internet. It allows you to offload your entire storage infrastructure into the cloud, where you can take advantage of Amazon S3's scalability and pay-as-you-go pricing to handle your growing storage needs. The content can be anything such as files, or you can host media such as photos videos and so on. You can also use it as a software delivery platform where customers can download your software. These contents can be distributed either directly from S3 or via Amazon CloudFront.

- **Data lake**   Amazon S3 is becoming extremely popular as a *data lake* solution. A data lake is a central place for storing massive amounts of data that can be processed, analyzed, and consumed by different business units in an organization. Any raw, semiprocessed, or processed data can be stored in S3. It is extremely popular in the world of big data as a big data store to keep all kinds of data. Whether you're storing pharmaceutical or financial data or multimedia files such as photos and videos, Amazon S3 can be used as your big data object store. Amazon Web Services offers a comprehensive portfolio of services to help you manage big data by reducing costs, scaling to meet demand, and increasing the speed of innovation. S3 is often used with EMR, Redshift, Redshift Spectrum, Athena, Glue, and QuickSight for running big data analytics.

- **Private repository**   Using Amazon S3 you can create your own private repository like with Git, Yum, or Maven.

Amazon S3 Basic Concepts

This section covers some Amazon S3 basic terminology and concepts that you will learn about throughout this chapter.

Just like you store water in a bucket, in the cloud you store the objects of the object store in a bucket. So, a *bucket* is actually a container for storing objects in Amazon S3. You can compare a bucket to a folder on a computer where you store various files. You can create multiple folders inside a folder, and in an S3 bucket you can create multiple folders. The name of the bucket must be unique, which means you cannot have two buckets with the same name even across multiple regions. Any object can be uniquely accessible from the bucket using a URL. For example, say an object name is `ringtone.mp3`, and it has been stored in the bucket `newringtones`. The file will be accessible using the URL http://newringtones.s3.amazonaws.com/ringtone.mp3. The bucket serves the following purposes:

- Organizes the Amazon S3 namespace at the highest level
- Identifies the account responsible for charges
- Plays a role in access control
- Serves as the unit of aggregation for usage reporting

You can create buckets in any region you want. By default, the data of a bucket is not replicated to any other region unless you do it manually or by using cross-region replication. S3 buckets allow versioning. If you use versioning, whenever an object is added to a bucket, a unique version ID is assigned to the object.

Objects are the fundamental entries stored in Amazon S3. Put simply, anything you store in an S3 bucket is called an *object,* and an object consists of data and metadata. The data portion stores the actual data in Amazon S3. Metadata is a set of name-value pairs describing the object. The metadata also includes additional information such as last-modified date, file type, and so on. An object is uniquely identified within a bucket by a name or key and by a version ID.

Using a key, you can uniquely identify an object in a bucket, which means that every object in a bucket has only one key. You can identify any object in an S3 bucket with a unique combination of bucket, key, and version ID. For example, to understand how you can use a key to identify an object, say the URL of the object of S3 bucket is http://s3.amazonaws.com/2017-02/pictures/photo1.gif. In this case, the name of the key is `2017-02/pictures/photo1.gif`. When you combine the key with the version of the file (photo1.gif), you can uniquely define the particular object.

You can create an S3 bucket in any region where the service is available. You may want to create an object in a *region* that is near to you to optimize the latency and get a better user experience. You can also choose a region for data compliance purposes or to minimize the cost. Note that the object stored in the region never leaves the region unless you explicitly transfer it to a different region. For example, if you store a file in the region US East, the file will never leave the region US East unless you move the file manually or use cross-region replication and move the file to another region, say, USA West. As of this writing, Amazon S3 supports the following regions:

- The US East (N. Virginia) region uses Amazon S3 servers in Northern Virginia.
- The US East (Ohio) region uses Amazon S3 servers in Columbus, Ohio.
- The US West (N. California) region uses Amazon S3 servers in Northern California.
- The US West (Oregon) region uses Amazon S3 servers in Oregon.
- The Canada (Central) region uses Amazon S3 servers in Canada.
- The Asia Pacific (Mumbai) region uses Amazon S3 servers in Mumbai.
- The Asia Pacific (Seoul) region uses Amazon S3 servers in Seoul.
- The Asia Pacific (Singapore) region uses Amazon S3 servers in Singapore.

- The Asia Pacific (Sydney) region uses Amazon S3 servers in Sydney.

- The Asia Pacific (Tokyo) region uses Amazon S3 servers in Tokyo.

- The EU (Frankfurt) region uses Amazon S3 servers in Frankfurt.

- The EU (Ireland) region uses Amazon S3 servers in Ireland.

- The EU (London) region uses Amazon S3 servers in London.

- The South America (São Paulo) region uses Amazon S3 servers in São Paulo.

S3 is accessible from an application programming interface (API), which allows developers to write applications on top of S3. The fundamental interface for S3 is a Representational State Transfer (REST) API. Although S3 supports the Simple Object Access Protocol (SOAP) in HTTPS mode only, SOAP support over Hypertext Transfer Protocol (HTTP) is deprecated. It is recommended that you use REST over SOAP since new Amazon S3 features will not be supported for SOAP.

REST APIs rely on a stateless, client-server, cacheable communications protocol, and in virtually all cases, the HTTP protocol is used. Using a REST API, you should be able to perform all kinds of operations in an S3 bucket including create, read, update, delete, and list. The REST API allows you to perform all operations in an S3 bucket with standard HTTP/HTTPS requests. Since HTTPS is more secure than HTTP, whenever using an API request with S3, always prefer HTTPS over HTTP to make sure that your request and data are secure.

The primary or most commonly used HTTP verbs (or *methods,* as they are properly called) are POST, GET, PUT, PATCH, and DELETE. These correspond to create, read, update, and delete (CRUD) operations, respectively. You can use these HTTP verbs with the corresponding actions in S3, as shown in Table 2-1.

In addition to APIs, lots of SDKs are available in various platforms including in browsers, on mobile devices (Android and iOS), and in multiple programming languages (Java, .NET, Node.js, PHP, Python, Ruby, Go, C++). A mobile SDK and IoT device SDK are also available. You can use these SDKs with the combination APIs as per your programming language to simplify using AWS services in your applications.

The AWS command-line interface (CLI) is a unified tool to manage all your AWS services. Using the AWS CLI, you can control multiple AWS services from the command line and automate them through scripts. The AWS CLI is often used by Amazon S3 in conjunction with REST APIs and SDKs. The CLI gives you the ability to perform to all the S3 operations from a command line. The AWS CLI can be invoked by using aws

HTTP Verb	CRUD Operations in Amazon S3
GET	Read
PUT	Create
DELETE	Delete
POST	Create

Table 2-1 HTTP Verbs and Their Corresponding Actions in Amazon S3 Using the REST API

from the command line. (Of course, you have to install and configure the AWS CLI before you can start using it.) S3 operations via the AWS CLI can be performed by using the `aws s3` command. For example, if you want to create a bucket, the command is `aws s3 mb`. Similarly, to remove a bucket, you can use `aws s3 rb`.

```
$ aws s3 mb s3://bucket-name
$ aws s3 rb s3://bucket-name
```

Steps for Installing AWS Command Line Interface

The primary distribution method for the AWS Command Line Interface (CLI) on Linux, Windows, and macOS is pip, a package manager for Python that provides an easy way to install, upgrade, and remove Python packages and their dependencies.

The AWS CLI can be installed on Linux, Windows, and macOS. The primary distribution method is pip, a package manager for Python through in which you can install and upgrade Python-based packages including the AWS CLI. To install the AWS CLI, you should have Python 2 version 2.6.5+ or Python 3 version 3.3+. If you already have pip and a supported version of Python, you can install the AWS CLI with the following command:

```
$ pip install awscli --upgrade --user
```

```
Verify that the AWS CLI installed correctly by running aws --version.
```

```
joyjeetb$ aws --version
aws-cli/1.11.75 Python/2.7.10 Darwin/16.7.0 botocore/1.5.38
```

Amazon S3 Data Consistency Model

It must be noted that Amazon S3 is a web store and not a file system. The S3 service is intended to be a "write once, read many" use case. Therefore, the architecture is a little bit different from a traditional file system or storage area network (SAN) architecture.

The S3 infrastructure consists of multiple load balancers, web servers, and storage across multiple availability zones. The entire architecture is redundant, and the data is stored in multiple storage locations across multiple availability zones (AZs) to provide durability. Figure 2-2 shows the S3 infrastructure.

Figure 2-2 shows how a file is written in S3. This example shows only two AZs, whereas in real life there could be more than that. For example Amazon S3 Standard uses a minimum of three AZ's to store the data. Similarly, there could be multiple load balancers and storage. Now when you write an object, you first connect to one of the load balancers. From there you connect to one of the API endpoints on the web server, and then the data is stored in a redundant fashion in multiple AZs across multiple storages, which makes sure your data is protected. The exception to this is Amazon S3-One Zone Infrequent Access, where the data is stored in a single AZ. Once that is done, indexing will happen, and the indexes are also stored in multiple storage locations across multiple AZs. If for any reason a load balancer goes down or if a web server goes down, the S3 request will choose a different load balancer or web server to process the request. Similarly, if a storage unit goes down or the storage containing the index goes down, the data or the index will

Figure 2-2
Amazon S3
infrastructure

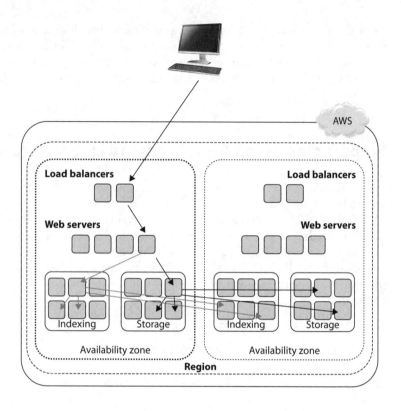

be served from a redundant storage unit. If the whole AZ goes down, failover will take place, and therefore the content will be served from a different AZ since the entire system is replicated across multiple AZs. This is the "write once, read many" architecture at work.

Let's explore the consistency model of S3. Whenever you write a new object, the data will be synchronously stored across multiple facilities before returning success. This provides read-after-write consistency.

For all other objects (apart from new ones), S3 is an eventually consistent system. In an eventually consistent system, the data is automatically replicated and propagated across multiple systems and across multiple AZs within a region, so sometimes you will have a situation where you won't be able to see the updates or changes instantly, or if you try to read the data immediately after update, you may not be able to see all the changes. If a PUT request is successful, your data is safely stored, and therefore there is no need to worry about the data since after a while you will be able to see it. Here are some examples of this:

- A process writes a new object to Amazon S3 and immediately attempts to read it. Until the change is fully propagated, Amazon S3 might report "key does not exist."

- A process writes a new object to Amazon S3 and immediately lists keys within its bucket. Until the change is fully propagated, the object might not appear in the list.

- A process replaces an existing object and immediately attempts to read it. Until the change is fully propagated, Amazon S3 might return the prior data.

- A process deletes an existing object and immediately attempts to read it. Until the deletion is fully propagated, Amazon S3 might return the deleted data.

- A process deletes an existing object and immediately lists keys within its bucket. Until the deletion is fully propagated, Amazon S3 might list the deleted object.

In the case of an update, updates to a single key are atomic. For example, if you PUT to an existing key, a subsequent read might return the old data or the updated data, but it will never write corrupted or partial data. Also, it should be noted that Amazon S3 does not support object locking, which means if there are requests to update the same file concurrently (PUT request), the request with the latest time stamp wins. Though this functionality is not available in S3, you can achieve this by building an object locking mechanism into your application.

Amazon S3 Performance Considerations

It is important to understand the best practice for partitioning if the workload you are planning to run on an Amazon S3 bucket is going to exceed 100 PUT/LIST/DELETE requests per second or 300 GET requests per second. In this case, you need to make sure you follow the partitioning guidelines so you don't end up with any performance bottleneck. You want to able to provide users with a better experience and be able to scale as you grow. Amazon S3 scales to support very high request rates. To do so, internally S3 automatically partitions all your buckets.

As you studied earlier, the name of an S3 bucket is unique, and by combining the bucket name and object name (key), every object can be identified uniquely across the globe. Moreover, the object key is unique within a bucket, and the object keys are stored in UTF-8 binary, with a maximum size of 1,024 bytes. Let's say you have a bucket named `awsbook` and you have the image image2.1.jpg in it in the folder chapter2/image. In this case, this is how it will look:

```
Bucket          Object Key
awsbook         chapter2/image/image2.1.jpg
```

Please note that the object key is `chapter2/image/image2.1.jpg` and not just the name of the file, which is image2.1.jpg. S3 automatically partitions based on the key prefix.

Say you have 20 objects in the bucket `awsbook`, as shown next. In this scenario, S3 is going to do the partitioning based on the key prefix. In this case, it is `c`, the first word of the key `chapter`, which is shown in bold in the following example:

```
chapter2/image/image2.1.jpg
chapter2/image/image2.2.jpg
chapter2/image/image2.3.jpg
chapter3/image/image3.1.jpg
chapter3/image/image3.2.jpg
chapter3/image/image3.3.jpg
chapter3/image/image3.4.jpg
```

```
chapter4/image/image4.1.jpg
chapter4/image/image4.2.jpg
chapter4/image/image4.3.jpg
chapter4/image/image4.4.jpg
chapter5/image/image5.1.jpg
chapter5/image/image5.2.jpg
chapter6/image/image6.1.jpg
chapter6/image/image6.2.jpg
chapter7/image/image7.1.jpg
chapter7/image/image7.2.jpg
chapter7/image/image7.3.jpg
chapter8/image/image8.1.jpg
chapter8/image/image8.2.jpg
```

In this case, everything falls under the same partition, here `awsbook/c`, since the partitioning key is `c`. Now imagine a scenario where you have millions of objects. The performance of the objects in this bucket is definitely going to take a hit. In this scenario, a better way would be to partition the objects with a different key so that you get better performance.

To address this problem, you can change the chapter name to start with a number such as 2chapter, 3chapter, 4chapter, and so on, as shown next. What you have done here is to simply change one character, which changes the partitioning strategy.

```
2chapter/image/image2.1.jpg
2chapter/image/image2.2.jpg
2chapter/image/image2.3.jpg
3chapter/image/image3.1.jpg
3chapter/image/image3.2.jpg
3chapter/image/image3.3.jpg
3chapter/image/image3.4.jpg
4chapter/image/image4.1.jpg
4chapter/image/image4.2.jpg
4chapter/image/image4.3.jpg
4chapter/image/image4.4.jpg
5chapter/image/image5.1.jpg
5chapter/image/image5.2.jpg
6chapter/image/image6.1.jpg
6chapter/image/image6.2.jpg
7chapter/image/image7.1.jpg
7chapter/image/image7.2.jpg
7chapter/image/image7.3.jpg
8chapter/image/image8.1.jpg
8chapter/image/image8.2.jpg
```

By doing this, you have distributed your objects into the following partitions instead of just one partition:

```
awsbook/2
awsbook/3
awsbook/4
awsbook/5
awsbook/6
awsbook/7
awsbook/8
```

A few other ways of implementing the partitioning for performance would be to reverse the key name string and to add a hex hash prefix to the key name. Let's see an example of each approach.

Reverse the Key Name String

Say you are doing massive uploads from your application, and with every set of uploads, the sequence of the application IDs increases by 1. This is a common scenario at many organizations.

```
applicationid/5213332112/log.text
applicationid/5213332112/error.text
applicationid/5213332113/log.text
applicationid/5213332113/error.text
applicationid/5213332114/log.text
applicationid/5213332114/error.text
applicationid/5213332115/log.text
applicationid/5213332115/error.text
```

In this case, since the application ID starts with 5, everything will fall under the same partition, which is `applicationid/5`. Now you are simply going to reverse the key to solve the partitioning issue.

```
applicationid/2112333125/log.text
applicationid/2112333125/error.text
applicationid/3112333125/log.text
applicationid/3112333125/error.text
applicationid/4112333125/log.text
applicationid/4112333125/error.text
applicationid/5112333125/log.text
applicationid/5112333125/error.text
```

By simply reversing the keys, S3 will create multiple partitions in this case, thereby improving the performance.

```
applicationid/2
applicationid/3
applicationid/4
applicationid/5
```

Adding a Hex Hash Prefix to a Key Name

In many scenarios, you will notice that by reversing the key or by changing a few characters, you will not get an optimal partitioning strategy. In that case, you can add a hash string as a prefix to the key name to introduce some randomness. You can compute an MD5 hash of the character sequence, pick a specific number of characters, and assign them as the prefix to the key name. For example, instead of reversing the keys this time, you will use a hex hash prefix. The hash prefix is shown in bold.

```
applicationid/112a5213332112/log.text
applicationid/c9125213332112/error.text
applicationid/2a825213332113/log.text
applicationid/7a2d5213332113/error.text
applicationid/c3dd5213332114/log.text
applicationid/8ao95213332114/error.text
applicationid/z91d5213332115/log.text
applicationid/auw85213332115/error.text
```

If you are planning to use a hash key, you may want to do it carefully because of randomness in the algorithm. If you have too many objects, you will end up with too many partition keys. For example, if you use a 4-character hex hash, there are 65,536 possible character combinations, so you will be sending 65,536 list bucket requests with each specific prefix, which is a combination of a four-digit hash and the date. In fact, you don't need more than two or three prefix characters in your hash. Say you are targeting 100 operations per second and have 25 million objects stored per partition; a 4-character hex has a partition that could support millions of operations per second. This is a pretty big number, and in most cases you probably do not need to support this big of a number.

Encryption in Amazon S3

Let's talk about the encryption features of Amazon S3. There are two main ways of securing the data: encryption of data in transit and encryption of data at rest. Encryption of data in transit means securing the data when it is moving from one point to other, and encryption of data at rest means securing the data or the objects in S3 buckets when the objects remain idle in the S3 bucket and there is no activity going on with them.

If you upload the data using HTTPS and use SSL-encrypted endpoints, the data is automatically secured for all the uploads and downloads, and the data remains encrypted during transit.

If the data is encrypted before being uploaded to an S3 bucket using an S3-encrypted client, the data will already be encrypted in transit. An Amazon S3 encryption client is used to perform client-side encryption for storing data securely in S3. Data encryption is done using a one-time randomly generated content encryption key (CEK) per S3 object. The encryption materials specified in the constructor will be used to protect the CEK, which is then stored alongside the S3 object. You can obtain the Amazon S3 encryption client from http://docs.aws.amazon.com/AWSJavaSDK/latest/javadoc/com/amazonaws/services/s3/AmazonS3EncryptionClient.html.

Let's talk about securing the data at rest.

With Amazon S3 Server Side Encryption (SSE), Amazon S3 will automatically encrypt your data on write and decrypt your data on retrieval. This uses Advanced Encryption Standard (AES) 256-bit symmetric keys, and there are three different ways to manage those keys.

- **SSE with Amazon S3 Key Management (SSE-SE)**   In this case, Amazon S3 will encrypt your data at rest and manage the encryption keys for you. Each object is encrypted using a per-object key. The per-object key is encrypted using a master key, and the master key is managed using S3 key management. The master key is rotated on a monthly basis. You can turn on that option from the S3 console or from the command line or via the SDK, and you don't have to do anything other than that for key management. Everything else is taken care of by Amazon.

- **SSE with customer-provided keys (SSE-C)**   With SSE-C, Amazon S3 will encrypt your data at rest using the custom encryption keys that you provide. To use SSE-C, simply include your custom encryption key in your upload request, and Amazon S3 encrypts the object using that key and securely stores the encrypted data at rest. Similarly, to retrieve an encrypted object, provide your custom encryption key, and Amazon S3 decrypts the object as part of the retrieval. Amazon S3 doesn't store your encryption key anywhere; the key is immediately discarded after Amazon S3 completes your requests.

- **SSE with AWS Key Management Service KMS (SSE-KMS)**   With SSE-KMS, Amazon S3 will encrypt your data at rest using keys that you manage in AWS KMS. Using AWS KMS for key management provides several benefits. With AWS KMS, there are separate permissions for the use of the master key, providing an additional layer of control as well as protection against unauthorized access to your object stored in Amazon S3. AWS KMS provides an audit trail so you can see who used your key to access which object and when, as well as view failed attempts to access data from users without permission to decrypt the data. Additionally, AWS KMS provides additional security controls to support customer efforts to comply with PCI-DSS, HIPAA/HITECH, and FedRAMP industry requirements.

Amazon S3 Access Control

Access control defines who is going to have what access in an S3 bucket. There are several ways to provide access to an S3 bucket, and access control is all about managing the access. You can define various rules specifying who can access which aspects of your S3 service, and by doing that you have total control over S3. In addition, by using access control, you have very fine manual control over the objects stored in S3. You will see a few examples in this chapter, but first let's discuss all the ways of managing the access control in an S3 bucket. There are three main ways of using access control.

Access Policies

By creating an Identity and Access Management policy, you can provide fine-grained control over objects in S3 because an IAM policy helps you control who can access your data stored in S3. You can create an IAM policy and assign that policy to either a user, a group, or a role. You will explore more about users, groups, and roles in Chapter 5. Say you create an S3 full access policy and assign it to a particular group that has ten members. Now all ten users of that particular group will have full access to the S3 bucket. There are a lot of other things that can be done using IAM and S3; for example, you can choose which S3 bucket can be shared with which IAM user, you can allow a particular user to access a particular bucket, you can allow a specific user or all the users to read objects from a specific bucket or from a few buckets, and you can have a policy to allow your customers or partners to drop objects in a particular bucket.

Let's see a few examples of what these policies look like. It is assumed you have a working knowledge of JavaScript Object Notation (JSON). Before you can start writing a policy, you need to know what an Amazon resource name (ARN) is. ARNs uniquely identify AWS resources. An ARN is needed to specify a resource unambiguously across all of AWS, such as in IAM policies, API calls, and so on. This is what an ARN looks like:

```
arn:partition:service:region:account-id:resource
arn:partition:service:region:account-id:resourcetype/resource
```

partition is the partition that the resource is in. For standard AWS regions, the partition is aws. If you have resources in other partitions, the partition is aws-partitionname. For example, the partition for resources in the China (Beijing) region is aws-cn.

service is the service namespace that identifies the AWS product (for example, Amazon S3, IAM, or Amazon RDS). For Amazon S3, the service will be s3.

region is the region the resource resides in. This is optional; some ARNs do not require a region, so you can omit it in that case.

account is the ID of the AWS account that owns the resource, without the hyphens. For example, it can be 331983991. This is optional; some ARNs do not require an account.

resource, resourcetype:resource, or resourcetype/resource is the content; this part of the ARN varies by service. It often includes an indicator of the type of resource—for example, an IAM user or Amazon RDS database—followed by a slash (/) or a colon (:), followed by the resource name itself.

Let's see a few examples of how an S3 ARN looks. Please note that S3 does not require an account number or region in ARNs.

```
arn:aws:s3:::bucket_name
arn:aws:s3:::bucket_name/key_name
arn:aws:s3:::my_bucket_forawsbook
arn:aws:s3:::my_bucket_forawsbook/chapter1.doc
arn:aws:s3:::my_bucket_forawsbook/*
arn:aws:s3:::my_bucket_forawsbook/images/*
```

 TIP   You can also use a policy variable to make things simpler. For example, instead of manually putting in the username, you can use the variable ${aws:username}, so when the policy is executed, the username is replaced with the actual username. This is helpful when you want to assign a policy to a group.

Now let's see an example of how a policy looks. Say you want to provide put and get permission to the S3 bucket my_bucket_forawsbook. The policy looks something similar to this:

```
{
    "Version":"2017-06-07",
    "Statement":[
        {
            "Effect":"Allow",
            "Action":[
                "s3:PutObject",
                "s3:GetObject"
            ],
            "Resource":"arn:aws:s3:::my_bucket_forawsbook/${aws:username}/*"
        }
    ]
}
```

In this example, Effect is the effect of the policy, Allow or Deny. Action lists the actions allowed or denied by this policy. Resource is the AWS resource that this policy applies to.

In Lab 2-3, you will generate a bucket policy using the AWS Policy Generator (https://awspolicygen.s3.amazonaws.com/policygen.html).

Bucket Policies

You can also create policies at the bucket level, which is called a *bucket policy*. Bucket policies also allow fine-grained control over S3 buckets. Using a bucket policy, you can incorporate user restrictions without using IAM. You can even grant other AWS accounts or IAM user permissions for buckets or any folders or objects inside it. When you create a bucket policy, any object permissions apply only to the objects that the bucket owner creates. A very common use case of a bucket policy would be that you can grant read-only permission to an anonymous user to access any object from a particular bucket. This is useful if you are planning to host a static web site in S3 and want everyone to be able to access the web site; you simply grant `GetObject` access. In the following example, you are giving access to all users for the S3 bucket `staticwebsite`. You will learn more about static web site hosting in S3 later in this chapter.

```
{
  "Version":"2017-06-07",
  "Statement":[
    {
      "Sid":"AddPerm",
      "Effect":"Allow",
      "Principal": "*",
      "Action":["s3:GetObject"],
      "Resource":["arn:aws:s3:::staticwebsite/*"]
    }
  ]
}
```

In the previous example, by specifying the principal with a wildcard (*), the policy grants anonymous access. You can even do some fine-grained control using a bucket policy. For example, if for your S3 bucket you want to allow access from only from a particular region and want to deny access from another region, you can do this by specifying a condition to include and not include an IP address range.

```
{
  "Version":"2017-06-07",
  "Statement":[
    {
      "Sid":"AddPerm",
      "Effect":"Allow",
      "Principal": "*",
      "Action":["s3:GetObject"],
      "Resource":["arn:aws:s3:::staticwebsite/*",
"Condition": {
        "IpAddress": {"aws:SourceIp": "74.140.213.0/24"},
        "NotIpAddress": {"aws:SourceIp": "74.140.213.188/32"}
    }
  }
  ]
}
```

A few other real-life uses of bucket policies would be granting permissions to multiple accounts with more conditions, making MFA authentication mandatory by using a policy, granting permission only when the origin is Amazon CloudFront, restricting access to a specific HTTP referrer just like you restricted access for a particular IP access in the previous example, and granting cross-account permissions to upload objects while ensuring the bucket owner has full control.

Access Control List

The third option is to use an access control list (ACL). Each bucket and object inside the bucket has an ACL associated with it. ACLs apply access control rules at the bucket or object level in S3. Unlike an IAM policy or bucket policy, an ACL does not allow fine-grained control. Rather, it allows coarse-grained control. An ACL is a list of grants identifying the grantee and permission granted. For example, you can grant permissions such as basic read-write permissions only to other AWS accounts, not users in your account.

Please note that bucket policies and access control lists are called *resource-based policies* since you attach them to your Amazon S3 resources.

Amazon S3 Storage Class

Amazon S3 offers a variety of storage class designs to cater to different use cases. Depending on your use case and needs, you can choose the appropriate storage class in an S3 bucket to store the data. You can also move the files from one storage class to another storage class. You can also configure lifecycle policies and rules to automatically move files from one storage class to other. Once you create a policy and enable it, the files will be moved from one storage class to the other automatically.

These are storage classes offered by Amazon S3.

- **Amazon S3 Standard**   Amazon S3 Standard is the default storage. It offers high durability, availability, and performance and is used for frequently accessed data. This is the most common use case of S3 and is used for a variety of purposes including web sites, content storage, big data analytics, mobile applications, and so on. The S3 Standard is designed for durability of 99.999999999 percent (11 nines) of objects and 99.99 percent availability over a given year and comes with the S3 SLA for availability. It supports SSL encryption of data in transit and at rest, data lifecycle policies, cross-region replication, and event notifications. The files in Amazon S3 Standard are synchronously copied across three facilities and designed to sustain the loss of data in two facilities.

- **Amazon S3 Standard Infrequent Access (IA)**   IA is an Amazon S3 storage class that is often used for storing data that is accessed less frequently. It provides the same durability over a given year (99.999999999 percent) and inherits all the S3 features including concurrent facility fault tolerance, SSL encryption of data in transit and at rest, data lifecycle policies, cross-region replication, and event notifications. This storage class provides 99.9 percent availability over a given year. The price of this storage class is much cheaper than Amazon S3 Standard, which makes it economical for long-term storage, backups, and disaster recovery use cases. Using lifecycle policies, you can move the files from Amazon S3 Standard to IA.

TIP The storage class is simply one of several attributes associated with each Amazon S3 object. The objects stay in the same S3 bucket (Standard versus IA) and are accessed from the same URLs when they transition from Standard to IA, and vice versa. There is no need to change the application code or point to a different URL when you move the files from one storage class to the other.

- **Amazon S3 Reduced Redundancy Storage (RRS)**   Amazon S3 RRS is a storage option that is used to store noncritical, nonproduction data. It is often used for storing data that can be easily reproduced such as if you are doing video encoding and are required to keep copies of the same file in different resolution modes, say, 1080p, 720p, 360p, and so on. You can keep the master copy of the file in Amazon S3 Standard and keep all the files with different resolutions in Amazon S3 RRS. Amazon S3 RRS is designed to provide 99.99 percent durability and 99.99 percent availability of objects over a given year. It is designed to sustain the loss of data in a single facility.

NOTE Amazon keeps reducing the prices of its services. With the latest price cut, the cost of Amazon S3 RRS is now almost similar to Amazon S3 Standard. Therefore, instead of storing files in Amazon S3 RRS, you may want to store them in Amazon IA, which is much cheaper than Amazon S3 RRS.

- **Amazon S3 One Zone-Infrequent Access (S3 One Zone-IA)**   Amazon S3 One Zone-IA is a new storage class for storing data that is accessed less frequently, but requires rapid access when needed. Amazon S3 One Zone-IA stores data in a single AZ and not like S3 Standard where the data is stored in a minimum of three Availability Zones (AZs). S3 One Zone-IA offers the same high durability, high throughput, and low latency of Amazon S3 Standard and S3 Standard-IA but it costs 20 percent less than storing it in S3 Standard-IA. The S3 One Zone-IA storage class is set at the object level and can exist in the same bucket as S3 Standard and S3 Standard-IA, allowing you to use S3 Lifecycle Policies to automatically transition objects between storage classes without any application changes.

- **Amazon Glacier**   Amazon Glacier is the storage class mainly used for data archiving. This also provides 99.999999999 percent durability of objects and supports SSL encryption of data in transit and at rest, and so on. Since it is mainly used for archiving the data, there are three main options for retrieving data with varying access times and cost. These are expedited, standard, and bulk retrievals. The expedited retrievals allow for very quick retrieval of data in the range of one to five minutes. Standard takes about three to five hours to retrieve the data, and bulk enables you to retrieve large amounts of data such as petabytes of data in a day (five to twelve hours). Amazon Glacier is much cheaper than all the other storage classes. You will study Amazon Glacier in more detail later in this chapter.

You can move the files from one storage class to another in a couple of ways:

- By creating a lifecycle policy
- By running the S3 copy (`aws s3 cp`) command from the AWS CLI

- From the Amazon S3 console
- From an SDK

Versioning of Objects in Amazon S3

Versioning allows you to maintain multiple versions of the same file. Say you have enabled versioning and then upload ten different versions of the same file. All those files will be stored in an S3 bucket, and every file will be assigned a unique version number. When you look at the S3 bucket, you will see only one file name and won't see all ten versions since all ten different versions of the file have the same name. But behind the scenes, S3 stores all the different versions, and with the version option, you can actually look at and download each version of the file. This is really helpful if you accidentally delete a file or if you accidentally update a file and want to go back to a previous version. Versioning is like an insurance policy; you know that regardless of what happens, your files are safe. With versioning, not only can you preserve the files and retrieve them, but you also can restore every version. Amazon S3 starts preserving the existing files in a bucket anytime you perform a PUT, POST, COPY, or DELETE operation on them with versioning enabled.

By default, GET requests will retrieve the most recently written version, or if you download a file directly from the console by default, it will show you only the latest version of the file. If you want to retrieve the older version of a file, you need to specify the version of the file in the GET request.

You can use versioning in conjunction with lifecycle rules to move the old versions of the files to a different class of storage. For example, you can write a rule to move all the old version files to Glacier after 30 days and then have them deleted from Glacier after an additional 30 days. Now you have a total of 60 days to roll back any change. Once you enable versioning, you can't disable it. However, you can suspend versioning to stop the versioning of objects.

TIP Versioning is always done at the bucket level. Say you have thousands of objects in an Amazon S3 bucket and you want to enable versioning for only a few files. In that case, create a separate bucket with only the files for which you want to enable versioning. This way you will avoid versioning thousands of files from your previous S3 bucket.

Amazon S3 Object Lifecycle Management

Using lifecycle management, you can get the best out of S3 in terms of performance as well as cost. You can create various policies according to your needs and can move the files that are stored in Amazon S3 from one storage class to another. You can perform two main kinds of actions with a lifecycle policy.

- **Transition action** This means you can define when the objects can be transitioned to another storage class. For example, you may want to copy all older log files after seven days to S3-IA.

- **Expiration action**   In this case, you define what is going to happen when the objects expire. For example, if you delete a file from S3, what are you going to do with that file?

There are several reasons why you need to have a lifecycle policy in place. For example, you may have a compliance requirement to store all the data that is older than seven years in an archival storage, you may have a rule to archive all the financial and healthcare records, or you may want to create an archive with all the database backups that must be retained for a compliance reason for *n* number of years. You can also create policies to move the files from one storage class to another and then delete them. For example, after a week, you could move all the log files from Amazon S3 to Amazon S3-IA then after one month move all the log files from Amazon S3-IA to Amazon Glacier, and finally after a year delete all the log files from Amazon Glacier.

 TIP   Lifecycle rules are attached to a bucket. If you want to apply the rules to a few files, prefix the files with a unique prefix and then enable the lifecycle rule on the prefix.

Amazon S3 Cross-Region Replication

By using cross-region replication (CRR), you can automatically replicate the objects residing in an S3 bucket to a different region. So if you want to automatically copy the files from one region to another, you need to enable cross-regional replication. CRR allows asynchronous copying of objects.

Many organizations need to keep copies of critical data in locations that are hundreds of miles apart. This is often because of a mandatory compliance requirement and disaster recovery considerations. To do so, you can make copies of your S3 bucket in a different AWS region. Using cross-region replication, you can automatically copy all the files from one region to another region. With cross-region replication, every object uploaded to a particular S3 bucket is automatically replicated to the destination bucket, which is located in a different AWS region.

As an example, say you have a bucket called `jbawsbook` and you want to enable cross-region replication on it. Go to the console and select the S3 bucket. Then go to the Management tab and click Replication, and then click the button Get Started, as shown in Figure 2-3.

The versioning must be enabled in the source and target buckets. If you don't enable versioning, you won't be able to do the cross-region replication. You will get an error, "The bucket doesn't have versioning enabled" (Figure 2-4). So, follow these steps:

1. Click Enable versioning and click Next, as shown in Figure 2-4.

2. Then click Select A Source; there are two options: Whole Bucket, which means that all the objects of the bucket will be replicated in a different region, and Prefix In This Bucket, which means you can restrict replication to a subset of the objects in the bucket using a prefix, as shown in Figure 2-5. Under Status, Enabled is selected by default, which means the rule starts to work as soon as

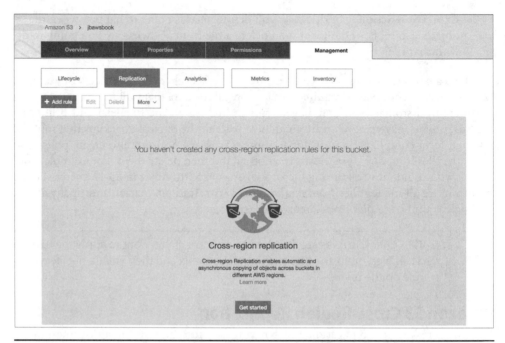

Figure 2-3 Enabling CRR

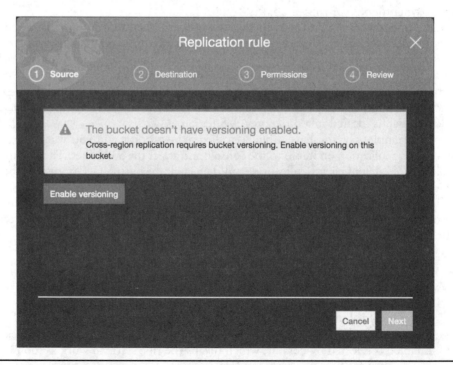

Figure 2-4 Enabling versioning

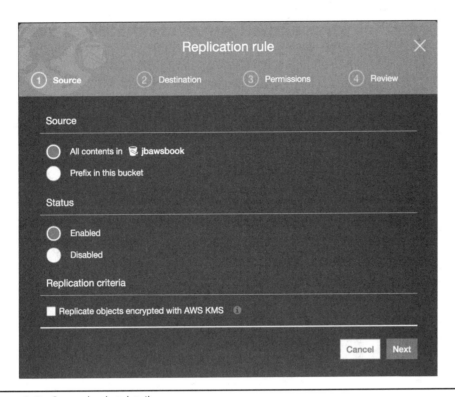

Figure 2-5   Source bucket details

you save it. If you want to enable the rule later, select Disabled. If you want to replicate the objects, which are encrypted with AWS KMS, select Replicate Objects Encrypted with AWS KMS.

3. Choose the Destination bucket where you want to replicate the files. (You must create the target bucket and enable versioning on it before trying this.) The bucket can be either in this account or in another account. Choose an option accordingly. You have the option to select a different class of storage for replicating the files. By default the files are replicated to the same storage class, but from the console you can choose one of the following storage classes: Standard, Standard-IA, One Zone-IA, or Reduced Redundancy. Selecting Change the Object Ownership to Destination Bucket Owner, you can change the object ownership. In order to do so you have to provide the account ID and bucket name. This is shown in Figure 2-6. Note you can't use CRR to replicate the content to two buckets that are in the same region.

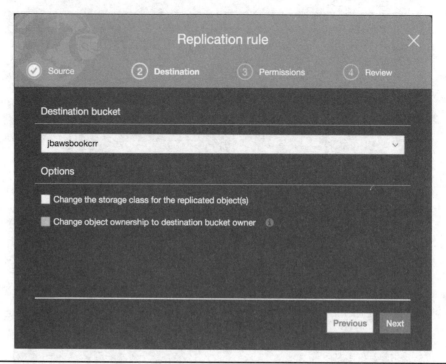

Figure 2-6   Destination bucket details

4. You need to set up an IAM role so that S3 can list and retrieve objects from the source bucket and replicate them to the destination bucket. Using roles you can also replicate objects owned by separate AWS accounts. If you already have an IAM role, you can select the same one from the next screen (see Figure 2-7). If you don't have an IAM role, you can create one by selecting the Create New Role option in the next screen. You will explore IAM in detail in Chapter 5.

5. Click Next and then Save, and you are all set. See Figure 2-7.

The CRR copies only the new objects. If you have preexisting files in the bucket, you must copy them manually from the source to the destination using an S3 copy or via the CLI or SDK.

If you want to monitor the replication status, you can do so by using the HEAD operation on a source object. The HEAD operation retrieves metadata from an object without returning the object itself. This operation is useful if you are interested only in an object's metadata. To use HEAD, you must have read access to the object. Covering the HEAD operation in more detail is beyond the certification objective; however, if you want to learn more about it, refer to the Amazon S3 API guide.

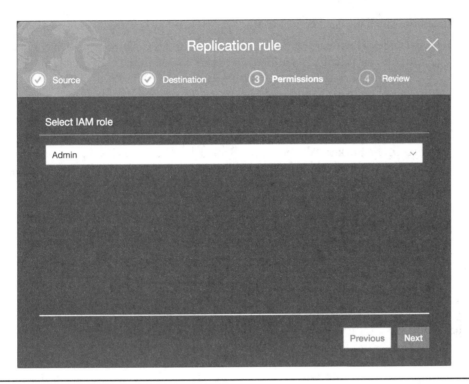

Figure 2-7   IAM details

Static Web Site Hosting in Amazon S3

You can host a static web site on Amazon S3. A static web site is one where the content does not change and remains static. A static web site may contain some client-side scripts, but the content of the web site is almost stagnant all the time. By contrast, a dynamic web site is one where the content changes frequently, and a lot of server-side processing happens by running scripts built on PHP, JSP, and so on. Amazon S3 does not support server-side scripting.

It is easy to host a static web site on Amazon S3. Using the following steps, you should be able to host your static web site on Amazon S3 in a few minutes:

1. Sign in to the AWS management console and open the Amazon S3 console at https://console.aws.amazon.com/s3/.

2. In the Bucket Name list, choose the name of the bucket that you want to enable static web site hosting for.

3. Choose Properties.

4. Choose Static Web Site Hosting. After you enable your bucket for static web site hosting, web browsers can access all of your content through the Amazon S3 web site endpoint for your bucket.

5. Choose Use This Bucket To Host.

- For Index Document, type the name of the index document, which is typically index.html. When you configure a bucket for web site hosting, you must specify an index document. Amazon S3 returns this index document when requests are made to the root domain or any of the subfolders.

- Choose Save.

6. Add a bucket policy to the web site bucket that grants everyone access to the objects in the bucket. When you configure a bucket as a web site, you must make the objects that you want to serve publicly readable. To do so, you write a bucket policy that grants everyone s3:GetObject permission. You will create this bucket policy as part of Lab 2-3.

Amazon Glacier

Amazon Glacier is a low-cost cloud storage service that is mainly used for data archiving and long-term backup. Just like S3, Glacier is extremely secure and durable and provides the same security and durability as S3. The best part about Glacier is it is extremely low in cost. You can store data in Amazon Glacier for as little as $0.004 per gigabyte per month, which is another reason why it's becoming popular these days. These are the most common use cases of Glacier in the industry currently:

- **Magnetic tape replacement**   Managing tape archives is a pretty painful activity, and if you have a compliance requirement to archive all old data, you end up maintaining a library of magnetic tape drives. Creating a tape library needs a huge capital investment and of course specialized maintenance. Often customers ship the tape archives to a different location to create a redundant backup. The shipping costs also add to the cost of managing the tape libraries and are often overlooked. Sometimes when restoring the magnetic tape you realize the tape has gone bad and you can't retrieve the data from it. Amazon Glacier has zero up-front costs, so you don't have to incur a huge capital expenditure to use it. In addition, there is no maintenance overhead like with magnetic tape, and you get the same durability as S3. Therefore, customers are replacing their table library footprint with Amazon Glacier.

- **Healthcare/life sciences/scientific data storage**   With the advancement in life sciences such as genomic data, a single sequence of genomes can take up to a terabyte of data. Also, if more data is available for running the analytics, the better results scientists will get to run their research. The same applies to scientists in other areas. They need to generate, analyze, and archive all the data, and Glacier is the best place to store all of it. In addition, even hospitals have to meet compliance requirements; they need to keep all the patients' records, which sometimes can be petabytes of data. Amazon Glacier helps you to achieve this at a low cost.

- **Media assets archiving/digital preservation** Media assets such as video of news coverage and game coverage can grow to several petabytes quickly. Glacier is the best place to archive all these media assets. If you need to redistribute/rebroadcast them, you can quickly move them to Amazon S3. Similarly, you can use Glacier to archive audio, e-books, and so on.
- **Compliance archiving/long-term backup** Many organizations have a compliance requirement to archive all the data that is *x* years old. Similarly, many organizations have an internal policy to keep a long-term backup of several files, though it may not be a compliance requirement. Amazon Glacier Vault Lock helps you set compliance controls to meet your compliance objectives. You will learn more about Amazon Glacier Vault Lock in the next section.

Amazon Glacier Key Terminology

This section will define some key terminology used in Amazon Glacier.

When you upload data in Amazon Glacier, you store it as an *archive*. Even if you store one file, that will still be an archive with a single file. It is recommended that you aggregate your files and then upload them to Amazon Glacier. You can use popular tools such as TAR or ZIP to do this. By consolidating your data into a single file as an archive, your cost will be much lower than storing single files as separate archives. Like with Amazon S3, there is no limit to how many files you can store in Amazon Glacier. A single Amazon Glacier archive can be anything from 1 byte to 40TB, and there is no limit on how many of these you can upload. Please note that archives are write-once, which means once you create an archive, you won't be able to modify the files in it. Therefore, the data stored in an archive is immutable, meaning that after an archive is created, it cannot be updated. If you want to update or edit the contents, you need to download them and modify and re-upload them in Glacier. If you are planning to upload large archives (100MB or bigger), it is recommended that you use the multipart upload capability where the files are broken into smaller chunks and uploaded individually. Once all the smaller chunks are successfully uploaded, they are combined to make a single archive. The max archive size that can be uploaded in a single upload request is 4GB.

Every vault has a unique address. The format looks like the following:

https://<region-specific endpoint>/<account-id>/vaults/<vault-name>/archives/<archive-id>

A *vault* is like a safe deposit box or locker. You can group multiple archives and put them in a vault. You can say a vault is like a container for an archive. A vault gives you the ability to organize your data residing in Amazon Glacier. You can set different access policies for each vault, thereby allowing different people to access different vaults. You can use IAM and create the vault-level access policies. You can create up to 1,000 vaults per account per region. For the ease of managing your vault, AWS provides you with the ability to tag your vault. If you want to delete a vault, it should not contain any archive. If it contains an archive, then you need to delete the archive first before deleting the vault.

Amazon Glacier Vault Lock allows you to easily deploy and enforce compliance controls on individual Glacier vaults via a lockable policy. You can specify controls such as Write Once Read Many (WORM) in a Vault Lock policy and lock the policy from future edits. Once locked, the policy becomes immutable, and Glacier will enforce the prescribed controls to help achieve your compliance objectives.

Glacier maintains a cold index of archives refreshed every 24 hours, which is known as an *inventory* or *vault inventory.*

Whenever you want to retrieve an archive and vault inventory, you need to submit a Glacier *job,* which is going to run behind the scenes to deliver you the files requested. This operation is an asynchronous operation in Amazon Glacier. For each job, Amazon Glacier maintains all the information related to the job such as type of the job, creation date, status of the job, completion date, and so on. As soon as the job is finished, you should be able to download the job output, which is your files. Amazon Glacier also supports notifications; therefore, when the Glacier job is finished, you can be notified. You can configure Amazon Simple Notification Service with Amazon Glacier, which allows you to create notifications once a Glacier job is finished.

Accessing Amazon Glacier

There are three ways to access Amazon Glacier:

- You can access it directly via the Amazon Glacier API or SDK.
- You can access it via Amazon S3 lifecycle integration. You can create various lifecycle policies to move the files to Glacier. For example, you can write a policy that says to move any file residing in S3 that is more than one year old to Glacier, move any file that is more than three months old to Glacier, and so on.
- You can access it via various third-party tools and gateways.

Uploading Files to Amazon Glacier

Uploading files to Amazon Glacier is pretty simple. You can use the Internet directly to upload the files. You can also upload the files to Glacier from your corporate data center using AWS Direct Connect. If you have a large number of files or a huge data set, you can use AWS Snowball to ship your files and then upload them to Glacier.

To upload a file in Glacier first, you need to create a vault, which is the container where your data will be stored. You can visualize this vault as a safety deposit box that you often see in a bank. Vault names must be unique within an account and within the region in which the vault is being created. During the creation of a vault, you can also enable notifications.

Then you need to create an access policy that you can attach directly to your Glacier vault (the resource) to specify who has access to the vault and what actions they can perform on it.

The next step is to create the archives and upload them to the vault. For large archives, Amazon Glacier provides a multipart upload API that enables you to upload an archive in parts. Amazon also provides you with SDKs for Java and .NET to upload files to Glacier. Whenever you upload an archive, Amazon internally creates an archive ID to uniquely identify the archive.

Retrieving Files from Amazon Glacier

There are three ways to retrieve data from Amazon Glacier:

- **Standard**   This is a low-cost option for retrieving data in just a few hours. Typically it takes about three to five hours to retrieve the data. The standard retrieval cost is $0.01 per gigabyte.

- **Expedited**   This is designed for occasional urgent access to a small number of archives. Using expedited retrieval, the data can be accessed almost instantly within one to five minutes. The expedited retrieval cost is $0.03 per gigabyte.

- **Bulk**   This is the lowest-cost option optimized for large retrievals, up to petabytes of data. It takes between five to twelve hours to retrieve the data. The bulk retrieval cost is $0.0025 per gigabyte.

Retrieving files from Glacier is simple. All the jobs are done in a four-step process.

1. You submit a retrieval job. While submitting the retrieval job, you can specify whether it is standard, expedited, or bulk retrieval. The moment you submit the retrieval job, you get a unique job ID that you can use to track the retrieval job.

2. Depending on the type of job you have submitted, it can take from a few minutes to a few hours to complete the job.

3. Once the job is completed, you get a notification that the job has been completed.

4. You can now download the output.

If you have enabled the lifecycle policy of S3, you can also restore the data using life-cycle management.

Amazon Elastic Block Store

Amazon Elastic Block Store (EBS) offers persistent storage for Amazon EC2 instances. A persistent storage means the storage is independent outside the life span of an EC2 instance. EBS volumes provide durable block-level storage for use with Amazon EC2 instances. Amazon EBS volumes are network-attached and continue independently after the life of an instance. Amazon EBS volumes are highly available, highly reliable volumes that can be leveraged as an Amazon EC2 instance's boot partition or attached to a running Amazon EC2 instance as a standard block device. Once you attach an EBS volume to an EC2 instance, the EBS volume can be used as a physical hard drive of a server (of course, you may have to format the volume before using it). You can attach multiple EBS volumes to an EC2 instance. This gives you a great advantage since you can separate the boot volumes from the data volume. You can have one EBS volume for the data and another EBS volume for the boot volume and attach both of them to the same EC2 instance. An EBS volume can be attached to only one EC2 server at a time. You cannot attach or mount the same EBS volume to multiple EC2 instances. But at any point in time you can detach an EBS volume from an EC2 instance and can mount it to a different EC2 instance. Since EBS volumes are part of a particular AZ, you can detach and reattach an EBS volume between instances within the same AZ. You can't detach and reattach EBS volumes across different AZs.

Once you attach the EBS volume to the EC2 instance, you can create a file system on top of that. After creating the file system, you can run any kind of workload you want to run on those servers. You can run any type of workload on EBS volumes such as databases, applications, big data workloads, NoSQL databases, web sites, and so on.

EBS volumes can also be used as a boot partition. When EBS volumes are used as a boot partition, then Amazon EC2 instances can be stopped and subsequently restarted, enabling you to pay only for the storage resources used while maintaining your instance's state. Also, since the EBS volumes persist after the restart, all the data that you store in the EBS volume stays as is. Amazon EBS volumes offer greatly improved durability over local Amazon EC2 instance stores.

Amazon EBS provides the ability to create point-in-time consistent snapshots of your volumes that are then stored in Amazon S3 and automatically replicated across multiple availability zones. These snapshots can be used as the starting point for new Amazon EBS volumes and can protect your data for long-term durability. You can also easily share these snapshots with co-workers and other AWS developers or to another account. The snapshot can also be copied across multiple regions. Therefore, if you are planning for disaster recovery, data center migration, or geographical expansion or you want to leverage multiple AWS regions, you can use EBS snapshots to get your data quickly and provision the infrastructure.

Features of Amazon EBS

The following are the main features of Amazon EBS:

- **Persistent storage**   As discussed previously, the volume's lifetime is independent of any particular Amazon EC2 instance.
- **General purpose**   Amazon EBS volumes are raw, unformatted block devices that can be used from any operating system.
- **High availability and reliability**   Amazon EBS volumes provide 99.999 percent availability and automatically replicate within their availability zones to protect your applications from component failure. It is important to note that EBS volumes are not replicated across multiple AZs; rather, they are replicated within different facilities within the same AZ.
- **Encryption**   Amazon EBS encryption provides support for the encryption of data at rest and data in transit between EC2 instances and EBS volumes.
- **Variable size**   Volume sizes range from 1GB to 16TB and are allocated in 1GB increments.

- **Easy to use**   Amazon EBS volumes can be easily created, attached, backed up, restored, and deleted.

- **Designed for resiliency**   The annual failure rate (AFR) of Amazon EBS is between 0.1 percent to 0.2 percent.

AWS Block Storage Offerings

There are three types of block storage offerings that AWS provides:

- Amazon EC2 instance store
- Amazon EBS SSD-backed volume
- Amazon EBS HDD-backed volume

Amazon EC2 Instance Store

An Amazon EC2 instance store is the local storage of an EC2 instance. It is local to the instance, and unlike EBS volumes, it can't be mounted into different servers. The instance store is ephemeral, which means all the data stored in the instance store is gone the moment the EC2 instance is shut down. The data neither persists nor is replicated in the instance store. Also, there is no snapshot support for the instance store, which means you won't be able to take a snapshot of the instance store. The instance store is available in a solid-state drive (SSD) or hybrid hard drive (HDD).

Amazon EBS Volumes

Amazon EBS provides multiple options that allow you to optimize storage performance and cost for any workload you would like to run. These options are divided into two major categories: SSD-backed storage, which is mainly used for transactional workloads such as databases and boot volumes, and HDD-backed storage, which is for throughput-intensive workloads such as log processing and mapreduce.

Amazon EBS-Backed Volume   Elastic volumes are a feature of Amazon EBS that allow you to dynamically increase capacity, tune performance, and change the type of live volumes with no downtime or performance impact. You can simply use a metric from CloudWatch and write a Lambda function to automate it. (You will learn about Cloud-Watch and Lambda later in this book.) This allows you to easily right-size your deployment and adapt to performance changes.

Amazon EBS SSD-Backed Volume   The SSD-backed volumes are of two types, General-Purpose SSD (gp2) and Provisioned IOPS SSD (io1). SSD-backed volumes include the highest performance io1 for latency-sensitive transactional workloads and gp2, which balances price and performance for a wide variety of transactional data.

Before going deep into the types of volume, it is important to understand the concept of IOPS. The performance of a block storage device is commonly measured and quoted in a unit called IOPS, short for input/output operations per second. A drive spinning at 7,200 RPM can perform at 75 to 100 IOPS, whereas a drive spinning at 15,000 RPM will deliver 175 to 210. The exact number will depend on a number of factors including the access pattern (random or sequential) and the amount of data transferred per read or write operation.

General-Purpose SSD   General-Purpose SSD delivers single-digit millisecond latencies, which is actually a good use case for the majority of workloads. gp2s can deliver between 100 to 10,000 IOPS. gp2 provides great performance for a broad set of workloads, all at a low cost. They reliably deliver three sustained IOPS for every gigabyte of configured storage. For example, a 100GB volume will reliably deliver 300 IOPS. The volume size for gp2 can be anything from 1GB to 16TB. It provides the maximum throughput of 160Mb per volume. You can run any kind of workload in gp2; however, some use cases that are a good fit for gp2 are system boot volumes, applications requiring low latency, virtual desktops, development and test environments, and so on.

The General-Purpose SSDs under 1TB have the ability to burst the IO. This means if you are not using the IOPS, they will get accumulated as IO credit and will be used as IO during peak loads. Let's see an example to understand this. Say you have a 100GB EBS volume; at 3 IOPS per gigabyte you can expect a total of 300 IOPS. Now whenever you are not using 300 IOPS, the system accumulates the unused IO and keeps it as IO credits. When you are running a peak workload or when there is a heavy activity, it will use the IO credits that it has accumulated, and you will see a lot more IO. The IO can burst up to 3,000 IOPS. When all the IO credits are over, it is going to revert to 300 IOPS. Since the max limit for burst is 3,000 IOPS, volumes more than 1TB in size won't get the benefit of it. By the way, each volume receives an initial IO credit balance of 5.4 million IO credits, which is good enough to sustain the maximum burst performance of 3,000 IOPS for 30 minutes. This initial credit balance provides a fast initial boot cycle for boot volumes and provides a better bootstrapping experience.

Provisioned IOPS SSD   If you have an IO-intense workload such as databases, then you need predictable and consistence IO performance. Provisioned IOPS is designed to cater to that requirement. When you create an EBS volume with Provisioned IOPS, you can specify the IOPS rate, and EBS volumes deliver within 10 percent of the Provisioned IOPS performance 99.9 percent of the time in a given year. You can create an io1 volume between 4GB to 16TB and can specify anything between 100 to 20,000 IOPS per volume. The ratio for volume versus Provisioned IOPS is 1:50. For example, if you have a volume of 100GB, then the IOPS you can provision with that will be 100*50, which is 5,000 IOPS. Since there is a limit of 20,000 IOPS per volume, even if the size of the volume is 1TB, the maximum IOPS you can provision with that volume would be 20,000 only. If you need more Provisioned IOPS, then you should distribute your workload on multiple EBS volumes. You can also use technologies such as RAID on top of multiple EBS volumes to stripe and mirror the data across multiple volumes. (Please note that RAID is irrespective of the type of EBS volume.) The maximum throughput per volume you will get is 320MB per second, and the maximum IOPS an instance can have is 75,000. Provisioned costs more than the general-purpose version, and it is based on the volume size as well as the amount of IOPS reserved. It can be used for database workloads such as Oracle, PostgreSQL, MySQL, Microsoft SQL Server, Mongo DB, and Cassandra; running mission-critical applications; or running production databases, which needs sustained IO performance and so on.

Amazon EBS HDD-Backed Volume   HDD-backed volumes include Throughput Optimized HDD (st1), which can be used for frequently accessed, throughput-intensive workloads; and HDD (sc1), which is for less frequently accessed data that has the lowest cost.

Throughput-Optimized HDD   Throughput-Optimized HDD (st1) is good when the workload you are going to run defines the performance metrics in terms of throughput instead of IOPS. The hard drives are based on magnetic drives. There are lots of workloads that can leverage this EBS volume such as data warehouses, ETL, log processing, mapreduce jobs, and so on. This volume is ideal for any workload that involves sequential IO. Any workload that has a requirement for random IO should be run either on general-purpose or on Provisioned IOPS depending on the price/performance need.

Like the General-Purpose SSDs, Throughput-Optimized HDD also uses a burst-bucket model for performance. In this case, it is the volume size that determines the baseline for the throughput of the volume. It bursts 250MB per second per terabyte up to 500Mb per second. The capacity of the volume ranges from 500GB to 16TB.

Cold HDD

Just like st1, Cold HDD (sc1) also defines performance in terms of throughput instead of IOPS. The throughput capacity is less compared to sc1; therefore, the prices are also very cheap for sc1. This is a great use case for noncritical, cold data workloads and is designed to support infrequently accessed data. Similar to st1, sc1 uses a burst-bucket model, but in this case the burst capacity is less since overall throughput is less.

EBS offers snapshot capabilities that can be used to back up EBS volumes. You can take a snapshot at any point in time when a volume is in use without any outages. The snapshot will back up the data that resides on the EBS volume, so if you have any data cached in the application, the snapshot won't be able to take the backup. To ensure a consistent snapshot, it is recommended that you detach the EBS volume from the EC2 instance, issue the snapshot command, and then reattach the EBS volume to the instance. You can take a snapshot of the root volume as well. In that case, it is recommended that you shut down the machine first and then take it. You can store the snapshots in Amazon S3. There is no limit to the number of snapshots you can take. Each snapshot is uniquely identified by name.

Amazon Elastic File System

As the name suggests, Amazon Elastic File System (EFS) provides a file system interface and file system semantics to Amazon EC2 instances. When EFS is attached to an EC2 instance, it acts just like a local file system. EFS is also a shared file system, which means you can mount the same file system across multiple EC2 instances, and EFS shares access to the data between multiple EC2 instances, with low latencies.

The following are the attributes of EFS:

- **Fully managed**   It is a fully managed file system, and you don't have to maintain any hardware or software. There is no overhead of managing the file system since it is a managed service.

- **File system access semantics**   You get what you would expect from a regular file system, including read-after-write consistency, locking, the ability to have a hierarchical directory structure, file operations like appends, atomic renames, the ability to write to a particular block in the middle of a file, and so on.

- **File system interface** It exposes a file system interface that works with standard operating system APIs. EFS appears like any other file system to your operating system. Applications that leverage standard OS APIs to work with files will work with EFS.

- **Shared storage** It is a shared file system. It can be shared across thousands of instances. When an EFS is shared across multiple EC2 instances, all the EC2 instances have access to the same data set.

- **Elastic and scalable** EFS elastically grows to petabyte scale. You don't have to specify a provisioned size up front. You just create a file system, and it grows and shrinks automatically as you add and remove data.

- **Performance** It is built for performance across a wide variety of workloads. It provides consistent, low latencies, high throughput, and high IOPS.

- **Highly available and durable** The data in EFS is automatically replicated across AZs within a region. As a result, your files are highly available, accessible from multiple AZs, and also well protected from data loss.

Figure 2-8 shows the foundation on which EFS is built. As you can see, it aims to be highly durable and highly available. Since your data is automatically available in multiple AZs, EFS is designed to sustain AZ offline conditions. It is superior to traditional NAS availability models since the data is mirrored across multiple AZs. Therefore, it is appropriate for running mission-critical production workloads.

Simplicity is the foundation of EFS. You can create an EFS instance in seconds. There are no file layers or hardware to manage. EFS eliminates ongoing maintenance and the constant upgrade/refresh cycle. It can be seamlessly integrated with existing tools and apps. It works with the NFS protocol. Using a direct connect and VPC, you can also mount EFS on your on-premise servers via the NFS 4.1 protocol. It is a great use case if you want to transfer a large number of data from the servers running on your premise to the AWS cloud. Also, if you have a workload on your premise that needs additional compute, you can leverage EFS and EC2 servers to offload some of the application workload processing to the cloud. You can even use EFS to back up files to the cloud.

Since EFS is elastic, the file system automatically grows and shrinks automatically as you add or remove files. You don't have to specify any capacity up front or provision anything, and there is no limit to the number of files you can add in the file system. You just pay for the storage space you use. There are no minimum fees or minimum commitment.

Figure 2-8
Foundation on which Amazon EFS is built

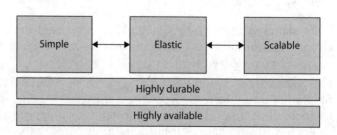

Since EFS is scalable, the throughput and IOPS scale automatically as file systems grow. There is no need to reprovision, adjust performance settings, or do anything in order for your file system to grow to petabyte-scale. The performance aspect is taken care of automatically as you add files. EFS has been designed in such a way that with each gigabyte of stored files you get a particular amount of throughput and IOPS, and as a result, you get consistent performance and are able get low latencies. EFS supports thousands of concurrent NFS connections.

Using Amazon Elastic File System

The first step in using Amazon EFS is to create a file system. The file system is the primary resource in EFS where you store files and directories. You can create ten file systems per account. Of course, like any other AWS service, you can increase this limit by raising a support ticket. To access your file system from instances in a VPC, you create mount targets in the VPC. A mount target is an NFS v4 endpoint in your VPC. A mount target has an IP address and a DNS name you use in your mount command. You need to create a separate mount target from each AZ. Now you can run the mount command on the file system's DNS name to mount the EFS on your EC2 instance. When the EFS is mounted, the file system appears like a local set of directories and files.

To summarize, these are the steps:

1. Create a file system.

2. Create a mount target in each AZ from which you want to access the file system.

3. Run the mount command from the EC2 instance on the DNS name of the mount of EFS.

4. Start using the EFS.

Figure 2-9 shows the process of creating an EFS instance.

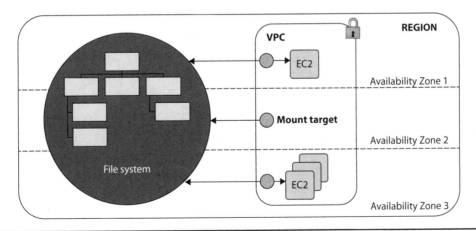

Figure 2-9 Amazon EFS creation

The EFS instance can be administered via the AWS management console or via the AWS command-line interface (CLI) or AWS software development kit (SDK), which provides EFS support for Java, Python, PHP .NET, and others. AWS also provides APIs that allow you to administer your EFS file systems via the three options mentioned.

Since EFS provides predictive performance, it serves the vast majority of file workloads, covering a wide spectrum of performance needs from big data applications that are massively parallelized and require the highest possible throughput to single-threaded, latency-sensitive workloads.

There are lot of places where it can be used. Some of the most common use cases of EFS are genomics, big data analytics, web serving, home directories, content management, media-intensive jobs, and so on.

Performance Mode of Amazon EFS

General-purpose mode is the default for Amazon EFS. It is optimized for latency-sensitive applications and general-purpose file-based workloads. This mode is the best option for the majority of use cases.

Max I/O mode is optimized for large-scale and data-heavy applications where tens, hundreds, or thousands of EC2 instances are accessing the file system. It scales to higher levels of aggregate throughput and operations per second with a trade-off of slightly higher latencies for file operation.

You can use Amazon CloudWatch metrics to get visibility into EFS's performance. You can use CloudWatch to determine whether your application can benefit from the maximum I/O. If not, you'll get the best performance in general-purpose mode.

On-Premise Storage Integration with AWS

If you have to transfer a large amount of data from your data centers, uploading it to S3 might not be a good choice. When you are planning to transfer more than 10TB of data, you can integrate your on-premise storage with AWS. AWS offers a couple of options through which you can move your data to the cloud. From a certification point of view, this topic is not important, but as a solutions architect, you should know about these offerings.

AWS Storage Gateway

The AWS Storage Gateway (SGW) service is deployed as a virtual machine in your existing environment. This VM is called a *storage gateway*, and you connect your existing applications, storage systems, or devices to this storage gateway. The storage gateway provides standard storage protocol interfaces so apps can connect to it without changes. The gateway in turn connects to AWS so you can store data securely and durably in Amazon S3 Glacier.

The gateway optimizes data transfer from on-premises to AWS. It also provides low-latency access through a local cache so your apps can access frequently used data locally. The service is also integrated with other AWS services such as CloudWatch, CloudTrail, and IAM. Therefore, you can leverage these services within the storage gateway running on-premise. The storage gateway supports three storage interfaces, as described here:

- The *file gateway* enables you to store and retrieve objects in Amazon S3 using industry-standard file protocols. Files are stored as objects in your S3 buckets and accessed through a Network File System (NFS) mount point. Ownership, permissions, and timestamps are durably stored in S3 in the user metadata of the object associated with the file. Once objects are transferred to S3, they can be managed as native S3 objects, and bucket policies such as versioning, lifecycle management, and cross-region replication apply directly to objects stored in your bucket.

- The *volume gateway* presents your applications with disk volumes using the iSCSI block protocol. Data written to these volumes can be asynchronously backed up as point-in-time snapshots of your volumes and stored in the cloud as Amazon EBS snapshots. You can set the schedule for when snapshots occur or create them via the AWS Management Console or service API. Snapshots are incremental backups that capture only changed blocks. All snapshot storage is also compressed to minimize your storage charges. When connecting with the block interface, you can run the gateway in two modes: cached and stored. In cached mode, you store your primary data in Amazon S3 and retain your frequently accessed data locally. With this mode, you can achieve substantial cost savings on the primary storage, minimizing the need to scale your storage on-premises, while retaining low-latency access to your frequently accessed data. You can configure up to 32 volumes of 32TB each, for a total 1PB storage per gateway. In stored mode, you store your entire data set locally while performing asynchronous backups of this data in Amazon S3. This mode provides durable and inexpensive off-site backups that you can recover locally or from Amazon EC2.

- The *tape gateway* presents the storage gateway to your existing backup application as an industry-standard iSCSI-based virtual tape library (VTL), consisting of a virtual media changer and virtual tape drives. You can continue to use your existing backup applications and workflows while writing to a nearly limitless collection of virtual tapes. Each virtual tape is stored in Amazon S3. When you no longer require immediate or frequent access to data contained on a virtual tape, you can have your backup application archive it from the virtual tape library into Amazon Glacier, further reducing storage costs.

AWS Snowball and AWS Snowball Edge

Snowball is an AWS import/export tool that provides a petabyte-scale data transfer service that uses Amazon-provided storage devices for transport. Previously, customers had to purchase their own portable storage devices and use these devices to ship their data. With Snowball, customers are now able to use highly secure, rugged, Amazon-owned network-attached storage (NAS) devices, called *Snowballs,* to ship their data. Once the Snowballs are received and set up, customers are able to copy up to 80TB data from their on-premises file system to the Snowball via the Snowball client software and a 10Gbps network interface. Snowballs come with two storage sizes: 50TB and 80TB. Prior to transfer to the Snowball, all the data is encrypted by 256-bit GSM encryption by the client. When customers finish transferring their data to the device, they simply ship the Snowball back to an AWS facility where the data is ingested at high speed into Amazon S3.

AWS Snowball Edge, like the original Snowball, is a petabyte-scale data transfer solution, but it transports more data, up to 100TB of data, and retains the same embedded cryptography and security as the original Snowball. In addition, Snowball Edge hosts a file server and an S3-compatible endpoint that allows you to use the NFS protocol, S3 SDK, or S3 CLI to transfer data directly to the device without specialized client software. Multiple units may be clustered together, forming a temporary data collection storage tier in your data center so you can work as data is generated without managing copies. As your storage needs scale up and down, you can easily add or remove devices to/from the local cluster and return them to AWS.

AWS Snowmobile

AWS Snowmobile is a secure, exabyte-scale data transfer service used to transfer large amounts of data into and out of AWS. Each Snowmobile instance can transfer up to 100PB. When you order a Snowmobile, it comes to your site, and AWS personnel connect a removable, high-speed network switch from Snowmobile to your local network. This makes Snowmobile appear as a network-attached data store. Once it is connected, the secure, high-speed data transfer can begin. After your data is transferred to Snowmobile, it is driven back to AWS where the data is loaded into the AWS service you select, including S3, Glacier, Redshift, and others.

Chapter Review

In this chapter, you learned about the various storage offerings from AWS.

Amazon S3 is the object store that has 99.99999999999 percent durability. S3 can be used for a variety of purposes. The objects are stored in a bucket in S3, and the name of bucket must be unique. S3 has different classes of storage. Amazon S3 Standard is the default storage. IA is an Amazon S3 storage class that is often used for storing data that is accessed less frequently. Amazon S3 RRS is a storage option that is used to store noncritical data where you get less durability compared to S3 Standard. S3 One Zone-IA stores data in a single AZ Amazon Glacier is the storage class mainly used for data archiving.

Amazon Elastic Block Store (EBS) offers persistent storage for Amazon EC2 instances. It is the block storage that can be used in AWS. EBS can be based on SSD or HDD. The SSD-backed volumes are of two types: General-Purpose SSD (gp2) and Provisioned IOPS SSD (io1). HDD-backed volumes include Throughput Optimized HDD (st1), which can be used for frequently accessed, throughput-intensive workloads; and HDD (sc1), which is for less frequently accessed data that has the lowest cost. Some EC2 instances also have a local storage built in that is called the *instance store*. The instance store is ephemeral, and it is gone whenever you terminate the instance.

Amazon Elastic File System provides a shared file system across many EC2 instances. EFS shares access to the data between multiple EC2 instances, with low latencies. If you need a shared file system for your applications, you can use EFS.

Amazon Storage Gateway can be integrated with your applications running on-premise to the storage on AWS so you can transfer the data from your data center to AWS.

AWS Snowball and AWS Snowball Edge are devices that can be used to ship a large amount of data to AWS. AWS Snowball has a capacity of either 50TB or 80TB, whereas Snowball Edge has a capacity of 100TB.

Amazon Snowmobile is an exabyte-scale data transfer service. Each Snowmobile can transfer up to 100PB. It is delivered to your site container.

Lab 2-1: Creating, Moving, and Deleting Objects in Amazon S3

This lab helps you navigate the AWS console and use the Amazon S3 service using the AWS management console. In this lab, you will do the following:

- Create a bucket in Amazon S3
- Add an object in Amazon S3
- View an object in Amazon S3
- Cut, copy, and paste the file from one bucket to another
- Make an object public and access the object from a URL
- Download the object from Amazon S3 to a local machine
- Delete an object in Amazon S3

If you don't have an account with AWS, you need to open one before you can start working on the labs. To create an account, go to https://aws.amazon.com/console/ and in the top-right corner click Create An AWS Account. You can sign up using your e-mail address or phone number. You will require a credit card to sign up for an AWS account. AWS offers most of its service for free for one year under the Free Tier category. Please read the terms and condition of the Free Tier to understand what is included for free and what is not. You should be up and running with an AWS account in a couple of minutes.

1. Log in to your AWS account. Once you log in to your account, you will notice at the top-right side your default AWS region. Click the region; you will notice a drop-down list. Choose the region of choice where you want to host your bucket.

2. From the console, choose S3 from AWS Service.

3. Click Create Bucket.

4. In Bucket Name, put a unique name for your bucket. To create a bucket, you are not charged anything. It's only when you upload stuff in your bucket that you are charged (you won't be charged if you are within the Free Tier limit).

5. In Region, choose US East (N. Virginia).

6. In Copy Settings From An Existing Bucket, don't type anything. Click Next.

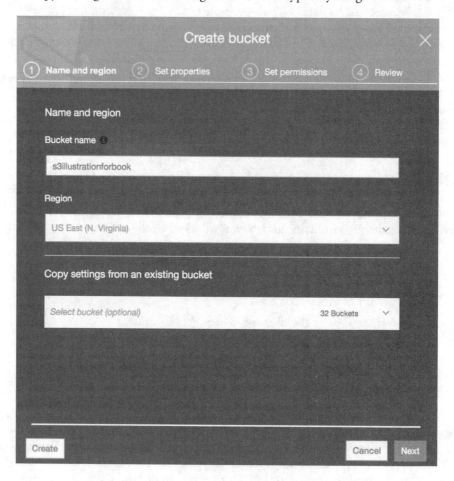

7. Leave the defaults for Versioning, Logging, and Tags; then click Next.

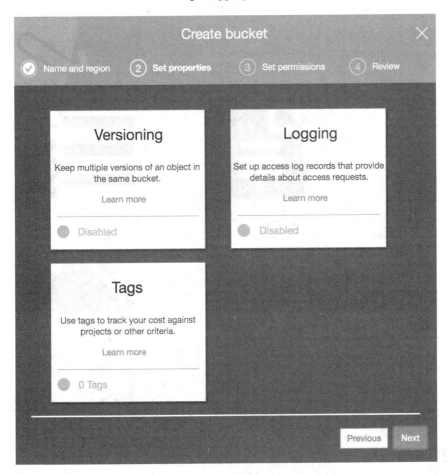

8. On the next screen, called Manage Users, leave Manage Public Permissions and Manage System Permissions at the defaults and click Next.

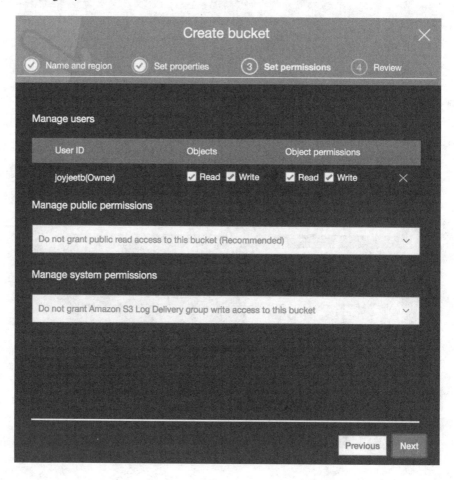

9. Click Create Bucket. Now the bucket will be created for you. Next, you will add an object in the newly created bucket.

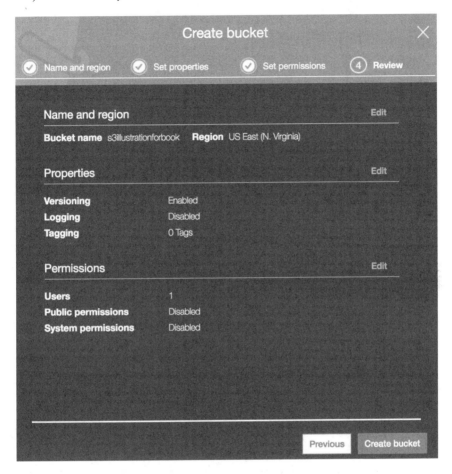

10. You should be able to see the newly created bucket; click it. You will see a couple of options such as Upload, Create Folder, More, and so on.

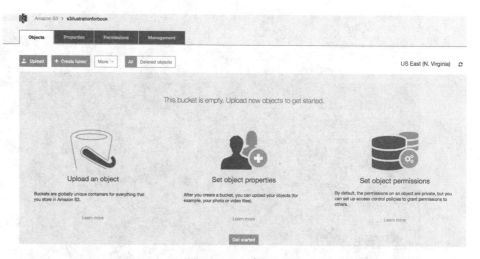

11. Click Upload and upload a few files. Keep everything at the defaults in the next three screens and upload the files.

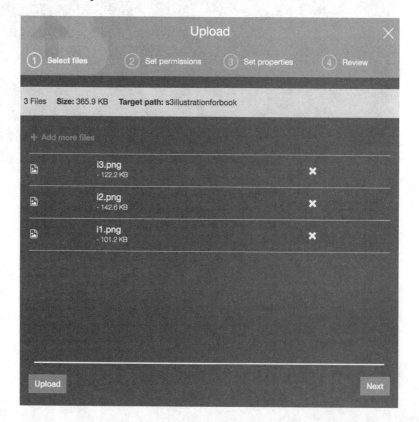

12. Click Create Folder and create a folder with a name of your choice.

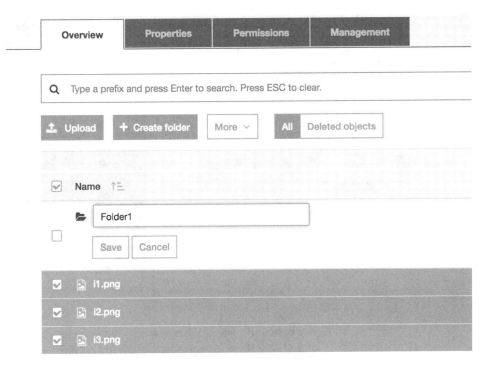

13. Go to the folder and upload a few files.

14. Go to your S3 bucket and select a file that you have uploaded. Notice the pop-up on the right once the file is selected. It has all the information related to the object you have uploaded.

15. With the file selected, click More on the top and browse all the options.

16. Do the same for the files you have created under the folder.

17. Now go to the original file you have created (the first file), select the file, and click More. Click the Copy option. Go to the new folder you have created, click More, and click Paste. You will notice the file is now copied to the new folder.

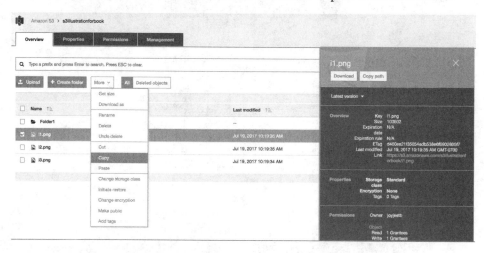

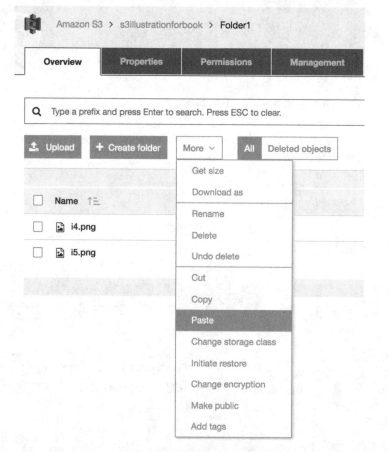

18. In the same way, try Cut and Paste. By cutting and pasting, you can copy the files from one bucket to other.

19. Go to the new folder, select the file, click More | Download, and save the file to your local machine. The file will be stored in your local machine.

20. Again, from the new folder, select the file from the S3 bucket, and click More | Make Public.

21. Reselect the file, and from the right side on the Object tab, select the URL for the file. Now you have made your file publicly accessible from anywhere in the world.

22. Copy the URL and paste it in a different browser window. You will notice that now you can download the file without even logging to S3. Since the file is public, anyone who has this URL can download the file.

23. Keep the file selected, and from S3 bucket click More | Delete.

The file will be deleted from the S3 bucket.
Congratulations! You have finished the first lab on S3.

Lab 2-2: Using Version Control in Amazon S3

In this lab, you will do the following:

- Create an Amazon S3 bucket and enable versioning
- Upload multiple versions of the same file
- Delete a file
- Restore the file after deletion

Log in to the AWS admin console, and from Services select Amazon S3.

1. Repeat steps 1 to 6 from Lab 2-1.

2. In the Versioning window, click the Versioning box. A window will appear asking you to select Enable Versioning or Suspend Versioning.

3. Choose Enable Versioning and click Save; then click Next.

4. Leave everything at the defaults on the next two screens.

5. Click Create Bucket. Now you will have the newly created bucket with versioning on. By the way, you can enable versioning on existing buckets as well. Try that and see how it works.

6. Now create a text file called s3versiontest.text and insert some text in it. For simplicity insert *California* in the text file and save it.

7. Upload the file in the newly created bucket.

8. From your local machine, replace the word *California* with *Texas* in the s3versiontest .text file.

9. Upload the file again.

10. Repeat steps 8 and 9 a couple of times, every time replacing the text with a new state name.

11. Go to the S3 bucket; you will see there is only one file called s3versiontext.text.

12. Select the file. On the right you will notice a button called Latest Version. Click it, and you will notice all the file versions.

13. Download the files with different versions to your local machine. Download them with different names and don't overwrite the files on your local machine since the file name will be the same. Compare the files; you will notice that file with the text *California*, *Texas*, and other states all are there.

14. Select the file and click More | Delete.

15. Go to the S3 bucket, and you will see a button Deleted Objects.

16. Click Deleted Objects, and you will notice your deleted file is there.

17. Select the file and click More | Undo Delete. You have now restored the deleted file successfully.

18. Create another S3 bucket without enabling versioning.

19. Repeat steps 6 to 8.

20. Download the file. You will notice that file has been overwritten, and there is no option to download the previous version of the file.

21. Repeat step 10, and download each file; you will notice each time the file gets overwritten.

22. Try to repeat steps 14 to 17.

You will realize that the button Deleted Objects does not exist, which means you can no longer restore a deleted file if versioning is not enabled.

This completes the second lab.

Lab 2-3: Using the Bucket Policy Generator for Amazon S3

In this lab, you will generate a bucket policy using the AWS Policy Generator. The AWS Policy Generator is a tool that enables you to create various policies and use them to control access to AWS products and resources.

1. Go to the URL https://awspolicygen.s3.amazonaws.com/policygen.html.
2. In the Select Policy Type drop-down list, select S3 Bucket Policy.
3. In Add Statement(s), do the following:
   a. Set Effect to Allow.
   b. Set Principal to * (this gives access to everyone).
   c. Set AWS Service to Amazon S3.
   d. In Actions, select GetObject.
   e. In ARN, enter **arn:aws:s3:::staticweb site/***.
4. Click the button Add Statement.
5. Click Generate Policy. You will notice that the system has generated the following policy for you. You can use this policy to grant anonymous access to your static web site.

```
{
  "Id": "Policy1497312378082",
  "Version": "2012-10-17",
  "Statement": [
    {
      "Sid": "Stmt1497312298007",
      "Action": [
        "s3:GetObject"
      ],
      "Effect": "Allow",
      "Resource": "arn:aws:s3:::staticwebsite/*",
      "Principal": "*"
    }
  ]
}
```

Questions

1. What is the main purpose of Amazon Glacier? (Choose all that apply.)
   A. Storing hot, frequently used data
   B. Storing archival data
   C. Storing historical or infrequently accessed data
   D. Storing the static content of a web site
   E. Creating a cross-region replication bucket for Amazon S3

2. What is the best way to protect a file in Amazon S3 against accidental delete?

    A. Upload the files in multiple buckets so that you can restore from another when a file is deleted

    B. Back up the files regularly to a different bucket or in a different region

    C. Enable versioning on the S3 bucket

    D. Use MFA for deletion

    E. Use cross-region replication

3. Amazon S3 provides 99.999999999 percent durability. Which of the following are true statements? (Choose all that apply.)

    A. The data is mirrored across multiple AZs within a region.

    B. The data is mirrored across multiple regions to provide the durability SLA.

    C. The data in Amazon S3 Standard is designed to handle the concurrent loss of two facilities.

    D. The data is regularly backed up to AWS Snowball to provide the durability SLA.

    E. The data is automatically mirrored to Amazon Glacier to achieve high availability.

4. To set up a cross-region replication, what statements are true? (Choose all that apply.)

    A. The source and target bucket should be in a same region.

    B. The source and target bucket should be in different region.

    C. You must choose different storage classes across different regions.

    D. You need to enable versioning and must have an IAM policy in place to replicate.

    E. You must have at least ten files in a bucket.

5. You want to move all the files older than a month to S3 IA. What is the best way of doing this?

    A. Copy all the files using the S3 copy command

    B. Set up a lifecycle rule to move all the files to S3 IA after a month

    C. Download the files after a month and re-upload them to another S3 bucket with IA

    D. Copy all the files to Amazon Glacier and from Amazon Glacier copy them to S3 IA

6. What are the various way you can control access to the data stored in S3? (Choose all that apply.)

    A. By using IAM policy

    B. By creating ACLs

    C. By encrypting the files in a bucket

    D. By making all the files public

    E. By creating a separate folder for the secure files

7. How much data can you store on S3?

   A. 1 petabyte per account

   B. 1 exabyte per account

   C. 1 petabyte per region

   D. 1 exabyte per region

   E. Unlimited

8. What are the different storage classes that Amazon S3 offers? (Choose all that apply.)

   A. S3 Standard

   B. S3 Global

   C. S3 CloudFront

   D. S3 US East

   E. S3 IA

9. What is the best way to delete multiple objects from S3?

   A. Delete the files manually using a console

   B. Use multi-object delete

   C. Create a policy to delete multiple files

   D. Delete all the S3 buckets to delete the files

10. What is the best way to get better performance for storing several files in S3?

    A. Create a separate folder for each file

    B. Create separate buckets in different region

    C. Use a partitioning strategy for storing the files

    D. Use the formula of keeping a maximum of 100 files in the same bucket

11. The data across the EBS volume is mirrored across which of the following?

    A. Multiple AZs

    B. Multiple regions

    C. The same AZ

    D. EFS volumes mounted to EC2 instances

12. I shut down my EC2 instance, and when I started it, I lost all my data. What could be the reason for this?

    A. The data was stored in the local instance store.

    B. The data was stored in EBS but was not backed up to S3.

    C. I used an HDD-backed EBS volume instead of an SSD-backed EBS volume.

    D. I forgot to take a snapshot of the instance store.

13. I am running an Oracle database that is very I/O intense. My database administrator needs a minimum of 3,600 IOPS. If my system is not able to meet that number, my application won't perform optimally. How can I make sure my application always performs optimally?

    A. Use Elastic File System since it automatically handles the performance

    B. Use Provisioned IOPS SSD to meet the IOPS number

    C. Use your database files in an SSD-based EBS volume and your other files in an HDD-based EBS volume

    D. Use a general-purpose SSD under a terabyte that has a burst capability

14. Your application needs a shared file system that can be accessed from multiple EC2 instances across different AZs. How would you provision it?

    A. Mount the EBS volume across multiple EC2 instances

    B. Use an EFS instance and mount the EFS across multiple EC2 instances across multiple AZs

    C. Access S3 from multiple EC2 instances

    D. Use EBS with Provisioned IOPS

15. You want to run a mapreduce job (a part of the big data workload) for a noncritical task. Your main goal is to process it in the most cost-effective way. The task is throughput sensitive but not at all mission critical and can take a longer time. Which type of storage would you choose?

    A. Throughput Optimized HDD (st1)

    B. Cold HDD (sc1)

    C. General-Purpose SSD (gp2)

    D. Provisioned IOPS (io1)

Answers

    1. B, C. Hot and frequently used data needs to be stored in Amazon S3; you can also use Amazon CloudFront to cache the frequently used data. Amazon Glacier is used to store the archive copies of the data or historical data or infrequent data. You can make lifecycle rules to move all the infrequently accessed data to Amazon Glacier. The static content of the web site can be stored in Amazon CloudFront in conjunction with Amazon S3. You can't use Amazon Glacier for a cross-region replication bucket of Amazon S3; however, you can use S3 IA or S3 RRS in addition to S3 Standard as a replication bucket for CRR.

    2. C. You can definitely upload the file in multiple buckets, but the cost will increase the number of times you are going to store the files. Also, now you need to manage three or four times more files. What about mapping files to applications? This does not make sense. Backing up files regularly to a different bucket can help you to restore the file to some extent. What if you have uploaded a new file just after taking the backup? The correct answer is versioning since enabling versioning maintains all the versions of the file and you can restore from any version even if you have deleted the file. You can definitely use MFA for delete, but what if even with MFA you delete a wrong file? With CRR, if a DELETE request is made without specifying an object version ID, Amazon S3 adds a delete marker, which cross-region replication replicates to the destination bucket. If a DELETE request specifies a particular object version ID to delete, Amazon S3 deletes that object version in the source bucket, but it does not replicate the deletion in the destination bucket.

3. **A, C.** By default the data never leaves a region. If you have created an S3 bucket in a global region, it will always stay there unless you manually move the data to a different region. Amazon does not back up data residing in S3 to anywhere else since the data is automatically mirrored across multiple facilities. However, customers can replicate the data to a different region for additional safety. AWS Snowball is used to migrate on-premises data to S3. Amazon Glacier is the archival storage of S3, and an automatic mirror of regular Amazon S3 data does not make sense. However, you can write lifecycle rules to move historical data from Amazon S3 to Amazon Glacier.

4. **B, D.** Cross-region replication can't be used to replicate the objects in the same region. However, you can use the S3 copy command or copy the files from the console to move the objects from one bucket to another in the same region. You can choose a different class of storage for CRR; however, this option is not mandatory, and you can use the same class of storage as the source bucket as well. There is no minimum number of file restriction to enable cross-region replication. You can even use CRR when there is only one file in an Amazon S3 bucket.

5. **B.** Copying all the files using the S3 copy command is going to be a painful activity if you have millions of objects. Doing this when you can do the same thing by automatically downloading and re-uploading the files does not make any sense and wastes a lot of bandwidth and manpower. Amazon Glacier is used mainly for archival storage. You should not copy anything into Amazon Glacier unless you want to archive the files.

6. **A, B.** By encrypting the files in the bucket, you can make them secure, but it does not help in controlling the access. By making the files public, you are providing universal access to everyone. Creating a separate folder for secure files won't help because, again, you need to control the access of the separate folder.

7. **E.** Since the capacity of S3 is unlimited, you can store as much data you want there.

8. **A, E.** S3 Global is a region and not a storage class. Amazon CloudFront is a CDN and not a storage class. US East is a region and not a storage class.

9. **B.** Manually deleting the files from the console is going to take a lot of time. You can't create a policy to delete multiple files. Deleting buckets in order to delete files is not a recommended option. What if you need some files from the bucket?

10. **C.** Creating a separate folder does not improve performance. What if you need to store millions of files in these separate folders? Similarly, creating separate folders in a different region does not improve the performance. There is no such rule of storing 100 files per bucket.

11. **C.** Data stored in Amazon EBS volumes is redundantly stored in multiple physical locations in the same AZ. Amazon EBS replication is stored within the same availability zone, not across multiple zones.

12. **A.** The only possible reason is that the data was stored in a local instance store that is not persisted once the server is shut down. If the data stays in EBS, then it does not matter if you have taken the backup or not; the data will always persist. Similarly, it does not matter if it is an HDD- or SSD-backed EBS volume. You can't take a snapshot of the instance store.

13. **B.** If your workload needs a certain number of workload, then the best way would be is to use a Provisioned IOPS. That way, you can ensure the application or the workload always meets the performance metric you are looking for.

14. **B.** Use an EFS. The same EBS volume can't be mounted across multiple EC2 instances.

15. **B.** Since the workload is not critical and you want to process it in the most cost-effective way, you should choose Cold HDD. Though the workload is throughput sensitive, it is not critical and is low priority; therefore, you should not choose st1. gp2 and io1 are more expensive than other options like st1.

Virtual Private Cloud

In this chapter you will

- Understand what a virtual private cloud is
- Find out what components make up a virtual private cloud
- Learn how to connect multiple virtual private clouds
- Learn how to connect Amazon Virtual Public Cloud (VPC) with your corporate data center

In real life, customers have lots of data centers, and in those data centers they run lots of applications. Sometimes these applications are integrated with lots of other things, and they often talk to each other. For example, a typical three-tier application may have a web tier, an app tier, and a database tier. All three tiers will talk with each other but also with all the connected applications. An OLTP system may interact with a data warehouse system; similarly, an OLTP system may have a reporting system, and so on. Some of the applications may be behind a firewall, and some of them may be directly exposed to the Internet. For example, the database tier will always be inside a private subnet, and no one from the Internet will be able to access it, whereas some applications such as corporate web servers or Internet suppliers (i-suppliers) can be accessed from the Internet. Similarly, networking plays an important role in how applications are going to talk to each other. If you change the IP address of one server, it may not be able to talk with another server. This raises these important questions: How do you start to migrate to the cloud? What happens to the networking? How do some of the applications sitting on your corporate data center connect/interact with the applications running on the cloud? How do you segregate networking in the cloud? How do you make sure that some of the applications running in the cloud have Internet connectivity while others run in the private subnet with no Internet connectivity? How do you make sure that you can extend the same IP range to the cloud? When you launch an EC2 instance, you get a 32-bit random number as an IP address. How do you make sure that the IP address is close to the IP address of your data center? Well, Amazon VPC tries to answer all these questions. So, what exactly is Amazon VPC?

Amazon VPC allows you to create your own virtual private cloud. In other words, it allows you to logically isolate a section of the cloud. You can provision any resource in this logically isolated region, and you have complete control over the networking. You can also say that Amazon VPC is your own data center in the cloud, and when you connect your data center and Amazon VPC with a virtual private network (VPN) or Direct Connect, it becomes an extension of your data center in the cloud. In Amazon VPC you have complete control over how you want to configure the networking. You can use your IP address, select your own IP range, create multiple subnets however you want, carve out private subnets and public subnets, and configure route tables and network gateways however you'd like.

Thus, Amazon VPC solves all the problems discussed previously. It gives you complete freedom to host your applications in the cloud and at the same time lets them talk with the applications running in your data center seamlessly. In the previous example of a three-tier application, you can have the web tier running in a public subnet within Amazon VPC and can have the app and the database tiers running on a private subnet in the same VPC. You can have an additional layer of control by using security groups and network access control lists, which you will learn about in this chapter.

Let's examine what you can do using VPC.

By connecting your data center with Amazon VPC, it becomes your own data center in the cloud. You can treat it the same way you treat the data centers on your company's premises. You can have Amazon VPC connect with the Internet or just have it talk to your own data center. You can bring your own network, create your own subnets, and configure customer routing rules in VPC. In short, you can do the following things by having a virtual private network:

- You can have some of the applications running in the cloud within VPC and some of the applications running on-premise.

- You can create multiple subnets within VPC. You can create a public subnet by providing it with Internet access and can keep the resource isolated from the Internet by creating a private subnet.

- You can have dedicated connectivity between your corporate data center and VPN by using Direct Connect. You can also connect your data center using a hardware virtual private network via an encrypted IPsec connection.

- If you need more than one VPC, you can create multiple VPCs and can connect each one of them by VPC peering. This way you can share the resources across multiple VPCs and accounts.

- You can connect to resources such as S3 using a VPC endpoint.

Amazon VPC Components and Terminology

Amazon VPC consists of multiple objects and concepts. Before discussing them, I'll cover why VPC was created in the first place. Without VPC, there would be no way to isolate your resources running on the cloud. For example, if you have deployed thousands of servers in the cloud, you need to manage IP namespaces more diligently so that there is no overlap between the IP addresses and so that you can seamlessly connect them from the resources running on your premises. Without VPC, it becomes difficult to manage the IP namespaces for thousands of servers.

Amazon VPC

As discussed, Amazon VPC gives you your own private space in the cloud. When you create a VPC, you have the option of carving out your own data center in the cloud. The first step of creating a VPC is deciding the IP range by providing a Classless Inter-Domain Routing (CIDR) block. VPC now supports both IPv4 and IPv6, so you can have both IP ranges as part of your VPC. When you choose an IPv4 CIDR range, you can choose anything between /16, which corresponds to 65,536 IP addresses (for example 10.0.0.0/16), and /28, which corresponds to 16 IP addresses. If you choose IPv6, the size of the IPv6 CIDR block is fixed to /56. The range of IPv6 addresses is automatically allocated from Amazon's pool of IPv6 addresses; at this time, you cannot select the range yourself. As of now, having a CIDR block for IPv6 is optional; however, you need an IPv4 CIDR block. It is important to note that once you create a VPC, you can't alter the size of it. If you create a VPC with a small size and later realize that you need more IP addresses, you can create a new VPC with a bigger IP address range and then migrate your applications from the old VPC to the new one.

A VPC is limited to a region, which means you can't have a VPC spanning regions. Within a VPC, you have all the AZs that are part of the region where the VPC belongs. Figure 3-1 shows a VPC spanning three AZs within a region with a CIDR block of /16. This figure also shows the main route table of the virtual private cloud. You will study route tables later in this chapter.

Subnet

Subnet is short for *subnetwork*, which is a logical subdivision of an IP network. With subnetting you can divide a network into multiple networks. With VPC you can create various subnets as per your needs. The most common ones are public subnets, private subnets, and VPN-only subnets. A public subnet is created for resources that need to be connected to the Internet. A private subnet is created for resources that do not need to be connected to the Internet, and a VPN-only subnet is created when you want to connect your virtual private cloud with your corporate data center. You can also create different subnets to isolate the type of workload, such as a subnet for the development environment, a subnet for the production environment, and so on.

EXAM TIP There will be a few questions about Amazon VPC, private subnets, and public subnets. You should be able to articulate which workload is a good fit for which subnet; for example, the web tier goes to a public subnet, the database tier goes to a private subnet, and so on.

With VPC you can define a subnet using a CIDR block. The smallest subnet you can create within VPC is /28, which corresponds to 16 available IP addresses. If you use IPv6 and create a subnet using /64 as the CIDR block, you get 18,446,744,073,709,551,616 IP addresses. It must be noted that a subnet is tied to only one availability zone. You cannot have a subnet span multiple AZs; however, a VPC can span multiple AZs in a region. If you have three AZs in a VPC, for example, you need to create a separate subnet in each AZ, such as Subnet 1 for AZ1, Subnet 2 for AZ2, and Subnet 3 for AZ3. Of course,

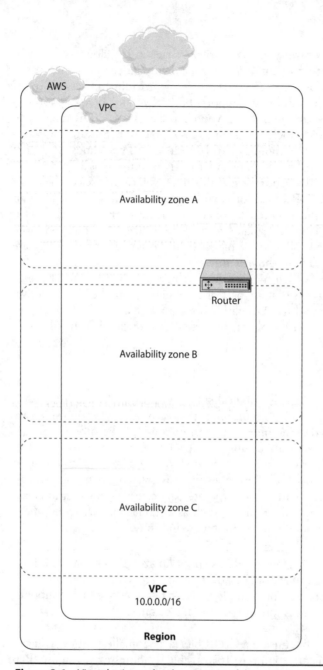

Main Route Table

Destination	Target
10.0.0.0/16	Local

VPC route table aka main route table

Figure 3-1 Virtual private cloud consisting of three AZs

within an AZ you can have multiple subnets. A virtual private cloud is tied to a region, which means you can't have the same VPC spanning multiple regions. The following are the key takeaways about subnets:

- Subnets are AZ specific. For multiple AZs, create multiple subnets.
- VPC are region specific. For multiple regions, create different VPCs.

When you create a VPC, you need to provide a CIDR block for the IP address range for VPC. It can be as big as /16, which can have 65,536 IP addresses. Now when you create multiple subnets, you must take into account the CIDR block of the VPC. Say you create the VPC with /16, and within VPC you create three subnets with /18, which has 16,384 IP addresses each. By doing this you have exhausted 49,152 IP addresses. Now you have only 65,536 − 49,152 IP addresses left for creating new subnets. At this point, you won't be able to create a new subnet with /17, which has 32,768 IP addresses; however, you should be able to create new subnets between /19 and /28. If you create more than one subnet in a VPC, the CIDR blocks of the subnets cannot overlap. There are lots of tools available to calculate the subnets of the CIDR block; for example, see www.subnet-calculator.com/cidr.php.

for each subnet

X X X Ø
. 1
. 2
. 3
you use

. 255

Table 3-1 contains the CIDR block and number of IP addresses available.

NOTE From any subnet AWS reserves, the first four IP addresses and the last IP address are for internal networking purposes, and they are not available for your usage. Always keep this in mind while calculating the number of IP addresses in a subnet. For example, in a subnet with a CIDR block of 10.0.0.0/24, the following five IP address are reserved: 10.0.0.0, 10.0.0.1, 10.0.0.2, 10.0.0.3, and 10.0.0.255.

Table 3-1 CIDR Block and Available IP Addresses	CIDR Block	Number of IP Addresses
	/28	16
	/27	32
	/26	64
	/25	128
	/24	254
	/23	510
	/22	1022
	/21	2046
	/20	4094
	/19	8190
	/18	16,382
	/17	32,766
	/16	65,536

Route Table

A *route table* is a table consisting of certain rules known as *routes* that determine where the traffic is directed. A route table contains all the information necessary to forward a packet along the best path toward its destination. A route table can be compared to a real-life route. For example, if you want to go to San Jose from San Francisco, which route would you take? A route table will provide that information. Every subnet should have a route table. For example, if the subnet of a VPC contains an Internet gateway in the route table, that subnet has access to the Internet. Similarly, if a subnet does not have an Internet gateway in the route table, any servers that are part of that subnet won't be able to access the Internet. Each subnet must have a route table at any time. However, you can associate multiple subnets with the same route table. Whenever you create a subnet, it is automatically associated with the main route table of the VPC if you don't associate it with any other route table. If you look at Figure 3-1, you will see the entry from the route table as 10.0.0.0/16 local. This is VPC's route table, and it will be automatically added in all the subnets' route tables you create within the VPC. (Please note 10.0.0.0/16 is an example; your IP address range will be different in real life.) This VPC's default route table (known as the main route table) is created automatically, and you can't modify it. VPC comes with an implicit router that is not visible. Since the CIDR blocks for IPv4 and IPv6 are different, the corresponding routes are also treated separately. Thus, a route with a destination of, say, 0.0.0.0/0 for all IPv4 addresses won't cater the destination of all IPv6 addresses; you must add another entry with a destination of CIDR ::/0 for all IPv6 addresses.

As discussed previously, when you create a VPC, Amazon VPC automatically creates the main route table. If you do not want to use the main route table, you can create your own custom route tables and use one of them instead of using the main route table. A best practice would be to keep the main route table of the VPC in an original state with only the local route and assign a custom route table for each subnet you have created. That way, you can have better control over the routes of outgoing traffic.

If you later add a virtual private gateway, Internet gateway, NAT device, or anything like that in your VPC, you must update the route table accordingly so that any subnet that wants to use these gateways can take advantage of them and have a route defined for them.

Table 3-2 shows what an entry in the route table looks like for a VPC.

Table 3-2 Entry in Route Table for a VPC	Destination	Target
	10.0.0.0/16	Local
	2011:dc8:1234:1c00::/56	Local
	172.31.0.0/16	pcx-1d2e1f2c
	0.0.0.0/0	igw-11aa33cc
	::/0	eigw-aacc1133

If you look at the routing table, you will notice there are only two columns: Destination and Target. The target is where the traffic is directed, and the destination specifies the IP range that can be directed to the target. As shown in Table 3-2, the first two entries are Local, which indicates internal routing within VPC for IPv4 and IPv6 for the CIDR block. The third one is the routing option for VPC peering, which means the traffic can go to another VPC with the CIDR block 172.31.0.0/16. The fourth one represents the Internet gateway. By allocating an IP range of 0.0.0.0/0, you are allowing all the traffic (IPv4) to go to the Internet gateway. (It also means that you can have a public subnet in your virtual private cloud.) The last line means you are again allowing all traffic, this time IPv6, to go to an egress-only Internet gateway. Similarly, you can add the entries for any destination and target where you want the traffic to go. For example, if you want to allow the traffic of the private subnet to access the NAT gateway, then just add the entry in the route table of the private subnet to route the traffic to the NAT gateway, as shown in this example:

```
Destination Target
10.0.0.0/0  nat-gateway-112a01
```

Internet Gateway

An *Internet gateway* (IG) is a component of VPC that allows your VPC to communicate with the Internet. When you attach an IG in your VPC, you can connect directly to the Internet from the subnets where you have added the IG in the route table. It must be noted that an IG is a horizontally scaled, redundant, and highly available component in VPC. An IG supports both IPv4 and IPv6 traffic. It's simple to attach an IG; you just add the entry for the IG in the routing table and you are all set. In the previous example of a routing table, the entry 0.0.0.0/0 igw-11aa33cc shows how an entry for the IG is added in the routing table. When you add an IG in your VPC, then you can make any of the subnets inside that VPC accessible to the Internet just by adding the IG in the subnet's route table. If Amazon VPC does not have an IG in the route table, then you won't be able to make any of the subnets accessible to the Internet.

For example, say the CIDR block for the virtual private cloud is 10.0.0.0/16 (IPv4) and 2600:1f14:880:f400 (IPv6), and the CIDR block for the subnet where you would like to enable the Internet access is 10.0.0.0/24. In this case, you want to provide Internet access to only the IPv4 traffic and not the IPv6 traffic within the subnet. The entries from the route table will look like Tables 3-3 and 3-4.

Table 3-3 Route Table for VPC	Destination	Target
	10.0.0.0/16	Local
	2600:1f14:880:f400::/56	Local
	0.0.0.0/0	igw-11aa33cc
	::/00	igw-11aa33cc

[handwritten: SUBNET DEFINED 10.0.0.0/16 ACCESSABLE to Internet]

Table 3-4	Destination	Target
Route Table for Subnet	10.0.0.0/16	Local
	2600:1f14:880:f400::/56	Local
	0.0.0.0/0	igw-11aa33cc

Say now you have another subnet, a private subnet, with the CIDR block 10.0.1.0/24 and you don't want to provide Internet access to any IP address residing in this subnet. So, the entry in the route table for the private subnet will look something like Table 3-5.

A target of "local" means only local traffic can flow within the virtual private cloud and no other traffic is allowed.

Deleting an Internet gateway is pretty simple; you just delete the IG via the console. From the list of services, select VPC, choose the Internet gateway from the left pane, select the IG you want to delete, and click the Delete button. If you want to restrict Internet access from a subnet where you allowed access previously, simply remove the routing table entry for the IG for that subnet.

Network Address Translation

In real life, you will be creating multiple subnets for different use cases, some public and some private. Say you have created a database inside a private subnet, which means there is no way the database server can access the Internet. It remains completely secluded. If you want to do some firmware updates in the database server or if you want to download some database patches, how do you download them? Network Address Translation (NAT) tries to solve that problem. Using a NAT device, you can enable any instance in a private subnet to connect to the Internet, but this does not mean the Internet can initiate a connection to the instance. The reverse is not true. This is how a NAT device works. A NAT device forwards traffic from the instances in the private subnet to the Internet and then sends the response to the instances. When traffic goes to the Internet, the source IPv4 address is replaced with the NAT device's address; similarly, when the response traffic goes to those instances, the NAT device translates the address back to those instances' private IPv4 addresses. This is another reason why it is called *address translation*. Please note that NAT devices can be used only for IPv4 traffic; they can't be used for IPv6. There are two types of NAT devices available within AWS.

- NAT instances
- NAT gateways

[handwritten: SUBNET DEFINED 10.0.1.0/24 NOT ACCESSBLE TO INTERNET]

Table 3-5	Destination	Target
Route Table Entry for Private Subnet	10.0.0.0/16	Local
	2600:1f14:880:f400::/56	Local

[handwritten: Lack of IGW for this subnet means no internet access]

Table 3-6	Destination	Target
Route Table with Entry for Internet Gateway	10.0.0.0/16	Local
	0.0.0.0/0	igw-11aa33cc

NAT Instances

By using a NAT instance in a public subnet, you can have the instance running in the private subnet initiate outbound traffic to the Internet or to some other AWS service. Let's see an example to understand it better. Say you have two subnets: public and private. You are running the web servers in the public subnet and the database server in the private subnet. Now if you want to provide Internet access to the database server because you want to download database patches, you need to create a NAT instance in the public subnet and route the database server's Internet traffic via the NAT instance running in the public subnet. By doing that, the database server will be able to initiate the connection to the Internet, but the reverse is not allowed (meaning no one will be able to connect to the database server from the Internet using NAT). Say you have created the VPC with the CIDR block 10.0.0.0/16, so the routing table for the VPC will look something like Table 3-6. As you can see, you have attached an Internet gateway to the VPC.

Say you have created the public subnet 10.0.0.0/24 and have two web servers with the IP addresses 10.0.0.5 and 10.0.0.6. You have created a private subnet with subnet 10.0.1.0/24, which is running a database server with the IP address 10.0.1.5. Now you have to create a NAT instance in the public subnet to provide Internet access to the database. Say you have created the NAT instance with the IP address 10.0.0.7 and it has an instance ID of nat-0093abx. The routing tables in the private and public subnets will look something like Table 3-7 and Table 3-8. To run an NAT instance, you also need an elastic IP address and need to associate it with the NAT instance.

Now the routing table in the public subnet (Table 3-7) will be the same since you are allowing Internet traffic to everything running in the public subnet. Since you are attaching the Internet gateway to 0.0.0.0/16, both the web servers 10.0.0.5 and 10.0.0.6 and the NAT instance 10.0.0.7 will be able to connect to the Internet.

The routing table in the private subnet won't have the Internet gateway but will have the NAT gateway attached to it. The entries should look like Table 3-8.

If you look carefully, you will find that you have been given the instance ID of the NAT instance, which is nat-0093abx and is mapped to 10.0.0.7. What happens if the NAT instance goes down? Yes, the database server won't be able to connect to the Internet since the NAT instance is a single point of failure. To solve this problem, customers do a variety of things such as have redundant NAT instances in different

Table 3-7	Destination	Target
Routing Table in Public Subnet	10.0.0.0/16	Local
	0.0.0.0/0	igw-11aa33cc

Table 3-8	Destination	Target
Routing Table in Private Subnet	10.0.0.0/16	Local
	0.0.0.0/0	nat-0093abx

AZs, use NAT instances in an active-passive manner across different AZs, use a script to monitor the NAT instance, start a new one if an existing one fails, and so on. But sometimes these options involve a lot of administration overhead and the solution is not easy. To make life simpler, AWS came up NAT gateways to address all the previously mentioned problems.

NAT Gateways

A NAT gateway performs the same function as that of a NAT instance, but it does not have the same limitations as a NAT instance. Moreover, it is a managed service and therefore does not require administration overhead. If you plan to use a NAT gateway, then you must specify an elastic IP address (to associate it with the NAT gateway while creating it). When a NAT gateway is created, it is created in a specific AZ in a redundant fashion. In the previous example of a NAT instance, the database server will now access the Internet via the NAT gateway instead of the NAT instance; similarly, the routing table in the private subnet will reflect the entry for the NAT gateway instead of the NAT instance.

A NAT gateway is preferred over a NAT instance since it provides better availability and bandwidth. If today you are using a NAT instance, you can replace that with a NAT gateway. If you want to use the same elastic IP address for a NAT gateway, you need to de-associate it first from the NAT instance and then re-associate it with the NAT gateway.

EXAM TIP You should be familiar with when to use a NAT gateway over a NAT instance.

Egress-Only Internet Gateway

Similar to NAT gateways, an egress-only IG is a component of your VPC, which allows Amazon VPC to communicate with the Internet for IPv6 traffic. Please note it's egress only, which means outbound only, and it prevents the Internet from initiating an IPv6 connection with your instances. The use case for a NAT gateway and an egress-only gateway is the same, and both of them serve the same purpose. The only difference is that a NAT gateway handles IPv4 traffic, and an egress-only gateway handles the IPv6 traffic. When you use an egress-only Internet gateway, you put the entry of the egress-only Internet gateway in the routing table (Table 3-9).

TIP Please note that NAT instances, NAT gateways, and egress-only Internet gateways are *stateful*. They forward traffic from the instances in the subnet to the Internet or other AWS services and then send the response to the instances. You will learn about stateful and stateless later in the "Security Group" and "Network Access Control List" sections.

	Destination	Target
Table 3-9 Routing Table with Egress-Only IG	10.0.0.0/16	Local
	2600:1f14:880:f400::/56	Local
	::/0	egw-id

Elastic Network Interface

During the course of your journey to the cloud, there are going to be many use cases where you need to create a network interface or multiple network interfaces and attach them to an instance. You might have to create a management network, use a security or network appliance in your VPC, or create a highly availability solution. The Elastic Network Interface (ENI) gives you the ability to create one or more network interfaces and attach them to your instance. At any time, you can detach the network interface from the instance and re-attach to either the same one or a different instance. Again, when you move a network interface from one instance to another, network traffic is redirected to the new instance. This ENI is a virtual network interface that you can attach to an instance in Amazon VPC. An ENI can have the following attributes:

- A MAC addresses
- One public IPv4 address
- One or more IPv6 addresses
- A primary private IPv4 address
- One or more secondary private IPv4 addresses
- One elastic IP address (IPv4) per private IPv4 address
- One or more security groups
- A source/destination check flag and description

As the name suggests, they are elastic; therefore, you can attach or detach them from an instance anytime, and you can reattach the ENI to a different instance. Whenever you move the ENI from one instance to the other, all the traffic is redirected to the new instance. Also, the attributes of the ENI follow along with it, which means when you assign an ENI to an instance, all the attributes of the ENI are propagated to that instance, and when you detach, they are gone. Again, when you reattach the ENI to a new instance, the new instance gets all the attributes of the ENI.

You cannot change the default network interface of any instance, which is also known as a *primary network interface* (eth0). You can create an additional network interface. The number of ENIs you can attach to a particular instance varies from instance to instance type. ENI doesn't impact the network bandwidth to the instance. For example, adding an ENI cannot be used as a method to increase or double the network bandwidth.

Elastic IP Address

An elastic IP (EIP) address is designed for applications running on the cloud. Every time you launch a new EC2 instance in AWS, you get a new IP address. Sometimes it becomes a challenge since you need to update all the applications every time there is an IP address change. There could be several reasons you would be spinning up a new instance. For example, you might be upgrading to a different instance type, you might be shutting down the instances at night when there is no activity, and so on. So, instead of changing the IP address for all applications every time, what you need to do is obtain an EIP and associate that with the EC2 instance and map the EIP with the application. Now whenever the IP address of the EC2 instance changes, you just need to repoint the new EC2 instance to the EIP, and applications can connect using the same EIP. Another benefit is if the instance running the application fails, you can quickly start another instance and remap the EIP to the new instance.

Thus, an EIP is a static IP address. If your application has a need for a static IP address, an EIP addresses that issue. Please note at this moment that an EIP supports only IPv4 and does not support IPv6. Also note an EIP is a public IPv4 IP address, which means it is reachable from the Internet. For example, say your instance does not have a public IP address; you can simply map it to an EIP and have the instance talk with the Internet. The following are the three steps to use an EIP:

1. Allocate one EIP to your account from the console.

2. Associate the EIP either with your instance or with a network interface.

3. Start using it.

 EXAM TIP You should know when to use an EIP versus when to use a public IP address.

Since EIP can be easily transferred from one instance to other, at any point of time you can disassociate an elastic IP address from a resource and re-associate it with a different resource. When you disassociate an EIP and don't re-associate it with any other resource, it continues to remain in your account until you explicitly release it from your account.

 NOTE There is no charge for using an EIP so long you associate the EIP with a running instance. If you allocate one EIP in your account and don't associate it with any active instance, you may be charged a fee. This is because IPv4 IP addresses are limited and currently are scarce public resources. This ensures a fair usage of EIPs. An elastic IP address is for use in a specific region only.

Security Group

A *security group* is like a virtual firewall that can be assigned to any instance running in a virtual private cloud. A security group defines what traffic can flow inside and outside a particular instance. Since it is instance specific, you can have different security groups for different instances. The security group is applied at the instance level and not at the subnet level. Therefore, even within a subnet, you can have different security groups for different instances. You can attach up to five different security groups to each instance. You can even attach the same security group to a different instance. A security group is stateful and consists of IP addresses, ports, and protocols via which you can provide the inbound and outbound rules for the traffic.

Let's see an example to understand this. Say you have a database running on an EC2 instance inside the private subnet and you have two web servers running in two EC2 instances in a public subnet. You also have a load balancer on top of the web servers that balances the traffic across both web servers. Now when the users log into the application, they go to the URL of the load balancer, and the load balancer decides which web server it should direct the traffic to. In this scenario, only the load balancer should have access to the web servers; you may also want to open an SSH port for the admins to log into the web server for doing operational work. Thus, for the web servers you are going to create a security group and assign it to both the EC2 instances hosting the web servers. In this security group, you will add entries only for the load balancer and SSH port. Now any traffic flowing to/from the web servers will be filtered using the security group. The traffic that is not coming from the load balancer or from the SSH port that you have open will be denied. Similarly, you can create a security group for the database server allowing it to access traffic from the web servers. You can similarly configure the security group for the load balancer allowing it to access traffic from anywhere.

At any time, you can modify the rules of the security group and can allow/block traffic. You can specify only allow rules. There are no deny rules, so the only way to block traffic is to not allow it. You can have separate rules for incoming and outgoing traffic. Whenever you make any changes to a security group, the changes are reflected in the instance immediately and automatically. In other words, you don't have to run any script in the instance or reboot the instance to reflect the changes.

Security groups are *stateful*. This means if you send a request from your instance, and vice versa, traffic is allowed. For example, if you allow incoming traffic via SSH on port 22, the outgoing traffic via SSH on port 22 will be allowed. When you create a security group, by default no incoming traffic is allowed there because you need to add the entry for whatever traffic you want inbound. By default all the outbound traffic is allowed, so if you want to block certain outbound traffic, you need to put an entry in the security group for it. Or if you want to allow only certain outbound traffic, you can remove the default rule, which allows all outgoing traffic and adds a rule to send only the desired traffic. Even if you allow two instances as part of the same security group, they won't be able to talk to each other unless you explicitly add the rules to allow the traffic. The only exception is the default security group.

 NOTE   Security groups are always associated with the network interface, which means if you change the security group of an instance, it's going to change the security group of the primary network associated with it.

Inbound			
Source	**Protocol**	**Port Range**	**Comments**
The security group ID (sg-xxxxxxxx)	All	All	Allow inbound traffic from instances assigned to the same security group.
Outbound			
Destination	**Protocol**	**Port Range**	**Comments**
0.0.0.0/0	All	All	Allow all outbound IPv4 traffic.
::/0	All	All	Allow all outbound IPv6 traffic. This rule is added by default if you create a VPC with an IPv6 CIDR block or if you associate an IPv6 CIDR block with your existing VPC.

Table 3-10　Default Security Groups

Amazon VPC always comes with a default security group. If you don't attach any security group to your EC2 instance, it is automatically associated with the security group of VPC. You can't delete the default security group; however, you can change the rules for the default security group.

Table 3-10 shows what the default security group looks like.

Let's see an example of how the security group of the web server should look. The web server accepts incoming traffic from the Internet. It also connects to the database server on the back end and accepts incoming traffic from there. You also need to allow SSH access to the administrator for maintenance activities. So, in this case, you will give the following access:

Inbound

- HTTP on port 80 from anywhere, since this is a web server and running on a public domain
- SSH on port 22 only from the corporate network, so you need to provide the CIDR block of the network's IP address range
- MYSQL/Aurora on port 3306, since the web server needs to accept incoming traffic from the database server so that the IP address is in the CIDR block of the network's IP address range

Outbound

- HTTP on port 80 to anywhere, so 0.0.0.0/0
- Only to the database tier, so MySQL Aurora on 3306 on corporate network

Figure 3-2 shows the console.

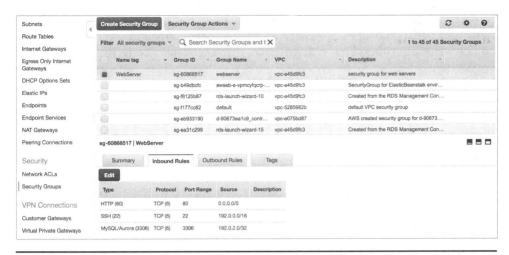

Figure 3-2   Security group

Network Access Control List

In the previous section, you learned about security groups. You saw that security groups can be applied at the instance level, but what if you want to have an additional firewall at a subnet level for your VPC? What if you want to have an additional layer of control? A network access control list (NACL) solves that problem. An NACL is a layer of security that acts as a firewall at the subnet level. Since an NACL is optional, you have the option of configuring it or not.

Put simply, an NACL is stateless and a combination of IP address, port, protocol, and allow/deny for a subnet.

Amazon VPC comes with a default NACL that can be modified. It allows all inbound and outbound IPv4 and IPv6 traffic (if applicable). You can create a custom NACL and associate it with a subnet. By default, each custom NACL denies all inbound and outbound traffic until you add rules. Since ACLs are associated with subnets, each subnet in your VPC must be assigned an NACL. If you don't explicitly associate a subnet with an NACL, the subnet is automatically associated with the default NACL. You can associate an NACL with multiple subnets; however, a subnet can be associated with only one NACL at a time. When you associate an NACL with a subnet, the previous association is removed. If you remember, you can attach multiple instances to the same security group.

NACLs contain a numbered list of rules that are evaluated in order to decide whether the traffic is allowed to a particular subnet associated with the NACL. Rules are evaluated starting with the lowest numbered rule. As soon as a rule matches traffic, it's applied regardless of any higher-numbered rule that may contradict it. The highest number that you can use for a rule is 32766. It is recommended that you create rules with numbers that are multiples of 100 so that you can insert new rules if you need to do so later.

NACLs are stateless; responses to allowed inbound traffic are subject to the rules for outbound traffic (and vice versa). An NACL has separate inbound and outbound rules, and each rule can either allow or deny traffic. If you remember correctly, security groups are stateful.

In addition to the rule number, NACL supports protocols, which means you can specify any protocol that has a standard protocol number, and you can choose to allow or deny specific traffic. Figure 3-3 shows the relationship between the security group and the NACL.

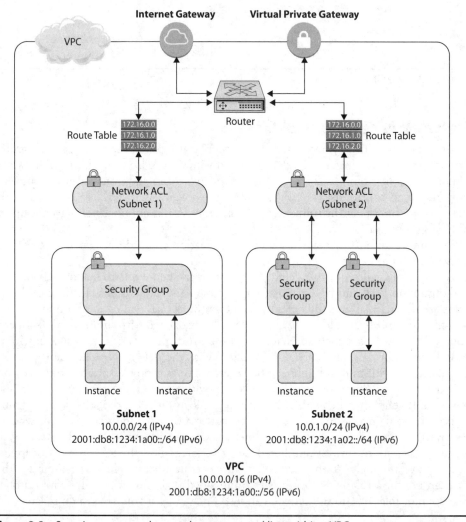

Figure 3-3   Security groups and network access control lists within a VPC

Let's quickly compare NACLs and security groups so that you understand the differences.

- A security group can be applied only at the instance level, whereas an NACL can be applied at the subnet level. So, if you have ten instances within a subnet, NACL rules are going to be applied for all ten instances.

- A security group is stateful (return traffic is allowed by default), whereas an NACL is stateless (return traffic is not allowed by default).

- A security group supports allow rules only; you can't specify a deny rule explicitly. An NACL allows both allow and deny rules.

- In a security group, all the rules are evaluated before deciding whether to allow the traffic, whereas in NACLs the rule number gets precedence.

EXAM TIP It is important to understand the difference between security groups and NACLs. You should be able to articulate when to use a security group over an NACL and vice versa.

There are some limits on the number of security groups you can have. But again, these limits are not hard limits and can be raised by a support request.

- You can have 500 security groups per VPC per region.

- You can have 50 inbound and 50 outbound rules in each security group.

- The maximum security groups you can have per network interface is 5; however, you can raise the number to 16 by contacting AWS Support.

Note that Amazon keeps increasing the limit; the limits are as of this writing. Please check the Amazon web site for the current numbers.

Amazon VPC Peering

There are many scenarios where you will need to create multiple VPCs for different purposes. For example, you may have different VPCs for running your production and nonproduction workloads, or you may want to create a separate management virtual private cloud. If there are different AWS accounts in your organization, then there will be multiple virtual private clouds. How do you connect the different virtual private clouds so that resources running inside the separate VPC's can talk to each other? VPC peering helps to connect one virtual private cloud to another and route the traffic across the virtual private clouds using a private IPv4 or IPv6 address. Once you establish VPC peering, the instances running on both the VPCs communicate with each other as if they were in the same network. VPC peering can be done only for virtual private clouds within a region. You can't peer VPCs across regions. Not only can you peer multiple VPCs running in your account, but you can also peer VPCs running across different accounts. Figure 3-4 shows two VPCs being peered.

Figure 3-4
VPC peering

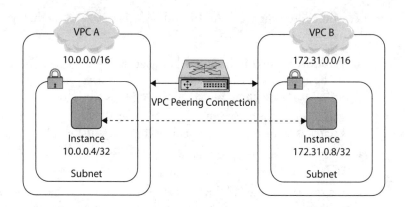

Internally AWS uses its infrastructure of a VPC to create a VPC peering connection. VPC peering is not any kind of gateway or a VPN connection; it relies on special hardware. Since AWS uses the internal infrastructure to peer VPCs, there is no single point of failure or throttling of bandwidth when the traffic flows across multiple virtual private clouds.

Here are the steps to peer a VPC:

1. Say you want to peer VPC A and VPC B. The first step is that the owner of VPC A sends a request to VPC B to create the VPC. VPC A and VPC B can be part of the same account or a different account. If you are planning to peer two VPCs, then you can't have a CIDR block that overlaps with requester's VPC CIDR block since it's going to cause a conflict in the IP address. Once the owner of VPC B gets the request, the owner needs to accept the VPC peering connection to activate the VPC peering connection.

2. The owner of each VPC, in this case VPC A and VPC B, needs to add a route to one or more of their VPC's route tables that point to the IP address range of the other VPC (the peer VPC). VPC peering connectivity is also controlled via route tables referencing the peering connection as a target for routes. Figure 3-5 shows how the entries in the route table look for VPC peering.

Figure 3-5
Route table
entries for
peered VPC

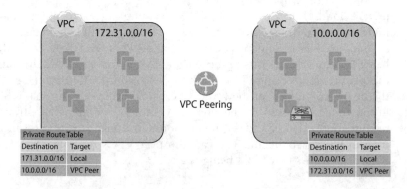

Figure 3-6
Three VPCs for peering

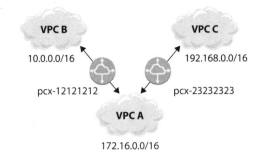

3. Optionally you might be required to update the security group rules associated with your instance to make sure the traffic from the peered VPC can reach your instance. Similarly, you may have to modify your VPC connection to enable DNS hostname resolution. By default, if instances on either side of a VPC peering connection address each other using a public DNS hostname, the hostname resolves to the instance's public IP address.

A VPC peering connection is a one-to-one relationship between two VPCs. You can create multiple VPC peering connections for each VPC that you own, but transitive peering relationships are not supported. Say you have three VPCs such as A, B, and C. Now say VPC A is paired with VPC B and VPC A is again paired with VPC C. Now if you want to establish a connection between VPC B and VPC C, you need to explicitly peer them. You can't use VPC A as a transit point for peering between VPC B and VPC C. Figure 3-6 shows the three VPCs.

Amazon VPC Endpoint

There are many services of AWS that run outside VPC. For example, S3 is a regional service and doesn't run inside VPC. Now if you want your VPC to connect to S3, you need to connect it either via the Internet or via your corporate data center. What a VPC endpoint does is give you the ability to connect to VPC and S3 directly using a private connection. Therefore, the traffic never leaves the Amazon network. Currently, the VPC endpoint is available only for S3 and DynamoDB. Soon there will be more services that can be connected via a VPC endpoint. The VPC endpoint is actually a virtual device that scales horizontally and is redundant, providing high availability. To use a VPC endpoint, you don't need a public IPv4 address or Internet gateway, NAT device/gateway, or virtual private gateway in your VPC.

It's easy to configure a VPC endpoint. These are the steps:

1. To create an endpoint, you must specify the VPC in which you want to create the endpoint and the service to which you want to establish the connection. You can also attach a policy to the endpoint and specify the route tables that will be used by the endpoint. (You will learn more about policies in Chapter 5.)

2. Specify one or more route tables to control the routing of traffic between your VPC and the other service.

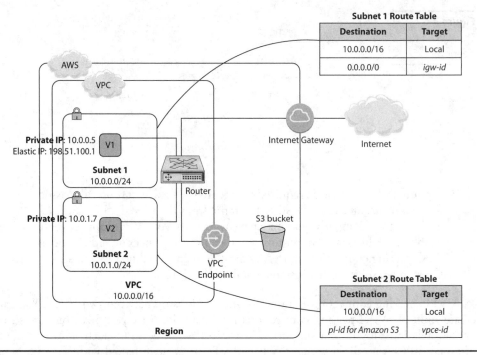

Figure 3-7   VPC endpoint for S3

Let's look at an example to understand the use of VPC endpoints. Say inside VPC you have two subnets: a private subnet and a public subnets. The public subnet has access to the Internet. Now if you want to connect to S3 from the private subnet, the only way to do this would be to access S3 via the public subnet that is attached to the Internet gateway. Now if you have a VPC endpoint, you can simply add an entry for that in the routing table of the private subnet and directly communicate with it, as shown in Figure 3-7. Table 3-11 shows what the entry for the VPC endpoint will look like in the routing table of the private subnet.

 EXAM TIP   You should know the use cases for using VPC endpoints.

Table 3-11	Destination	Target
VPC Endpoint	10.0.0.0/16	local
	pl-68a54001(com .amazonaws-us-west-2.s3)	vpc-endpoint-id

By using VPC endpoints, you save a lot of money. For example, if you have an EC2 instance in a private subnet and it has to access S3, with a VPC endpoint you can directly connect the EC2 instance running in a private subnet to S3, and since EC2 and S3 are connected via the endpoints, there are no data transfer charges. If there is no endpoint, the EC2 instance running in a private subnet needs to reach S3 via a bastion host running on the public subnet. The traffic has to leave VPC to access S3 since S3 is a regional service and is accessible via the Internet. There will be some data transfer charges for the traffic entering VPC, which you can completely save by using the endpoint.

DNS and VPC

The Domain Name System (DNS) is the equivalent of the phone book of the Internet. DNS servers maintain a directory of domain names and translate them to IP addresses. People don't always remember an IP address; rather, most of the time they use a domain name, so DNS servers are absolute necessary. A DNS hostname is a name that uniquely names a computer; it's composed of a hostname and a domain name.

Amazon provides DNS servers that are used to resolve the address of any instance running inside VPC. Public IPv4 addresses enable communication over the Internet, and private IPv4 addresses enable communication within an internal network (within VPC). Whenever you launch an instance into the default VPC, you will notice that the instance will have a public DNS hostname that corresponds to the public IPv4 address and a private DNS hostname that corresponds to the private IPv4 address of the instance. If you launch an instance in a custom VPC or nondefault VPC, then the instance will have a private DNS hostname, and the instance may have a public DNS hostname depending on the DNS attributes specified in VPC. There are two main DNS attributes that define whether an instance can have a public DNS hostname. If both the attributes are true, then the instance gets a public DNS hostname. If one of the attributes is not true, it doesn't get a public DNS hostname.

Attribute	Description
enableDnsHostnames	Indicates whether the instances launched in VPC get public DNS hostnames.
	If this attribute is true, instances in VPC get public DNS hostnames, but only if the enableDnsSupport attribute is also set to true.
enableDnsSupport	Indicates whether DNS resolution is supported for the VPC.

If this attribute is false, the Amazon-provided DNS server in VPC that resolves public DNS hostnames to IP addresses is not enabled. If this attribute is true, queries to the Amazon-provided DNS server at the 169.254.169.253 IP address, or the reserved IP address at the base of the VPC IPv4 network range plus two, will succeed. The attributes are from VPC, and you should be able to see them at the summary page of the VPC.

A public DNS hostname looks like ec2-*public-ipv4-address*.compute-1.amazonaws .com for the us-east-1 region, and it looks like ec2-*public-ipv4-address*.*region*.amazonaws.com for other regions. A private DNS hostname looks like ip-*private-ipv4-address*.ec2.internal for the us-east-1 region and like ip-*private-ipv4-address.region*.compute.internal for other regions. At this time, Amazon does not provide the DNS hostnames for IPv6 addresses.

You can also use your own DNS server and create a new set of DHCP options for your VPC. Let's understand what the DHCP options mean.

DHCP Option Sets

Dynamic Host Configuration Protocol (DHCP) option sets are used to specify host configurations for instances in your VPC, including the default domain name and DNS server for your instances. AWS recommends that you create a DHCP options set for your AWS Directory Service directory and assign the DHCP options set to the VPC that your directory is in. This allows any instances in that VPC to point to the specified domain and DNS servers to resolve their domain names.

For your VPC, Amazon automatically creates and associates a DHCP option set. It also sets two options in it that are domain name servers defaulted to AmazonProvidedDNS (which is an Amazon DNS server) and the domain name for your region. Please note that every VPC must have only one DHCP option set assigned to it. Once you create a DHCP option set, you can't modify it. If you need to specify different DHCP options, you'll need to create a new DHCP option set. Once you've associated a new DHCP option set, new instances launched in VPC will automatically start using the settings in the newer DHCP option set. Instances that are already running in VPC will pick up the new options when their DHCP lease is renewed.

For assigning your own domain name to your instances, you need to create a custom DHCP option set and assign it to your Amazon VPC. Using the standards of DHCP, you can pass configuration information to hosts on a TCP/IP network. The option field of DHCP contains the configuration parameters; you can provide the following values to them:

- **domain-name-servers** The IP addresses of domain name servers (up to four when specifying multiple domain name servers, separated by comma) or AmazonProvidedDNS. The default DHCP option set specifies AmazonProvidedDNS. If you want your instance to use a custom DNS hostname as specified in domain-name, you must set domain-name-servers to a custom DNS server.

- **domain-name** The domain name. If you're using AmazonProvidedDNS in us-east-1, specify ec2.internal. If you're using AmazonProvidedDNS in another region, specify region.compute.internal (for example, ap-northeast-1.compute .internal). Otherwise, specify a custom domain name (for example, amazon.com).

- **ntp-servers** The IP addresses of up to four Network Time Protocol (NTP) servers.

- **netbios-name-servers** The IP addresses of NetBIOS name servers (you can provide up to four of them).

- **netbios-node-type** The NetBIOS node type (1, 2, 4, or 8). It is recommended that you specify two. At this time, broadcast and multicast are not supported.

Connecting to a VPC

Once you have created a VPC in the cloud, the next step is to connect your corporate data center to VPC. Once you connect your corporate data center with VPC, VPC becomes an extension to your data, and traffic can easily move in and out between the corporate data center and VPC. There are multiple ways via which you can connect to VPC.

In this section, you will learn various ways of connecting to VPC. Before digging into this, you need to be aware of two terms that will be used when discussing how to connect to VPC.

- **Virtual private gateway**   By default, instances that you launch in a virtual private cloud can't communicate with a corporate data center on your own network. Since there is no way the corporate data center can reach the VPC (the exception is if you have any instance running in a public subnet, then you can reach it via the Internet), you can enable access to your network from your VPC by attaching a virtual private gateway to the VPC and then creating a custom route table, updating your security group rules, and so on. A virtual private gateway is the VPN concentrator on the Amazon side of the VPN connection. A virtual private gateway take cares of the Amazon side, but what about your own data center? The customer gateway takes care of that.

- **Customer gateway**   A customer gateway is a physical device, or it could be a software application on your corporate data center or your side of the VPN connection. It is the anchor on your side of that connection.

There are four main private connectivity options for a VPC and your corporate data center.

- **AWS hardware VPN**   You can create an IPsec, hardware VPN connection between your VPC and your remote network. Internet Protocol Security (IPsec) is a protocol suite for securing IP communications by authenticating and encrypting each IP packet of a communication session. On the AWS side of the VPN connection, a *virtual private gateway* provides two VPN endpoints for automatic failover. You configure your *customer gateway,* which is the physical device or software application on the remote side of the VPN connection. AWS supports both static and dynamic BGP-based and VPN connections. (Border Gateway Protocol [BGP] is the protocol used to exchange routing information on the Internet.) If you decide to use a static VPN connection, you will need to manually specify the routes to the remote corporate network. However, if your equipment supports BGP, I highly recommend that it's used. This would mean that the IP routes, called *prefixes,* are advertised dynamically over BGP and maintained automatically if they change in the corporate environment. If BGP is used, you should be aware that it has a maximum prefix limit of 100. Therefore, if you have more than that within your network, then you can aggregate them or alternatively simply announce a default route. Every VPN connection is actually provisioned as two IPsec tunnels, terminating in two different availability zones.

- **AWS Direct Connect**   AWS Direct Connect provides a dedicated private connection from your corporate data center to your VPC. Direct Connect consists of dedicated, private pipes into AWS. Each AWS region is associated with at least one Direct Connect location. These locations are large colocation facilities such as Equinix or Coresite with large concentrations of customers. AWS has private connectivity with these colocations. If you have a footprint in these locations, it's an easy cross connect into Direct Connect to hook up with AWS. If you don't have a footprint in the colocation, then you can work with one of AWS's telco partners to establish last-mile connectivity. Using Direct Connect, you get consistent network performance. You can combine this connection with an AWS hardware VPN connection to create an IPsec-encrypted connection.

- **VPN CloudHub**   If you have more than one remote network (for example, multiple branch offices), you can create multiple AWS hardware VPN connections via your VPC to enable communication between these networks. If you use the AWS VPN CloudHub configuration, multiple sites can access your VPC or securely access each other using a simple hub-and-spoke model. You configure each customer gateway to advertise a site-specific prefix (such as 10.0.0.0/24, 10.0.1.0/24) to the virtual private gateway. The virtual private gateway routes traffic to the appropriate site and advertises the reachability of one site to all other sites.

- **Software VPN**   You can create a VPN connection to your remote network by using an Amazon EC2 instance in your VPC that's running a software VPN appliance. AWS does not provide or maintain software VPN appliances; however, you can choose from a range of products provided by partners and open source communities. You can also purchase a software VPN from the marketplace.

Most of the enterprises establish a direct connection to an AWS network. By doing this, you can have greater bandwidth and a bigger pipe between your data center and the AWS network. To get redundancy, customers often use two direct connections. If you can't start with two direct connections, you can start with one direct connection and one VPN connection for failover purposes. Many customers initially start with a virtual private network and gradually establish a direct connection when their traffic increases.

VPC Flow Logs

Amazon VPC flow logs enable you to capture information about the IP traffic going to and from network interfaces in your VPC. Flow log data is stored using Amazon Cloud-Watch logs. After you've created a flow log, you can view and retrieve its data in Amazon CloudWatch logs.

Flow logs can help you with a number of tasks such as troubleshooting why specific traffic is not reaching an instance, which in turn can help you diagnose overly restrictive security group rules. You can also use flow logs as a security tool to monitor the traffic that is reaching your instance.

There is no additional charge for using flow logs; however, standard CloudWatch Logs charges apply.

Flow logs can be created for network interfaces, subnets, and VPCs.

Default VPC

In every account, a VPC is created in each region by default. This is called the *default VPC*. This is created to provide simplicity and convenience and to help you jumpstart to AWS. You may or may not want a default VPC. Even if you don't want to use the default VPC, AWS recommends not deleting it since that can create problems later. If you accidentally delete the default VPC, you can re-create it by logging a support ticket. The default VPC comes precreated with the following features:

- Dynamic private IP
- Dynamic public IP
- AWS-provided DNS names
- Private DNS name
- Public DNS name

You can also do the following in the default VPC:

- Create additional subnets and change routing rules
- Create additional network controls (security groups, NACLs, routing)
- Set hardware VPN options between corporate networks

In a default VPC, instances in default subnets have security group–controlled public and private IPs.

Labs on VPC

In this section, you will do a few hands-on labs on VPC.

Lab 3-1: Using the VPC Wizard

In this lab, you will use the VPC Wizard to create a VPC. Using the VPC Wizard, you can create four different types of virtual private cloud.

- A virtual private cloud with a single public subnet
- A virtual private cloud with public and private subnets
- A virtual private cloud with public and private subnets and hardware VPC access
- A virtual private cloud with a private subnet only and hardware VPN access

If you want a VPC with a single public subnet, then choose the first option. Once you create a VPC using the VPC Wizard, you can always modify it as per your requirements. For example, if you have created a VPC using the first option and then later want to add a public subnet, you can do it, or if you want to add a private subnet, you can do that. Choose the second option if you want to create a VPC with public and private subnets. The wizard creates one subnet for each, and you can always add more subnets when you need them. If you want to connect your data center using a hardware-based VPN and need a VPC with a private and public subnet, choose the third option. If you want to connect your data center using a hardware-based VPN but need a VPC with only a private subnet, choose the fourth option.

You can always create a VPC manually if your needs are different from the options provided in the wizard. The VPC Wizard just helps you get started quickly. In this lab, you will create a VPC with the VPC Wizard using the first two options.

To start, log into the AWS console and select the region where you want to create the VPC. From Services, choose VPC. Click Start VPC Wizard to start the VPC Wizard.

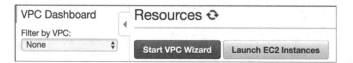

Select the first option on the left called VPC With A Single Public Subnet and click Select.

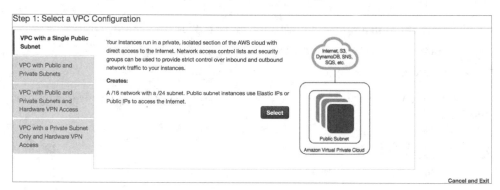

The next screen prompts you for a lot of inputs and shows all the options. Let's examine them one by one.

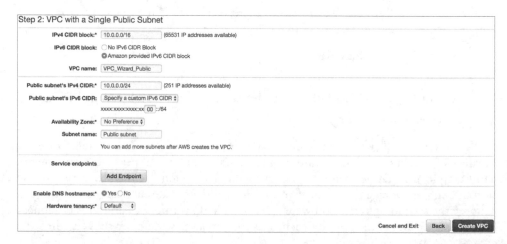

The first option prompts you for the CIDR block for the VPC. Please enter **10.0.0.0/16**, as shown in this example. Though the total number of IP addresses is /16, which is 65,536, AWS reserves five IP addresses for internal usage, as discussed previously. That's why the screen displays that 65,531 IP addresses available to you.

The next option is for the IPv6 CIDR block. At this time, you can't choose the CIDR block for IPv6; you need to go with the Amazon-provided IPv6 CIDR block, so choose the second option.

The next option is for the VPC name; you can enter any desired name for the VPC. In this example, I have chosen the name VPC_Wizard_Public.

The next option is for the CIDR block for the IPv4 public subnet. Please enter **10.0.0.0/24** for this.

The next option is for the CIDR block for the IPv6 public subnet. This field is optional. Optionally you can have IPv6's CIDR in a public subnet.

If you choose to have an IPv6 CIDR for a public subnet, you won't be able to provide the CIDR number manually. Amazon will automatically allocate the CIDR block for you.

The next option is to select an availability zone. If you don't choose an AZ (No Preference), the VPC will span all the AZs in that region. You can manually choose an AZ where you want to create the VPC, but the VPC will be restricted only to that AZ. This is not recommended since the VPC will become a single point of failure; you may still do this if you have a special requirement, however.

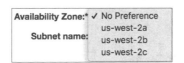

For this example, don't choose an AZ. Select No Preference.

The next option is for the subnet name. Choose Public Subnet for this option.

The next option is for the service endpoint. As discussed previously, you can add an S3 endpoint or a DynamoDB endpoint to your VPC to enable direct connectivity with that service. In this example, let's add an S3 endpoint. Click Add Endpoint. Select Add Endpoint.

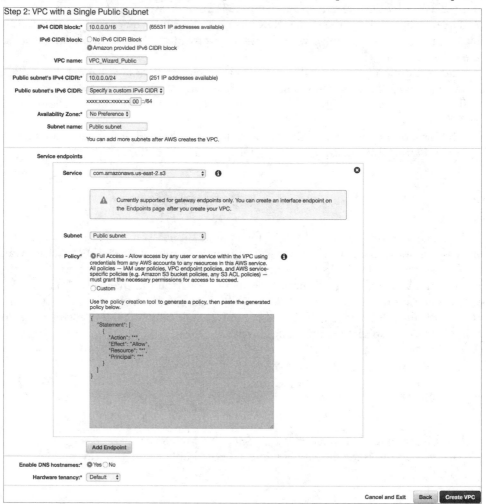

The next option is Enable DNS Hostnames; click Yes for this option.

The last option is Hardware Tenancy. You can choose either Default or Dedicated. You can run instances in your VPC on single-tenant dedicated hardware. Select Dedicated to ensure that instances launched in this VPC are dedicated tenancy instances regardless of the tenancy attribute specified at launch. Select Default to ensure that instances launched in this VPC use the tenancy attribute specified at launch. You will learn more about dedicated instances in Chapter 4. For now, choose Default and click Create VPC. Within a few minutes, the VPC will be created for you, and you will get a confirmation stating this. Hit OK.

Now go back to the console, and click VPC on the left side of the menu. Select your VPCs; you can now see the newly created VPC from the console.

Before looking at various options of the newly created VPC, let's work through the second lab exercise, and after that we will look at all the options.

Lab 3-2: Creating a VPC with Public and Private Subnets

For this lab, you will invoke the VPC Wizard again. Start the VPC Wizard, choose the second option from the left (VPC With Public And Private Subnets), and click Select.

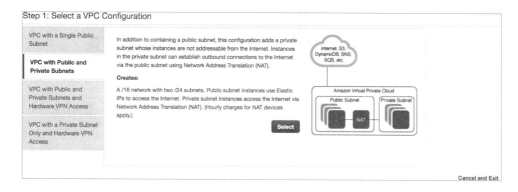

The next screen prompts you to fill out the options. In this example, you won't use IPv6; therefore, you won't choose the IPv6 option. You will also notice that the wizard then prompts you for the private subnet details as well as the public subnet details. Input all the information shown here.

Step 2: VPC with Public and Private Subnets

IPv4 CIDR block:*	10.0.0.0/16 (65531 IP addresses available)
IPv6 CIDR block:	◉ No IPv6 CIDR Block
	○ Amazon provided IPv6 CIDR block
VPC name:	VPC_Public_Private
Public subnet's IPv4 CIDR:*	10.0.0.0/24 (251 IP addresses available)
Availability Zone:*	No Preference ⬍
Public subnet name:	Public subnet
Private subnet's IPv4 CIDR:*	10.0.1.0/24 (251 IP addresses available)
Availability Zone:*	No Preference ⬍
Private subnet name:	Private subnet
	You can add more subnets after AWS creates the VPC.

Specify the details of your NAT gateway (NAT gateway rates apply).   Use a NAT instance instead

Elastic IP Allocation ID:*	
Service endpoints	
	Add Endpoint
Enable DNS hostnames:*	◉ Yes ○ No
Hardware tenancy:*	Default ⬍

                                               Cancel and Exit   Back   Create VPC

Since I have already discussed all the options in the previous lab, I won't repeat myself here. You will notice that the wizard prompts you for the elastic IP allocation ID. As discussed in this chapter, if you want the instances running in the private subnet to communicate with the Internet for downloading patches and firmware updates, you need to have either a NAT gateway or a NAT instance. If you want to use a NAT gateway (which is always preferred over a NAT instance), you need to provide an elastic IP. Since you don't have any elastic ID associated, the wizard will show "No results found." when you click Elastic IP Allocation ID.

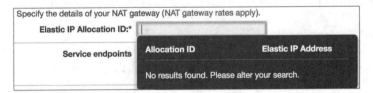

So, let's allocate an EIP and then come back to this VPC Wizard. On a separate browser tab, go to the VPC Dashboard and then choose Elastic IPs from the left menu.

Then click Allocate New Address.

The console displays an additional message. Click Allocate.

The system allocates an EIP for you and shows you the IP address of the EIP. In this example, the system has allocated 13.59.15.253.

Click OK, which will take you back to the screen for the EIP. Now from the console you will be able to see the new EIP and the allocation ID mapped to it.

Note the EIP and the allocation ID. Now go back to the VPC Wizard in the other browser window. You will notice that when you click Elastic IP Allocation ID, the system will display the newly created EIP along with its allocation ID.

Make sure the EIP being displayed matches with the one you have created.

You can also use a NAT instance in lieu of a NAT gateway. If you choose to do so, click Use A NAT Instance Instead. The system will prompt you for the instance type for running the NAT instance and the key pair name (you will learn about key pairs in Chapter 4).

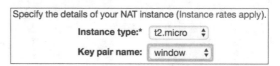

In this example, you will use a NAT gateway and not a NAT instance. Don't select the NAT instance option; stick with the NAT gateway for this example.

For the rest of the options, keep the defaults. Now the filled options should look similar to this:

Click Create VPC. Once the VPC has been created, you will get a success screen.

Now let's explore all the options of the VPC in the final lab of this chapter.

Lab 3-3: Exploring All the Options in a Virtual Private Cloud

Once your VPCs are created, you may notice that several things have been created for you. The next set of steps will walk you through the various VPC objects and components that were created for you by the VPC Wizard.

Click Your VPCs. This will show you all the VPCs you have created.

Clicking the Your VPCs link lists your VPCs and is a good location to obtain the VPC IDs for your VPCs. If you create multiple VPCs, they will be listed here. You will see the VPC_Wizard_Public and VPC_Public_Private instances, which are the ones you created in Lab 3-1 and Lab 3-2. Clicking a VPC will bring up details about the VPC such as the IP address block (CIDR), DHCP options set, route table, network ACL, hardware tenancy (whether VPC physical hardware will be shared [default] or dedicated to you), and DNS configuration information.

Also note the presence of a default VPC listed in the Your VPCs list. The last one shows the default VPC. As of December 2013, AWS creates a default VPC in each region. The default VPC includes one subnet per availability zone, a default security group, an Internet gateway, and other networking elements.

Let's now focus on the VPCs created and look at the components. First select the VPC VPC_Wizard_Public from Lab 3-1. If you remember correctly, this VPC has only one public subnet. Once you select the VPC, you will notice the bottom portion of the page shows all the details about it.

If you look at the Summary tab, you will see details about the newly created VPC. Similarly, you will see one of the VPCs you created in Lab 3-2. Do you notice any difference?

Now click Subnets on the left. Clicking the Subnets link lists all of your VPC subnets and allows you to create additional subnets within your VPC with the Create Subnets button. Clicking a subnet will bring up the subnet details, including its subnet address range (CIDR), availability zone, and associated route table and NACLs. Clicking the tabs underneath brings up relevant information about the subnet. Click the public subnet from the VPC VPC_Wizard_Public created by the VPC Wizard.

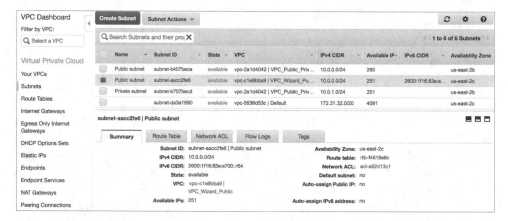

Now click the tab Route Table. You will see the route table.

You will notice that this subnet's default route of (0.0.0.0) IPv4 and ::/0 IPv6 is the Internet gateway. Internet gateways can be identified by the "igw" prefix in their IDs; in this example, it's igw-ac69a5c4. This route makes this subnet your public subnet because it is publicly routable through the Internet gateway. You will also notice that this subnet has a VPC endpoint attached with S3 vpce-e6c5038f. Of course, it has the local route for the VPC as well.

Now look at the route table of the public subnet of VPC VPC_Public_Private.

You will notice that it has just the subnet's default route of 0.0.0.0 as the Internet gateway and of course the local route for the VPC. Can you now figure out the difference between the two? While creating the second VPC with the VPC Wizard, you selected the public subnet, but you didn't select the IPv6 and VPC endpoint. That's the reason those components are missing from this routing table.

Now let's look at the routing table of the private subnet of the VPC VPC_Public _Private.

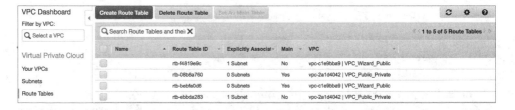

You will notice the routing table has just a NAT gateway assigned to it in addition to the local route. This subnet's default route (0.0.0.0) is the NAT gateway identified by the "nat-" prefix in its ID. In this example, it is nat-0502466cccd46cfdc. This route makes this subnet your private subnet because it is not routing through the Internet gateway. Instead, all client connections to the Internet are directed to, and proxied by, your NAT gateway in the public subnet.

When you created the VPC in the second lab, you created a public subnet and a private subnet. Let's note the routing table ID for both. In this case, they are rtb-ebbda283 and rtb-08b8a760 for public and private, respectively.

Now from the left side of the menu of the main VPC page in the console, click Route Tables. Clicking the Route Tables link lists all of your VPC route tables, allows you to modify and associate the route tables to subnets, and allows you to create additional route tables within your VPC with the Create Route Table button. Notice that two route tables were created by the VPC Wizard, and these are the same route tables that were displayed in the subnet details in the previous section. Notice the "Main" and "Explicitly Associated With" columns.

The subnet designated as the Main subnet (Main = Yes) is the default route table for the listed VPC. This means that all subnets that are not explicitly associated with a more specific route table will use this route table by default. The Explicitly Associated With column displays the number of subnets explicitly associated with the route table. In this example, you can see that the routing table specified as rtb-ebbda283 has (Main = No) and the routing table specified as rtb-08b8a760 has (Main = Yes), which means the routing table in the public subnet has Main = No and the routing table in the private subnet has Main = Yes.

Notice that the selected route table is *not* the Main route table (Main = No) and its default route (0.0.0.0) is the Internet gateway. This means your public subnet is explicitly associated with this route table (click the Subnet Associations tab to verify this). Notice there is another route table associated with the VPC; you will see the default route (0.0.0.0) is your NAT gateway.

So, what does all this mean? By default, the VPC Wizard created two subnets and two route tables. The public subnet is associated with a route table that directs traffic by default out to the Internet. The private subnet is not associated with a specific route table and therefore inherits the Main route table rules, which direct traffic by default to the NAT gateway in the "public" subnet.

Also note that the rules in the Main route table determine how subnets will be treated by default. Since the Main route table is a private route table (it does not route any traffic to the Internet gateway), all new subnets created in this VPC will be private subnets by default. They will remain private until they are explicitly associated with a public route table (e.g., one that routes traffic directly to the Internet gateway).

The Internet gateway that is created by the VPC Wizard can also be viewed from the VPC Dashboard by clicking the Internet Gateway link at the left. The Internet gateways associated with their respective VPCs are shown here.

Internet gateways can also be independently created, attached to, and detached from VPCs on this page. This page allows you to add or remove the Internet gateway capabilities to/from your VPCs after the VPC has been created.

The DHCP Options Sets link in the VPC Dashboard allows you to control some DHCP options that the VPC-provided DHCP service will present to your instances when they boot. By default the VPC Wizard created a DHCP options set that tells your VPCs to use the AWS-provided DNS service for domain name resolution.

VPC allows you to create and attach new DHCP options to your VPCs, including setting your domain name, DNS servers, time (NTP) servers, and Microsoft Windows NetBIOS name servers and node types. If you want to create a new one, click the Create DHCP Options Set button. You'll see a screen where you can configure a new DHCP options set.

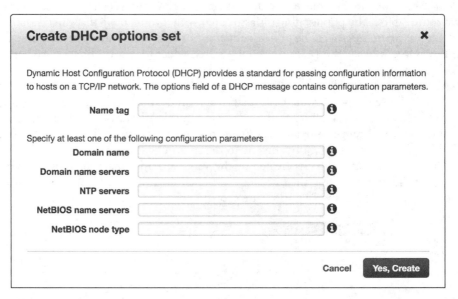

Remember that during the first lab you added an S3 endpoint. From the VPC Dashboard page you should be able to view the S3 endpoint attached to the VPC. If you forgot to attach a VPC endpoint during the VPC creation and want to attach it later, you can do so by clicking the button Create Endpoint at the top.

The VPC Wizard has also created a NAT gateway for you. As previously mentioned, a NAT gateway is a managed service that enables EC2 instances in private subnets to reach the Internet without publicly exposing the instances. It uses NAT to map the private IP address of an EC2 instance to the shared public IP address of the NAT gateway and remaps return traffic to the instance. NAT gateways have built-in redundancy and automatically scale capacity up to 10Gbps based on demand. You can view the NAT gateways assigned to your VPC by clicking the NAT gateway in the VPC Dashboard.

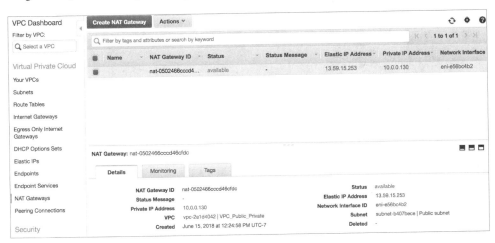

Similarly, from the VPC Dashboard, you should be able to create an egress-only Internet gateway, elastic IPs, and VPC peering connection. You can also view the network ACLs and the security group that have been created by running the VPC Wizard.

Chapter Review

In this chapter, you learned what Amazon VPC is. VPC allows you to have your own virtual private cloud and logically isolate a section in the cloud. You can provision any resource in this logically isolated region, and you have complete control over the networking.

You can connect to a VPC either with a virtual private network or with Direct Connect. By subnetting you can divide a network into multiple networks. Inside a VPC, you can create various subnets per your needs. The most common configuration consists of a public subnet, a private subnet, and a VPN-only subnet. Route tables are tables consisting of certain rules known as routes that determine where the traffic is directed. An Internet gateway is a component of your VPC that allows your VPC to communicate with the Internet. By using a network address translator, you can enable any instance in a private subnet to connect to the Internet. There are two types of NAT devices available within AWS NAT instances and NAT gateways. Similar to a NAT gateway, an egress-only Internet gateway is a component of your VPC that allows your VPC to communicate with the Internet for IPv6 traffic. The Elastic Network Interface gives you the ability to create network interfaces and attach them to your instance. An EIP gives you a static public IP address. A security group is like a virtual firewall that can be assigned to any instance running in a virtual private client. An NACL is a layer of security that acts as a firewall at the subnet level. VPC peering can be used to connect multiple VPCs. The VPC endpoint gives you the ability to connect to VPC and S3 directly using private connectivity. Amazon VPC flow logs enable you to capture information about the IP traffic going to and from network interfaces in your VPC. In every account, a VPC is created in each region by default. This is called the default VPC. This is created to provide simplicity and convenience and to help you get started with AWS. You can connect to a VPC from your corporate data center in one of four ways.

- AWS hardware VPN
- AWS Direct Connect
- VPN CloudHub
- Software VPN

Questions

1. You have created a VPC with two subnets. The web servers are running in a public subnet, and the database server is running in a private subnet. You need to download an operating system patch to update the database server. How you are going to download the patch?

   A. By attaching the Internet Gateway to the private subnet temporarily

   B. By using a NAT gateway

   C. By using peering to another VPC

   D. By changing the security group of the database server and allowing Internet access

2. What is the maximum size of the CIDR block you can have for a VPC?

   A. 16

   B. 32

   C. 28

   D. 10

3. How many IP addresses are reserved by AWS for internal purposes in a CIDR block that you can't use?

   A. 5

   B. 2

   C. 3

   D. 4

4. You have a web server and an app server running. You often reboot your app server for maintenance activities. Every time you reboot the app server, you need to update the connect string for the web server since the IP address of the app server changes. How do you fix this issue?

   A. Allocate an IPv6 IP address to the app server

   B. Allocate an Elastic Network Interface to the app server

   C. Allocate an elastic IP address to the app server

   D. Run a script to change the connection

5. To connect your corporate data center to AWS, you need at least which of the following components? (Choose two.)

   A. Internet gateway

   B. Virtual private gateway

   C. NAT gateway

   D. Customer gateway

6. You want to explicitly "deny" certain traffic to the instance running in your VPC. How do you achieve this?

   A. By using a security group

   B. By adding an entry in the route table

   C. By putting the instance in the private subnet

   D. By using a network access control list

7. You have created a web server in the public subnet, and now anyone can access the web server from the Internet. You want to change this behavior and just have the load balancer talk with the web server and no one else. How do you achieve this?

   A. By removing the Internet gateway

   B. By adding the load balancer in the route table

   C. By allowing the load balancer access in the NACL of the public subnet

   D. By modifying the security group of the instance and just having the load balancer talk with the web server

8. How can your VPC talk with DynamoDB directly?

   A. By using a direct connection

   B. By using a VPN connection

   C. By using a VPN endpoint

   D. By using an instance in the public subnet

9. The local route table in the VPC allows which of the following?

   A. So that all the instances running in different subnet within a VPC can communicate to each other

   B. So that only the traffic to the Internet can be routed

   C. So that multiple VPCs can talk with each other

   D. So that an instance can use the local route and talk to the Internet

10. What happens to the EIP address when you stop and start an instance?

   A. The EIP is released to the pool and you need to re-attach.

   B. The EIP is released temporarily during the stop and start.

   C. The EIP remains associated with the instance.

   D. The EIP is available for any other customer.

Answers

1. **B**. The database server is running in a private subnet. Anything running in a private subnet should never face the Internet directly. Even if you peer to another VPC, you can't really connect to the Internet without using a NAT instance or a NAT gateway. Even if you change the security group of the database server and allow all incoming traffic, it still won't be able to connect to the Internet because the database server is running in the private subnet and the private subnet is not attached to the Internet gateway.

2. **A**. The maximum size of a VPC you can have is /16, which corresponds to 65,536 IP addresses.

3. **A**. AWS reserves five IP address for internal purposes, the first four and the last one.

4. **C**. Allocating an IPv6 IP address won't be of any use because whenever the server comes back, it is going to get assigned another new IPv6 IP address. Also, if your VPC doesn't support IPv6 and if you did not select the IPv6 option while creating the instance, you may not be able to allocate one. The Elastic Network Interface helps you add multiple network interfaces but won't get you a static IP address. You can run a script to change the connection, but unfortunately you have to run it every time you are done with any maintenance activities. You can even automate the running of the script, but why add so much complexity when you can solve the problem simply by allocating an EIP?

5. **A, C**. To connect to AWS from your data center, you need a customer gateway, which is the customer side of a connection, and a virtual private gateway, which is the AWS side of the connection. An Internet gateway is used to connect a VPC with the Internet, whereas a NAT gateway connects to the servers running in the private subnet in order to connect to the Internet.

6. D. By using a security group, you can allow and disallow certain traffic, but you can't explicitly deny traffic since the deny option does not exist for security groups. There is no option for denying particular traffic via a route table. By putting an instance in the private subnet, you are just removing the Internet accessibility of this instance, which is not going to deny any particular traffic.

7. D. By removing the Internet gateway, a web connection via the load balancer won't be able to reach the instance. You can add the route for a load balancer in the route table. NACL can allow or block certain traffic. In this scenario, you won't be able to use NACL.

8. C. Direct Connect and VPN are used to connect your corporate data center to AWS. DynamoDB is a service running in AWS. Even if you use an instance in a public subnet to connect with DynamoDB, it is still going to use the Internet. In this case, you won't be able to connect to DynamoDB, bypassing the Internet.

9. A. The traffic to the Internet is routed via the Internet gateway. Multiple VPCs can talk to each other via VPC peering.

10. C. Even during the stop and start of the instance, the EIP is associated with the instance. It gets detached when you explicitly terminate an instance.

Introduction to Amazon Elastic Compute Cloud

In this chapter, you will

- Learn the benefits of Amazon EC2
- Go through the Amazon EC2 instance types and features
- Walk through the steps for using Amazon EC2
- See the pricing for Amazon EC2
- Understand what shared tenancy, dedicated hosts, and dedicated instances are
- Explore instances and AMIs
- Learn about virtualization in an AMI
- Go through the instance life cycle
- Learn how to connect to an instance
- Learn about security groups

Amazon Elastic Compute Cloud (EC2) provides almost infinite compute capability in the cloud, and it is not only reliable but secure. You can run any kind of workload in the Amazon cloud and don't have to invest a lot of capital expenditures to get computing resources. The model for cloud computing is pay as you go, which means you pay just for the resources that you are going use on an hourly basis. Therefore, to procure new servers, you don't really have to wait months to get a budget approved. As a result, you can deploy your applications faster as well as innovate quickly. Amazon's EC2 ecosystem is designed to scale; as a result, whenever there is a spike in the traffic of your workload, you can quickly spin off additional servers almost instantly, and when the traffic reduces, you can get rid of those servers. For example, say for your normal business during weekdays you need a server with 16 CPUs, but on the weekend you are expecting twice that traffic. You can provision an extra 16 CPUs only for the weekend, and when Monday comes, you can get rid of that server. You have to pay for the additional server only for the hours on Saturday and Sunday.

When you spin off servers in Amazon EC2, you have complete control over the type of storage you want to use, the network configurations, the security configuration, and so on. The EC2 web interface allows you to configure a server in a minimal amount of time. Imagine a traditional deployment model where you have to provision a server. The operating system installation takes a couple of hours, not including the time it takes to configure the storage and network. If you added all of this time together, it would be a couple of days of effort. With Amazon EC2, the time required to obtain and boot the new server is a matter of minutes. Since now it takes only a few minutes to deploy a server, you can actually deploy hundreds or thousands of servers almost instantly, and since this model is very scalable, you can quickly scale up or scale down depending on your workload or traffic volume.

You have the choice of multiple instance types, operating systems, and software packages. Amazon EC2 allows you to select a configuration of memory, CPU, instance storage, and boot partition size that is optimal for your choice of operating system and application. For example, your choice of operating systems includes numerous Linux distributions and Microsoft Windows Server.

These are the operating system supported by EC2:

- Windows 2003R2, 2008/2008R2, 2012/2012R2, 2016
- Amazon Linux
- Debian
- SUSE
- CentOS
- Red Hat Enterprise Linux
- Ubuntu

Benefits of Amazon EC2

When you deploy a new application or a new workload on your data center (in other words, on-premise), it takes a few months just to provision the hardware, whereas if you decide to host your workload on Amazon EC2, it is almost instant. Similarly, you get several benefits when you choose to host your application or workload on Amazon EC2.

The following are the benefits of EC2:

- **Time to market** The biggest advantage of running an EC2 server is the time to market. You can deploy any server almost instantly, and as a result you don't have to wait for weeks or months to get a new server. This also facilitates innovation because you can quickly get the resources for your new project. If the project ends, you can simply get rid of the servers and start a new project with new resources.

- **Scalability** Another benefit of running EC2 is scalability; you can scale up and scale down at any point of time depending on your workload. In the past, you always had to over-provision the resources just to make sure that you would be able to support the peak demand. But with EC2 servers you don't have to over-provision the resources; you just provision the resources that are needed for your business, and whenever there is additional growth or a spike, you can quickly deploy additional servers that can take care of the additional demand. EC2 Auto Scaling technologies allow you to automatically scale up or scale down applications depending on the needs. In this way, you get the best of both worlds. You not only maximize the performance but also minimize the cost.

- **Control**   You have complete control over the servers just like you have control over the servers in your data center. You can start and stop the service at any point of time, and you have the root access to the servers. You can interact with the servers just like you interact with any other machine. You can control or reboot the servers remotely using web service APIs, and you can also access them using the Amazon console.

- **Reliable**   EC2 offers a reliable environment where replacement instances can be rapidly and predictably commissioned. EC2's service level agreement is 99.95 percent availability for each region.

- **Secure**   The entire infrastructure of Amazon is secure; in fact, security is a highest priority job for Amazon. Everything that operates under the EC2 cloud is secure. You can create an EC2 resource in conjunction with Amazon VPC to provide security and networking functionality for your compute resources.

- **Multiple instance type**   Amazon EC2 allows you to select from a variety of instances. You can choose the instance on the basis of operating system, software package, CPU storage size or memory, and so on. You can also choose an instance from the Amazon Marketplace where various third-party vendors offer their prepackaged servers.

- **Integration**   Amazon EC2 is integrated with most of the AWS services such as S3, VPC, Lambda Redshift, RDS, EMR, and so on. Using EC2 and the other services of AWS, you can get a complete solution for all of your IT needs.

- **Cost effective**   Since you pay only for the usage of the server on an hourly basis or per second depending on which instance you run, you don't really have to pay a huge capital expense when you provision servers on EC2.

Amazon EC2 Instance Types and Features

Amazon EC2 offers a variety of instance types to choose from, which can fit any type of workload depending on the use case. You can choose from various combinations of CPU, memory, networking, and storage to deploy your server. When you create a new instance, the *instance type* that you specify determines the hardware of the host computer used for your instance. There are various instance types offered by Amazon, and each instance type offers different types of compute, memory, and storage capabilities grouped into an instance family. You can choose an instance depending on your workload. For example, if your workload is compute intense, you can choose a compute-optimized EC2 instance, and if your workload is memory intense, you can choose a memory-optimized instance. Since EC2 runs on virtualization, each instance type supports either paravirtual (PV) or hardware virtual machine (HVM). The virtualization depends on the type of Amazon Machine Image (AMI) used to launch it. You will learn about AMI and virtualization later in this chapter.

You will notice that there are two types of instances that are available within the EC2 ecosystem: current-generation instances and previous-generation instances. Current-generation instances contain the latest of everything (for example, the latest version of chipsets, memory, processor, and so on), whereas the previous generation consists of the machines that are one or two generations older than the current one. Amazon still supports them because of backward compatibility, and there are many users who have optimized their applications around the previous-generation machines. The current-generation instance will always have a higher number than a previous-generation instance.

Let's examine the various types of instances offered by Amazon EC2. The instance types are broadly divided into the following categories:

- General purpose
- Compute optimized
- Memory optimized
- Storage optimized
- Advanced computing

General Purpose (T2, M5, M4, and M3)

The general-purpose instances provide a balance of computer memory and network resources and are a pretty good choice for many applications. Some of the general-purpose instances, such as T2, provide burstable performance, which means these instances provide a baseline level of CPU performance with the ability to burst above the baseline. The way it works is that T2 instances accrue CPU credits when they are idle and use the CPU credits when they are active. The instance provides burstable performance depending on how many CPU credits it has accrued over a period of time. T2 is suitable for workloads that do not use full CPU utilization. Some of the use cases can be web server, development environments, and so on. Other general-purpose instances are M5, M4, and M3, which can be used for lot of things such as building web sites, development environments, build servers, code repositories, microservices, test and staging environments, and so on. M5, M4, and M3 do not provide burstable performance like T2.

Compute Optimized (C5, C4, and C3)

If you have an application or workload that is heavy on compute, a compute-optimized instance is ideal for that. A compute-optimized instance has high-performance processors, and as a result any application that needs a lot of processing power benefits from these instances. Some good use cases for the compute-optimized workload are media transcoding, applications supporting a large number of concurrent users, long-running batch jobs, high-performance computing, gaming servers, and so on.

Memory Optimized (X1e, X1, R4, and R3)

The memory-optimized instances are ideal if the workload you are planning to run has a lot of memory requirements. Any application that processes large data sets in memory will benefit by using the memory-optimized instance. Some good use cases for memory-optimized instances are running in memory databases such as a SAP HANA or Oracle database in-memory, NoSQL databases like MongoDB and Cassandra, big data processing engines like Presto or Apache Spark, high-performance computing (HPC) and Electronic Design Automation (EDA) applications, Genome assembly and analysis, and so on.

Storage Optimized (H1, I3, and D2)

Storage-optimized instances can be used for the workloads that require high sequential read and write access to very large data sets on local storage. Since they are optimized at storage, they deliver many thousands of low-latency, random I/O operations per second (IOPS). Some use cases for the storage-optimized instance could be running a relational database that is I/O bound, running an I/O-bound application, NoSQL databases, data warehouse applications, MapReduce and Hadoop distributed caches for in-memory databases like Redis, and so on. You can also select a high I/O instance and dense storage instances depending on workload.

Advanced Computing (P3, P2, G3, and F1)

If you have high-processing computing requirements, for example, you want to run machine learning algorithms, molecular modeling, genomics, computation of fluid dynamics, computational finance, and so on, then an advanced computing instance is going to give you the most bang for the buck. These advanced computing instances provide access to hardware-based accelerators such as graphic processing units (GPUs) or field programmable gate arrays (FPGAs), which enable parallelism and give high throughput. The advanced computing also includes GPU compute instances and GPU graphics instances.

Let's discuss some of the key features of the Amazon EC2 instance.

Processor Features

The EC2 instances use an Intel processor, so they in turn use all the processor features that Intel provides. Some of the processor features that are often seen in the EC2 instances are as follows:

- **Intel AES New Instructions (AES-NI)**   This encryption instruction applies the Advanced Encryption Standard (AES) algorithm better compared to the original one and provides faster data protection and greater security. All the current-generation EC2 instances have this feature.

- **Intel Advanced Vector Extensions**   Intel AVX instructions improve performance for applications such as image and audio/video processing. They are available on instances launched with HVM AMIs.

- **Intel Turbo Boost Technology**   Intel Turbo Boost Technology provides more performance when needed.

Network Features

EC2-Classic is the original release of Amazon EC2. With this platform, instances run in a single, flat network that is shared with other customers. Many of the newer instance types are not available today in EC2-Classic; therefore, you must launch those instances in Amazon VPC only. Amazon VPC brings lots of networking enhancements that are not available in EC2-Classic. Examples are assigning multiple private IPv4 addresses to an instance, assigning IPv6 addresses to an instance, changing the security groups, adding the NACL rules, and so on.

Please note that EC2-Classic does not apply for anyone getting started with AWS anymore. All accounts are automatically enabled with the default Amazon VPC now. Amazon VPC allows customers with great control of the IP address space, the ability to segment with subnets, the ability to provide network-level security, and so on.

You can also launch an instance in a placement group to maximize the bandwidth and get better network performance. A placement group is a logical grouping of instances within a single AZ. If you have an application or workload that needs low-latency or high-network throughput, the placement group is going to provide you with that benefit. This is also known as cluster networking. R4, X1, M5, M4, C5, C4, C3, I2, P3, P2, G3, and D2 instances support cluster networking. Since AWS keeps on adding instance type, you should check AWS website to find the latest on instance type supported. When launched in a placement group, EC2 instances can utilize up to 10Gbps for single flow and 25Gbps for multiflow traffic in each direction. To use a placement group, first you need to create a placement group and then start launching multiple instances in your placement group. There is no charge for creating a placement group; only when you start an instance in a placement group are you billed for the usage of the instance. It is recommended that you use the same type of instance in a placement group, although it is possible to use multiple instance types in the same placement group. A placement group cannot span multiple AZs, and also the name of a placement group must be unique within your AWS account. You cannot move an existing or running instance in a placement group. To get the maximum benefit for your placement group, you should choose an instance type that supports "enhanced networking." Enhancement networking provides higher bandwidth, higher packet per second (PPS) performance, and lower inter-instance latencies. It uses single root I/O virtualization (SR-IOV), which is a method of device virtualization that provides higher I/O performance and lower CPU utilization and thus provides high-performance networking capabilities. Since there is no additional cost for using enhanced networking, you should look for an instance that supports enhanced networking and put it in a placement group.

Storage Features

Amazon provides a variety of storage that you can use along with the EC2 instance depending on your workload requirement. The block storage that you attach along with the EC2 instance is known as Elastic Block Storage (EBS). When you attach an EBS volume, it becomes the primary storage, and you can use it like any other physical hard drive. The EBS volume persists independently for the life span of the Amazon EC2 instance. Amazon provides three types of volumes. You can choose any one of them depending on your workload and computation requirements. This has already been discussed in details in Chapter 2.

- **General purpose**   This is the general-purpose EBS volume backed up by solid-state drives (SSDs) and can be used for any purpose. This is often used as the default volume for all the EC2 instances.

- **Provisioned IOPS (PIOPS)**   If you have a computing need for a lot of I/O, for example, running a database workload, then you can use a provisioned IOPS-based EBS volume to maximize the I/O throughput and get the IOPS that your application or database may need. PIOPS costs a little bit more than the general-purpose EBS volumes since you get more IOPS compared to a general-purpose EBS volume.

- **Magnetic**   Magnetic hard drives provide the lowest cost per gigabyte for all the volume time. They are idle for running a development workload, a non-mission-critical workload, or any other workload where data is accessed frequently.

Some of the EC2 instances also include a local disk in the physical hardware, which is also known as an *instance store*. The instance store is ephemeral storage and persists only until the end of the EC2 instance's life. If you shut down the machine, the instance store is gone; therefore, you should not keep any important data in an instance store.

You will notice that some instances are EBS optimized. EBS-optimized instances enable EC2 instances to fully use the IOPS provisioned on an EBS volume. EBS-optimized instances deliver dedicated throughput between Amazon EC2 and Amazon EBS, with options between 500Mbps and 14,000Mbps depending on the instance type used. The dedicated throughput minimizes contention between Amazon EBS I/O and other traffic from your EC2 instance, providing the best performance for your EBS volumes.

Some instances support a cluster networking feature. If you launch instances that support cluster networking in a common cluster placement group, they are placed into a logical cluster that provides high-bandwidth, low-latency networking between all instances in the cluster.

Steps for Using Amazon EC2

It is pretty easy to spin off an EC2 instance. Using the following steps, you should be able to launch an EC2 instance quickly:

1. Select a preconfigured Amazon Machine Image. You can also create your custom AMI and later use that to launch an instance.

2. Configure the networking and security (virtual private cloud, public subnet, private subnet, and so on).

3. Choose the instance type.

4. Choose the AZ, attach EBS, and optionally choose static EIP.

5. Start the instance and you are all set.

Pricing for Amazon EC2

Amazon provides multiple pricing options, depending on the duration of the instance and your payment flexibility. The instances are divided into three categories from a pricing perspective.

- On-demand instance
- Reserved instance
- Spot instance

On-Demand Instance

This is the most popular pricing model of an EC2 instance. In this model, you pay just for the usage on a flat hourly rate or per-second billing. There are no up-front costs or hidden costs or anything else. Say if you create an instance and use it for ten hours and later discard the instance, you need to pay only for ten hours. There is no commitment or minimum term involved; as a result, you can scale up or down at any point of time. If you are developing a new application and don't know how many resources it is going to take, an on-demand instance is a great way to start.

 NOTE Effective October 2, 2017, usage of Linux instances that are launched in the on-demand, reserved, and spot forms will be billed in one-second increments with a minimum of 60 seconds. Similarly, provisioned storage for EBS volumes will be billed in one-second increments with a minimum of 60 seconds. This means if you use an EC2 instance for five minutes, you will be charged only for five minutes.

Reserved Instance

A reserved instance provides up to a 75 percent discount compared to an on-demand instance. If you already know how many resources your workload is going to take and for how long, a reserved instance is going to provide the maximum cost benefit. One of the best use cases of instances is running the production workload. Say you know that your production server is going to take 16 CPUs and you need this production server configuration for at least a year. You can reserve the capacity for a year and get the discount compared to an on-demand instance. A reserved instance is ideal when you know your application has a pretty steady state or is predictable in terms of performance. Since reserves require either a one-year or three-year commitment, it is important to know the nature of the workload before committing to a reserved instance. Multiple payment options are available when you reserve an instance. You can either pay for it in full, which is called *up-front reserved,* or make a partial payment up front, which is called *partial up-front reserved.* Or you can pay nothing in advance, and everything gets billed into a monthly billing cycle that is called *no up-front reserved.* Thus, you can have the following pricing model for a reserved instance:

1 year, no up-front costs, reserved
1 year, partial up-front costs, reserved
1 year, all up-front costs, reserved 3 years, no up-front costs, reserved
3 years, partial up-front costs, reserved
3 years, all up-front costs, reserved

The reserved instance is divided into two subcategories: standard reserved instance and convertible reserved instance. The standard reserved instance is the regular one you have just studied. The convertible reserved instance provides better flexibility if your compute requirement changes over the given period of time. A convertible reserved instance provides you with the ability and flexibility to exchange the instance from one class of family to another class if your computing need changes. You can purchase the reserved instance for only three years. Please note that standard and convertible reserved instances can be purchased to apply to instances in a specific availability zone or to instances in a region.

For convertible reserved instances, the following are the payment options:

3 years, no up-front costs, convertible
3 years, partial up-front costs, convertible
3 years, all up-front costs, convertible

Spot Instance

As you are probably aware, AWS has the largest compute capabilities among all the different cloud providers, and often some of the excess compute capacity is unused. AWS gives you the ability to bid for the unused capacity, and you can get up to a 90 percent discount compared to on-demand pricing. This pricing model is called *spot pricing,* and the instance created using the spot pricing model is called a *spot instance.* The spot instance runs on the bidding model, and you can bid for the spot pricing. The spot price fluctuates based on supply and demand, and if someone overbids, you then lose the instance at a very short notice. Therefore, you must be careful when choosing the type of workload you are going to run in the spot instance. Spot instances are great for workloads that can restart from where they failed, in other words, for running non-mission-critical projects. Often customers add a few spot instances along with on-demand instances to provide additional horsepower.

Shared Tenancy, Dedicated Hosts, and Dedicated Instances

EC2 runs on a virtualized environment; therefore, it is possible that on the same physical machine another customer might be running a different EC2 instance. AWS never over-provisions the resources, which means if you create a server with 16 CPUs, for sure you are going to get 16 CPUs; however, sometimes because of some compliance requirement, you may have to segregate your instances even at the physical level. Dedicated hosts and dedicated instances solve this problem.

Shared Tenancy

This is the default behavior when you launch an instance in EC2. In this case, you run the EC2 instances on multitenant hardware. Dedicated instances are the most popular in Amazon's EC2 ecosystem.

Dedicated Host

A dedicated host means it is a physical server exclusively assigned to you. Dedicated hosts can help you reduce costs by allowing you to use your existing server-bound software licenses, including Windows Server, SQL Server, and SUSE Linux Enterprise Server. If you want, you can also carve as many virtual machines (VMs) as you want depending on the capacity of the physical server. It can be purchased on-demand or on a reservation basis.

Dedicated Instance

In this case, you run the EC2 instances on single-tenant hardware. Dedicated instances are Amazon EC2 instances that run in a virtual private cloud on hardware that's dedicated to a single customer. Your dedicated instances are physically isolated at the host hardware level from instances that belong to other AWS accounts.

Instances and AMIs

An Amazon Machine Image is a blueprint that has all the details of the software configuration of the server that you are going to launch in the Amazon cloud (Figure 4-1). For example, an AMI may have details of the operating system, the application server, the applications running in it, and so on. When you launch an instance or server using an AMI, it inherits all the qualities of the AMI. You can launch as many instances as you want from an AMI.

The AMI contains a blueprint about the root volume for the instance, and the root volume contains information about the operating system and various other software running on top of the operating system, such as application servers or the Linux, Apache, MySQL, and PHP (LAMP) stack or any other custom application.

Figure 4-1
Launching one or
many instances
from AMI

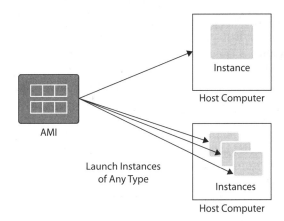

It also has the launch permission information that controls what AWS accounts can use the AMI to launch the instance. Launch permissions fall into the following categories:

- *Public*: The owner grants launch permissions to all AWS accounts.
- *Explicit*: The owner grants launch permissions to specific AWS accounts.
- *Implicit*: The owner has implicit launch permissions for an AMI.

It has block device mapping information that specifies which volume needs to be attached or will be attached when the instance is launched.

As discussed previously, various types of instances are available from Amazon Web Services. You can choose from a compute-intensive instance or an all-memory intensive instance and so on. Using a single AMI, you can launch different types of instances. You can choose an instance type depending on the workload you are going to run. Once you launch the instance, you will get an EC2 server according to the specifications you specify during the launch, and you can log into the system exactly the way you log in to a system on your premise. You can run all the commands that you normally run on a system that run on-premise or at your data center. For example, if you launch a Linux server, you can connect to it by putty, and you can run all the standard Linux commands that you normally run on a Linux server. Similarly, if you launch a Windows server, you can connect to it using RDP, and you can run all the Windows commands that you would on a Windows server in your data center.

Please note there is a limit on the number of instances you can start in a particular region. The limit depends on the instance type. But again, this limit is a soft limit, and with a support ticket you should be able to increase the limit at any time.

Instance Root Volume

An instance root device contains the image that is used to boot the instance. When EC2 was launched initially, all the root devices used to get launched from S3 since the instance root used to be backed up at S3. If the instance root device is backed up by S3, it is called an instance store–backed AMI. After the introduction of Amazon EBS, the images are backed up by an EBS volume because whenever an instance is launched, the root device for the instance is launched from the EBS volume, which is created from an EBS snapshot. It is also known as an Amazon EBS–backed AMI.

Now you can launch an instance either from an instance store–backed AMI or from an Amazon EBS–backed AMI. If you launch an instance that is backed up by instance store, then when the instance is launched, the image that is used to boot the instance is copied to the root volume. As long as the instance is running, all the data in the instance store volume persists. But whenever the instance is terminated, all the data is gone. Please note instance store–backed instances do not support the stop action; therefore, you can't stop that instance. If an instance store–backed instance fails or terminates, the data residing on the instance store cannot be restored. Therefore, it is important if you are using an instance store, you should back up your data to a persistent storage regularly and/or on your instance stores across multiple availability zones. The only exception is when the instance is rebooted, data in the instance store persists. Figure 4-2 shows instance creation backed up by an instance store.

On the other hand, if you launch an instance that is backed up any Amazon EBS–backed instance, the data always persists. These instances support the stop action, and the instance can be stopped and restarted without losing any data. Even if the instance terminates or fails, you don't lose the data. Since the instance root volume runs out of an EBS volume, you can even attach the root volume of your instance to a different running instance for debugging or any other purpose, such as changing the size of instance or modifying the properties of the instance.

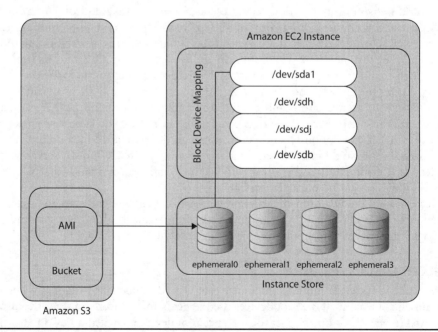

Figure 4-2 Instance creation backed by an instance store

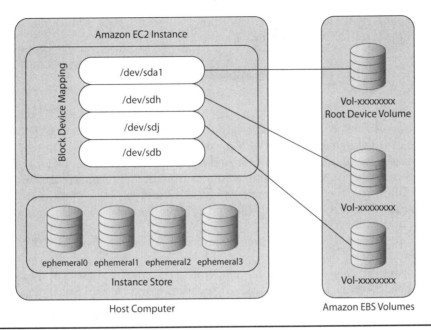

Figure 4-3 Instance creation backed up EBS volume

When you use an instance with instance store, you can't detach an instance store volume from one instance and re-attach it to a different instance.

It is recommended that you use an instance that is backed up by EBS, but in case you need to use an AMI that is backed up by instance store, please don't store any data in the instance store. Rather, attach an EBS volume to it and store all your data in the EBS volume. By doing this, even if you lose the instance, the EBS volume is going to retain all the data, which you can again mount to any other instance and get the data. Figure 4-3 shows instance creation backed up by an EBS volume.

Obtaining an AMI

There are many ways you can obtain an AMI for your use. AWS publishes many AMIs with many common software configurations that are available for public use. There are a lot of AMIs that are available via the community. A lot of developers also create their own AMI and make it available for public use; you can even use them. You can also create your own AMI and publish it to the developer community. In the community images, you will see a wide variety of different AMIs available. You can choose any one of them depending on your usage. For example, if you need pre-install Linux, Apache, MySQL, and PHP, you can quickly search AMIs with the LAMP stack and use that to create your EC2 instance. As soon as the instance is created, the LAMP stack is already deployed for you. You just need to start the web server, and then you are all set.

As discussed previously, irrespective of how you choose your AMI, either it will be backed up Amazon EBS or it will be backed up by instance store.

 TIP You can convert an instance store–backed Linux AMI that you own to an Amazon EBS–backed Linux AMI; you can't do that with Windows-based AMIs.

You can also create your AMI and save it as a template to launch further instances. You can also distribute your AMIs with the developer community. You can take a public AMI, make customizations on top of it, and then save it as a custom AMI for your own use or distribute it to a different team in your organization or to an external community. If you want to keep the AMI for your own use, make sure you keep it private so that only you can use it. When you create an AMI, you have the choice to back it up either via EBS volume or by instance store.

The image created by the developer community is called a *shared AMI*. When you share an AMI with the developer community, that will also be called a shared AMI. Since anyone can create the AMI and share it with the developer community, as a result Amazon does not vouch for those AMIs. If you want to use a shared AMI, you should be careful because you don't know who has created the AMI and whether it has any bugs. You can also leverage AWS forums to ask any questions about a shared AMI.

Please note an AMI is a regional resource. If you want to share an AMI to a different region, you need to copy the AMI to a different region and then share it. You can also share an AMI with specific accounts without making it public (when you make an AMI public, everyone has access to it). For example, if you want to share it to multiple friends or multiple clients, sharing with AWS IDs is the way to go.

The AWS Marketplace is an online store where you can buy software that runs on AWS. You can also purchase an AMI from the AWS Marketplace. When you purchase an AMI from the AWS Marketplace, you launch it in the same way as you would for any other AMI. The marketplace is integrated with EC2; therefore, it is easy and simple to launch an AMI from the marketplace. The instance is charged according to the rates set by the owner of the AMI, as well as the standard usage fees for the software running on top of it, if any. You can also create your own AMI and sell it to the AWS Marketplace.

Once you're done with the AMI, you can deregister it. Once you deregister it, you won't have access to it, and you will not be able to create any instances from it.

Virtualization in AMI

Linux Amazon Machine Images use one of two types of virtualization.

- Hardware Virtual Machine (HVM)
- Paravirtual (PV)

The main difference between them is how they boot and how they take advantage of the hardware extensions in the context of CPU, memory, and storage to provide better performance.

HVM AMI

HVM AMI executes the master boot records of the root block device and then presents a fully virtualized set of hardware to the operating system. As a result, the operating system runs directly on top of the VM as it is without any modification similar to the way it runs on a bare-metal hardware.

HVM AMIs are presented with a fully virtualized set of hardware and boot by executing the master boot record of the root block device of your image. This virtualization type provides the ability to run an operating system directly on top of a virtual machine without any modification, as if it were run on the bare-metal hardware. The Amazon EC2 host system emulates some or all of the underlying hardware that is presented to the guest. The EC2 server emulates some or all of the underlying hardware that is presented to the guest. As a result of this, the performance becomes really fast since HVM guests can take full advantage of all the hardware extensions that provide fast access to the underlying hardware on the host system.

All current-generation instance types support HVM AMIs. The CC2, CR1, HI1, and HS1 previous-generation instance types support HVM AMIs.

PV AMI

PV AMIs boot with a boot loaded called PV-GRUB. It starts the boot cycle and loads the kernel specified in the menu.lst file on your image. Paravirtual guests can run on host hardware that does not have explicit support for virtualization. But unfortunately, they can't really take advantage of special hardware extensions that HVM can take such as enhanced networking or GPU processing and so on.

The C3 and M3 current-generation instance types support PV AMIs. The C1, HI1, HS1, M1, M2, and T1 previous-generation instance types support PV AMIs.

Amazon recommends you use an HMV image to get the maximum performance when you launch your instance. Also, you should always use a current-generation instance over a previous-generation instance to get the latest and greatest hardware (CPU, memory, and so on) features.

Instance Life Cycle

Since you are going to work with the instance on a day-to-day basis, it is important for you to understand the overall life cycle for an instance. Let's understand all the phases of an EC2 instance.

Launch

When you launch an instance, immediately it enters into the "pending" state. The AMI you specify at the launch is used to boot the instance. The hardware on which it gets booted up depends on the type of hardware that you select for the instance type. Before starting the instance, a few health checks are performed to make sure that there are no issues with the hardware and the instance can come online without any issues. Once the instance is up and running and is ready for you, it enters into the "running" state.

As soon as it is in the running state, the instance is ready for all practical purposes, and you can connect to it and start using it. At this moment, the billing starts, and you are billed for each hour of usage. When the instance reaches the running state, you are still liable to pay the bill, even if you don't connect and use it.

Start and Stop

If the health check fails, the instance does not get started. At that time, you can either start a new instance or try to fix the issue. If there are no issues with the health check, the instance starts normally, and you can start using it thereafter.

You can stop an instance only if it is backed up by an EBS-backup instance. You can't stop an instance backed by an instance store. When you stop your instance, it enters the stopping state and then the stopped state. Amazon doesn't charge you once the instance is in a stopped state or if you stop it. Since the data resides in the EBS volumes, you are charged for the EBS volumes. You can also modify an instance type by upgrading it to new or bigger hardware by stopping it and then starting it on a new instance.

Reboot

You can reboot an instance that is either backed up by instance store or backed by EBS. A reboot is similar to rebooting an operating system. All the data is saved after the reboot; even the data in the instance store is saved, and nothing is lost. The IP address, machine type, and DNS name all remain the same after the reboot. You can reboot the instance either via the Amazon console or via CLI and API calls.

Termination

If you do not need the instance anymore, you can terminate it. As soon as you terminate the instance, you will see that the status changes to "shutting down" or "terminated." The moment the instance is shut down, the billing stops, and you don't have to pay anything after that. If the instance has termination protection enabled, you may have to perform an additional step, or you may have to disable termination protection to terminate the environment. Termination protection is a helpful feature that can protect an instance against accidental termination. If you enable the termination protection, then before terminating, the system will prompt you with "Do really want to terminate the instance?"

You will notice that even after the termination of the instance, it remains visible in the console for a little while. This is normal behavior, and after a while the entry is automatically deleted.

You can either delete the EBS volume associated with the instance or preserve the EBS volume associated with the instance. The Amazon EBS volume supports the DeleteOn-Termination attribute. This attribute controls whether the volume is deleted or preserved when you terminate the instance. The default behavior is to delete the root device volume and preserve any other EBS volumes.

Retirement

When AWS determines there is an irreparable hardware failure that is hosting the instance, then the instance is either retired or scheduled to be retired. As soon as the instance reaches its retirement date, it is stopped or terminated by AWS. If the instance is a backed EBS volume, you have all the data stored in the EBS volume, and therefore you can start the instance any time by choosing a different hardware. If the instance's root volume is backed up by the instance store, you must take the backup of all the files stored in the instance store before it gets terminated or you will lose all the data.

Connecting to an Instance

Once you launch an instance successfully, the next step is to connect to it. To connect to it, you need the connection details of the instance. The same can be obtained by logging into the console and going to the EC2 home page. Select the instance and then click Actions | Connect. A connection pop-up will open with all the connection details, as shown in Figure 4-4.

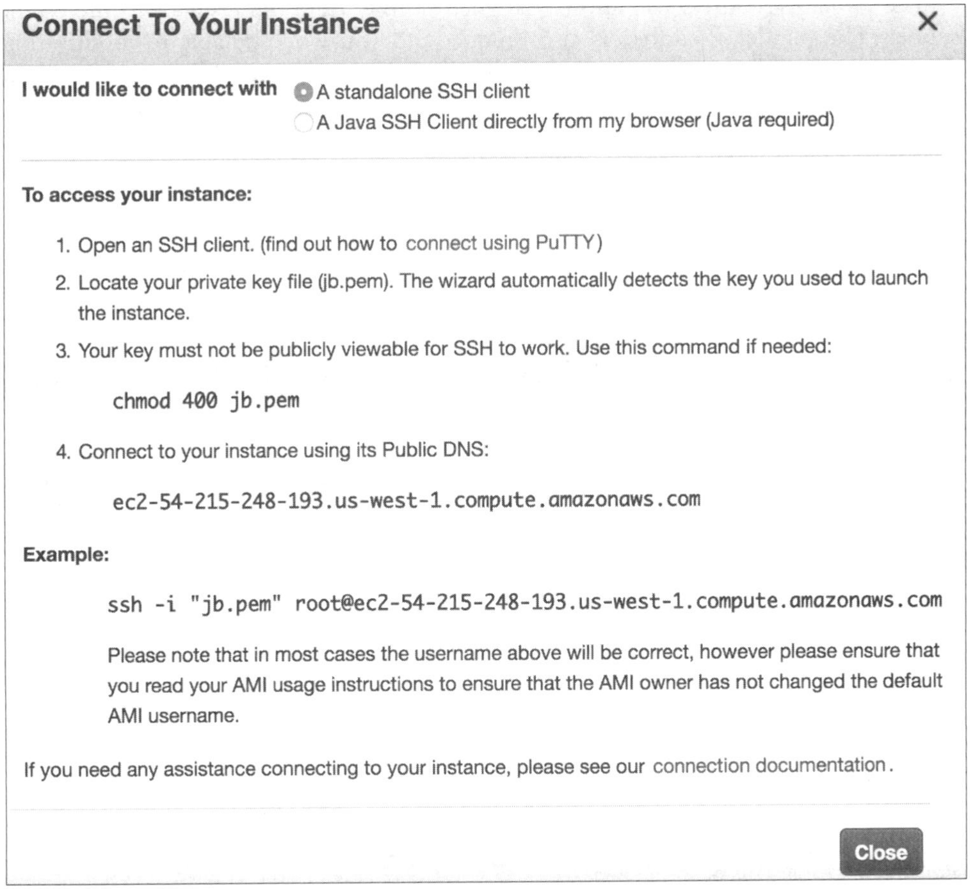

Connect To Your Instance   ✕

I would like to connect with ⦿ A standalone SSH client
                                   ◯ A Java SSH Client directly from my browser (Java required)

To access your instance:

1. Open an SSH client. (find out how to connect using PuTTY)
2. Locate your private key file (jb.pem). The wizard automatically detects the key you used to launch the instance.
3. Your key must not be publicly viewable for SSH to work. Use this command if needed:

   ```
   chmod 400 jb.pem
   ```

4. Connect to your instance using its Public DNS:

   ```
   ec2-54-215-248-193.us-west-1.compute.amazonaws.com
   ```

Example:

```
ssh -i "jb.pem" root@ec2-54-215-248-193.us-west-1.compute.amazonaws.com
```

Please note that in most cases the username above will be correct, however please ensure that you read your AMI usage instructions to ensure that the AMI owner has not changed the default AMI username.

If you need any assistance connecting to your instance, please see our connection documentation.

[Close]

Figure 4-4   Connection details for an EC2 instance

If you launch the instance in the public subnet, it will be assigned a public IP address and public DNS name via which you can reach the instance from the Internet. Besides the public IP address, it will also be an allocated private IP address and private DNS. If you choose the IPv6 IP address, then it will be allocated a public IPv6 IP address as well.

This is how all IPs look:

- **Public DNS (IPv4)**   ec2-34-210-110-189.us-west-2.compute.amazonaws.com
- **IPv4 public IP**   34.210.110.189
- **Private DNS**   ip-10-0-0-111.us-west-2.compute.internal
- **Private IPs**   10.0.0.111

The public DNS name is automatically created by AWS during the instance creation and stays with the instance for its tenure. You won't be able to change the public DNS associated with an instance. You can find the public DNS from the EC2 console main page and then select the instance for which you are querying the details, as shown in Figure 4-5.

The public IP address will also be assigned if you create the instance in the public subnet. The public IP address is also unique, and you won't be able to modify this. The public IP address will persist for the life span of the instance. If you terminate the instance, the public IP address will automatically be disassociated, and you can't associate the same public IP address in any other server even if you terminate an instance. If you want to associate an IP address from one server from another server, then you can do it via an elastic IP address.

Optionally you can also assign an EIP address to an EC2 instance. I already discussed EIP in the previous chapter, so I am not going to discuss this again. EIP address can be moved from one instance to other.

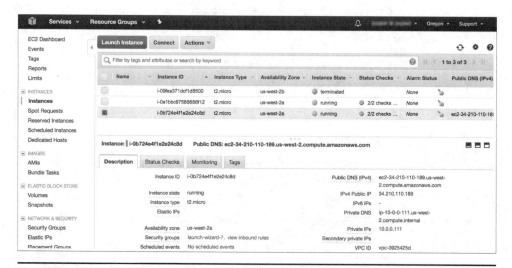

Figure 4-5   Public DNS of an EC2 Instance

If you create the instance in a private subnet, then it will be allocated a private IP address and a private DNS.

If you look at Figure 4-4, you will notice that to connect to an instance, the console prompts you to download a private key in your local machine and then change the permission in it. Amazon EC2 uses the public-private key concept used in cryptography to encrypt and decrypt the login information. In cryptography a public key is used to encrypt the data, and the private key associated with it is used to decrypt the data. You need the private key to connect to an EC2 instance. There are multiple ways of creating the key pair (a combination of public and private keys is called a *key pair*). You can create it via the AWS console or via the AWS command-line interface or by API. AWS customers can also bring their own keys and upload them in the system. The keys that Amazon EC2 uses are 2,048-bit SSH-2 RSA keys. You can have up to 5,000 key pairs per region.

Once you download the private key, you can connect to the EC2 instance using the instructions shown in Figure 4-4. You must be wondering where the public key is kept. The public key is stored inside the EC2 instance in the ~/.ssh/authorized_keys directory.

```
[ec2-user@ip-10-0-0-75 .ssh]$ pwd
/home/ec2-user/.ssh
[ec2-user@ip-10-0-0-75 .ssh]$ ls
authorized_keys
[ec2-user@ip-10-0-0-75 .ssh]$ file authorized_keys
authorized_keys: OpenSSH RSA public key
[ec2-user@ip-10-0-0-75 .ssh]$
```

The connect details screen will also tell which user to use to log in to the instance. By default the user will be ec2-user for Amazon Linux, and it will be a different user for a different Linux distribution. After the initial login using the keys, you can configure SSO and log in via LDAP.

In the case of a Windows-based EC2 instance, the server generates a random password for the administrator account and encrypts the password using the public key. The first time a user logs in, the password is decrypted using the private key, and immediately after that, the user is prompted to change their password.

Security Group

A *security group* acts as a virtual firewall that controls the traffic for one or more instances. When you launch an instance, you associate one or more security groups with the instance. You add rules to each security group that allow traffic to or from its associated instances. You can modify the rules for a security group at any time; the new rules are automatically applied to all instances that are associated with the security group. When you decide whether to allow traffic to reach an instance, you evaluate all the rules from all the security groups that are associated with the instance.

The rules of a security group control the inbound traffic that's allowed to reach the instances that are associated with the security group and the outbound traffic that's allowed to leave them.

The following are the characteristics of security group rules:

- By default, security groups allow all outbound traffic.
- You can't change the outbound rules for an EC2-Classic security group.
- Security group rules are always permissive; you can't create rules that deny access.
- Security groups are stateful—if you send a request from your instance, the response traffic for that request is allowed to flow in regardless of the inbound security group rules. For VPC security groups, this also means that responses to allowed inbound traffic are allowed to flow out, regardless of outbound rules.
- You can add and remove rules at any time. Your changes are automatically applied to the instances associated with the security group after a short period.
- When you associate multiple security groups with an instance, the rules from each security group are effectively aggregated to create one set of rules. You use this set of rules to determine whether to allow access.

For each rule, you specify the following:

- **Protocol** This is the protocol to allow. The most common protocols are 6 (TCP), 17 (UDP), and 1 (ICMP).
- **Port range** For TCP, UDP, or a custom protocol, this is the range of ports to allow. You can specify a single port number (for example, 22) or a range of port numbers (for example, 7000 to 8000).
- **ICMP type and code** For ICMP, this is the ICMP type and code.
- **Source or destination** This is the source (inbound rules) or destination (outbound rules) for the traffic. Specify one of these options:
  - An individual IPv4 address. You must use the /32 prefix after the IPv4 address, for example, 203.0.113.1/32.
  - (VPC only) An individual IPv6 address. You must use the /128 prefix length, for example, 2001:db8:1234:1a00::123/128.
  - A range of IPv4 addresses, in CIDR block notation, for example, 203.0.113.0/24.
  - (VPC only) A range of IPv6 addresses, in CIDR block notation, for example, 2001:db8:1234:1a00::/64.
  - Another security group. This allows instances associated with the specified security group to access instances associated with this security group. This does not add rules from the source security group to this security group. You can specify one of the following security groups:
    - The current security group.
    - **EC2-Classic** A different security group for EC2-Classic in the same region.

- **EC2-Classic**   A security group for another AWS account in the same region (add the AWS account ID as a prefix, for example, 111122223333 /sg-edcd9784).
- **EC2-VPC**   A different security group for the same VPC or a peer VPC in a VPC peering connection.

When you specify a security group as the source or destination for a rule, the rule affects all instances associated with the security group. Incoming traffic is allowed based on the private IP addresses of the instances that are associated with the source security group (and not the public IP or elastic IP addresses). If your security group rule references a security group in a peer VPC and the referenced security group or VPC peering connection is deleted, the rule is marked as stale.

If there is more than one rule for a specific port, you apply the most permissive rule. For example, if you have a rule that allows access to TCP port 22 (SSH) from IP address 203.0.113.1 and another rule that allows access to TCP port 22 from everyone, everyone has access to TCP port 22.

Amazon Elastic Container Service

Amazon Elastic Container Service (ECS) is a container management service that allows you to manage Docker containers on a cluster of Amazon EC2. Amazon ECS is highly scalable, it is fast, and it allows you to start, stop, manage, and run the containers easily and seamlessly. Using Amazon ECS, you can easily launch any container-based application with simple API calls.

Containers are similar to hardware virtualization (like EC2), but instead of partitioning a machine, containers isolate the processes running on a single operating system. This is a useful concept that lets you use the OS kernel to create multiple isolated user space processes that can have constraints on them like CPU and memory. These isolated user space processes are called *containers*. Using containers you can build your own application, share the image with others, deploy the image quickly, and do lots of other things quickly. Containers are portable, which makes the development life cycle simpler. The same image can run on the developer's desktop as well as in the production server. The image is consistent and immutable; therefore, no matter where it runs or whenever you start it, it's always the same. The entire application is self-contained, and the image is the version that makes deployments and scaling easier because the image includes the dependencies. Containers are very efficient. You can allocate exactly the amount of resources (CPU, memory) you want, and at any point in time you can increase or decrease these resources depending on your need.

Containers enable the concept of microservices. Microservices encourage the decomposition of an app into smaller chunks, reducing complexity and letting teams move faster while still running the processes on the same host. If you are planning to run a microservice architecture, a container should be your first choice.

Often it is seen that once developers start deploying their applications on containers, the tasks of managing and scaling the containers become challenging. For example, if there are 200 developers and everyone is trying to deploy the part of their code using containers, managing these 200 containers becomes really challenging. A couple of the problems often faced are: What, happens when a container dies? How do you know whether the host where you are putting the containers has enough resources? Managing the state of the cluster, hosting the containers is critical for the successful deployment of the containers and applications running inside it. Flexible scheduling is another challenge that is often faced. Amazon ECS solves all these problems.

Amazon ECS handles the complexity of cluster and container management so you don't have to install and operate your own cluster management infrastructure. Amazon has built several core distributed systems primitives to support its needs. Amazon ECS is built on top of one of these primitives. Amazon exposes this state management behind a simple set of APIs that give the details about all the instances in your cluster and all the containers running on those instances. Amazon ECS APIs respond quickly whether you have a cluster with one instance and a few containers or a dynamic cluster with hundreds of instances and thousands of containers. These are some of the benefits of running containers on Amazon ECS:

- Eliminates cluster management software. There is no need to install any cluster management software.
- You can easily manage clusters for any scale.
- Using ECS you can design fault-tolerant cluster architecture.
- You can manage cluster state using Amazon ECS.
- You can easily control and monitor the containers seamlessly.
- You can scale from one to tens of thousands of containers almost instantly.
- ECS gives you the ability to make good placement decisions about where to place your containers.
- ECS gives you the intel about the availability of resources (CPU, memory).
- At any time you can add new resources to the cluster with EC2 Auto Scaling.
- It is integrated with other services such as Amazon Elastic Container Registry, Elastic Load Balancing, Elastic Block Store, Elastic Network Interfaces, Virtual Private Cloud, IAM, and CloudTrail.

 EXAM TIP ECS has been recently added to the Associate certification. You should be able to articulate the advantages of running ECS and what kind of applications you would be hosting in ECS.

Lab 4-1: Using EC2

This lab will walk you through launching, configuring, and customizing an EC2 virtual machine to run a web server. You will successfully provision and start an EC2 instance using the AWS Management Console.

Creating a New Key Pair

In this lab, you will need to create an EC2 instance using an SSH key pair. The following steps outline how to create a unique SSH key pair for you to use in this lab:

1. Sign into the AWS Management Console and open the Amazon EC2 console at https://console.aws.amazon.com/ec2.

2. In the upper-right corner of the AWS Management Console, confirm you are in the desired AWS region (e.g., Oregon).

3. Click Key Pairs in the Network & Security section near the bottom of the leftmost menu. This will display a page to manage your SSH key pairs.

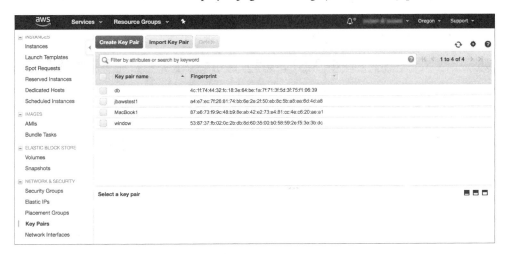

4. To create a new SSH key pair, click the Create Key Pair button at the top of the browser window.

5. In the resulting pop-up window, type **[First Name]**-**[Last Name]**-**awslab** in the Key Pair Name text box and click Create.

6. The page will download the file joyjeet-banerjee-awslab.pem to the local drive. Follow the browser instructions to save the file to the default download location.

Remember the full path to the file.pem file you just downloaded. You will use the key pair you just created to manage your EC2 instances for the rest of the lab.

Launching a Web Server Instance

In this example, you will launch a default Amazon Linux instance with an Apache/PHP web server installed on initialization.

1. Click EC2 Dashboard toward the top of the left menu.

2. Click Launch Instance.

3. In the Quick Start section, select the first Amazon Linux AMI and click Select.

4. Select the general-purpose t2.micro instance type and click Next: Configure Instance Details.

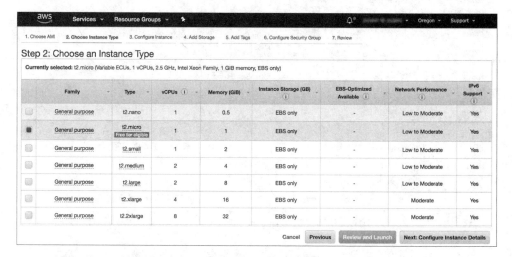

5. On the Configure Instance Details page, expand the Advanced Details section at the bottom of the page, and type the following initialization script information into the User Data field. (You can use SHIFT-ENTER to create the necessary line break, or alternatively you could type this into Notepad and copy and paste the results.) Then click Next: Add Storage. This will automatically install and start the Apache web server on launch.

#include https://s3.amazonaws.com/jbawsbook/bootstrap.sh

Click Next: Add Storage to accept the default storage device configuration.

6. Next, (Add Tags) choose a "friendly name" for your instance. This name, more correctly known as a *tag*, will appear in the console once the instance launches. It makes it easy to keep track of running machines in a complex environment. Name yours according to this format: [Name] Web Server.

7. Then click Next: Configure Security Group.

8. You will be prompted to create a new security group, which will be your firewall rules. On the assumption you are building out a web server, name your new security group **[Your Name] Web Tier**, and confirm an existing SSH rule exists that allows TCP port 22 from anywhere. Click Add Rule.

9. Select HTTP from the Type drop-down menu, and confirm TCP port 80 is allowed from anywhere. Click Add Rule.

10. Click the Review and Launch button after configuring the security group.

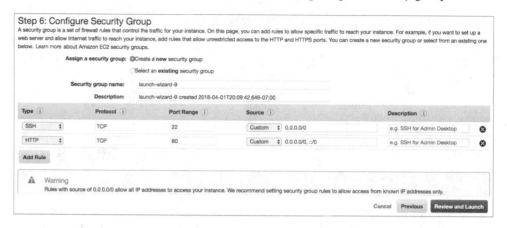

11. Review your choices and then click Launch.

12. Select the [YourName]-awslab key pair that you created at the beginning of this lab from the drop-down and select the "I acknowledge" check box. Then click the Launch Instances button.

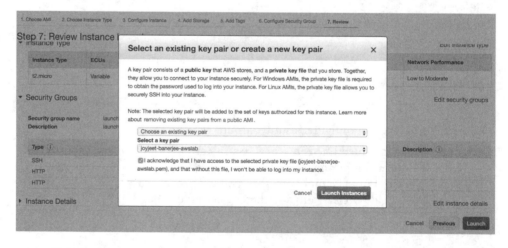

13. Click the View Instances button in the lower-right portion of the screen to view the list of EC2 instances. Once your instance has launched, you will see your web server as well as the availability zone the instance is in and the publicly routable DNS name.

14. Select the check box next to your web server name to view details about this EC2 instance.

Browsing the Web Server

To browse the web server, follow these steps:

1. Wait for the instance to pass the status checks to finish loading.

2. Open a new browser tab and browse the web server by entering the EC2 instance's public DNS name into the browser. The EC2 instance's public DNS name can be found in the console by reviewing the Public DNS name line.

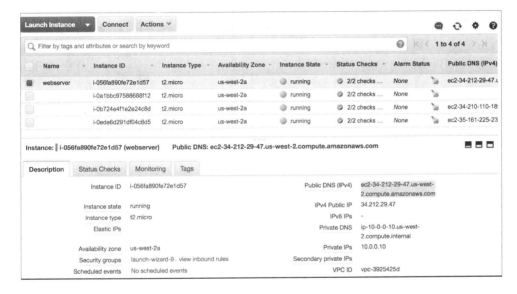

3. You should see a web site with the details of the EC2 instance, the instance ID, and the availability zone.

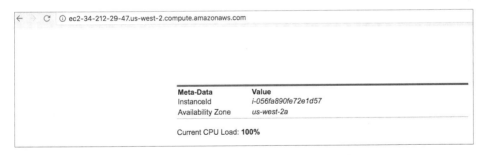

Great job! You have deployed a server and launched a web site in a matter of minutes.

Lab 4-2: Creating an EBS Instance and Attaching It to an EC2 Instance

1. In this lab, you will create a new provisioned IOPS-based EBS volume and then attach it to an existing EC2 instance. Go to the AWS console and select EC2.

2. Make sure you are in the correct region.

3. In the left menu, select Volumes under Elastic Block Store.

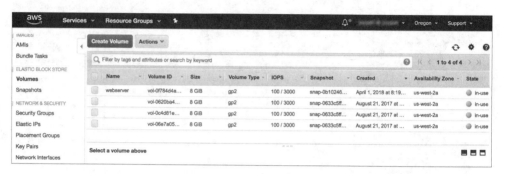

4. Click Create Volume at the top.

5. For Volume Type, select Provisioned IOPS.

6. For Size, select 10.

7. For IOPS, select 100.

8. For Availability Zone, choose the AZ where your EC2 instance is running. In this example, we have chosen us-east-1b.

9. Leave the defaults for the rest of the settings except Tags. Select the Add Tags To Your Volume box.

10. Add a tag to uniquely identify this volume. In this example, we have added Name for Key and EBSforBook for Value.

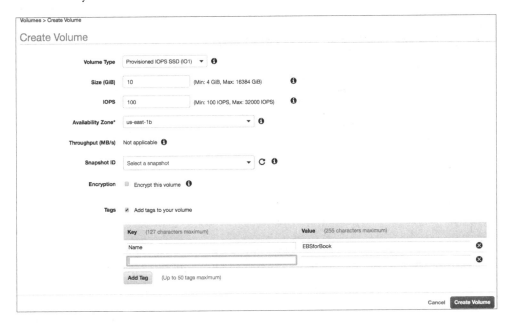

11. Click Create Volume. You will see an alert about a volume being created successfully and with the volume ID.

12. You have successfully created the volume. Now mount it to a running EC2 instance by clicking the EBS volume.

13. Select the new volume you have created and click Actions | Attach Volume.

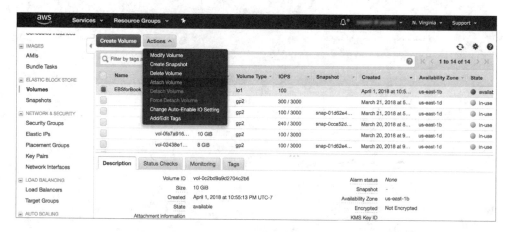

14. To attach the volume, you need the instance ID and device name. You can obtain the instance ID from the instance detail page of the EC2 instance. The instance detail page will also show you the existing devices that are in use. Choose a device name that is not in use. The system will prompt you for a device name. You can use that as well.

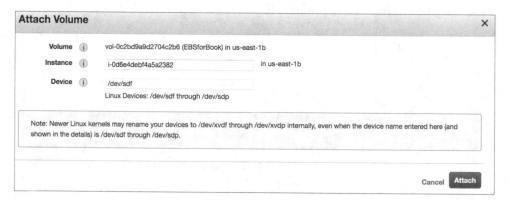

15. The volume is already added in the EC2 instance, so go to the details page from the EC2 instance to see the new volume.

16. Go to the EBS volume page to see the details for this volume. Look at State; it should say that it's in use. Now look at the attachment information; you will see where it is attached.

17. Select this volume and take a snapshot. Click Volume | Actions | Create Snapshot.

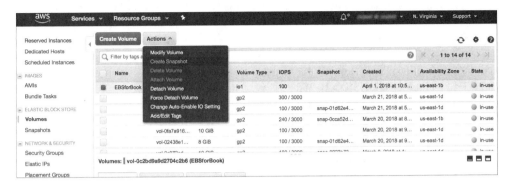

18. The Create Snapshot window will open; provide the description for the snapshot. You will notice that Encrypted will show as Not Encrypted since the EBS volume is not encrypted. Add a tag and create the snapshot.

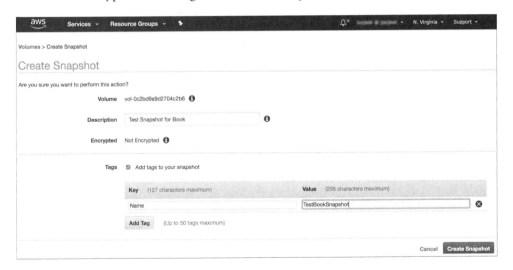

19. The snapshot will be created, and you will get the ID of the snapshot.

20. Now use this snapshot to create another EBS volume and then attach it to a new EC2 instance. Try it yourself. By doing this, you should be able to create a clone of any EBS volume and should be able to mount it to any other EC2 instance.

Lab 4-3: Creating an EBS Instance and Mounting Across Two EC2 Instances in Different AZs

1. In this lab, you will create an EFS instance and mount it across two EC2 instances in different AZs. Go to the AWS console and select EFS.

2. Choose the region of your choice from the top-right corner and click Create File System.

3. Select the VPC where you want to create the EFS instance. You can create the EFS instance across the VPC's AZ. In this case, you will use the VPC that has only two AZs. Therefore, you should be able to create the mount target only in those two AZs. If you choose the default AZ in the Virginia region, you should be able to create six mount targets since there are six availability zones in Virginia.

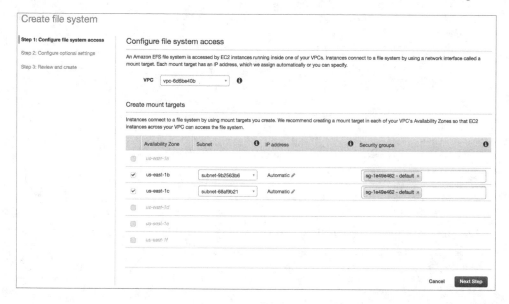

4. Add tags to the file system so that you can uniquely identify it. In this case, we have added Name for Key and EFSbook for Value.

5. Under Choose Performance Mode, select General Purpose since you are going to attach this EFS to only two EC2 instances. When you have many servers and you need faster input/output, choose Max I/O.

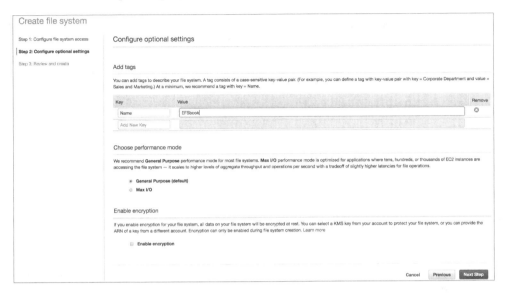

6. Deselect Enable Encryption since you are not going to encrypt the EFS instance.

7. Review the details and click Create File System.

8. It will take a few minutes to create the file system. Once the file system has been created, you will see the details on the confirmation screen.

9. Now that the EFS has been created, the next step is to mount it across EC2 instances. If you look at the previous illustration carefully, you will notice it has an instructions link for mounting an Amazon EC2 instance. Click the link, and you will see the detailed instructions.

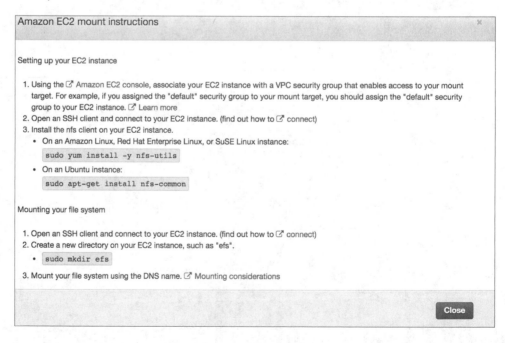

10. Log in to the EC2 instance from a terminal.

11. Install the NFS client on the EC2 instance. You can do this by running the following command on an Amazon Linux, Red Hat Enterprise Linux, or SUSE Linux instance:

```
sudo yum install -y nfs-utils
```

Or you can run the following command on an Ubuntu instance:

```
sudo apt-get install nfs-common
```

12. Make a directory where you will mount the EFS instance (say efs) by running this command:

```
sudo mkdir efs
```

13. Mount the EFS instance by running the following command:

```
sudo mount -t nfs -o nfsvers=4.1,rsize=1048576,wsize=1048576,hard,timeo
=600,retrans=2 file-system-id.efs.aws-region.amazonaws.com:/ efs-mount-
point
```

14. Once the file system is mounted, create a file and save it.

15. Now mount the EFS instance from a second EC2 instance in a different AZ. You should be able to access the file that you have created and saved in the EFS instance from the first EC2 instance.

Chapter Review

In this chapter, you learned that there are five types of EC2 instances available: general purpose, compute optimized, memory optimized, storage optimized, and advanced computing. You learned how you can use a placement group to reduce the latency across instances. A placement group is a logical grouping of instances within a single AZ. You also learned that three types of EBS volumes can be attached to the EC2 instance: a general-purpose EBS volume backed up by solid-state drives, a provisioned IOPS-based EBS volume to maximize the I/O throughput, and a magnetic hard drive that provides the lowest cost per gigabyte. You learned about EBS-optimized instances that deliver dedicated throughput between Amazon EC2 and Amazon EBS volumes. You learned about the pricing model of EC2, which can be either on-demand (on an hourly or a per-second basis depending on the instance type) or a reserved instance (where you can reserve the instance in advance) and spot instances (where you bid for the unused compute). The default behavior of EC2 is shared tenancy, where you run EC2 instances on multitenant hardware. You can also host the EC2 instance on a dedicated host as well as on a dedicated instance. A dedicated host is a physical server exclusively assigned to you, and a dedicated instance is where you run the EC2 instances on single-tenant hardware. An Amazon machine image is a blueprint that has all the details of the software configuration of the server that you are going to launch in the Amazon cloud. An instance root device contains the image that is used to boot the instance. Linux AMIs use one of two types of virtualization: paravirtual and hardware virtual machine. Amazon Elastic Container Service is a container management service that allows you to manage Docker containers on a cluster of Amazon EC2 instances.

Questions

1. You know that you need 24 CPUs for your production server. You also know that your compute capacity is going to remain fixed until next year, so you need to keep the production server up and running during that time. What pricing option would you go with?

    A. Choose the spot instance

    B. Choose the on-demand instance

    C. Choose the three-year reserved instance

    D. Choose the one-year reserved instance

2. You are planning to run a database on an EC2 instance. You know that the database is pretty heavy on I/O. The DBA told you that you would need a minimum of 8,000 IOPS. What is the storage option you should choose?

    A. EBS volume with magnetic hard drive

    B. Store all the data files in the ephemeral storage of the server

    C. EBS volume with provisioned IOPS

    D. EBS volume with general-purpose SSD

3. You are running your application on a bunch of on-demand servers. On weekends you have to kick off a large batch job, and you are planning to add capacity. The batch job you are going to run over the weekend can be restarted if it fails. What is the best way to secure additional compute resources?

    A. Use the spot instance to add compute for the weekend

    B. Use the on-demand instance to add compute for the weekend

    C. Use the on-demand instance plus PIOPS storage for the weekend resource

    D. Use the on-demand instance plus a general-purpose EBS volume for the weekend resource

4. You have a compliance requirement that you should own the entire physical hardware and no other customer should run any other instance on the physical hardware. What option should you choose?

    A. Put the hardware inside the VPC so that no other customer can use it

    B. Use a dedicated instance

    C. Reserve the EC2 for one year

    D. Reserve the EC2 for three years

5. You have created an instance in EC2, and you want to connect to it. What should you do to log in to the system for the first time?

    A. Use the username/password combination to log in to the server

    B. Use the key-pair combination (private and public keys)

   C. Use your cell phone to get a text message for secure login

   D. Log in via the root user

6. What are the characteristics of AMI that are backed up by the instance store? (Choose two.)

   A. The data persists even after the instance reboot.

   B. The data is lost when the instance is shut down.

   C. The data persists when the instance is shut down.

   D. The data persists when the instance is terminated.

7. How can you make a cluster of an EC2 instance?

   A. By creating all the instances within a VPC

   B. By creating all the instances in a public subnet

   C. By creating all the instances in a private subnet

   D. By creating a placement group

8. You need to take a snapshot of the EBS volume. How long will the EBS remain unavailable?

   A. The volume will be available immediately.

   B. EBS magnetic drive will take more time than SSD volumes.

   C. It depends on the size of the EBS volume.

   D. It depends on the actual data stored in the EBS volume.

9. What are the different ways of making an EC2 server available to the public?

   A. Create it inside a public subnet

   B. Create it inside a private subnet and assign a NAT device

   C. Attach an IPv6 IP address

   D. Allocate that with a load balancer and expose the load balancer to the public

10. The application workload changes constantly, and to meet that, you keep on changing the hardware type for the application server. Because of this, you constantly need to update the web server with the new IP address. How can you fix this problem?

   A. Add a load balancer

   B. Add an IPv6 IP address

   C. Add an EIP to it

   D. Use a reserved EC2 instance

Answers

1. **D**. You won't choose a spot instance because the spot instance can be taken away at any time by giving notice. On-demand won't give you the best pricing since you know you will be running the server all the time for next year. Since you know the computation requirement is only for one year, you should not go with a three-year reserved instance. Rather, you should go for a one-year reserved instance to get the maximum benefit.

2. **C**. The magnetic hard drive won't give you the IOPS number you are looking for. You should not put the data files in the ephemeral drives because as soon as the server goes down, you will lose all the data. For a database, data is the most critical component, and you can't afford to lose that. The provisioned IOPS will give you the desired IOPS that your database needs. You can also run the database with general-purpose SSD, but there is no guarantee that you will always get the 8,000 IOPS number that you are looking for. Only PIOPS will provide you with that capacity.

3. **A**. Since you know the workload can be restarted from where it fails, the spot instance is going to provide you with the additional compute and pricing benefit as well. You can go with on-demand as well; the only thing is you have to pay a little bit more for on-demand than for the spot instance. You can choose a PIOPS or GP2 with the on-demand instance. If you choose PIOPS, you have to pay much more compared to all the other options.

4. **B**. You can create the instance inside a VPC, but that does not mean other customers can't create any other instance in the physical hardware. Creating a dedicated instance is going to provide exactly what you are looking for. Reserving the EC2 instance for the instance for one or three years won't help unless you reserve it as a dedicated instance.

5. **B**. The first time you log in to an EC2 instance, you need the combination of the private and public keys. You won't be able to log in using a username and password or as a root user unless you have used the keys. You won't be able to use multifactor authentication until you configure it.

6. **A, B**. If an AMI is backed up by an instance store, you lose all the data if the instance is shut down or terminated. However, the data persists if the instance is rebooted.

7. **D**. You can create the placement group within the VPC or within the private or public subnet.

8. **A**. The volumes are available irrespective of the time it takes to take the snapshot.

9. **A**. If you create an EC2 instance in the public subnet, it is available from the Internet. Creating an instance inside a private subnet and attaching a NAT instance won't give access from the Internet. Attaching an IPv6 address can provide Internet accessibility provided it is a public IPv6 and not private. Giving load balance access to the public won't give the EC2 access to the public.

10. **C**. Even if you reserve the instance, you still need to remap the IP address. Even with IPv6 you need to remap the IP addresses. The load balancer won't help because the load balancer also needs to be remapped with the new IP addresses.

Identity and Access Management and Security on AWS

[handwritten: STS = Security Token Service
CloudTrail
Cognito = web identity Federation
(3rd party identity provider)]

In this chapter, you will

- Be introduced to IAM
- Learn about different types of security credentials
- Understand users, groups, and roles
- Learn some IAM best practices
- Take a look at AWS platform compliance
- Understand the shared security model

AWS Identity and Access Management (IAM) allows you to control individual (users) and group access to all the AWS resources in a secured way. Using IAM, you can define what each user can access in the AWS cloud. For example, you can specify which users have administrator access, which users have read-only access, which users can access certain AWS services, and so on. Using the IAM service, you can choose the services that specific users are going to use and what kind of privileges users should have. In a nutshell, you control both authentication and authorization on the AWS resources through identity and access management. In addition, you can audit and log the users, continuously monitor them, and review account activity.

Authentication

IAM offers the following authentication features:

- **Managing users and their access**   You can create and manage users and their security such as access keys, passwords, and multifactor authentication. You can also manage the permissions for a user and thus get granular control over what operations the user can perform.

- **Managing federated users and their access** Using IAM, you can manage federated users. Using federation you can use single sign-on (SSO) to access the AWS resources using the credentials of your corporate directory. AWS supports Security Assertion Markup Language (SAML) as well as non-SAML-based options such as AWS Directory Service for Microsoft Active Directory to exchange identity and security information between an identity provider (IdP) and an application. Using an IdP, you don't have to manage your own user identities or create custom sign-in code. An IdP does that for you. Your external users sign in through a well-known identity provider, such as Login with Amazon, Facebook, Google, and many others, and you can give those external identities permissions to use AWS resources in your account.

Authorization

Using IAM, you can authorize with granularity who can do what. Therefore, you can implement the concepts of least privilege and segregation of duties. In AWS, authorization is mainly done using IAM policies. An IAM policy is a piece of code written in JavaScript Object Notation (JSON) where you can define one or more permissions. These permissions define which resources and which actions or operations the IAM entity is allowed. This policy can be attached to any IAM entity such as a user, group, or role. The policy defines what actions an IAM entity can take, which resources to use, what the effect will be when the user requests access to a resource, and so on. By using an IAM policy, you can get fine-grained access control for any IAM entity, and you can attach any number of policies to an entity. A policy can even be attached to multiple entities. If you want to give Amazon RDS read-only access to your developers, then you can create a policy called RDSRO and attach all the developers to this policy. Alternatively, if all your developers are part of a particular group (which is typical), attach the IAM policy to that group only. By doing that, you won't have to manually attach the policy to every developer account individually. A policy looks something like this:

```
{
    "Version": "2018-03-18",
    "Statement": [
      {
        "Effect": "Allow",
        "Action": ["s3:ListBucket"],
        "Resource": ["arn:aws:s3:::<Your_bucket_name>"]
      },
      {
        "Effect": "Allow",
        "Action": [
          "s3:GetObject"
        ],
        "Resource": ["arn:aws:s3:::<Your_bucket_name>/*"]
      }
    ]
}
```

If you look at the policy, you will find that by attaching this policy to a user, the user is going to have read-only access to S3, which means the user can view the bucket and get an object from the bucket but can't upload or put anything in the bucket.

Figure 5-1
How AWS IAM
determines
permissions

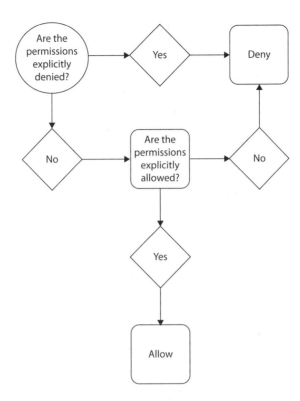

Using a policy, you can either allow or deny access to any resource for any IAM entity. When you create a user, there are no default permissions; all the permissions need to be explicitly given. In other words, all permissions are implicitly denied by default, which means unless you explicitly allow a permission, the IAM entity won't have access to anything. Of course, if you explicitly deny something, it will always be denied. Figure 5-1 shows how IAM determines permissions.

Auditing

AWS offers you tools that can help you with auditing. The AWS CloudTrail service records activity made on your account and delivers log files to your Amazon S3 bucket. You can access these logs directly from the console or via the command-line interface (CLI) and process them via some of the popular third-party tools like Splunk, SumoLogic, AlertLogic, Loggly, and DataDog. CloudTrail provides visibility into user activity by recording actions taken on your account. CloudTrail can log every API call and related event made. CloudTrail records important information about each action, including the following:

- Who made the request?
- When was the request made?
- What was the request about?

- Which resources were acted upon in response to the request?
- Where was the request made from and made to?

This information helps you to track changes made to your AWS resources and to troubleshoot operational issues. CloudTrail makes it easier to ensure compliance with internal policies and regulatory standards.

Types of Security Credentials

When you work with the AWS ecosystem, you can have various types of security credentials. It all depends on how you interact with the AWS ecosystem. For example, when you log in to the AWS console, you can use a combination of usernames and passwords, whereas when you log in to an Amazon EC2 environment, you use a key pair. These are the security credentials you are often going to use:

- **IAM username and password**   This will be used mainly for accessing the AWS Management Console.
- **E-mail address and password**   This is associated with your root account.
- **Access keys**   This is often used with the CLI, APIs, and SDKs.
- **Key pair**   This is used with Amazon EC2 for logging in to the servers.
- **Multifactor authentication**   This is an additional layer of security that can be used with the root account as well.

Temporary Security Credentials

In addition to these types of security credentials, AWS offers temporary security credentials. These security credentials are short-term and should never be used for long-term purposes. They can be configured to last for a few minutes to a few hours. Once the credentials expire, you won't be able to use them. If you are using these temporary credentials via an API, once they expire, AWS won't recognize the API or allow access when an API request is made with the security credentials.

The temporary security credentials work exactly like the long-term credentials; they are just short-lived. If you want to create and provide the temporary security credentials to your set of trusted users to control some of the AWS resources, you can use the AWS Security Token Service (AWS STS). These temporary security credentials won't be stored with a user; rather, they will be dynamically generated whenever a user requests them.

Temporary security credentials offer lots of advantages since they are short-lived and expire automatically; therefore, you can provide access to your AWS resources to users without having to define an AWS identity for them. Moreover, you do not have to distribute or embed long-term or permanent AWS security credentials with an application.

By using IAM, you can create users and groups and then assign permissions to the users using the least privilege principle. Let's first understand users, groups, and roles in detail.

Users

To log in to a laptop or an operating system, you need a username and password. Similarly, to use the AWS service, you need a user through which you log in to AWS and start working. A user can be an actual physical user, or it can be an application that needs access to the AWS service. Thus, you can say that an IAM user is an *entity* that you create in AWS to uniquely represent a person or a service; this entity interacts with AWS to do day-to-day work with AWS. An IAM user has a username and credentials. Whenever an IAM user is created, the user does not have any permission to do anything unless explicit permissions are granted to the user by an administrator or via federation. It is always recommended that you identify a few users as administrators and grant them admin privileges to AWS. Going forward, these administrators can grant permissions to other users via IAM. They can provide fine-grained access to each user depending on their job role. For example, if a person needs to access only the web servers, then the administrator can grant that user access to specific EC2 servers. Similarly, if a developer wants to work with a database, administrators can grant that user read-only information from RDS. When a user is created via IAM, the user doesn't have any security credentials either. The administrator needs to assign the security credentials followed by the permissions before the user can log in to the system.

These are the steps when creating a user via IAM:

1. Create a user via IAM.

2. Provide security credentials.

3. Attach permissions, roles, and responsibilities.

4. Add the user to one or more groups (covered in the next section).

The first time you create an AWS account, you create the AWS root account, which has unrestricted access to all the resources within AWS. The root account is a superuser account, and it can be compared to a root user of Unix, which is a superuser and has all the privileges. There is no way you can restrict any privileges from the root account; therefore, it is important to secure it. The root account also has your AWS billing information. After creating the root account, you should create an IAM user with administrative access and should never log in using the root account. In other words, you should do all your day-to-day work using the administrative account and not via the root account. Needless to say, the root credentials should not be shared with anyone and should be kept very secure. To sign in via root credentials, you have to use the e-mail ID associated with the account and a password. You can also set up multifactor authentication along with the root user to safeguard it.

Since you cannot use the root account for the day-to-day administration of your AWS account, you need to create an IAM user with administrative privileges. When you have hundreds or thousands of users who want to use the service or resources of AWS within your account, you don't share the root privilege with them; you rather create different IAM users with different privileges according to their job profile. These IAM users are part of the same AWS account and not separate accounts. These IAM users have their individual usernames and passwords to log in to the AWS console. You can also create an individual access key for each user so that the user can make programmatic requests to work with resources in your account. If users want to make programmatic calls to AWS from the AWS CLI or SDKs or API calls for individual AWS services, they need access keys, which you can create via IAM. When you create an access key, IAM returns the access key ID and secret access key that can be passed on to the user associated with it. Please note for security reasons the access key is accessible only at the time you create it. If a secret access key is lost, you must delete the access key for the associated user and create a new key.

When you sign in as the root user, you have complete, unrestricted access to all resources in your AWS account, including access to your billing information and the ability to change your password. This level of access is necessary when you initially set up the account. As mentioned, you should not use root user credentials for everyday access or share your root user credentials with anyone because doing so gives them unrestricted access to your account. It is not possible to restrict the permissions that are granted to the AWS account, so you should adhere to the best practice of using the root user only to create your first IAM user and then securely locking away the root user credentials.

Groups

IAM groups are similar to groups in a Unix operating system. If you are not familiar with Unix groups, don't worry. Say in your company there are 50 developers; every time a new developer joins, you give that person the same set of roles and responsibilities just like any other developer. Say for your organization there are 20 different roles and privileges your developer needs. So, when the developer joins the company, you provision the user using IAM and explicitly assign that person those 20 roles and privileges, and you keep on doing the same thing every time a new developer joins. However, instead of manually assigning these 20 roles and privileges every time a developer joins, you can create a group for developers and assign the 20 roles and privileges that all the developers use to this group. Now whenever a new developer joins, instead of explicitly assigning that person these roles and privileges, you can just add the user to the developer group. By doing this, the new developer will automatically inherit the 20 roles and privileges that the group has. You can create various groups as per the job specifications. For example, you can have a separate group for administrators, a separate group for DBAs, a separate group for developers, a separate group for folks from the DevOps team, and so on.

If someone is a DBA but needs developer access as well, you just need to assign this user to both the DBA and developer groups, and by doing that the person has access to both. Similarly, if a developer becomes a DBA, you can simply remove that user from the developer group and add the user to the DBA group.

These are the characteristics of IAM groups:

- A group consists of multiple roles and privileges, and you grant these permissions using IAM.
- Any user who is added to a group inherits the group's roles and privileges.
- You can add multiple users in a group.

- A user can be part of multiple groups.

- You can't add one group into another group. A group can contain only users and not other groups.

- There is no default group that automatically includes all users in the AWS account. However, you can create one and assign it to each and every user.

Roles

Role: delegate access to users, apps or services that don't have access to AWS resources

As you have learned, there can be two types of AWS users: IAM users who have a permanent identity in AWS and federated users who don't have permanent identities. Since IAM users have permanent identities associated to permissions, they can do any task associated with their permission. Since federated users do not have permanent identities, the way you control their permission is by creating a *role*. That does not mean you cannot associate an IAM user with a role; you can very well associate an IAM user with a role.

Using roles you can define a set of permissions to access the resources that a user or service needs, but the permissions are not attached to an IAM user or group. For example, a specific application can access S3 buckets by assuming a role. Similarly, a mobile application can access the EC2 server in the back end by assuming a role. The role can be assumed by applications or services during the execution or at runtime. Thus, an IAM role is similar to a user, in that it is an AWS identity with permission policies that determine what the identity can and cannot do in AWS. However, instead of being uniquely associated with one person, a role is intended to be assumable by anyone who needs it. Since a role doesn't have any credentials (password or access keys) associated with it, when a user is assigned a role or when an application assumes a role, the access keys or security credentials are created dynamically by AWS during runtime and are provided to the user or application. The advantage of this is that you don't have to share the long-term security credentials to the application that requires access to a particular resource. Therefore, you can say that a role is an IAM entity that defines a set of permissions for making AWS service requests.

These are some of the use cases where you would use roles:

- To delegate access to users, applications, or services that don't normally have access to your AWS resources

- When you don't want to embed AWS keys within the app

- When you want to grant AWS access to users who already have identities defined outside of AWS (for example, corporate directories)

- To grant access to your account to third parties (such as external auditors)

- So that applications can use other AWS services

- To request temporary credentials for performing certain tasks

When you create a role, you need to specify two policies. One policy governs who can assume the role (in other words, the *principal*). This policy is also called the *trust policy*.

The second policy is the *permission* or *access policy*, which defines what resources and action the principal or who is assuming the role is allowed access to. This principal can be anyone who would be assuming the role. It can be a third-party user, an AWS service such as EC2 or DynamoDB, an identity provider, and so on. The principal can even be an IAM user from a different account; of course, it can't be from your account.

IAM Hierarchy of Privileges

If you have to classify the AWS users into the hierarchy of privileges, it is going to follow this order, with the most powerful first and least powerful last:

- **AWS root user or the account owner** This user has unrestricted access to all enabled services and resources.
- **AWS IAM user** In this case, the user has limited permissions. The access is restricted by group and user policies.
- **Temporary security credentials** Access is restricted by generating identity and further by policies used to generate tokens.

IAM Best Practices

The following are some best practices for using IAM.

Use the IAM User

Immediately after creating the AWS account, create an IAM user for yourself and assign admin privileges. Lock down your root user. Never use the root user's access key for any programmatic requests to AWS. Create individual IAM users for anyone who needs access to your AWS account.

Create a Strong Password Policy

Set a strong password policy and make sure the password expires after 90 days. Make sure the password has at least one uppercase letter, one lowercase letter, one symbol, and one number; it should be a minimum of eight to ten characters.

Rotate Security Credentials Regularly

Use the Access Key Last Used to identify and deactivate credentials that have been unused in 90 or more days. Enable credential rotation for IAM users. Use the Credential Report to audit credential rotation.

Enable MFA

Enable MFA for root and critical accounts with superuser privileges. MFA provides an additional layer of protection, and using it will make sure your account is protected.

Manage Permission with Groups

Instead of assigning permission to individual users, create groups that relate to job functions and attach policies to groups. The biggest advantage of this is that it reduces the complexity of access management as the number of users grow. It also reduces the opportunity for a user to accidentally get excessive access. It is an easy way to reassign permissions based on a change in responsibility and to update permissions for multiple users.

Grant the Least Privileges

It is important to use the principle of least privilege for managing the users. Always start with a minimum set of permissions and grant additional permissions only as necessary. This minimizes the chances of accidentally performing privileged actions. Since it is easier to relax than to tighten up, you can always add privileges as and when needed.

Use IAM Roles

You should always use IAM roles to delegate cross-account access, to delegate access within an account, and to provide access for federated users. If you use roles, then there is no need to share security credentials or store long-term credentials, and you have a clear idea and have control over who has what access.

Use IAM Roles for Amazon EC2 Instances

If you have an application that runs on an Amazon EC2 instance and it needs to access other AWS services, you need to assign the application credentials. The best way to provide credentials to an application running on an EC2 instance is by using IAM roles.

Use IAM Policy Conditions for Extra Security

IAM policies allow access to a resource, but by using policy conditions, you can set up finer-grained conditions for the access. For example, using policy conditions, you can provide access on a particular day and time from a specified IP address.

Enable AWS CloudTrail

It is important that you have the ability to audit in your AWS ecosystem. You must ensure that AWS CloudTrail is enabled in all regions and that the AWS CloudTrail log file validation is enabled. It is also important to make sure that the Amazon S3 bucket of CloudTrail logs is not publicly accessible.

AWS Compliance Program

Amazon Web Services Compliance Program enables customers to understand the robust controls in place at AWS to maintain security and data protection in the cloud. As systems are built on top of AWS cloud infrastructure, compliance responsibilities will be shared.

By tying together governance-focused, audit-friendly service features with applicable compliance or audit standards, AWS Compliance features build on traditional programs, helping customers to establish and operate in an AWS security control environment. The IT infrastructure that AWS provides to its customers is designed and managed in alignment with security best practices and a variety of IT security standards, including the following:

- SOC 1/SSAE 16/ISAE 3402 (formerly SAS 70)
- SOC 2
- SOC 3
- FISMA, DIACAP, and FedRAMP
- DOD CSM Levels 1–5
- PCI DSS Level 1
- ISO 9001/ISO 27001
- ITAR
- FIPS 140-2
- MTCS Level 3

In addition, the flexibility and control that the AWS platform provides allows customers to deploy solutions that meet several industry-specific standards, including the following:

- Criminal Justice Information Services (CJIS)
- Cloud Security Alliance (CSA)
- Family Educational Rights and Privacy Act (FERPA)
- Health Insurance Portability and Accountability Act (HIPAA)
- Motion Picture Association of America (MPAA)

Many of these reports can be downloaded directly from the admin console from the Artifact menu in the Security, Identity & Compliance section. Some of these artifacts may need a nondisclosure agreement (NDA). If you need a report that needs an NDA, please work with your sales representative to start the process.

Shared Responsibility Model

Let's talk about how security in the cloud is slightly different than security in your on-premises data centers. When you move computer systems and data to the cloud, security responsibilities become shared between you and your cloud service provider. In this case, AWS is responsible for securing the underlying infrastructure that supports the cloud, and you're responsible for anything you put on the cloud or connect to the cloud. This shared security responsibility model can reduce your operational burden in many ways, and in some cases may even improve your default security posture without additional

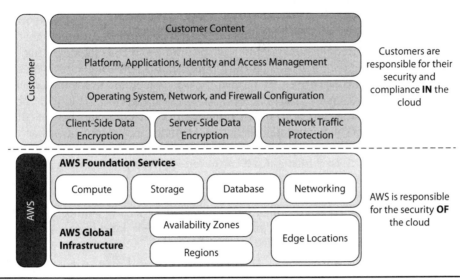

Figure 5-2   AWS shared responsibility model

action on your part. The infrastructure consists of the hardware, software, networking, and data centers that run AWS services. AWS is responsible for protecting this infrastructure. Since security is the topmost priority for AWS, no one can visit the data centers.

AWS follows the shared security model in which there are some elements that AWS takes responsibility for and other areas that customers must address. As shown in Figure 5-2, AWS is responsible for the security in the cloud, and customers are responsible for security and compliance in the cloud.

AWS Responsibility

As discussed regarding the shared responsibility model, there are some elements that AWS takes responsibility for and other areas that customers must address. These are AWS's responsibilities:

- **Physical security of data center**   Amazon has been building large-scale data centers for many years. It has strict controls in place for the physical security of the data centers. Amazon is responsible for the physical security of the data centers, and to do that, it logs and audits the employees who access the data center, ensures that proper video surveillance is in place, and protects the data center from fire by installing fire detection and suppression equipment. The data centers are designed to be fully redundant in terms of power. In addition, AWS has Uninterruptible Power Supply (UPS) units that provide backup power in the event of an electrical failure. AWS makes sure that the data center has proper climate control in place. AWS has segregation of duty in place, which means that any employee with physical access doesn't have logical privileges and that any employee who visits the data center does not have AWS console access.

- **Amazon EC2 security**   AWS is responsible for securing the host operating system where AWS has root access to the operating system. (For example, if you deploy your database on RDS, you don't have access to the operating system hosting the database.) Those administrators who have a business need to access the management plan of the host OS are required to use multifactor authentication to gain access. All these activities are logged and audited. For the guest operating system, where the virtual instances are controlled by you (the AWS customer), you have full root access or administrative control over accounts, services, and applications. AWS does not have any access rights to your instances or the guest OS. In this case, AWS can't even log in to your operating system. In addition to this, Amazon EC2 provides a complete firewall solution. AWS provides mandatory inbound firewalls with default deny mode in the form of security groups. You can configure the firewall using security groups. Multiple instances running on the same physical machines are isolated from each other via the Xen hypervisor.

- **Network security**   AWS is responsible for managing the network infrastructure, and it has implemented a world-class network infrastructure that is carefully monitored and managed. AWS has redundant network devices, including a firewall, to monitor and control internal and external communications. ACLs, or traffic flow policies, are established on each managed interface, which manage and enforce the flow of traffic. AWS also takes care of network monitoring and protection and has implemented a variety of tools to monitor server and network usage, port scanning activities, application usage, and unauthorized intrusion attempts. In addition, AWS has several strict controls in place; for example, IP spoofing is prohibited at the host OS level, packet sniffing is ineffective (protected at the hypervisor level), unauthorized port scanning is a violation of TOS and is detected/blocked, and inbound ports are blocked by default.

- **Configuration management**   Whenever new hardware is provisioned, configuration management software is installed. This software runs on all UNIX machines to validate that they are configured properly and all the software installed is in compliance with standards determined by the role assigned to the host. This software also makes sure that all updates are done in such a manner that they will not impact the customer. Configuration management makes sure that all the changes are authorized, logged, tested, approved, and documented. In addition, AWS also communicates to its customer via e-mail or through the AWS Service Health Dashboard (http://status.aws.amazon.com/) when there is a potential for a service to be affected.

- **Highly available data center**   AWS is responsible for making sure that all the data centers are highly available at all times. All data centers are always online and serving customers, and there is no concept of a cold data center. As a result, all the AZs are always active at any point in time. Every AZ has redundant architecture built in, which provides fault-tolerant services. In addition, you should also architect your application in such a way that it is leveraging multiple AZs.

- **Disk management**   AWS has proprietary disk management in place, which prevents customers from accessing each other's data. The way it is done is that the customer instances have no access to raw disk devices but instead are presented with virtualized disks. The disk virtualization layer automatically resets every block of storage used by the customer. All the hard drives are wiped prior to use. In addition, customers can encrypt the hard drives for additional security.

- **Storage device decommissioning**   Whenever a storage device comes to the end of its life, AWS uses DoD 5220.22-M ("National Industrial Security Program Operating Manual") and NIST 800-88 ("Guidelines for Media Sanitization") to wipe off all the data. Once the data has been wiped, the disks are degaussed and then finally physically destroyed.

Customer's Responsibility

The customer's responsibility differs depending on the type of services being used from AWS. Figure 5-3 shows the responsibilities if you are using AWS for Infrastructure as a Service (IaaS) such as EC2, VPC, networking, and so on. In that case, you are responsible for the following:

- **Operating system**   You are responsible for the management of the guest OS. It is your responsibility to make sure that the OS is regularly patched and has all the security updates and bug fixes.

- **Application**   You are responsible for managing any application that you run on top of AWS. Management includes encrypting data, managing application users and their privileges, and so on. You are also responsible for all the security and compliance of the application. For example, if your application needs to be PCI compliant, just deploying it into AWS (since the AWS infrastructure is PCI compliant) won't make it PCI compliant. You need to make sure that you deploy all the steps for being PCI compliant from the application tier as well.

Figure 5-3
Customer
responsible for
compliance of
application

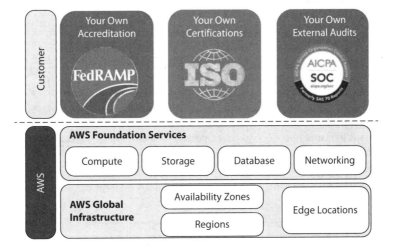

- **Firewall**   You need to make sure the proper firewalls at the OS level (security groups) and across the network level (NACL) are configured.

- **Network configuration**   VPC gives you the ability to run your own private data center in the cloud, but you are responsible for its configuration. Since AWS does not have access to your VPC or anything that you run within your VPC, it is your responsibility to make sure that it is secure and that the relevant people have the relevant access. Similarly, you need to make sure the resources you deploy on the VPC are configured correctly. (For example, the database server should not be configured in a public subnet.)

- **Service configuration**   You should have a proper service configuration in place so that you know who is installing what on the servers, or who is making what changes in your infrastructure.

- **Authentication and account management**   You are responsible for the authentication and account management for both AWS users and application users. You can use IAM to manage the AWS users, but for managing the application users, you may have to explore this on a case-to-case basis. For example, if you want to deploy SAP on AWS, you need to manage all the SAP users as well.

Figure 5-4 summarizes the AWS and customer's responsibility to make a fully compliant application.

In addition to IaaS, you can use AWS as a Platform as a Service (PaaS), which is also known as *container services*. If you host your database in RDS, or run your data warehouse in Redshift, or run your NoSQL database in DynamoDB, all the work related to hosting the operating system, managing OS firewalls, launching and maintaining instances, patching the guest OS or database, or replicating databases, and so on, is taken care of by AWS. You should protect your AWS account credentials and set up individual user accounts with Amazon IAM so that each of your users has their own credentials, and you can implement segregation of duties. You are also responsible for the data residing in these services such as RDS and encryption. Figure 5-5 summaries the responsibilities when using AWS in this way.

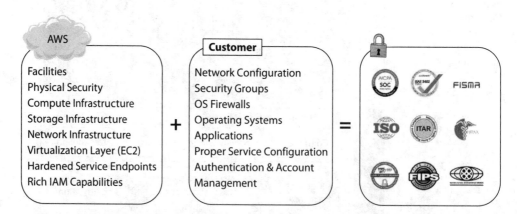

Figure 5-4   AWS and customer's responsibility for compliance

- Foundational Services—Networking, Compute, Storage
- AWS Global Infrastructure
- AWS API Endpoints
- Operating System
- Platform/Application

AWS

Customers

- Customer Data
- Firewall (VPC)
- Customer IAM (DB Users, Table Permissions)
- AWS IAM (Users, Groups, Roles, Policies)
- High Availability
- Data Protection (Transit, Rest, Backup)
- Scaling

Figure 5-5 AWS and customer's responsibility when using PaaS

In addition to PaaS, you can also use AWS like Software as a Service (SaaS), or *abstract services*. A common example for using AWS as a SaaS is S3. In this case, you just need to manage the data, and you are responsible for encrypting it. Figure 5-6 summaries the responsibilities when using AWS in this way.

The amount of security configuration work you have to do varies depending on which services you select and how sensitive your data is. However, there are certain security features—such as individual user accounts and credentials, SSL/TLS for data transmissions, and user activity logging—that you should configure no matter which AWS service you use. This is discussed in detail in Chapter 9.

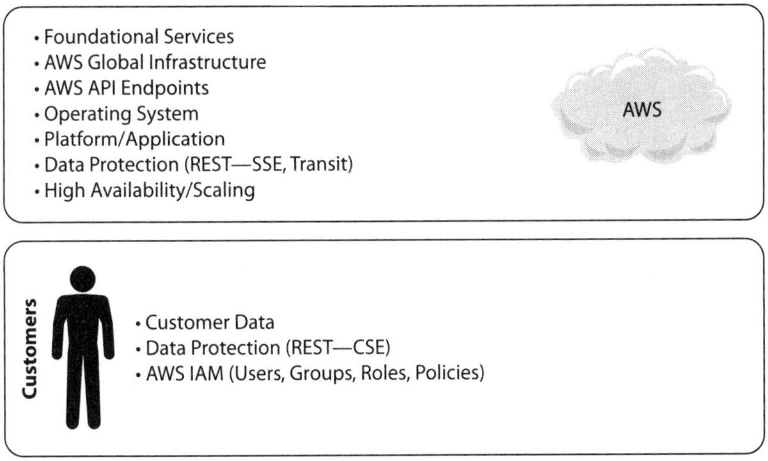

- Foundational Services
- AWS Global Infrastructure
- AWS API Endpoints
- Operating System
- Platform/Application
- Data Protection (REST—SSE, Transit)
- High Availability/Scaling

AWS

Customers

- Customer Data
- Data Protection (REST—CSE)
- AWS IAM (Users, Groups, Roles, Policies)

Figure 5-6 AWS and customer's responsibility when using SaaS

Lab 5-1: Creating IAM Users, Groups, and Roles

This lab will walk you through connecting to the instance and configuring security credentials so that you can interact with the AWS APIs and command-line tools. This lab will cover the following topics:

- Creating an IAM group and adding an IAM user to the group
- Exploring the properties of an IAM user
- Creating an IAM role for EC2

Let's start by creating a group first. To do that, go to the IAM dashboard in the AWS console. Search for IAM or select IAM under Security, Identity & Compliance.

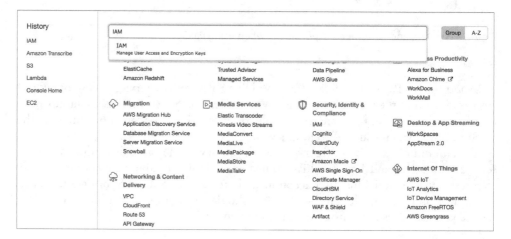

To create a group, select Groups on the left side and then click the Create New Group button.

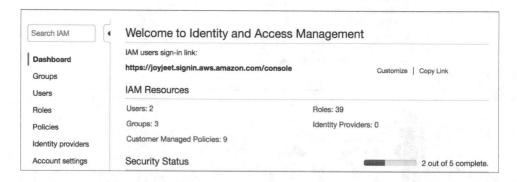

Type **PowerUser** into the Group Name text box and click Next Step.

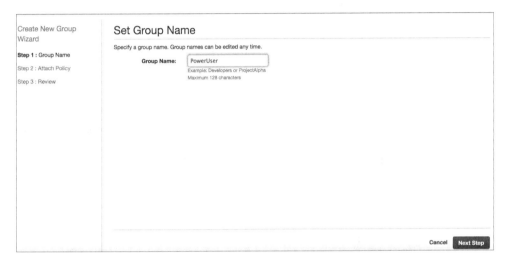

Type **Power** in the filtering text box and then select PowerUserAccess. Click Next Step.

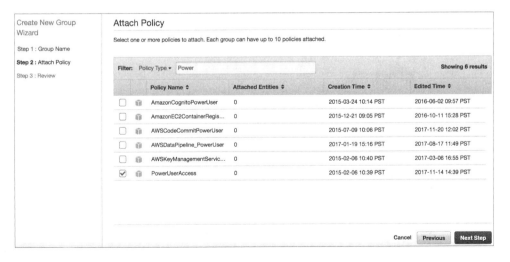

This will associate the PowerUserAccess IAM policy with your new group and allow group members to perform any AWS action except IAM management. Click Create Group.

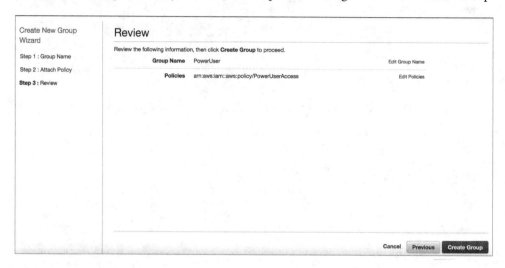

You should be able to see the newly created group from the console.

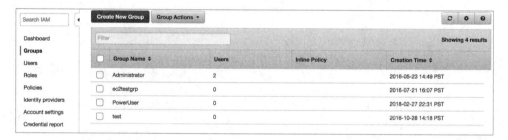

To create a user, select Users and then click the Add User button.

Enter **user1** in the first text box next to User Name. Select the check box next to Programmatic Access and click Next: Permissions.

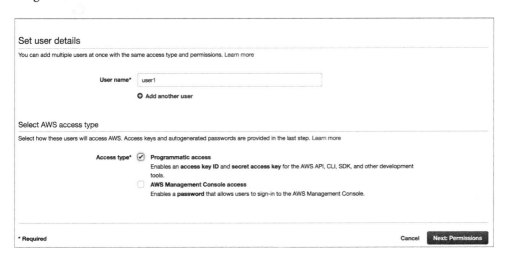

To add the user to the group, select Add User To Group and then click the check box next to the PowerUser group; click Next: Review.

Click Create User.

Click Close. Your new user and group have now been created, and your user is a member of your group.

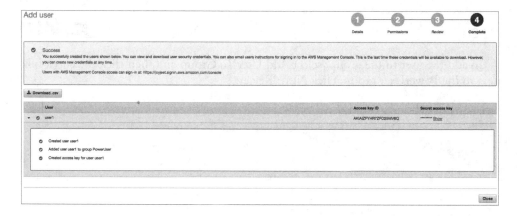

Managing IAM User Permissions and Credentials

Now that you have created your first IAM user and group, let's take a look at the IAM user properties. Click the Users option in the left menu and then select the user's account that you just created.

Notice that user1 is a member of the PowerUser group that you added user1 to.

Now select the Permissions tab to see the individual user and group policies that will be applied to this account. Note that this user has only the PowerUserAccess group policy applied to the account.

Now select the Security Credentials tab. This is where you can assign or change a user's console password and multifactor authentication device.

From here you can also create, rotate, or revoke a user's API access keys (for using the AWS command-line tools or other direct access to the AWS APIs through custom or third-party applications).

IAM Roles for Amazon EC2

Applications or command-line tools running on Amazon EC2 instances that make requests to AWS must sign all AWS API requests with AWS access keys. AWS IAM roles for EC2 instances make it easier for your applications and command-line tools to securely access AWS service APIs from EC2 instances. An IAM role with a set of permissions can be created and attached to an EC2 instance on launch. AWS access keys with the specified permissions will then be automatically made available on EC2 instances that have been launched with an IAM role. IAM roles for EC2 instances manage the process of securely distributing and rotating your AWS access keys to your EC2 instances so that you don't have to do this.

Using IAM roles for instances, you can securely distribute AWS access keys to instances and define permissions that applications on those instances use when accessing other services in AWS. Here are some things you should know about using IAM roles for instances:

- AWS access keys for signing requests to other services in AWS are automatically made available on running instances.

- AWS access keys on an instance are rotated automatically multiple times a day. New access keys will be made available at least five minutes prior to the expiration of the old access keys.

- You can assign granular service permissions for applications running on an instance that make requests to other services in AWS.

- You can include an IAM role when you launch on-demand, spot, or reserved instances.

- IAM roles can be used with all Windows and Linux AMIs.

CAUTION If you are using services that use instance metadata service (IMDS) with IAM roles, you should ensure that you do not expose your credentials when the services make HTTP calls on your behalf. Either you should include logic to ensure that these services cannot leak information from IMDS or you should have the appropriate firewall rules in place so that the services cannot access IMDS. Types of services that could expose your credentials include the following:

- HTTP proxies
- HTML/CSS validator services
- XML processors that support XML inclusion

To create an IAM role for EC2, click the Roles link on the left menu and click Create Role.

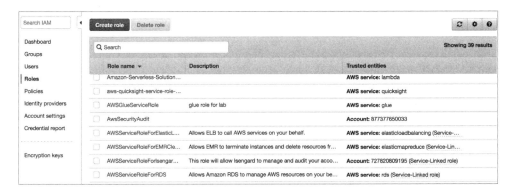

Select AWS Service as the type of trusted entry.

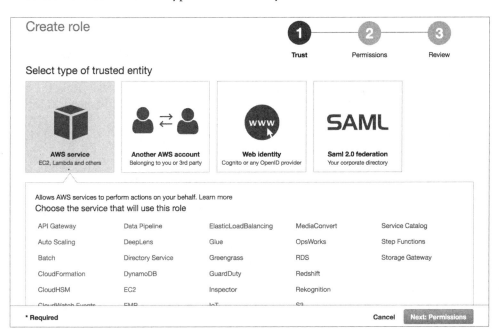

Select EC2 on the Select Your Use Case screen.

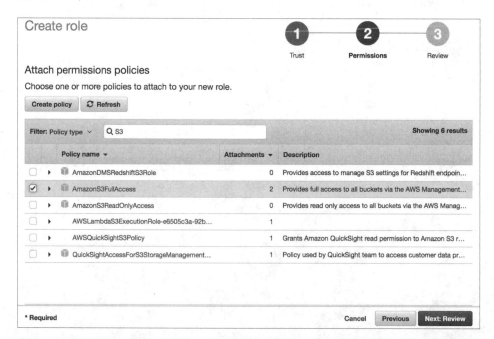

IAM supports several types of roles. Select the Amazon EC2 Service Role for this example, but know that IAM roles can be used to grant access to AWS services, other AWS accounts, and third-party identity providers.

You now need to set permissions for this new role. Type **S3** and then select Amazon S3FullAccess; click Next: Review.

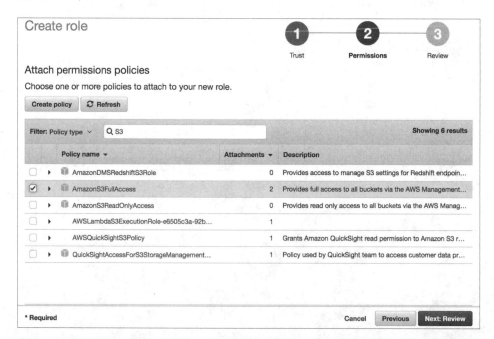

You now have the opportunity to review the role information. Give a name for the role you are going to create. In this case, name it **EC2S3Full**. Click Create Role.

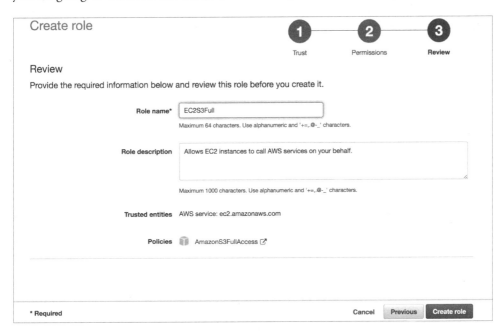

Now go to the Roles screen and search for that role. You will see that your role exists.

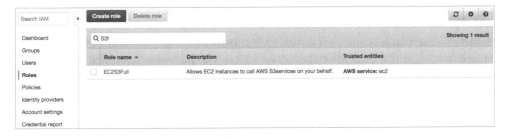

You can now use the newly created IAM role when you launch an EC2 instance. For example, in the EC2 console, you can select the role as part of the launch process. Once the instance is launched, applications and tools that access AWS services will automatically pick up temporary credentials made available to the instance by the infrastructure.

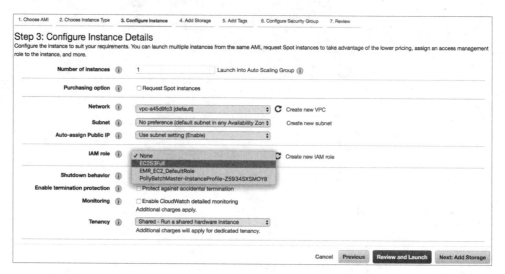

Congratulations! You have created your first IAM user, group, and role!

Chapter Review

In this chapter, you learned what AWS IAM is. IAM allows you to implement a comprehensive access control on AWS resources by giving you the ability to authenticate, authorize, and log all access. Therefore, you can implement the concepts of least privilege and segregation of duties. You can log every allow and deny in CloudTrail for troubleshooting or auditing purposes.

You can use AWS IAM to securely control individual and group access to your AWS resources. You can create and manage user identities (called IAM *users*) and grant permissions for those IAM users to access your resources. You can also grant permissions for users outside of AWS. Any AWS customer can use IAM because the service is offered at no additional charge. You will be charged only for the use of other AWS services by your users.

A user is a unique identity recognized by AWS services and applications. Similar to a login user in an operating system like Windows or UNIX, users have unique names and can identify themselves using familiar security credentials such as passwords or access keys.

A group is a collection of IAM users. You can manage group membership as a simple list and add users to or remove them from a group. A user can belong to multiple groups. Groups cannot belong to other groups.

An IAM role is an IAM entity that defines a set of permissions for making AWS service requests. IAM roles are not associated with a specific user or group. Instead, trusted entities assume roles, such as IAM users, applications, or AWS services such as EC2. IAM roles allow you to delegate access with defined permissions to trusted entities without having to share long-term access keys. You can use IAM roles to delegate access to IAM users managed within your account, to IAM users under a different AWS account, or to an AWS service such as EC2.

You also studied the shared security model in which AWS is responsible for protecting the infrastructure that runs all of the services offered in the AWS cloud. This infrastructure is composed of the hardware, software, networking, and facilities that run AWS cloud services.

Customer responsibility is determined by the AWS cloud services that a customer selects. This determines the amount of configuration work the customer must perform as part of its security responsibilities. For example, services such as Amazon Elastic Compute Cloud (Amazon EC2) are categorized as Infrastructure as a Service and, as such, requires the customer to perform all of the necessary security configuration and management tasks. If a customer deploys an Amazon EC2 instance, they are responsible for managing the guest operating system (including updates and security patches), any application software or utilities installed by the customer on the instances, and the configuration of the AWS-provided firewall (called a *security group*) on each instance.

Questions

1. Can you add an IAM role to an IAM group?

   A. Yes

   B. No

   C. Yes, if there are ten members in the group

   D. Yes, if the group allows adding a role

2. An IAM policy contains which of the following? (Choose two.)

   A. Username

   B. Action

   C. Service name

   D. AZ

3. What happens if you delete an IAM role that is associated with a running EC2 instance?

   A. Any application running on the instance that is using the role will be denied access immediately.

   B. The application continues to use that role until the EC2 server is shut down.

   C. The application will have the access until the session is alive.

   D. The application will continue to have access.

4. For implementing security features, which of the following would you choose?

   A. Username/password

   B. MFA

   C. Using multiple S3 buckets

   D. Login using the root user

5. Which is based on temporary security tokens? (Choose two.)

   A. Amazon EC2 roles

   B. Federation

   C. Username password

   D. Using AWS STS

6. You want EC2 instances to give access without any username or password to S3 buckets. What is the easiest way of doing this?

   A. By using a VPC S3 endpoint

   B. By using a signed URL

   C. By using roles

   D. By sharing the keys between S3 and EC2

7. An IAM policy takes which form?

   A. Python script

   B. Written in C language

   C. JSON code

   D. XML code

8. If an administrator who has root access leaves the company, what should you do to protect your account? (Choose two.)

   A. Add MFA to root

   B. Delete all the IAM accounts

   C. Change the passwords for all the IAM accounts and rotate keys

   D. Delete all the EC2 instances created by the administrator

9. Using the shared security model, the customer is responsible for which of the following? (Choose two.)

   A. The security of the data running inside the database hosted in EC2

   B. Maintaining the physical security of the data center

   C. Making sure the hypervisor is patched correctly

   D. Making sure the operating system is patched correctly

10. In Amazon RDS, who is responsible for patching the database?

    A. Customer.

    B. Amazon.

    C. In RDS you don't have to patch the database.

    D. RDS does not come under the shared security model.

Answers

  1. B. No, you can't add an IAM role to an IAM group.

  2. B, **C**. A policy is not location specific and is not limited to a user.

  3. A. The application will be denied access.

  4. A, **B**. Using multiple buckets won't help in terms of security. Similarly, leveraging multiple regions won't help to address the security.

  5. B, **D**. The username password is not a temporary security token.

  6. C. A VPC endpoint is going to create a path between the EC2 instance and the Amazon S3 bucket. A signed URL won't help EC2 instances from accessing S3 buckets. You cannot share the keys between S3 and EC2.

  7. C. It is written in JSON.

  8. A, **C**. Deleting all the IAM accounts is going to be a bigger painful task. You are going to lose all the users. Similarly, you can't delete all the EC2 instances; they must be running some critical application or something meaningful.

  9. A, **D**. The customer is responsible for the security of anything running on the hypervisor, and therefore the operating system and the security of data are the customer's responsibility.

  10. B. RDS does come under a shared security model. Since it is a managed service, the patching of the database is taken care of by Amazon.

CHAPTER 6

Auto Scaling

In this chapter, you will

- Learn what Auto Scaling is
- Understand the benefits of Auto Scaling
- Understand various Auto Scaling policies
- See how to set up Auto Scaling
- Learn what Elastic Load Balancing is
- Understand how Elastic Load Balancing works
- See the various types of load balancing

Auto Scaling is the technology that allows you to scale your workload up and down automatically based on the rules you define. It is one of the innovations that makes the cloud elastic and helps you customize per your own requirements. Using Auto Scaling, you don't have to over-provision the resources to meet the peak demand. Auto Scaling will spin off and configure new resources automatically and then take the resources down when the demand goes down. In this chapter, you'll learn all about the advantages of Auto Scaling.

On-premise deployments require customers to go through an extensive sizing exercise, essentially guessing at the resources required to meet peak workloads. Experience shows that it's almost impossible to get the sizing estimates right. Most often customers end up with under-utilized resources while under-estimating resources for peak workloads. Other times customers plan for the peak by over-provisioning the resources. For example, you might provision all the hardware for Black Friday at the beginning of the year since you get your capital budget during the start of the year. So, for the whole year those servers run only with, say, 15 to 20 percent CPU and achieve the peak during the Black Friday sale. In this case, you have wasted a lot of compute capacity throughout the year that could have been used for some other purpose.

With Amazon Web Services (AWS), you have the ability to spin servers up when your workloads require additional resources and spin them back down when demand drops. You can set up rules with parameters to ensure your workloads have the right resources.

You can integrate Auto Scaling with Elastic Load Balancing; by doing so you can distribute the work load across multiple EC2 servers.

Benefits of Auto Scaling

These are the main benefits of Auto Scaling:

- **Dynamic scaling**   The biggest advantage of Auto Scaling is the dynamic scaling of resources based on the demand. There is no limit to the number of servers you can scale up to. You can scale up from two servers to hundreds or thousands or tens of thousands of servers almost instantly. Using Auto Scaling you can make sure that your application always performs optimally and gets additional horsepower in terms of CPU and other resources whenever needed. You are able to provision them in real time.

- **Best user experience**   Auto Scaling helps to provide the best possible experience for your users because you never run out of resources and your application always performs optimally. You can create various rules within Auto Scaling to provide the best user experience. For example, you can specify that if the CPU utilization increases to more than 70 percent, a new instance is started.

- **Health check and fleet management**   You can monitor the health checks of your Elastic Compute Cloud (EC2) instances using Auto Scaling. If you are hosting your application on a bunch of EC2 servers, the collection of those EC2 servers is called a *fleet*. You can configure health checks with Auto Scaling, and if a health check detects there is a failure on an instance, it automatically replaces the instance. It reduces a lot of burden from you because now you don't have to manually replace the failed instance. It also helps to maintain the desired fleet capacity. For example, if your application is running on six EC2 servers, you will be able to maintain the fleet of six EC2 servers no matter how many times there is an issue with an EC2 server. Alternatively, if one or more servers go down, Auto Scaling will start additional servers to make sure you always have six instances running. When you configure Auto Scaling with Elastic Load Balancing (ELB), it is capable of doing ELB health checks as well. There are various kinds of health checks ELB can do, such as for hardware failure, system performance degradation, and so on. Detecting these failures on the fly while always managing a constant fleet of resources is really painful in the on-premise world. With AWS, everything is taken care of for you automatically.

- **Load balancing**   Since Auto Scaling is used to dynamically scale up and down the resources, it can take care of balancing the workload load across multiple EC2 instances when you use Auto Scaling along with ELB. Auto Scaling also automatically balances the EC2 instances across multiple AZs when multiple AZs are configured. Auto Scaling makes sure that there is a uniform balance of EC2 instances across multiple AZs that you define.

- **Target tracking**   You can use Auto Scaling to run on a particular target, and Auto Scaling adjusts the number of EC2 instances for you in order to meet that target. The target can be a scaling metric that Auto Scaling supports. For example, if you always want the CPU's utilization of your application server to remain at 65 percent, Auto Scaling will increase and decrease the number of EC2 instances automatically to meet the 65 percent CPU utilization metric.

In addition to scaling EC2, Auto Scaling can be used to scale up some other services. You can use application Auto Scaling to define scaling policies to scale up these resources. These are the other services where Auto Scaling can be used:

- EC2 spot instances
- EC2 Container Service (ECS)
- Elastic Map Reducer (EMR) clusters
- AppStream 2.0 instances
- DynamoDB

Let's see how Auto Scaling works in real life. Say you have an application that consists of two web servers that are hosted in two separate EC2 instances. To maintain the high availability, you have placed the web servers in different availability zones. You have integrated both the web servers with ELB, and the users connect to the ELB. The architecture will look something like Figure 6-1.

Everything is going well when all of a sudden you notice that there is an increase in the web traffic. To meet the additional traffic, you provision additional two web servers and integrate them with ELB, as shown in Figure 6-2. Up to this point you are doing everything manually, which includes adding web servers and integrating them with ELB. Also, if your traffic goes down, you need to bring down the instances manually since

Figure 6-1
Application
with two web
servers in two
different AZs

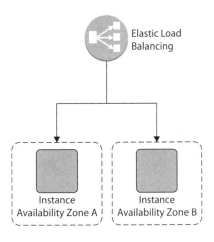

Elastic Load
Balancing

Instance
Availability Zone A

Instance
Availability Zone B

Figure 6-2
Adding two web
servers to the
application

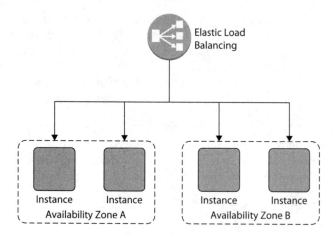

Auto Scaling Group

keeping them is going to cost you more. This is fine and manageable when you have smaller number of servers to manage and you can predict the traffic. What if you have hundreds or thousands of servers hosting the application? What if the traffic is totally unpredictable? Can you still add hundreds and thousands of servers almost instantly and then integrate each one of them with ELB? What about taking those servers down? Can you do it quickly? Not really. Auto Scaling solves this problem for you.

When you use Auto Scaling, you simply add the EC2 instances to an Auto Scaling group, define the minimum and maximum number of servers, and then define the scaling policy. Auto Scaling takes care of adding and deleting the servers and integrating them with ELB based on the usage. When you integrate Auto Scaling, the architecture looks something like Figure 6-3.

Figure 6-3
Adding all four
web servers as
part of Auto
Scaling

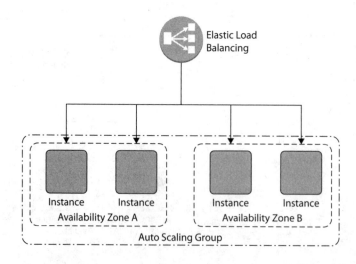

Launch Configuration

When you use Auto Scaling to scale up your instances, it needs to know what kind of server to use. You can define this by creating a *launch configuration*. A launch configuration is a template that stores all the information about the instance, such as the AMI (Amazon Machine Image) details, instance type, key pair, security group, IAM (Identity and Access Management) instance profile, user data, storage attached, and so on.

Once you create a launch configuration, you can link it with an Auto Scaling group. You can use the same launch configuration with multiple Auto Scaling groups as well, but an Auto Scaling group always has only one launch configuration attached to it. You will learn about Auto Scaling groups in the next section. Once you create an Auto Scaling group, you can't edit the launch configuration tied up with it; the only way to do this is to create a new launch configuration and associate the Auto Scaling group with the new launch configuration. The subsequent instances will be launched as per the new Auto Scaling group settings. For example, in your Auto Scaling group, say you have created a launch configuration with C4 large instances. You launch four C4 large instances as part of the initial launch. Then you remove the old configuration, create a new configuration, and add the new configuration as part of your Auto Scaling group. In your new configuration, you specify C4 extra-large instances. Now when the new instances are going to spin off, they will be C4 extra-large. Say the new Auto Scaling rule kicks in and the Auto Scaling group starts two more instances; the additional two new instances will be C4 extra-large. Now you will be running the fleet with four C4 large and two C4 extra-large instances. If one of the C4 large instances goes down because of a hardware fault, the replacement instance that the Auto Scaling group will launch will be a C4 extra-large and not C4 large since there is no entry of C4 large instance in the launch configuration anymore.

Auto Scaling Groups

An Auto Scaling group is the place where you define the logic for scaling up and scaling down. It has all the rules and policies that govern how the EC2 instances will be terminated or started. Auto Scaling groups are the collection of all the EC2 servers running together as a group and dynamically going up or down as per your definitions. When you create an Auto Scaling group, first you need to provide the launch configuration that has the details of the instance type, and then you need to choose the scaling plan or scaling policy. You can scale in the following ways:

- **Maintaining the instance level** This is also known as the default scaling plan. In this scaling policy, you define the number of instances you will always operate with. You define the minimum or the specified number of servers that will be running all the time. Auto Scaling groups make sure you are always running with that many instances. For example, if you define that you are always going to run six instances, whenever the instance goes down because of hardware failure or any issues, the Auto Scaling group is going to spin off new servers, making sure you are always operating with a fleet of six servers.

- **Manual scaling**   You can also scale up or down manually either via the console or the API or CLI. When you do the manually scaling, you manually add or terminate the instances. Manually scaling should be the last thing you would be doing since Auto Scaling provides so many ways of automating your scaling. If you still scale it manually, you are defying the Auto Scaling setup.

- **Scaling as per the demand**   Another usage of Auto Scaling is to scale to meet the demand. You can scale according to various CloudWatch metrics such as an increase in CPU, disk reads, disk writes, network in, network out, and so on. For example, you can have a rule that says if there is a spike of 80 percent and it lasts for more than five minutes, then Auto Scaling will spin off a new server for you. When you are defining the scaling policies, you must define two policies, one for scaling up and the other for scaling down.

- **Scaling as per schedule**   If your traffic is predictable and you know that you are going to have an increase in traffic during certain hours, you can have a scaling policy as per the schedule. For example, your application may have heaviest usage during the day, and hardly any activity at night. You can scale the application to have more web servers during the day and scale down during the night. To create an Auto Scaling policy for scheduled scaling, you need to create a scheduled action that tells the Auto Scaling group to perform the scaling action at the specified time.

To create an Auto Scaling group, you need to provide the minimum number of instances running at any time. You also need to set the maximum number of servers to which the instances can scale. In some cases, you can set a desired number of instances that is the optimal number of instances the system should be. Therefore, you tell Auto Scaling the following:

- If the desired capacity is greater than the current capacity, then launch instances.
- If the desired capacity is less than the current capacity, then terminate instances.

It is important that you know when the Auto Scaling group is increasing or decreasing the number of servers for your application. To do so, you can configure Amazon Simple Notification Service (SNS) to send an SNS notification whenever your Auto Scaling group scales up or down. Amazon SNS can deliver notifications as HTTP or HTTPS POST, as an e-mail, or as a message posted to an Amazon SQS queue.

There are some limits to how many Auto Scaling groups you can have. Since the number keeps on changing, it is recommended that you check the AWS web site for the latest numbers. All these numbers are soft limits, which can be increased with a support ticket.

Please note that an Auto Scaling group cannot span regions; it can be part of only one region. However, it can span multiple AZs within a region. By doing so, you can achieve a high availability architecture.

It is recommended that you use the same instance type in an Auto Scaling group since you are going to have effective load distribution when the instances are of the same type. However, if you change the launch configuration with different instance types, all the new instances that will be started will be of different types.

Let's talk about the scaling policy types in more detail. You can have three types of scaling policies.

Simple Scaling

Using simple scaling, you can scale up or down on the basis of only one scaling adjustment. In this mechanism, you select an alarm, which can be CPU utilization, disk read, disk write, network in or network out, and so on, and then scale up or down the instances on the occurrence of that particular alarm. For example, if the CPU utilization is 80 percent, you can add one more instance, or if the CPU utilization is less than 40 percent, you can take one instance down. You can also define how long to wait before starting or stopping a new instance. This waiting period is also called the *cooldown period*. When you create a simple scaling policy, you need to create two policies, one for scaling up or increasing the group size and another for scaling down or decreasing the group size. Figure 6-4 shows what a simple scaling policy looks like.

If you look at Figure 6-4, you will notice the policy is executed when the alarm occurs, so the first step is to create an alarm. By clicking Add New Alarm, you can create a new alarm from where you can specify whom to notify and the scaling conditions. Figure 6-5 shows an alarm created that sends a notification to the admin when the CPU goes up by 50 percent after one occurrence of five minutes.

Once you create the alarm, you need to define the action that adds an EC2 instance for scaling up and decreases an EC2 instance for scaling down; then you input the time before the next scale-up or scale-down activity happens, as shown in Figure 6-6. If you

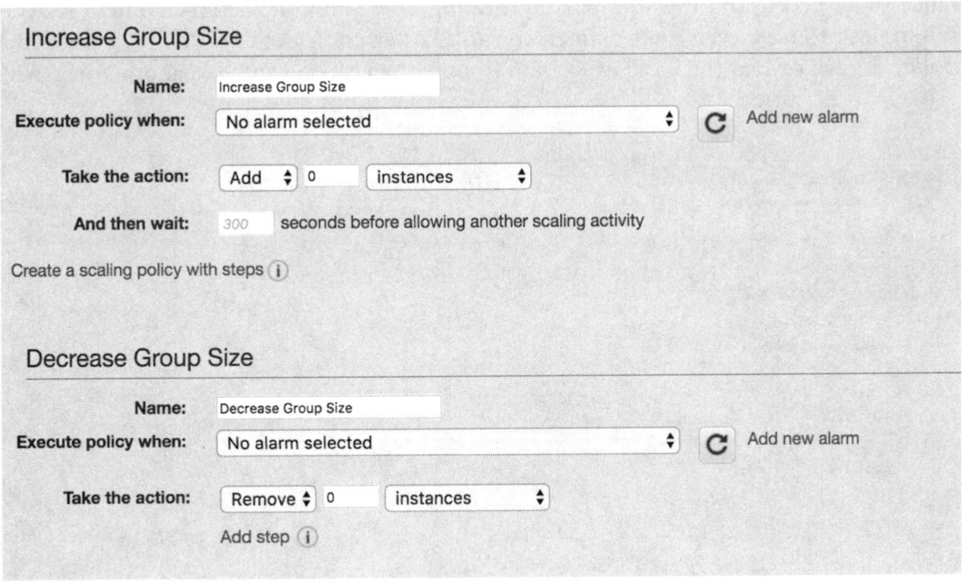

Figure 6-4   Simple scaling policy

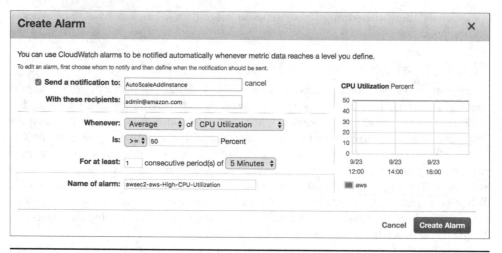

Figure 6-5 Creating an alarm

look at the top of Figure 6-6, you will see that I have chosen from one to six instances; therefore, the maximum instances I can scale up to is 6.

Simple Scaling with Steps

With simple scaling, as we have discussed, you can scale up or down based on the occurrence of an event, and every time Auto Scaling does the same action. Sometimes you might need to have even finer-grained control. For example, let's say you have defined a policy that says when the CPU utilization is more than 50 percent, add another instance.

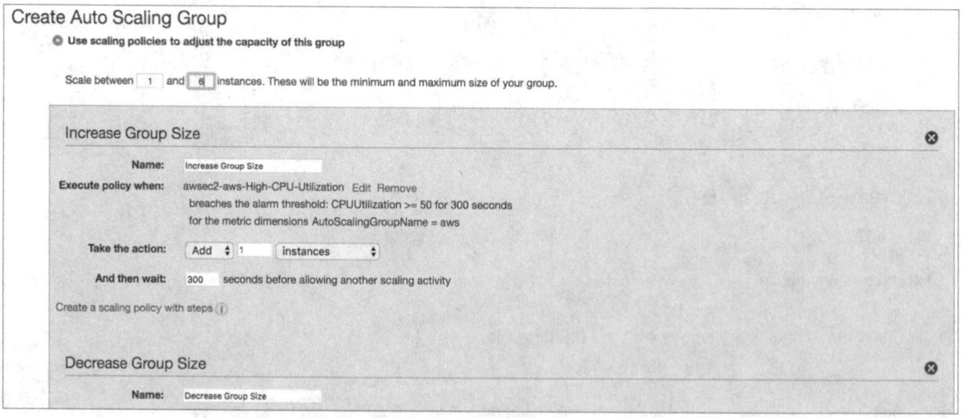

Figure 6-6 Simple scaling policy with all the parameters

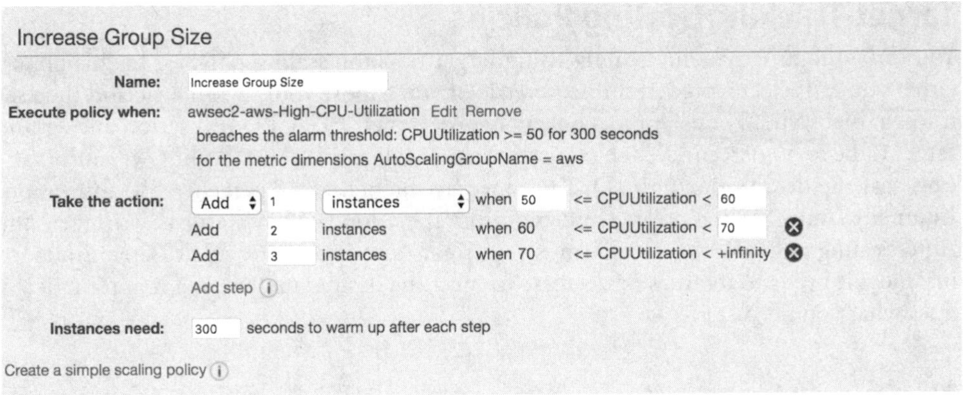

Increase Group Size

Name:	Increase Group Size
Execute policy when:	awsec2-aws-High-CPU-Utilization Edit Remove
	breaches the alarm threshold: CPUUtilization >= 50 for 300 seconds
	for the metric dimensions AutoScalingGroupName = aws

Take the action: Add ▲▼ 1 instances ▼ when 50 <= CPUUtilization < 60
           Add 2 instances when 60 <= CPUUtilization < 70 ✕
           Add 3 instances when 70 <= CPUUtilization < +infinity ✕
           Add step ⓘ

Instances need: 300 seconds to warm up after each step

Create a simple scaling policy ⓘ

Figure 6-7   Simple scaling with steps

However, you can have even more control. Specifically, you can specify that when the CPU utilization is between 50 percent to 60 percent, add two more instances, and when the CPU utilization is 60 percent or more, add four more instances. If you want to do this kind of advanced configuration, simple scaling with steps is the solution. With simple scaling with steps, you do everything just like simple scaling, but in the end you add a few more steps. Figure 6-6 showed the option Creating A Scaling Policy With Steps. Once you click this, the Add Step button is enabled, and from there you can define the additional steps, as shown in Figure 6-7.

When you are doing the scaling up or down using simple scaling or simple scaling with steps, you can change the capacity in the following ways:

- **Exact capacity**   You can provide the exact capacity to increase or decrease. For example, if the current capacity of the group is two instances and the adjustment is four, Auto Scaling changes the capacity to four instances when the policy is executed.

- **Chance in capacity**   You can increase or decrease the current capacity by providing a specific number. For example, if the current capacity of the group is two instances and the adjustment is four, Auto Scaling changes the capacity to six instances when the policy is executed.

- **Percentage change in capacity**   You can also increase or decrease the current capacity by providing a certain percentage of capacity. For example, if your current capacity is 10 instances and the adjustment is 20 percent when the policy runs, Auto Scaling adds two more instances, making it a total of 12. Please note that since in this case it is a percentage, the resulting number will not always be an integer, and Auto Scaling will round off the number to the nearest digit. Values greater than 1 are rounded down. For example, 13.5 is rounded to 13. Values between 0 and 1 are rounded to 1. For example, .77 is rounded to 1. Values between 0 and −1 are rounded to −1. For, example, −.72 is rounded to −1. Values less than −1 are rounded up. For example, −8.87 is rounded to −8.

Target-Tracking Scaling Policies

You can configure dynamic scaling using target-tracking scaling policies. In this policy, either you can select a predetermined metric or you choose your own metric and then set it to a target value. For example, you can choose a metric of CPU utilization and set the target value to 50 percent. When you create a policy like this, Auto Scaling will automatically scale up or scale down the EC2 instances to maintain a 40 percent CPU utilization. Internally, Auto Scaling creates and monitors the CloudWatch alarm that triggers the Auto Scaling policy. Once the alarm is triggered, Auto Scaling calculates the number of instances it needs to increase or decrease to meet the desired metric, and it automatically does what you need.

Termination Policy

Auto Scaling allows you to scale up as well as scale down. When you scale down, your EC2 instances are terminated; therefore, it is important to shut down in a graceful manner so that you have better control. You can decide how exactly you are going to terminate the EC2 servers when you have to scale down. Say, for example, that you are running a total of six EC2 instances across two AZs. In other words, there are three instances in each AZ. Now you want to terminate one AZ. Since in this case the instances are pretty much balanced across these two AZs, terminating any one of them from any one of the AZs should be fine. If you have to terminate two instances, it is important to shut down instances from each AZ so that you can have a balanced configuration. It should not happen that you are going to terminate two servers from a single AZ; then you would have three servers running from one AZ and one server running from a second AZ, making it an unbalanced configuration.

You can configure termination policies to terminate an instance. The termination policy determines which EC2 instance you are going to shut down first. When you terminate a machine, it deregisters itself from the load balancer, if any, and then it waits for the grace period, if any, so that any connections opened to that instance will be drained. Then the policy terminates the instance.

There could be multiple ways you can write down termination policies. One way would be to determine what is the longest running server you have in your fleet and then terminate it. The advantage of this is that since you're running the server for the longest time, it may be possible the server might not have been patched, or there might be some memory leaks happening on the server and so on.

You can also terminate the servers that are close to billing an hour. By terminating these servers, you are going to extract the maximum benefit from the Auto Scaling feature. For example, if you have two servers and one of them has been running for just five minutes and another one has been running for around 54 minutes, terminating the one that has been running for 54 minutes gives you more value for the money.

 NOTE AWS has now moved to a new billing model that is based on paying per second for certain instance types along with pay per hour. You should be aware of both concepts.

You can also terminate the oldest launch configuration. If you are running servers with some older version of AMIs and you were thinking of changing them, then it makes sense to get rid of the launch configuration and create a new launch configuration with the latest version of AMIs. Of course, if you remove the launch configuration, there is no impact on the running servers; only the new servers are going to reflect the change.

Elastic Load Balancing

ELB - Scoped at VPC level
Highly Avail in a region —

As you are probably aware, in an on-premise environment, the load balancer is a physical hardware that is responsible for routing the traffic and balancing the workload across multiple servers. Many applications use a load balancer in front of web servers to route the traffic, balance the workload, and provide the elasticity. But it is often seen that sometimes the load balancer itself becomes a single point of failure. What happens when your physical load balancer fails? Of course, the underlying application goes down until the load balancer is replaced. In addition, there are some additional challenges for managing the traditional load balancer. For example, you need to manually add or remove a server from the load balancer. The traditional load balancer is not capable of adding a new server dynamically if the traffic goes up. AWS Elastic Load Balancing is a fully managed service that solves all these problems for you. Elastic Load Balancing automatically distributes incoming application traffic across the multiple applications, microservices, and containers hosted on Amazon EC2 instances.

These are the advantages of Elastic Load Balancing:

- **Elastic** The biggest advantage of ELB is it is automatically scalable. You don't have to do anything manually when you are adding or deleting the instances; there is no manual intervention at all. In the traditional on-premise environment, when you deploy a load balancer you always have to configure it manually. For example, if you're planning to hook up the load balancer to ten different servers, you have to configure every server with the load balancer. Similarly, when you have to take a server down from the load balancer, you need to do that manually.

- **Integrated** ELB is integrated with various AWS services. As discussed previously in this chapter, ELB's integration with Auto Scaling helps to scale the EC2 instances and workload distribution. The integration plays a vital role since ELB and Auto Scaling are integrated; therefore, whenever a new server is started by Auto Scaling, it automatically gets registered with Elastic Load Balancing, and whenever the instance is terminated by Auto Scaling, it gets deregistered with Elastic Load Balancing. ELB can also be integrated with CloudWatch from where it gets all the metrics and decides whether to take an instance up or down or what other action to take. ELB can also be integrated with Route 53 for DNS failover.

- **Secured** ELB provides a lot of security features such as integrated certificate management and SSL decryption, port forwarding, and so on. These days, web site operators are expanding encryption across their applications and are often using HTTPS by default to secure all web traffic. ELB is capable of terminating

HTTPS/SSL traffic at the load balancer to avoid having to run the CPU-intensive decryption process on their EC2 instances. This can also help in mitigating a DDoS attack. In addition to this, ELB provides lots of predefined security policies that you can directly use. Just like an EC2 instance, you can also configure security groups for ELB that allows you to control incoming and outgoing traffic for ELB.

- **Highly available** ELB helps you to create the most highly available architecture. Using ELB you can distribute the traffic across Amazon EC2 instances, containers, and IP addresses. Using Elastic Load Balancing, you can deploy applications across multiple AZs and have ELB distribute the traffic across the multiple AZs. By doing this, if one of the AZs goes down, your application continues to run.

- **Cheap** ELB is cheap and cost-effective. If you have to deploy a load balancer in your own premises or even if you're planning to deploy a load balancer across multiple EC2 servers, it is going to cost you a lot. You also save some money on hiring people since a lot of stuff can be automated; for example, Auto Scaling saves network administrators a lot of time.

How ELB Works

Let's understand how a load balancer works. You might be wondering how a load balancer offers high availability. Is there a possibility of ELB going down? Internally, every single Elastic Load Balancing instance utilizes multiple AZs. Even if you do not deploy your application or workload across multiple AZs (which is always recommended), the load balancers that you are going to use will be always deployed across multiple AZs.

In Figure 6-8, you will notice that in the customer VPC, the EC2 instances are deployed in two different AZs. The customer also hooked up an ELB with both the EC2

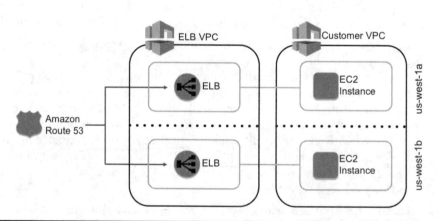

Figure 6-8 High availability for ELB

instances. Internally, there will be multiple load balancers deployed in a separate ELB VPC, spanning multiple AZs to provide a highly available architecture. This part will be transparent to you; you don't have to do anything to configure the high availability for the load balancer. AWS will manage everything for you automatically, and there is no separate charge for that. As a result, you get highly available load balancers with zero overhead of manageability.

Types of Load Balancers

There are three main load balancers that you can leverage using Amazon Web Services, covered next.

Network Load Balancer

TCP load balancer
SSL layer 4

The network load balancer (NLB), or the TCP load balancer, acts in layer 4 of the OSI model. This is basically a connection-based load balancing model. It can handle connections across Amazon EC2 instances, containers, and IP addresses based on IP data. In all cases, all the requests flow through the load balancer; then the load balancer handles those packets and forwards them to the back end as they are received. It does not look inside the packets. It supports both TCP and SSL. In a network load balancer, the client connection is always bound to a server connection, which means whenever a request comes, it will always be bound to a back-end instance. There is no header modification done, which means the load balancer does not make any changes or touch the packet. The network load balancer preserves the client-side source IP address, allowing the back end to see the IP address of the client. There are no X-Forwarded-For headers, proxy protocol prepends, source or destination IP addresses, or ports to request.

TCP + SSL

Application Load Balancer

HTTP + HTTPS   *layer 7*

The application load balancer (ALB) works on layer 7 of the OSI model. It supports HTTP and HTTPS. Whenever a package comes from an application, it looks at its header and then decides the course of action. The connection is terminated at the load balancer and pooled to the server. Multiple connections are opened in the server, and whenever the load balancer receives the requests, it forwards them using the connection pool. In the case of an application load balancer, the headers might be modified. For example, a header might be inserted, such as the X-Forwarded-For header containing the client IP address. The ALB is capable of doing content-based routing, which means if your application consists of multiple services, it can route to a specific service as per the content of the request. You can also do *host-based routing*, where you route a client request based on the Host field of the HTTP header, and *path-based routing*, where you can route a client request based on the URL path of the HTTP header.

Classic Load Balancer

The classic load balancer supports the classic EC2 instances. It supports both network and application load balancing. In other words, it operates on layer 4 as well as on layer 7 of the OSI model. If you are not using the classic EC2 instances, then you should use either an application or a network load balancer depending on your use case.

The X-Forwarded-For request header helps you identify the IP address of a client when you use an HTTP or HTTPS load balancer. Because load balancers intercept traffic between clients and servers, your server access logs contain only the IP address of the load balancer. To see the IP address of the client, use the X-Forwarded-For request header. Elastic Load Balancing stores the IP address of the client in the X-Forwarded-For request header and passes the header to your server.

Table 6-1 compares the features of all three types of load balancers.

You can configure a load balancer to be either external facing or internal facing. The load balancer is accessed from the Internet; it is called an *external load balancer*.

only balances classic EC2 instances on way out

Feature	Application Load Balancer	Network Load Balancer	Classic Load Balancer
Protocols	HTTP, HTTPS	TCP	TCP, SSL, HTTP, HTTPS
Platforms	VPC	VPC	EC2-Classic, VPC
Health checks	✔	✔	✔
CloudWatch metrics	✔	✔	✔
Logging	✔	✔	✔
Zonal fail-over	✔	✔	✔
Connection draining (deregistration delay)	✔	✔	✔
Load balancing to multiple ports on the same instance	✔	✔	
WebSockets	✔	✔	
IP addresses as targets	✔	✔	
Load balancer deletion protection	✔	✔	
Path-based routing	✔		
Host-based routing	✔		
Native HTTP/2	✔		
Configurable idle connection timeout	✔		✔
Cross-zone load balancing	✔		✔
SSL offloading	✔		✔
Sticky sessions	✔		✔
Back-end server encryption	✔		✔
Static IP		✔	
Elastic IP address		✔	
Preserve source IP address		✔	

Table 6-1 Comparison of the Three Types of Load Balancers

When the load balancer does not have any Internet access and rather is used internally, say to load balance a couple of instances running on a private subnet, then it is called an *internal load balancer*. Load balancers in EC2-Classic are always Internet-facing load balancers. When you create a load balancer within a VPC, you can either make it external facing or internal facing. To create an external-facing load balancer, you need to create it within the public subnet, and to create an internal-facing load balancer, you need to configure it for the private subnet.

external-facing-lb → within public subnet
internal-facing-lb → " private

Load Balancer Key Concepts and Terminology

As discussed previously, the load balancers are fully managed, scalable, and highly available. The application load balancer supports content-based routing; therefore, the biggest benefit from it is that it allows for multiple applications to be hosted behind a single load balancer. Let's see an example to understand this. In a classic load balancer, you can host only one application per ELB. If you wanted to host multiple applications, you had to use DNS. Say you have an application that takes care of all the orders on your web site, and you have another application that takes care of all the images of your web site. In this case, you would hook up two load balancers: one for the orders and another for the images. Then you use DNS to resolve. So, when you go to orders.example.com from a web browser, the DNS routes it to the application hosting the orders, and when you go to images.example.com in your browser, the application routes it to the application hosting the images. In this case, you have managed to load balance, as well as pay for two separate load balancers. See Figure 6-9.

Figure 6-9

Using two different load balancers for two applications

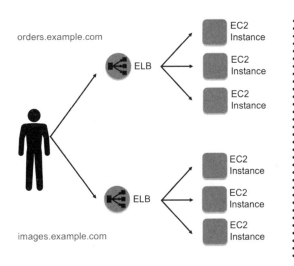

Now with the application load balancer in the same example, if you have orders in part of example.com, the load balancer does path-based routing, and it will reroute the traffic to the application hosting the orders. Similarly, if you have images in the path, it will route you to the application hosting the images. So, you are not using multiple load balancers here; rather, you are using just one load balancer and routing it to the respective application using path-based routing. This is shown in Figure 6-10.

Using path-based routing, you can have up to ten different sets of rules, which means you can host up to ten applications using one load balancer. The biggest benefit of this is you are paying only for one load balancer instead of ten, and of course you're managing only one load balancer.

The application load balancer provides native support for microservice and container-based architectures. Instances can be registered with multiple ports, allowing for requests to be routed to multiple containers on a single instance. In the case of classic EC2, you register an instance with the load balancer with an API. If you try to reregister that instance again, the system tells you that the instance is already registered and cannot be registered. With the application load balancer, you can register an instance with different ports multiple times. This is really helpful when you are running a container-based application because containers often give dynamic ports, and you can register any of the ports with an application load balancer. If you use Amazon ECS, it takes care of the register tasks automatically with the load balancer using a dynamic port mapping. Even if you are running a container but running multiple applications in multiple ports, you can register all of them in the load balancer since the port is different. You can even balance the load across multiple containers as well as across multiple EC2 instances using the application load balancer. Also, if you use containers instead of EC2 instances, you save more cost because for many of the use cases, you may not need a T2 micro instance; you can save the CPU cycles and don't have to pay for it. This is shown in Figure 6-11.

Figure 6-10
Using one
load balancer
for different
applications

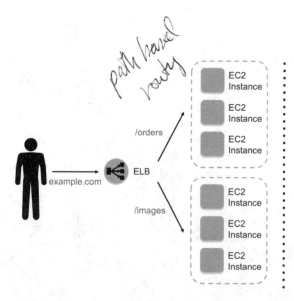

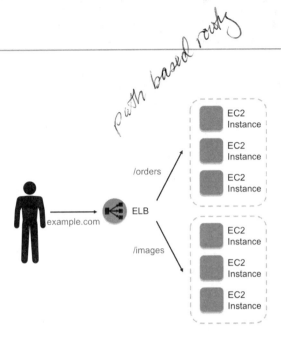

Figure 6-11
Load balancing
across EC2
and ECS

Now let's understand the core components of the load balancer.

Listeners

Listeners define the protocol and port on which the load balancer listens for incoming connections. Each load balancer needs at least one listener to accept incoming traffic and can support up to ten listeners. You can define all the routing rules on the listener. In the previous example of routing, where you used path-based routing, the routing was defined in the listener. For application load balancing, the listener supports the HTTP and HTTPS protocols, and for a network load balancer, the listener supports the TCP protocol. For both ALB and NLB, the ports between 1 and 65535 are supported. You can use WebSockets with your HTTP, HTTPS, and TCP listeners. Application load balancers also provide native support for HTTP/2 with HTTPS listeners. Using one HTTP/2 connection, you can send up to 128 requests in parallel. The load balancer converts these to individual HTTP/1.1 requests and distributes them across the healthy targets in the target group using the round-robin routing algorithm.

Target Groups and Target

The target groups are logical groupings of targets behind a load balancer. Target groups can exist independently from the load balancer. You can create a target group and keep it ready; you can keep on adding resources to the target group and may not immediately add it with the load balancer. You can associate it with a load balancer when needed. The target groups are regional constructs, which means you can allocate resources from only one region in a target group. The target group can be associated with the Auto Scaling group as well.

The target is a logical load balancing target, which can be an EC2 instance, microservice, or container-based application for an application load balancer and instance or an IP address for a network load balancer. When the target type is IP, you can specify IP addresses from one of the following CIDR blocks:

- The subnets of the VPC for the target group
- 10.0.0.0/8 (RFC 1918)
- 100.64.0.0/10 (RFC 6598)
- 172.16.0.0/12 (RFC 1918)
- 192.168.0.0/16 (RFC 1918)

EC2 instances can be registered with the same target group using multiple ports. A single target can be registered with multiple target groups.

Rules

Rules provide the link between listeners and target groups and consist of conditions and actions. When a request meets the condition of the rule, the associated action is taken. Rules can forward requests to a specified target group. In the previous example, you use a rule whenever you see an image in the path and route it to the application hosting the image. This is called a *path-based rule*. Whenever you do a path-based rule, the conditions have to be specified in the path pattern format. A path pattern is case sensitive, can be up to 128 characters in length, and can contain any of the following characters:

- A–Z, a–z, 0–9
- _ - . $ / ~ " ' @ : +
- & (using &)
- (matches zero or more characters)
- ? (matches exactly one character)

When you create a listener by default, it has a rule; however, you can add additional rules. The default rule does not have any conditions attached to it. Each rule has a priority attached to it.

The rule with the highest priority will be executed first, and the one with the lowest priority will be executed at the end. The default rule has the lowest-priority value; hence, it is evaluated last. Currently, the rule supports only one kind of action, which is forward; this forwards requests to the target group. There are two types of rule conditions: host and path. When the conditions for a rule are met, then its action is taken.

As of the writing of this book, load balancers can support up to ten rules. Support for 100 rules is on the road map of AWS.

Figure 6-12 shows the relationship between the listeners, target groups, targets, and rules.

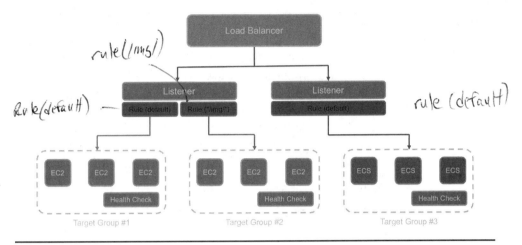

Figure 6-12 Relationship between listeners, target groups, targets, and rules

Health Check

When you consider a load balancer, you want to make sure the application it supports is highly available. To do so, you need to run a health check, which is going to check the target or target group at a certain interval of time defined by you to make sure the target or the target group is working fine. If any of the targets have issues, then health checks allow for traffic to be shifted away from the impaired or failed instances. For example, if your load balancer is hooked up to four EC2 instances and one of them has a spike in CPU usage, the health check will keep on failing. When this happens, the instance will be taken off the load balancer, and all the traffic will be redirected to a difference EC2 instance. If the server becomes healthy, the health check will pass, and the load balancer will redirect the traffic to that instance. If the server does not become healthy and the health check keeps on failing, then it will be replaced by a new EC2 instance.

For the interval at which the load balancer sent a check request switch, the target is called HealthCheckIntervalSeconds. With the health check request, you specify the port, protocol, and ping path. If the target responds before the response times out, the shell check is successful. If it does not respond and exceeds the threshold for consecutive failed responses, the load balancer marks it as a failure and takes the target out of service. You can customize the frequency, failure thresholds, and list of successful response codes. If there is a failure, then the detailed reasons for health check failures are now returned via the API and displayed in the AWS Management Console.

The application load balancer supports HTTP and HTTPS health checks, whereas the network load balancer supports TCP health checks.

The results of the health check can have the possible values shown in Table 6-2.

	Value	Description
Table 6-2 Various Health Check Status	Initial	The load balancer is in the process of registering the target or performing the initial health checks on the target.
	Healthy	The target is healthy.
	Unhealthy	The target did not respond to a health check or failed the health check.
	Unused	The target is not registered with a target group, the target group is not used in a listener rule for the load balancer, or the target is in an availability zone that is not enabled for the load balancer.
	Draining	The target is deregistering, and connection draining is in process.

Using Multiple AZs

Whenever you're building an application with Auto Scaling and ELB, it is recommended that you use multiple AZs whenever possible. This helps you craft a highly available architecture. Since ELB can distribute the traffic equally across multiple AZs, then why not leverage this feature and get the best out of the AWS ecosystem? Internally ELB always runs from multiple AZs, so even if one of the AZs goes down, there won't be any impact to Elastic Load Balancing since the traffic will be routed via a load balancer sitting in a different AZ. The DNS will route the traffic via a different AZ. So, if your application sits on only one AZ, if the AZ goes down, your application will fail but not the ELB. Figure 6-13 shows the routing of the ELB traffic via a different ELB.

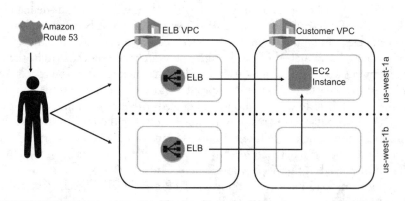

Figure 6-13   Routing of ELB via a different AZ

Now let's see an example when you run your application on a single AZ or on multiple AZs. So, you have an application that is running on six servers; if you run this application from a single AZ and it goes down, then your application goes down.

If you run this application from two different AZs, then you could be running three servers from each AZ. Now if one of the AZs goes down, you lose 50 percent of the capacity. In that case, you can quickly use Auto Scaling to spin off the new instance. In some cases, it can be possible that you are running a critical application and you cannot even afford to lose 50 percent of the capacity. In that case, you will provision six servers on each AZ to make sure even if one of the AZ goes down you are running with 100 percent of the capacity.

Now let's say you are going to use three different AZs to build your application. In this case, you will be running two instances from each AZ. Now if one of the AZ goes down, you will lose 33 percent of the resource, which means you are going to lose only two servers. In the same scenario of high availability, where you cannot afford to have any downtime, you are going to provision three servers at each AZ, so in the event of one of the AZs going down, you still will be running with six instances. In this scenario, you are deploying nine servers across three AZs, whereas in the previous scenario of two AZs, you have to deploy 12 servers across two AZs. So, sometimes deploying the applications in more AZs ends up being cheaper, as shown in Figure 6-14.

NOTE When you dynamically scale up or scale down, it is important to maintain the state information of the session. If you maintain that in the EC2 servers and that server goes down, you lose all the information. If you maintain the session information in the EC2 server and even one user is connected with that EC2 server, you can't take it down. Therefore, it is recommended you maintain the state information outside the EC2 servers so that Auto Scaling can dynamically scale up and down the EC2 servers. DynamoDB is a great way to maintain the session state that you should consider while designing the architecture.

Figure 6-14
Single AZ vs. two
AZs vs. three AZs

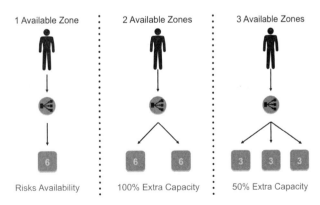

Sometimes using multiple AZs may have some issues or challenges such as if you are using a Java-based application. Often the application caches the server IP address in the DNS, and as a result, it redirects the traffic to the same instance every time. This causes an imbalance in the instance capacity since the proper load distribution does not happen. *Cross-zone load balancing* solves that problem.

Cross-zone load balancing distributes the requests evenly across multiple availability zones. Cross-zone load balancing is enabled by default in an application load balancer, and you don't have to do anything manually to configure it. If you are using a classic load balancer, you need to configure this manually if you are using an API or CLI to create the load balancer. If you are using the console to create the classic load balancer, this option is selected by default. With network load balancers, each load balancer node distributes traffic across the registered targets in its availability zone only. Moreover, there is no additional bandwidth charge for cross-zone traffic, so you don't have to pay anything extra for the data transfer across multiple AZs. This is useful when you are using ALB across multiple AZs.

Please note the cross-zone load balancing happens across the targets and not at the AZ level. Let's see an example to understand this. Say you have an imbalanced configuration with one instance running in one AZ and three instances running in the second AZ, and you have hooked up an ALB with both the AZs across all the four targets (instances). Now with cross-zone load balancing, the workload will be distributed equally across the four instances and not equally within the two AZs. This ensures that all the instances you have get an equal share of work.

In the case of the application load balancer, when the load balancer receives a request, it checks the priority order from the listener rule to determine which rule to apply. Once it decides which rule to apply, it selects a target from the target group and applies the action of the rule using a round-robin algorithm. The routing is performed independently for each target group, and it doesn't matter if the target is registered with multiple target groups.

In the case of a network load balancer, the load balancer receives a request and selects a target from the target group for the default rule using a flow hash algorithm, based on the protocol, source IP address, source port, destination IP address, and destination port. This provides session stickiness from the same source to the same destination for the traffic. With a sticky session, you can instruct the load balancer to route repeated requests to the same EC2 instance whenever possible. The advantage of this is that the EC2 instance can cache the user data locally for better performance.

With classic load balancers, the load balancer node that receives the request selects the least outstanding request's routing algorithm for HTTP and HTTPS listeners and selects a registered instance using the round-robin routing algorithm for TCP listeners.

Lab 6-1: Set Up Auto Scaling

In this lab, you will be doing the following:

- Create a launch configuration
- Create an Auto Scaling group
- Configure Auto Scaling notifications that are triggered when instance resources become too high or too low
- Create policies to scale up or scale down the number of currently running instances in response to changes in resource utilization

  1. Log in to the AWS console and select the desired region where you want to want your instances to be started.

  2. From the Services main page, select EC2.

  3. In the menu on the left, scroll down until you see Auto Scaling.

  4. Click Launch Configurations and then click Create Auto Scaling Group.

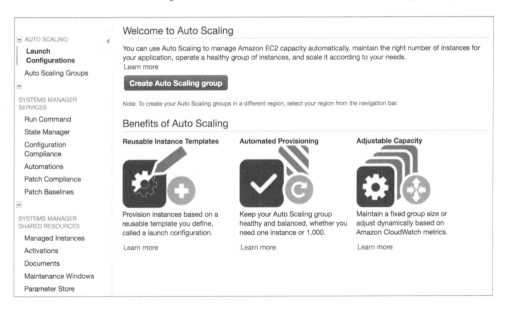

5. You will see this option if you have not created any Auto Scaling group previously. If you created an Auto Scaling group earlier, clicking Launch Configurations will take to a screen where you need to click Create Launch Configuration.

6. Click Create Launch Configuration.

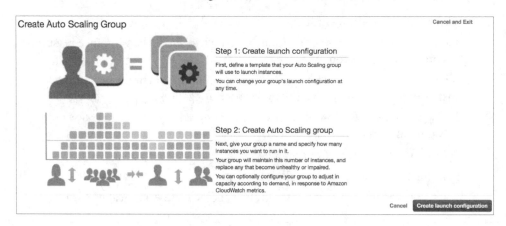

7. The Create Launch Configuration screen will be displayed.

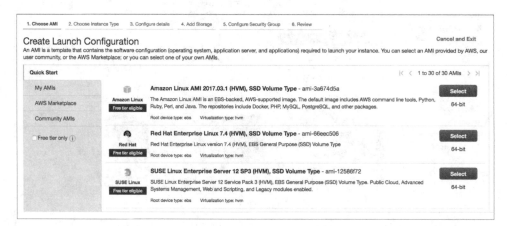

8. Select the AMI from where your EC2 instances will be started. Select Amazon Linux AMI, and on the next screen choose the t2.micro instance since it belongs to the free tier.

9. On the next screen, you need to provide the name of the launch configuration. Choose a unique name for your launch configuration. In this example, the name is AWS SA Book. Leave all other fields at the defaults and click Next. The next few screens will be exactly like that of creating an EC2 instance. You need to provide all the other details such as adding storage, configuring the security group, and so on. After providing all the details, click Create Launch Configuration.

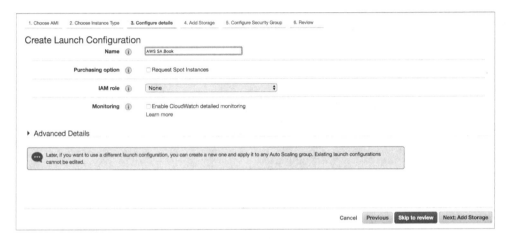

10. The system will prompt you to download the keys. If you already have a key pair, you can reuse it, or you can create a new one from this screen and then download it.

11. The system will now prompt you to create the Auto Scaling group. You need to provide the unique group name and group size (which is the number of instances the group should have at any time); this is also known as the desired capacity. For this example, enter **2** as the value for Start With *x* Instances. In the Network field, put the VPC name where you want this Auto Scaling group to run, and in the Subnet field, put the subnet details where you want the EC2 instances to be launched. In this example, I have chosen two different subnets across two different AZs. This is important because this is how you run the EC2 instances across multiple AZs using Auto Scaling.

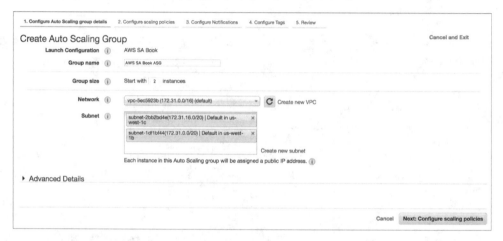

12. The next step is to configure the scaling policies. In this case, you will create a simple scaling policy. Select the option Use Scaling Policies to adjust the capacity of this group. Click Create A Simple Scaling Policy. For the option Scale Between *x* And *x* Instances, choose between 2 and 4. This will be the minimum size and maximum size of your group.

13. Create an alarm, as shown in Figure 6-5, for both scaling up and scaling down policy.

14. Now you need to create the two scaling policies. First, create the scaling up policy, and then create the scaling down policy. For increasing the group size, choose CPU as a metric and use a number greater than or equal to 60 percent CPU utilization. Set to add one instance and wait for 300 seconds before allowing another scaling activity. Similarly, create another policy for scaling down, choose the metric CPU, and select less than equal to 20 percent, and set the action of removing an instance.

15. The next step is to add a notification. In the field Send A Notification Topic, enter the topic **Auto Scale test**. For these recipients, put your e-mail address, and select all the check boxes: Launch, Terminate, Fail To Launch, and Fail To Terminate. Click Next.

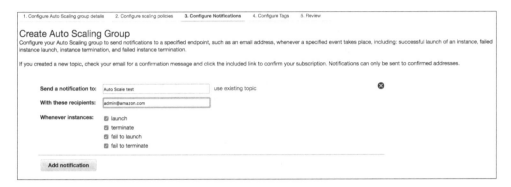

16. Now configure the tags. By using the tags, you should be able to uniquely identify the EC2 instances created by Auto Scaling. In the Key field, type the name, and in the Value field type **EC2AutoScaleLab**.

17. Click Review. This screen will show you all the options you have chosen. If it looks good, click Create Auto Scaling Group.

18. Once you click Create Auto Scaling Group, your Auto Scaling group will be created for you and will start two EC2 instances as part of the initial group.

19. Now log in to both instances and run the following command, which will increase your CPU, from the terminal:

```
stress --cpu 2 --timeout 600
```

20. Open another terminal and monitor using the top command. Once the CPU has spiked, keep monitoring your console. You will see that another EC2 instance will be started by the Auto Scaling group. Also, the moment the CPU spikes up to 60 percent, you will get an e-mail alert that the CPU is more than 60 percent. Similarly, you will get another e-mail notification when Auto Scaling has launched another instance. Now kill the command, and the CPU will go down. Observe from the console that Auto Scaling is going to shut down a server for you, and again you will get an e-mail notification.

Chapter Review

In this chapter, you learned that Auto Scaling is the technology that allows you to scale your workload automatically up and down based on the rules you define. Auto Scaling can be integrated with various AWS services. The most popular use case is with EC2. To use Auto Scaling for an EC2 instance, you need to create a launch configuration, which stores all the information about the instance such as the AMI details, instance type, key pair, security group, IAM instance profile, user data, storage attached, and so on. Then you create an Auto Scaling group, where you define the logic for scaling up and scaling down. It has all the rules and policies that govern how the EC2 instances will be terminated or started. To create an Auto Scaling group, you also need to define the minimum and maximum EC2 instances.

There are three types of scaling policy that you can have.

- **Simple scaling**   Using simple scaling, you can scale up or down on the basis of only one scaling adjustment. In this mechanism, you select an alarm, which can be either CPU utilization, disk read, disk write, network in, network out, and so on.

- **Simple scaling with steps**   With simple scaling with steps, you do everything just like simple scaling, but in the end you add a few more steps.

- **Target-tracking scaling policy**   In this policy, either you can select a predetermined metric or you choose your own metric and then set it to a target value. For example, you can choose the metric CPU utilization and set the target value to 50 percent.

You also learned about Elastic Load Balancing. Elastic Load Balancing balances the workload across multiple EC2 instances. There are three main load balancers you can leverage using Amazon Web Services.

- **Network load balancer**   This is also known as a TCP load balancer. It acts in the layer 4 of OSI model. This is basically a connection-based load balancing model.

- **Application load balancer**   The application load balancer works on layer 7 of the OSI model. It supports HTTP and HTTPS.
- **Classic load balancer**   The classic load balancer supports the classic EC2 instances.

Questions

[handwritten notes: Launch Config - What / Auto Scaly Grp - Where / Auto Scaling Policy - How / Launch Config] mand. / AS Grp]

1. Where do you define the details of the type of servers to be launched when launching the servers using Auto Scaling?

   A. Auto Scaling group

   B. Launch configuration

   C. Elastic Load Balancer

   D. Application load balancer

2. What happens when the Elastic Load Balancing fails the health check? (Choose the best answer.)

   A. The Elastic Load Balancing fails over to a different load balancer.

   B. The Elastic Load Balancing keeps on trying until the instance comes back online.

   C. The Elastic Load Balancing cuts off the traffic to that instance and starts a new instance.

   D. The load balancer starts a bigger instance.

3. When you create an Auto Scaling mechanism for a server, which two things are mandatory? (Choose two.)

   A. Elastic Load Balancing

   B. Auto Scaling group

   C. DNS resolution

   D. Launch configuration

4. You have configured a rule that whenever the CPU utilization of your EC2 goes up, Auto Scaling is going to start a new server for you. Which tool is Auto Scaling using to monitor the CPU utilization?

   A. CloudWatch metrics.

   B. Output of the top command.

   C. The ELB health check metric.

   D. It depends on the operating system. Auto Scaling uses the OS-native tool to capture the CPU utilization.

5. The listener within a load balancer needs two details in order to listen to incoming traffic. What are they? (Choose two.)

    A. Type of the operating system

    B. Port number

    C. Protocol

    D. IP address

6. Which load balancer is not capable of doing the health check?

    A. Application load balancer

    B. Network load balancer

    C. Classic load balancer

    D. None of the above

7. If you want your request to go to the same instance to get the benefits of caching the content, what technology can help provide that objective?

    A. Sticky session

    B. Using multiple AZs

    C. Cross-zone load balancing

    D. Using one ELB per instance

8. You are architecting an internal-only application. How can you make sure the ELB does not have any Internet access?

    A. You detach the Internet gateway from the ELB.

    B. You create the instances in the private subnet and hook up the ELB with that.

    C. The VPC should not have any Internet gateway attached.

    D. When you create the ELB from the console, you can define whether it is internal or external.

9. Which of the following is a true statement? (Choose two.)

    A. ELB can distribute traffic across multiple regions.

    B. ELB can distribute across multiple AZs but not across multiple regions.

    C. ELB can distribute across multiple AZs.

    D. ELB can distribute traffic across multiple regions but not across multiple AZs.

10. How many EC2 instances can you have in an Auto Scaling group?

    A. 10.

    B. 20.

    C. 100.

    D. There is no limit to the number of EC2 instances you can have in the Auto Scaling group.

Answers

1. **B**. You define the type of servers to be launched in the launch configuration. The Auto Scaling group is used to define the scaling policies, Elastic Load Balancing is used to distribute the traffic across multiple instances, and the application load balancer is used to distribute the HTTP/HTTS traffic at OSI layer 7.

2. **C**. When Elastic Load Balancing fails over, it is an internal mechanism that is transparent to end users. Elastic Load Balancing keeps on trying, but if the instance does not come back online, it starts a new instance. It does not wait indefinitely for that instance to come back online. The load balancer starts the new instance, which is defined in the launch configuration. It is going to start the same type of instance unless you have manually changed the launch configuration to start a bigger type of instance.

3. **B**, **D**. The launch configuration and the Auto Scaling group are mandatory.

4. **A**. Auto Scaling relies on the CloudWatch metrics to find the CPU utilization. Using the top command or the native OS tools, you should be able to identify the CPU utilization, but Auto Scaling does not use that.

5. **B**, **C**. Listeners define the protocol and port on which the load balancer listens for incoming connections.

6. **D**. All the load balancers are capable of doing a health check.

7. **A**. Using multiple AZs, you can distribute your load across multiple AZs, but you can't direct the request to go to same instance. Cross-zone load balancing is used to bypass caching. Using one ELB per instance is going to complicate things.

8. **D**. You can't attach or detach an Internet gateway with ELB, even if you create the instances in private subnet, and if you create an external-facing ELB instance, it will have Internet connectivity. The same applies for VPC; even if you take an IG out of the VPC but create ELB as external facing, it will still have Internet connectivity.

9. **B**, **C**. ELB can span multiple AZs within a region. It cannot span multiple regions.

10. **D**. There is no limit to the number of EC2 instances you can have in the Auto Scaling group. However, there might an EC2 limitation in your account that can be increased by logging a support ticket.

Deploying and Monitoring Applications on AWS

In this chapter, you will

- Learn about serverless applications
- Be introduced to AWS Lambda
- Learn about API Gateway
- Learn about Amazon Kinesis Data Steams, Amazon Kinesis Data Firehose, and Amazon Kinesis Data Analytics
- Explore Amazon CloudFront, Amazon Route 53, and AWS WAF
- Learn about AWS SQS, SNS, and Step Functions
- Learn about Elastic Beanstalk and AWS OpsWorks
- Understand Amazon Cognito
- Learn about Amazon Elastic MapReduce
- Learn about AWS CloudFormation
- Learn how to monitor the AWS services by exploring the monitoring services such as Amazon CloudWatch, AWS CloudTrail, AWS Config, VPC Flow Logs, and AWS Trusted Advisor
- Learn how to manage multiple AWS accounts using AWS Organization

[handwritten note: SWF - simple workflow service. step Function → replacement for SWF]

AWS Lambda

When you're building applications, you want them to deliver a great experience for your users. Maybe you want your application to generate in-app purchase options during a gaming session, rapidly validate street address updates, or make image thumbnails available instantly after a user uploads photos. To make this magic happen, your application needs back-end code that runs in response to events such as image uploads, in-app activity, web site clicks, or censor outputs. But managing the infrastructure to host and execute back-end code requires you to size, provision, and scale a bunch of servers; manage operating system updates; apply security patches; and then monitor all this infrastructure for performance and availability. Wouldn't it be nice if you could just focus on building great applications without having to spend a lot of time managing servers?

AWS Lambda is a compute service that runs your back-end code in response to events such as object uploads to Amazon S3 buckets, updates to Amazon DynamoDB tables, data in Amazon Kinesis Data Streams, or in-app activity. Once you upload your code to AWS Lambda, the service handles all the capacity, scaling, patching, and administration of the infrastructure to run your code and provides visibility into performance by publishing real-time metrics and logs to Amazon CloudWatch. All you need to do is write the code.

AWS Lambda is low cost and does not require any up-front investment. When you use AWS Lambda, you're simply charged a low fee per request and for the time your code runs, measured in increments of 100 milliseconds. Getting started with AWS Lambda is easy; there are no new language tools or frameworks to learn, and you can use any third-party library and even native ones. The code you run on AWS Lambda is called a *Lambda function*. You just upload your code as a ZIP file or design it in the integrated development environment in the AWS Management Console, or you can select prebuilt samples from a list of functions for common use cases such as image conversion, file compression, and change notifications. Also, built-in support for the AWS SDK makes it easy to call other AWS services. Once your function is loaded, you select the event source to monitor such as an Amazon S3 bucket or Amazon DynamoDB table, and within a few seconds AWS Lambda will be ready to trigger your function automatically when an event occurs. With Lambda, any event can trigger your function, making it easy to build applications that respond quickly to new information.

Is AWS Lambda Really Serverless?

AWS Lambda is a compute service, and the biggest advantage of using AWS Lambda is you don't have to provision or manage any infrastructure. It is a serverless service. I'll first explain what is meant by *serverless*. If the platform is to be considered serverless, it should provide these capabilities at a minimum:

- **No infrastructure to manage**   As the name *serverless* implies, there should not be any infrastructure to manage.

- **Scalability**   You should be able to scale up and down your applications built on the serverless platform seamlessly.

- **Built-in redundancy**   The serverless platform should be highly available at all times.

- **Pay only for usage**   On the serverless platform, you have to pay only when you are using the service; if you are not using the service, you don't have to pay anything. For example, by using Lambda, you are paying only when your code is running. If your code is not running, you don't pay anything.

If you study these four characteristics carefully, you will realize that many AWS services that you have studied elsewhere in the book are serverless. Specifically, these AWS services are serverless:

- Amazon S3
- Amazon DynamoDB

- Amazon API Gateway
- AWS Lambda
- Amazon SNS and SQS
- Amazon CloudWatch Events
- Amazon Kinesis

You may be wondering whether *serverless* is really serverless. Aren't there any servers running behind the scenes? You're right; serverless does not literally mean no servers. There are fleets of EC2 servers running behind the scenes to support the serverless infrastructure. AWS takes care of the provisioning, management, stability, and fault tolerance of the underlying infrastructure. AWS keeps everything ready for you; you just need to use the service. For example, for S3, all the infrastructure is already provisioned; you just need to upload your content. Similarly, for Lambda, you just need to execute your code. Since you don't have to deal with the server infrastructure in the back end, these services are called *serverless*.

implemented in Java/Python/C sharp (C#) Node.js/Go/Ruby/PowerShell

Understanding AWS Lambda

By using AWS Lambda, you get all the benefits obtained via a serverless platform. This means no servers to manage, continuous scaling, built-in redundancy, and a pay-for-usage model. With AWS Lambda, you are charged for every 100ms your code executes and the number of times your code is triggered. This cost is also based on the memory consumption. You don't pay anything when your code isn't running.

With Lambda, you can run code for virtually any type of application or back-end service. Lambda runs and scales your code with high availability. Each Lambda function you create contains the code you want to execute, the configuration that defines how your code is executed, and, optionally, one or more event sources that detect events and invoke your function as they occur.

An event source can be an Amazon SNS function that can trigger the Lambda function, or it can be an API Gateway event (covered in the next section of this book) that can invoke a Lambda function whenever an API method created with API Gateway receives an HTTPS request. There are lots of event sources that can trigger a Lambda function, such as Amazon S3, Amazon DynamoDB, Amazon Kinesis, Amazon CloudWatch, and so on. For the examination, you don't have to remember all the event sources.

Figure 7-1 shows what the simplest architecture of AWS Lambda looks like.

After you have configured an event source, as soon as the event occurs (the event can be an image upload, in-app activity, web site click, and so on), your code is invoked

Figure 7-1
Architecture of a running AWS Lambda function

(as a Lambda function). The code can be anything; it can be business logic or whatever end result you want. You will look at a couple of reference architectures using Lambda in the "Reference Architectures Using Serverless Services" section, which will give you more exposure to various use cases.

You can run as many Lambda functions in parallel as you need; there is no limit to the number of Lambda functions you can run at any particular point of time, and they scale on their own. Lambda functions are "stateless," with no affinity to the underlying infrastructure so that Lambda can rapidly launch as many copies of the function as needed to scale to the rate of incoming events. AWS Lambda allows you to decouple your infrastructure since it provides you with the ability to replace servers with microprocesses. As a result, building microservices using Lambda functions and API Gateway is a great use case.

With AWS Lambda, you can use the normal language and operating system features, such as creating additional threads and processes. The resources allocated to the Lambda function, such as memory, disk, runtime, and network usage, must be shared among all the processes the function uses. The processes can be launched using any language supported by Amazon Linux.

These are the simple steps you need to follow to use AWS Lambda:

1. Upload the code to AWS Lambda in ZIP format.

2. Schedule the Lambda function. Here you can specify how often the function will run or whether the function is driven by an event and, if yes, the source of the event.

3. Specify the compute resource for the event, which can be from 128MB to 3008MB of memory.

4. Specify the timeout period for the event.

5. Specify the Amazon VPC details, if any.

6. You are all set; just launch the function.

Figure 7-2 summarizes how Lambda works.

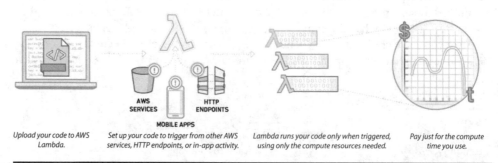

Upload your code to AWS Lambda.   Set up your code to trigger from other AWS services, HTTP endpoints, or in-app activity.   Lambda runs your code only when triggered, using only the compute resources needed.   Pay just for the compute time you use.

Figure 7-2 How AWS Lambda works

AWS Lambda supports the following languages:

- Java
- Node.js
- Python
- C#

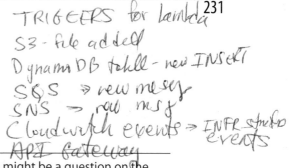

 EXAM TIP Remember these languages; there might be a question on the exam about the languages that AWS Lambda supports.

AWS Lambda Resource Limits per Invocation

It is important to know the resource limits of AWS Lambda so that you can find the right use case for Lambda, as shown in Table 7-1. For example, if you want a job to run for 12 hours, you won't be able to do that via AWS Lambda since the maximum execution duration per request is 300 seconds, or 5 minutes.

Also, there is a limit of 1,000 concurrent executions, but just like any other AWS service, you can increase the service limit by creating a support ticket or case.

Amazon API Gateway

Architecting, deploying, maintaining, and monitoring an API are time-consuming and challenging tasks. If you want to continuously improve as well, this is an even bigger challenge. Often you have to run different versions of the same APIs to maintain the backward compatibility of the APIs for all the clients. The effort required can increase

Resource	Limits
Memory allocation range	Minimum = 128MB Maximum = 3008MB (with 64MB increments) If the maximum memory use is exceeded, the function invocation will be terminated.
Ephemeral disk capacity (/tmp space)	512MB
Number of file descriptors	1,024
Number of processes and threads (combined total)	1,024
Maximum execution duration per request	300 seconds
Lambda function deployment package size (compressed .zip/.jar file)	50MB
Total size of all the deployment packages that can be uploaded per region	75GB

Table 7-1 AWS Lambda Resource Limits per Invocation

depending on which phase of the development cycle you are in (development, testing, or production).

Also, it is important to handle the access authorization aspect for every API. It is a critical feature for all APIs but complex to build and involves repetitive work. When an API is published and becomes successful, the next challenge is to manage, monitor, and monetize the ecosystem of third-party developers utilizing the API.

Other challenges of developing APIs are throttling requests to protect the back end, caching API responses, transforming requests and responses, and generating API definitions. Sometimes documentation with tools adds to the complexity.

Amazon API Gateway not only addresses those challenges but also reduces the operational complexity of creating and maintaining RESTful APIs.

API Gateway is a fully managed service that makes it easy for developers to define, publish, deploy, maintain, monitor, and secure APIs at any scale. Clients integrate with the APIs using standard HTTPS requests. API Gateway serves as a front door (to access data, business logic, or functionality from your back-end services) to any web application running on Amazon EC2, Amazon ECS, AWS Lambda, or on-premises environment. It has specific features and qualities that result in it being a powerful edge for your logic tier. Thus, you can use API Gateway in the following ways:

- To create, deploy, and manage a RESTful API to expose back-end HTTP endpoints, AWS Lambda functions, or other AWS services
- To invoke exposed API methods through the front-end HTTP endpoints

API Gateway is capable of handling all the tasks involved in processing hundreds of thousands of concurrent API calls. It takes care of any problem you have when managing an API. For example, it can do traffic management, it is able to handle the authorization and access control, it can take care of the monitoring aspect, it can do version control, and so on. It has a simple pay-as-you-go pricing model where you pay only for the API calls you receive and the amount of data transferred out. There are no minimum fees or startup costs.

Benefits of Amazon API Gateway

These are some of the benefits that you get by using Amazon API Gateway:

- **Resiliency and performance at any scale**   Amazon API Gateway can manage any amount of traffic with throttling so that back-end operations can withstand traffic spikes. You don't have to manage any infrastructure for API Gateway, and the infrastructure scales on its own depending on your needs.
- **Caching**   API Gateway provides the ability to cache the output of API calls to improve the performance of your API calls and reduce the latency since you don't have to call the back end every time. As a result, it provides a great user experience.
- **Security**   API Gateway provides several tools to authorize access to your APIs and control service operation access. You can also use the AWS native tools such as AWS Identity and Access Management (IAM) and Amazon Cognito

to authorize access to your APIs. API Gateway also has the capability to verify signed API calls. API Gateway leverages signature version 4 to authorize access to APIs.

- **Metering**   API Gateway helps you define plans that meter and restrict third-party developer access to your APIs. API Gateway automatically meters traffic to your APIs and lets you extract utilization data for each API key. (API keys are a great tool to manage the community of third-party developers interacting with the APIs.) API Gateway allows developers to create API keys through a console interface or through an API for programmatic creation. You can set permissions on API keys and allow access only to a set of APIs, or stages within an API. You also have the ability to configure throttling and quota limits on a per API key basis. Thus, API Gateway helps developers create, monitor, and manage API keys that they can distribute to third-party developers.

restrict access to Third party by payment

- **Monitoring**   Once you deploy an API, API Gateway provides you with a dashboard to view all the metrics and to monitor the calls to your services. It is also integrated with Amazon CloudWatch, and hence you can see all the statistics related to API calls, latency, error rates, and so on.

Swagger - open API Spec Prato

- **Lifecycle management**   API Gateway allows you to maintain and run several versions of the same API at the same time. It also has built-in stages. These enable developers to deploy multiple stages of each version such as the development stage, production stage, or beta stage.

- **Integration with other AWS products**   API Gateway can be integrated with AWS Lambda, which helps you to create completely serverless APIs. Similarly, by integrating with Amazon CloudFront, you can get protection against distributed denial-of-service (DDoS) attacks.

- **Open API specification (Swagger) support**   API Gateway supports open source Swagger. Using the AWS open source Swagger importer tool, you can import your Swagger API definitions into Amazon API Gateway. With the Swagger importer tool, you can create and deploy new APIs as well as update existing ones.

- **SDK generation for iOS, Android, and JavaScript**   API Gateway can automatically generate client SDKs based on your customer's API definition. This allows developers to take their APIs from concept to integration test in a client app in a matter of hours.

 EXAM TIP   Amazon API Gateway recently has been added to the associate examination; therefore, you should be able to identify the use cases of API Gateway and articulate the benefits of using API Gateway.

Amazon Kinesis

In the past few years, there has been a huge proliferation of data available to businesses. They are now receiving an enormous amount of continuous streams of data from a variety of sources. For example, the data might be coming from IoT devices, online gaming data, application server log files, application clickstream data, and so on. If you want to get insight from the data, you should be able to quickly process and analyze it. Having the ability to process and analyze becomes extremely important because that governs how you are going to serve your customers. For example, depending on a customer's purchase patterns, you can customize the promotions, or you can provide personal recommendations based on the patterns of the customer.

Real-Time Application Scenarios

There are two types of use case scenarios for streaming data applications.

- **Evolving from batch to streaming analytics**   You can perform real-time analytics on data that has been traditionally analyzed using batch processing in data warehouses or using Hadoop frameworks. The most common use cases in this category include data lakes, data science, and machine learning. You can use streaming data solutions to continuously load real-time data into your data lakes. You can also update machine learning models more frequently as new data becomes available, ensuring the accuracy and reliability of the outputs. For example, Zillow uses Amazon Kinesis Data Streams to collect public record data and MLS listings and then provides home buyers and sellers with the most up-to-date home value estimates in near real time. Zillow also sends the same data to its Amazon Simple Storage Service (S3) data lake using Kinesis Data Streams so that all the applications work with the most recent information.

- **Building real-time applications**   You can use streaming data services for real-time applications such as application monitoring, fraud detection, and live leaderboards. These use cases require millisecond end-to-end latencies, from ingestion to processing and all the way to emitting the results to target data stores and other systems. For example, Netflix uses Kinesis Data Streams to monitor the communications between all its applications so it can detect and fix issues quickly, ensuring high service uptime and availability to its customers. While the most commonly applicable use case is application performance monitoring, more real-time applications in ad tech, gaming, and IoT are falling into this category.

Differences Between Batch and Stream Processing

You need a different set of tools to collect, prepare, and process real-time streaming data than the tools that you have traditionally used for batch analytics. With traditional analytics, you gather the data, load it periodically into a database, and analyze it hours, days, or weeks later. Analyzing real-time data requires a different approach. Instead of running database queries over stored data, stream-processing applications process data continuously in real time, even before it is stored. Streaming data can come in at a blistering pace, and data volumes can increase or decrease at any time. Stream data–processing platforms have to be able to handle the speed and variability of incoming data and process it as it arrives, meaning often millions to hundreds of millions of events per hour.

The Amazon Kinesis family provides you with solutions to manage huge quantities of data and gain meaningful insights from it. Amazon Kinesis consists of the following products:

- Amazon Kinesis Data Streams
- Amazon Kinesis Data Firehose
- Amazon Kinesis Data Analytics

Amazon Kinesis Data Steams

Amazon Kinesis Data Streams enables you to build custom applications that process or analyze streaming data for specialized needs. Kinesis Data Streams can continuously capture and store terabytes of data per hour from hundreds of thousands of sources such as web site clickstreams, financial transactions, social media feeds, IT logs, and location-tracking events. With the Kinesis Client Library (KCL), you can build Kinesis applications and use streaming data to power real-time dashboards, generate alerts, implement dynamic pricing and advertising, and more. You can also emit data from Kinesis Data Streams to other AWS services such as Amazon S3, Amazon Redshift, Amazon EMR, and AWS Lambda.

Benefits of Amazon Kinesis Data Streams

These are the benefits of Amazon Kinesis Data Streams:

- **Real time**   Kinesis Data Streams allows for real-time data processing. With Kinesis Data Streams, you can continuously collect data as it is generated and promptly react to critical information about your business and operations.

- **Secure**   You can privately access Kinesis Data Streams APIs from Amazon Virtual Private Cloud (VPC) by creating VPC endpoints. You can meet your regulatory and compliance needs by encrypting sensitive data within Kinesis Data Streams using server-side encryption and AWS Key Management Service (KMS) master keys.

- **Easy to use**   You can create a Kinesis stream within seconds. You can easily put data into your stream using the Kinesis Producer Library (KPL) and build Kinesis applications for data processing using the Kinesis Client Library. An Amazon Kinesis Data Streams producer is any application that puts user data records into a Kinesis data stream (also called *data ingestion*). The Kinesis Producer Library simplifies producer application development, allowing developers to achieve high-write throughput to a Kinesis stream.

- **Parallel processing**   Kinesis Data Streams allows you to have multiple Kinesis applications processing the same stream concurrently. For example, you can have one application running real-time analytics and another sending data to Amazon S3 from the same stream.

- **Elastic**   The throughput of a Kinesis data stream can scale from megabytes to terabytes per hour and from thousands to millions of PUT records per second. You can dynamically adjust the throughput of your stream at any time based on the volume of your input data.

- **Low cost**   Kinesis Data Streams has no up-front cost, and you pay for only the resources you use.

- **Reliable**   Kinesis Data Streams synchronously replicates your streaming data across three facilities in an AWS region and preserves your data for up to seven days, reducing the probability of data loss in the case of application failure, individual machine failure, or facility failure.

Amazon Kinesis Data Firehose

Amazon Kinesis Data Firehose is the easiest way to load streaming data into data stores and analytics tools. It can capture, transform, and load streaming data into Amazon S3, Amazon Redshift, Amazon Elasticsearch, and Splunk, enabling near real-time analytics with the existing business intelligence tools and dashboards you're already using today. It is a fully managed service that automatically scales to match the throughput of your data and requires no ongoing administration. It can also batch, compress, and encrypt the data before loading it, minimizing the amount of storage used at the destination and increasing security.

You can easily create a Firehose delivery stream from the AWS Management Console or AWS SDK, configure it with a few clicks, and start sending data to the stream from hundreds of thousands of data sources to be loaded continuously to AWS—all in just a few minutes. With Amazon Kinesis Data Firehose, you pay only for the amount of data you transmit through the service. There is no minimum fee or setup cost.

Amazon Kinesis Data Firehose manages all underlying infrastructure, storage, networking, and configuration needed to capture and load your data into Amazon S3, Amazon Redshift, Amazon Elasticsearch, or Splunk. You do not have to worry about provisioning, deployment, ongoing maintenance of the hardware or software, or writing any other application to manage this process. Firehose also scales elastically without requiring any intervention or associated developer overhead. Moreover, Amazon Kinesis Data Firehose synchronously replicates data across three facilities in an AWS region, providing high availability and durability for the data as it is transported to the destinations.

Figure 7-3 shows how Kinesis Data Firehose works.

Capture and submit streaming data to Firehose.   Firehose transforms and loads streaming data continuously into S3, Redshift, and Amazon Elasticsearch domains.   Analyze streaming data using your favorite BI tools.

Figure 7-3   How Amazon Kinesis Data Firehose works

Benefits of Amazon Kinesis Data Firehose

These are the benefits of Amazon Kinesis Data Firehose:

- **Easy to use**   Amazon Kinesis Data Firehose provides a simple way to capture and load streaming data with just a few clicks in the AWS Management Console. You can simply create a Firehose delivery stream, select the destinations, and start sending real-time data from hundreds of thousands of data sources simultaneously. The service takes care of stream management, including all the scaling, sharding, and monitoring needed to continuously load the data to destinations at the intervals you specify.

- **Integrated with AWS data stores**   Amazon Kinesis Data Firehose is integrated with Amazon S3, Amazon Redshift, and Amazon Elasticsearch. From the AWS Management Console, you can point Kinesis Data Firehose to an Amazon S3 bucket, Amazon Redshift table, or Amazon Elasticsearch domain. You can then use your existing analytics applications and tools to analyze streaming data.

- **Serverless data transformation**   Amazon Kinesis Data Firehose enables you to prepare your streaming data before it is loaded to data stores. With Kinesis Data Firehose, you can easily convert raw streaming data from your data sources into formats required by your destination data stores, without having to build your own data-processing pipelines.

- **Near real time**   Amazon Kinesis Data Firehose captures and loads data in near real time. It loads new data into Amazon S3, Amazon Redshift, Amazon Elasticsearch, and Splunk within 60 seconds after the data is sent to the service. As a result, you can access new data sooner and react to business and operational events faster.

- **No ongoing administration**   Amazon Kinesis Data Firehose is a fully managed service that automatically provisions, manages, and scales compute, memory, and network resources required to load your streaming data. Once set up, Kinesis Data Firehose loads data continuously as it arrives.

- **Pay only for what you use**   With Amazon Kinesis Data Firehose, you pay only for the volume of data you transmit through the service. There are no minimum fees or up-front commitments.

Amazon Kinesis Data Analytics

Amazon Kinesis Data Analytics is the easiest way to process and analyze real-time, streaming data. With Amazon Kinesis Data Analytics, you just use standard SQL to process your data streams, so you don't have to learn any new programming language. Simply point Kinesis Data Analytics at an incoming data stream, write your SQL queries, and specify where you want to load the results. Kinesis Data Analytics takes care of running your SQL queries continuously on data while it's in transit and then sends the results to the destinations.

Data is coming at us at lightning speeds because of the explosive growth of real-time data sources. Whether it is log data coming from mobile and web applications, purchase data from e-commerce sites, or sensor data from IoT devices, the massive amounts of data can help companies learn about what their customers and clients are doing. By getting visibility into this data as it arrives, you can monitor your business in real time and quickly leverage new business opportunities—such as making promotional offers to customers based on where they might be at a specific time or monitoring social sentiment and changing customer attitudes to identify and act on new opportunities.

To take advantage of these opportunities, you need a different set of analytics tools for collecting and analyzing real-time streaming data than what has been available traditionally for static, stored data. With traditional analytics, you gather the information, store it in a database, and analyze it hours, days, or weeks later. Analyzing real-time data requires a different approach and different tools and services. Instead of running database queries on stored data, streaming analytics platforms process the data continuously before the data is stored in a database. Streaming data flows at an incredible rate that can vary up and down all the time. Streaming analytics platforms have to be able to process this data when it arrives, often at speeds of millions of events per hour.

Benefits of Amazon Kinesis Data Analytics

These are the benefits of Amazon Kinesis Data Analytics:

- **Powerful real-time processing**   Amazon Kinesis Data Analytics processes streaming data with subsecond processing latencies, enabling you to analyze and respond in real time. It provides built-in functions that are optimized for stream processing, such as anomaly detection and top-K analysis, so that you can easily perform advanced analytics.

- **Fully managed**   Amazon Kinesis Data Analytics is a fully managed service that runs your streaming applications without requiring you to provision or manage any infrastructure.

- **Automatic elasticity**   Amazon Kinesis Data Analytics automatically scales up and down the infrastructure required to run your streaming applications with low latency.

- **Easy to use**   Amazon Kinesis Data Analytics provides interactive tools including a schema editor, a SQL editor, and SQL templates to make it easy to build and test your queries for both structured and unstructured input data streams.

- **Standard SQL**   Amazon Kinesis Data Analytics supports standard SQL. There is no need to learn complex processing frameworks and programming languages.

- **Pay only for what you use**   With Amazon Kinesis Data Analytics, you pay only for the processing resources your streaming application uses. As the volume of input data changes, Amazon Kinesis Data Analytics automatically scales resources up and down and charges you only for the resources actually used for processing. There are no minimum fees or up-front commitments.

Use Cases for Amazon Kinesis Data Analytics

You can use Amazon Kinesis Data Analytics in pretty much any use case where you are collecting data continuously in real time and want to get information and insights in seconds or minutes rather than having to wait days or even weeks. In particular, Kinesis Data Analytics enables you to quickly build applications that process streams from end to end for log analytics, clickstream analytics, Internet of Things (IoT), ad tech, gaming, and more. The three most common usage patterns are time-series analytics, real-time dashboards, and real-time alerts and notifications.

Generate Time-Series Analytics

Time-series analytics enables you to monitor and understand how your data is trending over time. With Amazon Kinesis Data Analytics, you can author SQL code that continuously generates these time-series analytics over specific time windows. For example, you can build a live leaderboard for a mobile game by computing the top players every minute and then sending it to Amazon S3. Or, you can track the traffic to your web site by calculating the number of unique site visitors every five minutes and then send the processed results to Amazon Redshift.

Feed Real-Time Dashboards

You can build applications that compute query results and emit them to a live dashboard, enabling you to visualize the data in near real time. For example, an application can continuously calculate business metrics such as the number of purchases from an e-commerce site, grouped by the product category, and then send the results to Amazon Redshift for visualization with a business intelligence tool of your choice. Consider another example where an application processes log data, calculates the number of application errors, and then sends the results to the Amazon Elasticsearch Service for visualization with Kibana.

Create Real-Time Alarms and Notifications

You can build applications that send real-time alarms or notifications when certain metrics reach predefined thresholds or, in more advanced cases, when your application detects anomalies using the machine learning algorithm you provide. For example, an application can compute the availability or success rate of a customer-facing API over time and then send the results to Amazon CloudWatch. You can build another application to look for events that meet certain criteria and then automatically notify the right customers using Kinesis Data Streams and Amazon Simple Notification Service (SNS).

Reference Architectures Using Serverless Services

In this section, you will explore the reference architecture when using AWS Lambda, Amazon API Gateway, and Amazon Kinesis. This will help you to understand the practical implementation aspects of using serverless architecture.

Real-Time File Processing

You can use Amazon S3 to trigger AWS Lambda to process data immediately after an upload. For example, you can use Lambda to thumbnail images, transcode videos, index

Example: *Image Thumbnail Creation*

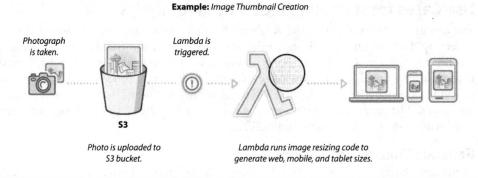

*Photograph
is taken.*

*Lambda is
triggered.*

S3

*Photo is uploaded to
S3 bucket.*

*Lambda runs image resizing code to
generate web, mobile, and tablet sizes.*

Figure 7-4 Reference architecture for real-time file processing

files, process logs, validate content, and aggregate and filter data in real time. Figure 7-4 shows the reference architecture for real-time file processing.

Real-Time Stream Processing

You can use AWS Lambda and Amazon Kinesis to process real-time streaming data for application activity tracking, transaction order processing, clickstream analysis, data cleansing, metrics generation, log filtering, indexing, social media analysis, and IoT device data telemetry and metering. Figure 7-5 shows the reference architecture for real-time stream processing.

Extract, Transformation, and Load (ETL) Processing

You can use AWS Lambda to perform data validation, filtering, sorting, or other transformations for every data change in a DynamoDB table and load the transformed data into another data store. Figure 7-6 shows the reference architecture for a data warehouse ETL.

Example: *Analysis of Streaming Social Media Data*

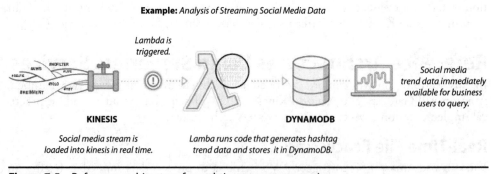

*Lambda is
triggered.*

KINESIS

DYNAMODB

*Social media
trend data immediately
available for business
users to query.*

*Social media stream is
loaded into kinesis in real time.*

*Lamba runs code that generates hashtag
trend data and stores it in DynamoDB.*

Figure 7-5 Reference architecture for real-time stream processing

Example: *Retail Data Warehouse ETL*

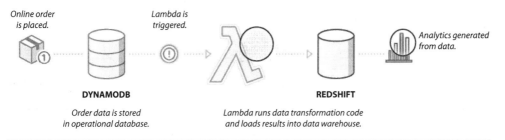

Figure 7-6   Reference architecture for data warehouse ETL

IoT Back Ends

This example leverages a serverless architecture for back ends using AWS Lambda to handle web, mobile, Internet of Things (IoT), and third-party API requests. Figure 7-7 shows the IoT back end.

Figure 7-8 shows the reference architecture for a weather application with API Gateway and AWS Lambda.

Amazon CloudFront

Cloud front = CDN
content delivery network

Amazon CloudFront is a global content delivery network (CDN) service that allows you to distribute content with low latency and provides high data transfer speeds. Amazon CloudFront employs a global network of edge locations and regional edge caches that cache copies of your content close to your viewers. In addition to caching static content, Amazon CloudFront accelerates dynamic content. Amazon CloudFront ensures that end-user requests are served by the closest edge location. It routes viewers to the best

Example: *Sensors in Tractor Detect Need for a Spare Part and Automatically Place Order*

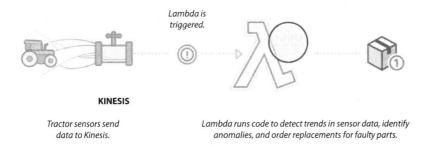

Figure 7-7   IoT back end

Example: *Weather Application*

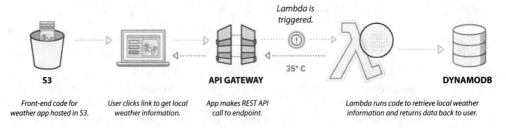

S3		API GATEWAY		DYNAMODB
Front-end code for weather app hosted in S3.	*User clicks link to get local weather information.*	*App makes REST API call to endpoint.*		*Lambda runs code to retrieve local weather information and returns data back to user.*

Figure 7-8   Reference architecture for a weather application using Amazon API Gateway and AWS Lambda

location. As a result, viewer requests travel a short distance, improving performance for your viewers. As of writing this book, Amazon CloudFront has 116 points of presence (105 edge locations and 11 regional edge caches) in 56 cities across 25 countries. When using Amazon CloudFront, there are no minimum usage commitments; you pay only for the data transfers and requests you actually use. Also, there is no data transfer charges for data transferred between AWS regions and CloudFront edge locations.

These are some of the use cases for Amazon CloudFront:

- **Caching static asset**   This is the most common use case for Amazon CloudFront. It helps in speeding up the delivery of your static content such as photos, videos, style sheets, and JavaScript content across the globe. The data is served to end users via edge locations.

- **Accelerating dynamic content**   Amazon CloudFront has a lot of network optimizations that accelerate the dynamic content. You can integrate CloudFront with your application or web site running on EC2 servers.

- **Helping protect against distributed denial-of-service (DDoS) attacks**   Amazon CloudFront can be integrated with AWS Shield and WAF, which can protect layers 3 and 4 and layer 7, respectively, against DDoS attacks. CloudFront negotiates TLS connections with the highest security ciphers and authenticates viewers with signed URLs.

- **Improving security**   Amazon CloudFront can serve the content securely with SSL (HTTPS). You can deliver your secure APIs or applications using SSL/TLS, and advanced SSL features are enabled automatically. CloudFront's infrastructure and processes are all compliant with PCI, DSS, HIPAA, and ISO to ensure the secure delivery of your most sensitive data.

- **Accelerating API calls**   Amazon CloudFront is integrated with Amazon API Gateway and can be used to secure and accelerate your API calls. CloudFront supports proxy methods such as POST, PUT, OPTIONS, DELETE, and PATCH.

- **Distributing software**   Amazon CloudFront is used for software distribution. By using Amazon CloudFront for the distribution of your software, you can provide a faster user experience since it is going to result in faster downloads. Since Amazon CloudFront scales automatically, you don't have to bother about how much content it can serve. You can make your software available right at the edge where your users are.

- **Streaming videos**   Amazon CloudFront can be used for video streaming both live and on demand. It is capable of streaming 4K video.

Amazon CloudFront Key Concepts

In this section, you will learn some Amazon CloudFront key terminology.

- **Edge location**   CloudFront delivers your content through a worldwide network of data centers called *edge locations*. These data centers are located in major cities across the globe. It is likely that an AWS region may not exist at a particular place where an edge location is present.

- **Regional edge location**   The regional edge caches are located between your origin web server and the global edge locations that serve content directly to your viewers. They are located between your origin web server and the global edge locations that serve content directly to your viewers. As objects become less popular, individual edge locations may remove those objects to make room for more popular content. Regional edge caches have a larger cache width than any individual edge location, so objects remain in the cache longer at the nearest regional edge caches. This helps keep more of your content closer to your viewers, reducing the need for CloudFront to go back to your origin web server and improving the overall performance for viewers. This regional edge cache feature is enabled by default, and you don't have to do anything manually to use this feature; it is not charged separately.

   NOTE   An origin web server is often referred to as an *origin*, which is the location where your actual noncached data resides.

- **Distribution**   A distribution specifies the location or locations of the original version of your files. A distribution has a unique CloudFront.net domain name (such as abc123.cloudfront.net) that you can use to reference your objects through the global network of edge locations. If you want, you can map your own domain name (for example, www.example.com) to your distribution. You can create distributions to either download your content using the HTTP or HTTPS protocol or stream your content using the RTMP protocol.

- **Origin**   CloudFront can accept any publicly addressable Amazon S3 or HTTP server, an ELB/ALB, or a custom origin server outside of AWS as an origin. When you create an origin, you must provide the public DNS name of the origin. For example, if you specify an EC2 server, it should be something like ec2-52-91-188-59.compute-1.amazonaws.com.

- **Behaviors**   Behaviors allow you to have granular control of the CloudFront CDN, enforce certain policies, change results based on request type, control the cacheablity of objects, and more. You can unleash the whole power of Amazon CloudFront using behaviors. The following sections discuss the important behaviors that can be configured with Amazon CloudFront.

Path Pattern Matching   You can configure multiple cache behaviors based on URL path patterns for the web site or application for which you are going to use Amazon CloudFront. The pattern specifies which requests to apply the behavior to. When Cloud-Front receives a viewer request, the requested path is compared with path patterns in the order in which cache behaviors are listed in the distribution, as in images/*.jpg and /images/*.jpg. The CloudFront behavior is the same with or without the leading /. Based on the path pattern, you can route requests to specific origins, set the HTTP/HTTPS protocol, set the header or caching options, set cookie and query string forwarding, restrict access, and set compression.

Headers   Using headers you can forward request headers to the origin cache based on the header values. You can detect the device and take actions accordingly. For example, you can have a different response if the user is coming from a laptop or mobile device. Similarly, you can have a different response based on the language; for example, a user can prefer Spanish but will accept British. You can also have a different response based on the protocol. For example, you can forward the request to different content based on the connection type.

Query Strings/Cookies   Some web applications use query strings to send information to the origin. A query string is the part of a web request that appears after a ? character; the string can contain one or more parameters separated by & characters. For example, the following query string includes two parameters, color=blue and size=small:

http://abc111xyz.cloudfront.net/images/image.jpg?*color=blue&size=small*

Now let's say your web site is available in three languages. The directory structure and file names for all three versions of the web site are identical. As a user views your web site, requests that are forwarded to CloudFront include a language query string parameter based on the language that the user chose. You can configure CloudFront to forward query strings to the origin and to cache based on the language parameter. If you configure your web server to return the version of a given page that corresponds with the selected language, CloudFront will cache each language version separately, based on the value of the language query string parameter.

In this example, if the main page for your web site is main.html, the following three requests will cause CloudFront to cache main.html three times, once for each value of the language query string parameter:

http://abc111xyz.cloudfront.net/main.html?*language=en*
http://abc111xyz.cloudfront.net/main.html?*language=es*
http://abc111xyz.cloudfront.net/main.html?language=fr

Signed URL or Signed Cookies If you move your static content to an S3 bucket, you can protect it from unauthorized access via CloudFront signed URLs. A signed URL includes additional information, for example, an expiration date and time, that gives you more control over access to your content. This is how the signed URL works. The web server obtains temporary credentials to the S3 content. It creates a signed URL based on those credentials that allow access. It provides this link in content returned (a signed URL) to the client, and this link is valid for a limited period of time. This additional information appears in a policy statement, which is based on either a canned policy or a custom policy. Via signed URLs, you can get additional control such as restricting access to content, getting subscriptions for your content, creating digital rights, creating custom policies, and so on.

Signed HTTP cookies provide the same degree of control as a signed URL by including the signature in an HTTP cookie instead. This allows you to restrict access to multiple objects (e.g., whole-site authentication) or to a single object without needing to change URLs. This is how it works. A Set-Cookie header is sent to the user after they are authenticated on a web site. That sets a cookie on the user's device. When a user requests a restricted object, the browser forwards the signed cookie in the request. CloudFront then checks the cookie attributes to determine whether to allow or restrict access.

Protocol Policy If you want CloudFront to allow viewers to access your web content using either HTTP or HTTPS, specify HTTP and HTTPS. If you want CloudFront to redirect all HTTP requests to HTTPS, specify Redirect HTTP to HTTPS. If you want CloudFront to require HTTPS, specify HTTPS Only.

Time to Live (TTL) You can control how long your objects stay in a CloudFront cache before CloudFront forwards another request to your origin. Reducing the duration allows you to serve dynamic content. Increasing the duration means your users get better performance because your objects are more likely to be served directly from the edge cache. A longer duration also reduces the load on your origin. You can set up minimum, maximum, and default TTL for all the objects. The time is specified in seconds. By default, each object automatically expires after 24 hours. You can also control the cache duration for an individual object, and you can configure your origin to add a Cache-Control max-age or Cache-Control s-maxage directive or an expires header field to the object.

Gzip Compression Gzip compression can be enabled on distributions; your pages can load more quickly because content will download faster, and your CloudFront data transfer charges may be reduced as well. You can configure Amazon CloudFront to automatically apply gzip compression when browsers and other clients request a compressed object with text and other compressible file formats. This means if you are already using Amazon S3, CloudFront can transparently compress this type of content. For origins outside S3, doing compression at the edge means you don't need to use resources at your origin to do compression. The resulting smaller size of compressed objects makes downloads faster and reduces your CloudFront data transfer charges.

You can create two types of distributions via CloudFront: web and RTMP. Web distribution is used for speeding up the distribution of static and dynamic content, for example, .html, .css, .php, and graphics files. RTMP distribution is used to speed up the distribution of your streaming media files using Adobe Flash Media Server's RTMP protocol. An RTMP distribution allows an end user to begin playing a media file before the file has finished downloading from a CloudFront edge location. Most of the behaviors mentioned earlier are applicable for web distribution, and some of them may not be applicable for RTMP distribution.

Geo Restriction

When a user requests your content, CloudFront typically serves the requested content regardless of where the user is located. If you need to prevent users in specific countries from accessing your content, you can use the CloudFront geo restriction feature to do one of the following:

- Allow your users to access your content only if they're in one of the countries on a whitelist of approved countries
- Prevent your users from accessing your content if they're in one of the countries on a blacklist of banned countries

Error Handling

You can configure CloudFront to respond to requests using a custom error page when your origin returns an HTTP 4xx or 5xx status code. For example, when your custom origin is unavailable and returning 5xx responses, CloudFront can return a static error page that is hosted on Amazon S3. You can also specify a minimum TTL to control how long CloudFront caches errors.

Amazon Route 53

Amazon Route 53 is the managed Domain Name Service (DNS) of Amazon. DNS translates human-readable names such as www.example.com into the numeric IP addresses such as 192.0.0.3 that servers/computers use to connect to each other. You can think of DNS as a phone book that has addresses and telephone numbers. Route 53 connects user requests to infrastructure running in AWS, such as Amazon EC2 instances, Elastic Load Balancing load balancers, or Amazon S3 buckets, and it can also be used to route users to infrastructure outside of AWS.

It is highly available and scalable. This is the only service that has a 100 percent SLA. This service is region independent, which means you can configure Route 53 with resources running across multiple regions. It is capable of doing DNS resolution within multiple regions and among AWS VPCs.

In addition to managing your public DNS record, Route 53 can be used to register a domain, create DNS records for a new domain, or transfer DNS records for an existing domain.

Amazon Route 53 currently supports the following DNS record types:

- A (address record)
- AAAA (IPv6 address record)

- CNAME (canonical name record)
- CAA (certification authority authorization)
- MX (mail exchange record)
- NAPTR (name authority pointer record)
- NS (name server record)
- PTR (pointer record)
- SOA (start of authority record)
- SPF (sender policy framework)
- SRV (service locator)
- TXT (text record)

In addition, Route 53 supports alias records (also known as *zone apex support*). The zone apex is the root domain of a web site (example.com, without the www). You use CloudFront to deliver content from the root domain, or zone apex, of your web site. In other words, you configure both http://www.example.com and http://example.com to point at the same CloudFront distribution. Since the DNS specification requires a zone apex to point to an IP address (an A record), not a CNAME (such as the name AWS provides for a CloudFront distribution, ELB, or S3 web site bucket), you can use Route 53's alias record to solve this problem.

Route 53 also offers health checks, which allow you to monitor the health and performance of your application, web servers, and other resources that leverage this service. Health checks of your resources with Route 53 are useful when you have two or more resources that are performing the same function. For example, you might have multiple Amazon EC2 servers running HTTP server software responding to requests for the example.com web site. Say you have multiple EC2 servers running across two regions. As long as all the resources are healthy, Amazon Route 53 responds to queries using all of your example.com resource sets (using all the EC2 servers). When a resource becomes unhealthy, Amazon Route 53 responds to queries using only the healthy resource record sets for example.com, which means if a few EC2 servers go down, Route 53 won't use them, or if an AZ goes down, Route 53 won't use the EC2 instances from the AZ that went down for the resources. It is going to leverage only the healthy EC2 servers from healthy AZs in a region.

Amazon Route 53 supports the following routing policies:

- **Weighted round robin**   When you have multiple resources that perform the same function (for example, web servers that serve the same web site) and you want Amazon Route 53 to route traffic to those resources in proportions that you specify (for example, one-quarter to one server and three-quarters to the other), you can do this using weighted round robin. You can also use this capability to do A/B testing, sending a small portion of traffic to a server on which you've made a software change (say 10 percent of the traffic going to the newly changed server and 90 percent of the traffic going to the old server).

- **Latency-based routing**   When you have resources in multiple Amazon EC2 data centers that perform the same function and you want Amazon Route 53 to respond to DNS queries with the resources that provide the best latency, you can use latency-based routing. It helps you improve your application's performance for a global audience. You can run applications in multiple AWS regions, and Amazon Route 53, using dozens of edge locations worldwide, will route end users to the AWS region that provides the lowest latency.

- **Failover routing**   When you want to configure active-passive failover, in which one resource takes all traffic when it's available and the other resource takes all traffic when the first resource isn't available, you can use failover routing. For example, you may have all your resources running from a particular region. When this region fails, you can do failover routing and point to a static web site running from a different region.

- **Geo DNS routing**   When you want Amazon Route 53 to respond to DNS queries based on the location of your users, you can use this routing. Route 53 Geo DNS lets you balance the load by directing requests to specific endpoints based on the geographic location from which the request originates. Geo DNS makes it possible to customize localized content, such as presenting detail pages in the right language or restricting the distribution of content to only the markets you have licensed.

AWS Web Application Firewall

AWS Web Application Firewall (WAF) is a web application firewall that protects your web applications from various forms of attack. It helps to protect web sites and applications against attacks that could affect application availability, result in data breaches, cause downtime, compromise security, or consume excessive resources. It gives you control over which traffic to allow or block to/from your web applications by defining customizable web security rules. The following are some of the use cases of AWS WAF:

- **Vulnerability protection**   You can use AWS WAF to create custom rules that block common attack patterns, such as SQL injection or cross-site scripting (XSS), and rules that are designed for your specific application.

- **Malicious requests**   Web crawlers can be used to mount attacks on a web site. By using an army of automated crawlers, a malicious actor can overload a web server and bring a site down. AWS WAF can protect against those malicious request. It can also protect from scrapers where someone tries to extract large amounts of data from web sites.

- **DDoS mitigation (HTTP/HTTPS floods)**   This helps protect web applications from attacks by allowing you to configure rules that allow, block, or monitor (count) web requests based on conditions that you define. These conditions include IP addresses, HTTP headers, HTTP body, URI strings, SQL injection, and cross-site scripting.

WAF is integrated with CloudFront. As a result, you can bring the added distribution capacity and scalability of a CDN to WAF. It helps to decrease the load of origin by blocking attacks close to the source, helps in distributing sudden spikes of traffic leveraging CDNs, and avoids single points of failures with increased redundancy of CDNs. WAF can be integrated with application load balancers (ALBs) as well, which can protect your origin web servers running behind the ALBs.

To use WAF with CloudFront or ALB, you need to identify the resource that can be either an Amazon CloudFront distribution or an application load balancer that you need to protect. You then deploy the rules and filters that will best protect your applications. Rules are collections of WAF filter conditions; it either can be one condition or can be a combination of two or more conditions. Let's understand this in detail.

Conditions define the basic characteristics that you want AWS WAF to watch for in web requests, and these conditions specify when you want to allow or block requests. For example, you may want to watch the script that looks malicious. If WAF is able to find it, it is going to block it. In this case, you create a condition that watches for the request. Let's take a look at all the conditions you can create using AWA WAF.

- Using cross-site scripting match conditions, you can allow or block the requests that appear to contain malicious scripts.
- Using IP match conditions, you can allow or block requests based on the IP addresses that they originate from.
- Using geographic match conditions, you can allow or block requests based on the country that they originate from.
- Using size constraint conditions, you can allow or block requests based on whether the requests exceed a specified length.
- Using SQL injection match conditions, you can allow or block requests based on whether the requests appear to contain malicious SQL code.
- Using string match conditions, you can allow or block requests based on strings that appear in the requests.
- Using regex matches, you can allow or block requests based on a regular expression pattern that appears in the requests.

Once you create the condition, you can combine these conditions into rules to precisely target the requests that you want to allow, block, or count.

There are two types of rules in AWS WAF: regular rules and rate-based rules. Regular rules use only conditions to target specific requests. For example, you can create a regular rule based on the following conditions: requests coming from 19.152.0.55 and requests that include SQL-like code. In this case, with a regular rule, you have included two conditions. When a rule includes multiple conditions, as in this example, AWS WAF looks for requests that match all conditions—that is, it ANDs the conditions together. Rate-based rules are similar to regular rules, with one addition: a rate limit in five-minute intervals. Say you specify the rate limit as 2,000; then the rate-based rules count the requests that arrive from a specified IP address every five minutes. The rule can trigger an action (block all IPs) that have more than 2,000 requests in the last five minutes.

You can combine conditions with the rate limit. In this case, if the requests match all of the conditions and the number of requests exceeds the rate limit in any five-minute period, the rule will trigger the action designated in the web ACL.

Creating a web access control list (web ACL) is the first thing you need to do to use AWS WAF. Once you combine your conditions into rules, you combine the rules into a web ACL. This is where you define an action for each rule. The action can be set to allow, block, or count. Now when a web request matches all the conditions in a rule, AWS WAF can either block the request or allow the request to be forwarded to Amazon CloudFront or an application load balancer.

Now that you understand the concept, let's look at the step-by-step process to configure a WAF from the console:

1. Name the web ACL.

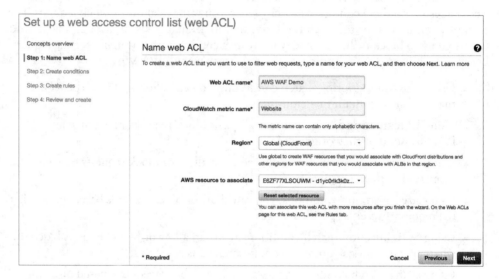

2. Create the conditions.

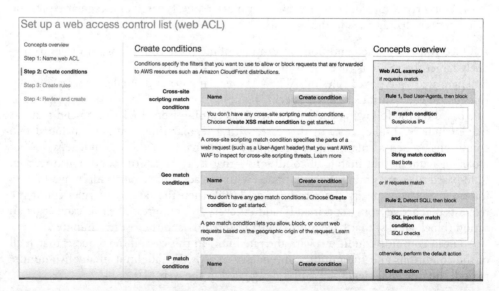

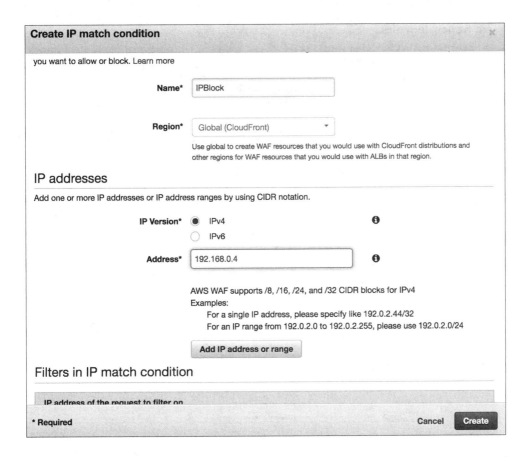

3. Create the rules.

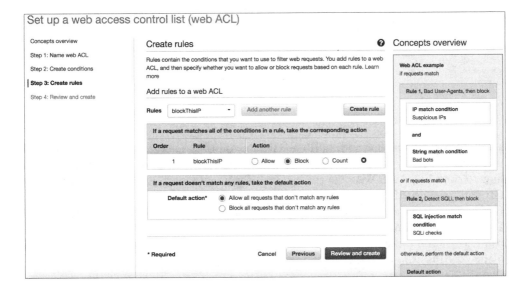

4. Review the rules.

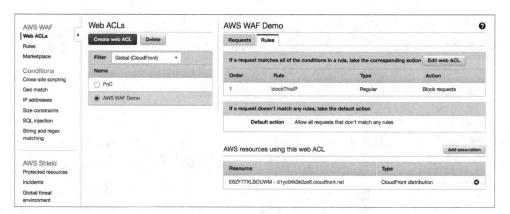

5. Confirm the rules.

AWA WAF resources can be managed with APIs. Therefore, you can do all kinds of actions using APIs such as adding IPs to a list. In addition to APIs, just like any other service, you can configure everything via the AWS console. The previous example showed how to configure AWS WAF via the AWS Management Console. AWS WAF configurations are propagated globally in one minute.

You can watch the real-time metrics using Amazon CloudWatch. One-minute metrics are available in CloudWatch. You can see how many requests were blocked, allowed, and counted, or you can apply your rules for analysis. You can also monitor all the changes made via APIs using CloudWatch.

Amazon Simple Queue Service

One of the challenges an architect faces when building new applications for the cloud or migrating existing applications is making them distributed. You need to address scalability, fault tolerance, and high availability, and you need to start thinking more deeply about things such as the CAP theorem, eventual consistency, distributed transactions, and design patterns that support distributed systems.

 NOTE The CAP theorem states that in a distributed data store it is impossible to provide more than two guarantees out of these three: consistency, availability, partition tolerance. This means either you can have consistency and availability or consistency and partition tolerance or availability and partition tolerance but not all three together.

Messaging can really help you in this case to achieve the goals. A *message queue* is a form of asynchronous service-to-service communication used in serverless and microservice architectures. Messages are stored on the queue until they are processed and deleted. Each message is processed only once, by a single consumer. Message queues can be used to decouple the processing of larger jobs into small parts that can be run independent of each other. This can help in terms of performance, making the batch job run faster, and can help during busy workloads.

When you are designing an architecture for the cloud, it is recommended to decouple the applications to smaller, independent building blocks that are easier to develop, deploy, and maintain. Message queues provide communication and coordination for these distributed applications. It can also simplify the coding of decoupled applications, at the same time improving performance, reliability, and scalability.

Message queues allow different parts of a system to communicate and process operations asynchronously. A message queue provides a *buffer,* which temporarily stores messages, and *endpoints,* which allow software components to connect to the queue to send and receive messages. You can put messages into a queue, and you can retrieve messages from a queue. The messages are usually small and can be things such as requests, replies, error messages, or just plain information. The software that puts messages into a queue is called a *message producer,* and the software that retrieves messages is called a *message consumer.* For sending a message, the producer adds a message to the queue. The message is stored on the queue until the receiver of the message (the consumer) retrieves the message and does something with it. Figure 7-9 shows the producer, queue, and consumer.

Amazon Simple Queue Service (Amazon SQS) is a fast, reliable, scalable, and fully managed queue service. Using Amazon SQS, you can quickly build message queuing applications that can run on any system. It can send, store, and receive messages between components. Like most AWS services, it's accessible through a web API, as well as SDKs in most languages.

These are some of the key features of Amazon SQS:

- SQS is redundant across multiple AZs in each region. Even if an AZ is lost, the service will be accessible.

- Multiple copies of messages are stored across multiple AZs, and messages are retained up to 14 days.

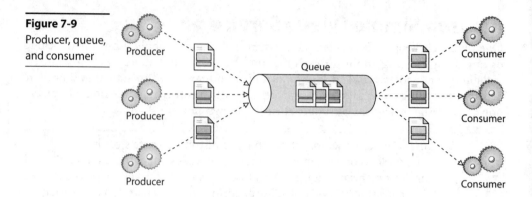

Figure 7-9
Producer, queue,
and consumer

- If your consumer or producer application fails, your messages won't be lost.

- Because of the distributed architecture, SQS scales without any preprovisioning. It scales up automatically as and when more traffic comes. Similarly, when the traffic is low, it automatically scales down.

- The messages can contain up to 256KB of text data, including XML, JSON, and unformatted text.

There are two types of SQS queues: standard and FIFO.

- **Standard**   This is the default queue type of Amazon SQS. It supports almost unlimited transactions per second. It supports at-least-once message delivery. It provides best-effort ordering that ensures that messages are generally delivered in the same order as they're sent and at nearly unlimited scale. Although a standard queue tries to preserve the order of messages, it could be possible that sometimes a message is delivered out of order. If your system needs order to be preserved, then instead of choosing standard, you should choose FIFO.

- **FIFO**   This is the second type of queue. A first in, first out (FIFO) queue guarantees first in, first out delivery and also exactly once processing, ensuring that your consumer application does not need to consider the message being delivered multiple times. In FIFO queues, the throughput is limited to 300 transactions per second.

These are the differences between standard queues and FIFO queues:

- Standard queues support a nearly unlimited number of transactions per second (TPS) per API action, whereas FIFO queues support up to 300 messages per second (300 send, receive, or delete operations per second). You can also batch 10 messages per operation (maximum). FIFO queues can support up to 3,000 messages per second.

- In standard queues, a message is delivered at least once, but occasionally more than one copy of a message is delivered, whereas in FIFO a message is delivered once and remains available until a consumer processes and deletes it. Duplicates aren't introduced into the queue.

- In standard queues, occasionally messages might be delivered in an order different from which they were sent, whereas in FIFO the order in which messages are sent and received is strictly preserved (i.e., first in, first out).

Let's understand some of the terminology and parameters that you need to know for configuring SQS.

When a producer sends a message to the queue, it is immediately distributed to multiple SQS servers across multiple AZs for redundancy. Whenever a consumer is ready to process the message, it processes the message from the queue. When the message is being processed, it stays in the queue and isn't returned to subsequent receive requests for the duration of *visibility timeout*. When the visibility timeout expires, the consumer deletes the message from the queue to prevent the message from being received and processed again. Thus, visibility timeout is the length of time (in seconds) that a message received from a queue will be invisible to other receiving components. The value must be between 0 seconds and 12 hours.

- **Message retention period** This is the amount of time that Amazon SQS will retain a message if it does not get deleted. The value must be between 1 minute and 14 days.

- **Maximum message size** This is the maximum message size (in bytes) accepted by Amazon SQS. It can be between 1KB and 256KB.

- **Delivery delay** This is the amount of time to delay or postpone the delivery of all messages added to the queue. It can be anywhere from 0 seconds to 15 minutes. If you create a delay queue, any messages that you send to the queue remain invisible to consumers for the duration of the delay period. For standard queues, the per-queue delay setting is *not retroactive*—changing the setting doesn't affect the delay of messages already in the queue. For FIFO queues, the per-queue delay setting is *retroactive*—changing the setting affects the delay of messages already in the queue.

- **Receive message wait time** Using this parameter, you can specify short polling or long polling. Short polling returns immediately, even if the message queue being polled is empty. When you set Receive Message Wait Time to 0 seconds, short polling is enabled. *Long polling* helps reduce the cost of using Amazon SQS by eliminating the number of empty responses (when there are no messages available for a ReceiveMessage request) and false empty responses (when messages are available but aren't included in a response) and returning messages as soon as they become available. When you specify the parameter between 1 and 20 seconds, long polling is enabled.

- **Content-based deduplication**   This parameter is applicable only for the FIFO queue. Using this parameter you use an SHA-256 hash of the body of the message (but not the attributes of the message) to generate the content-based message deduplication ID.

Amazon SQS supports *dead-letter queues*, which other queues (*source queues*) can target for messages that can't be processed (consumed) successfully. Sometimes messages can't be processed because of a variety of possible issues, such as erroneous conditions within the producer or consumer application or an unexpected state change that causes an issue with your application code. Dead-letter queues are useful for debugging your application or messaging system because they let you isolate problematic messages to determine why their processing doesn't succeed. By checking the parameter Use Redrive Policy, you can send messages into a dead-letter queue after exceeding the Maximum Receives setting. Using the parameter Maximum Receives, you can specify the maximum number of times a message can be received before it is sent to the dead-letter queue. The value of Maximum Receives can be between 1 and 1000. You can specify a queue name by adding one for the parameter Dead Letter Queue.

Using server-side encryption (SSE), you can transmit sensitive data in encrypted queues. SSE protects the contents of messages in Amazon SQS queues using keys managed in the AWS Key Management Service (AWS KMS). SSE encrypts messages as soon as Amazon SQS receives them. The messages are stored in encrypted form, and Amazon SQS decrypts messages only when they are sent to an authorized consumer.

Amazon Simple Notification Service

As the name suggests, Amazon Simple Notification Service (Amazon SNS) is a web service used to send notifications from the cloud. It is easy to set up and operate and at the same time highly scalable, flexible, and cost-effective. SNS has the capacity to publish a message from an application and then immediately deliver it to subscribers. It follows the publish-subscribe mechanism, also known as *pub-sub messaging*. It is a form of asynchronous service-to-service communication used in serverless and microservice architectures. In this model, any message published to a topic is immediately received by all the subscribers to the topic. Just like SQS, SNS is used to enable event-driven architectures or to decouple applications to increase performance, reliability, and scalability.

To use SNS, you must first create a "topic" identifying a specific subject or event type. A topic is used for publishing messages and allowing clients to subscribe for notifications. Once a topic is created, the topic owner can set policies for it such as limiting who can publish messages or subscribe to notifications or specifying which notification protocols are supported. To broadcast a message, a component called a *publisher* simply pushes a message to the topic. These topics transfer messages with no or very little queuing and push them out immediately to all subscribers. Figure 7-10 shows the publisher and subscriber model.

Subscribers are clients interested in receiving notifications from topics of interest; they can subscribe to a topic or be subscribed by the topic owner. Subscribers specify

Figure 7-10
Publisher and
subscriber model

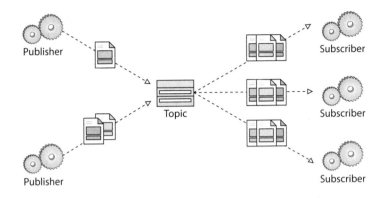

the protocol and endpoint (URL, email address, etc.) for notifications to be delivered. All components that subscribe to the topic will receive every message that is broadcast, unless a message filtering policy is set by the subscriber. The publishers and subscribers can operate independent of each other, which means publishers need not know who has subscribed to the messages, and similarly, the subscribers don't have to know from where the message is coming.

These are some of the features of Amazon SNS:

- It is reliable since the messages are stored across multiple AZs by default.
- It offers flexible message delivery over multiple transport protocols. It can be HTTP/HTTPS, e-mail, SMS, Lambda, and SQS where the message can be delivered.
- The messages can be delivered instantly or can be delayed. It follows push-based delivery, which means messages are automatically sent to subscribers.
- It provides monitoring capability. Amazon SNS and CloudWatch are integrated, so you can collect, view, and analyze metrics for every active Amazon SNS topic.
- It can be accessed from the AWS Management Console, AWS Command Line Interface (CLI), AWS Tools for Windows PowerShell, AWS SDKs, and Amazon SNS Query API.
- Amazon SNS messages can contain up to 256KB of text data with the exception of SMS, which can contain up to 140 bytes. If you publish a message that exceeds the size limit, Amazon SNS sends it as multiple messages, each fitting within the size limit. Messages are not cut off in the middle of a word but on whole-word boundaries. The total size limit for a single SMS publish action is 1,600 bytes.

With these three simple steps, you can get started with Amazon SNS:

- **Create a topic**   A topic is a communication channel to send messages and subscribe to notifications. It provides an access point for publishers and subscribers to communicate with each other.

- **Subscribe to a topic**   To receive messages published to a topic, you have to subscribe an endpoint to that topic. Once you subscribe an endpoint to a topic and the subscription is confirmed, the endpoint will receive all messages published to that topic.
- **Publish to a topic**   Publishers send messages to topics. Once a new message is published, Amazon SNS attempts to deliver that message to every endpoint that is subscribed to the topic.

There are several scenarios where you use SNS and SQS together.

Say you have uploaded a new video to S3. The moment a video is uploaded, it triggers a message to be published to the SNS topic and is then replicated and sent to SQS queues. This sends the S3 event to multiple Lambda functions to be processed independently. In this case, the processing can be encoding the video to a different format (360p, 480p, 720p, 1080p) in parallel.

You have an order management system. Whenever someone places an order, an SNS notification is created. It is then sent to the order queue (SQS) and processed by EC2 servers. You can again have different SQSs depending on the priority of the order, say, a high-priority SQS queue and a low-priority SQS queue. When the order goes to the high-priority queue, it will be shipped immediately, and when it goes to the low-priority queue, it will be shipped after two or three days.

AWS Step Fns replaced SWF

AWS Step Functions and Amazon Simple Workflow (SWF)

AWS Step Functions is a fully managed service that makes it easy to coordinate the components of distributed applications and microservices using visual workflow. It is really easy to use and scales down to little one-off shell-script equivalents and up to billions of complex multiphase tasks. Let's take a simple example to understand this. Say you are planning to go Europe for your next vacation. For your vacation, you need to do the following three tasks in sequence: book a flight, book a hotel, and book a rental car. For each step you are going to choose a different vendor. This is shown in Figure 7-11.

Now if you are not able to reserve a rental car because of the unavailability of it, you should be able to automatically cancel the hotel booking and flight ticket (Figure 7-12).

In this case, there are multiple ways of solving this problem.

You could create a function for each step and just link your functions together. That's not terrible, but it does not give you modular, independent functions that each does one thing well. If you invoke one Lambda from another and you do it synchronously, that doesn't scale because it might want to call another, and another, and so on, depending on how many steps you have. So, you can do it asynchronously, which is actually a better design, but then error handling gets hard. The more steps you add, the more difficult it is going to become to handle the error. Alternatively, you could keep track of your state by writing it into a database, say Amazon DynamoDB, or you could pass your state and control around through queues, but again both of those ideas take a lot of effort.

Figure 7-11
Steps for
vacation
planning

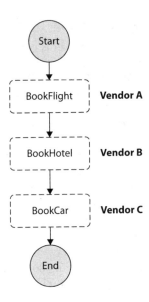

What if you can do this seamlessly? Thus, if you are designing a coordination solution, it must have several characteristics:

- It needs to scale out as demand grows. You should be able to run one execution or run thousands.
- You can never lose state.
- It deals with errors and times out and implements things like try/catch/finally.

Figure 7-12
Cancellation of
hotel and flight

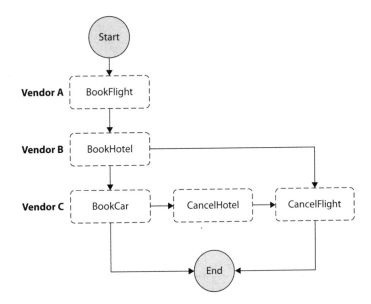

- It is easy to use and easy to manage.
- It keeps a record of its operation and is completely auditable.

With AWS Step Functions, you define your application as a state machine, a series of steps that together capture the behavior of the app. States in the state machine may be tasks, sequential steps, parallel steps, branching paths (choice), and/or timers (wait). Tasks are units of work, and this work may be performed by AWS Lambda functions, Amazon EC2 instances, containers, or on-premises servers; anything that can communicate with the Step Functions API may be assigned a task. When you start a state machine, you pass it input in the form of JSON, and each state changes or adds to this JSON blob as output, which becomes input to the next state. The console provides this visualization and uses it to provide near-real-time information on your state machine execution. The management console automatically graphs each state in the order of execution, making it easy to design multistep applications. The console highlights the real-time status of each step and provides a detailed history of every execution. Step Functions operate and scale the steps of your application and underlying compute for you to ensure your application executes reliably under increasing demand. Figure 7-13 shows the application lifecycle in AWS Step Functions.

As of writing this book, AWS Step Functions has seven state types:

- **Task**   This is a single unit of work. Task states do your work. These call on your application components and microservices. There are two kinds of task states: one pushes a call to AWS Lambda functions, and the other dispatches tasks to applications.

- **Choice**   Using the choice states, you can use branching logic to your state machines.

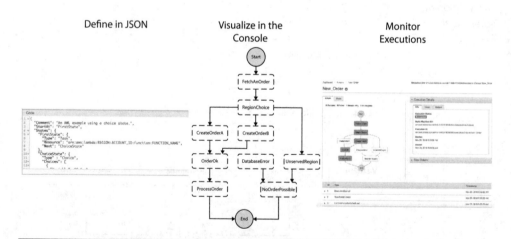

Figure 7-13   Application lifecycle in AWS Step Functions

- **Parallel**   Parallel states allow you to fork the same input across multiple states and then join the results into a combined output. This is really useful when you want to apply several independent manipulations to your data, such as image processing or data reduction.
- **Wait**   You can delay for a specified time by specifying wait in state.
- **Fail**   This stops an execution and marks it as a failure.
- **Succeed**   This stops an execution successfully.
- **Pass**   This passes its input to its output.

AWS Step Functions is replacing Amazon Simple Workflow Service (SWF). Amazon SWF continues to exist today for customers who have already built their application using Amazon SWF. If you are building a new application, then you should consider AWS Step Functions instead of SWF.

AWS Elastic Beanstalk

With Elastic Beanstalk, you can deploy, monitor, and scale an application on AWS quickly and easily. Elastic Beanstalk is the simplest and fastest way of deploying web applications. You just need to upload your code, and Elastic Beanstalk will provision all the resources such as Amazon EC2, Amazon Elastic Container Service (Amazon ECS), Auto Scaling, and Elastic Load Balancing for you behind the scenes. Elastic Beanstalk lets you focus on building applications without worrying about managing infrastructure. Although the infrastructure is provisioned and managed by Elastic Beanstalk, you maintain complete control over it.

If you don't have much AWS knowledge and want to deploy an application, you might do several tasks. You can start by creating a VPC and then create public and private subnets in different AZs, launch EC2 instances, integrate them with Auto Scaling and ELB, provision a database, and so on. Laying the infrastructure itself can become challenging, and on top of that, if you have to manage everything manually, it adds to more overhead. Elastic Beanstalk solves this problem.

An Elastic Beanstalk application consists of three key components. The environment consists of the infrastructure supporting the application, such as the EC2 instances, RDS, Elastic Load Balancer, Auto Scaling, and so on. An environment runs a single application version at a time for better scalability. You can create many different environments for an application. For example, you can have a separate environment for production, a separate environment for test/dev, and so on. The next component is the application version. It is nothing but the actual application code that is stored in Amazon S3. You can have multiple versions of an application, and each version will be stored separately. The third component is the saved configuration. It defines how an environment and its resources should behave. It can be used to launch new environments quickly or roll back configuration. An application can have many saved configurations.

AWS Elastic Beanstalk has two types of environment tiers to support different types of web applications:

- Web servers are standard applications that listen for and then process HTTP requests, typically over port 80.
- Workers are specialized applications that have a background processing task that listens for messages on an Amazon SQS queue. Worker applications post those messages to your application by using HTTP.

It can be deployed either in a single instance or with multiple instances with the database (optional) in both cases. When deployed with multiple instances, Elastic Beanstalk provisions the necessary infrastructure resources such as load balancers, Auto Scaling groups, security groups, and databases. It also configures Amazon Route 53 and gives you a unique domain name. The single instance is mainly used for development or testing purposes, whereas multiple instances can be used for production workloads.

Elastic Beanstalk configures each EC2 instance in your environment with the components necessary to run applications for the selected platform. You don't have to manually log in and configure EC2 instances. Elastic Beanstalk does everything for you. You can add AWS Elastic Beanstalk configuration files to your web application's source code to configure your environment and customize the AWS resources that it contains. The configuration files can be either a JSON file or YAML. Using these configuration files, you can customize your Auto Scaling fleet as well. You should never manually log in and configure EC2 instances since all the manual changes will be lost on scaling events. Figure 7-14 shows what a deployment in Elastic Beanstalk looks like.

AWS Elastic Beanstalk provides a unified user interface to monitor and manage the health of your applications. It collects 40+ key metrics and attributes to determine the health of your application. It has a health dashboard in which you can monitor the application. It is also integrated with Amazon CloudWatch.

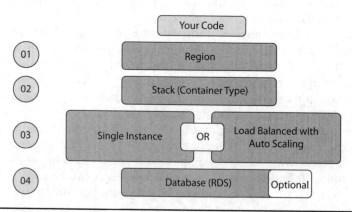

Figure 7-14   Deployment in AWS Elastic Beanstalk

AWS Elastic Beanstalk supports the following languages and development stacks:

- Apache Tomcat for Java applications
- Apache HTTP Server for PHP applications
- Apache HTTP Server for Python applications
- Nginx or Apache HTTP Server for Node.js applications
- Passenger or Puma for Ruby applications
- Microsoft IIS 7.5, 8.0, and 8.5 for .NET applications
- Java SE
- Docker
- Go

AWS OpsWorks

When you're building an application, you want to get new features out to your users fast, but having to manage all the infrastructure that your application needs and respond to changing conditions such as spikes in traffic can be error prone and hard to repeat if you're configuring everything manually. Wouldn't it be nice if you could automate operational tasks like software configuration, server scaling, deployments, and database setup so that you could focus on developing instead of doing all that heavy lifting?

AWS OpsWorks is a configuration management service that helps you deploy and operate applications of all shapes and sizes. OpsWorks allows you to quickly configure, deploy, and update your applications. It even gives you tools to automate operations such as automatic instant scaling and health monitoring. You have a lot of flexibility in defining your applications, architecture, and other things such as package installations, software configurations, and the resources your application needs such as storage databases or load balancers.

OpsWorks provides managed instances of Chef and Puppet. Chef and Puppet are automation platforms that allow you to use code to automate the configurations of your servers. OpsWorks lets you use Chef and Puppet to automate how servers are configured, deployed, and managed across your Amazon EC2 instances or on-premises compute environments.

OpsWorks offers three tools: AWS OpsWorks for Chef Automate, AWS OpsWorks for Puppet Enterprise, and AWS OpsWorks Stacks.

AWS OpsWorks for Chef Automate provides a fully managed Chef server and suite of automation tools that give you workflow automation for continuous deployment, automated testing for compliance and security, and a user interface that gives you visibility into your nodes and their status. The Chef server gives you full stack automation by handling operational tasks such as software and operating system configurations, package installations, database setups, and more. The Chef server centrally stores your configuration tasks and provides them to each node in your compute environment at any scale, from a few nodes to thousands of nodes. OpsWorks for Chef Automate is completely compatible with tooling and cookbooks from the Chef community and automatically registers new nodes with your Chef server.

AWS OpsWorks for Puppet Enterprise provides a managed Puppet Enterprise server and suite of automation tools giving you workflow automation for orchestration, automated provisioning, and visualization for traceability. The Puppet Enterprise server gives you full stack automation by handling operational tasks such as software and operating system configurations, package installations, database setups, and more. The Puppet Master centrally stores your configuration tasks and provides them to each node in your compute environment at any scale.

AWS OpsWorks Stacks lets you manage applications and servers on AWS and on-premises. Using OpsWorks Stacks, you model your entire application as a *stack* consisting of various layers. Layers are like blueprints that define how to set up and configure a set of Amazon EC2 instances and related resources.

OpsWorks provides prebuilt layers for common components, including Ruby, PHP, Node.js, Java, Amazon RDS, HA Proxy, MySQL, and Memcached. It also allows you to define your own layers for practically any technology and configure your layer however you want using Chef recipes. After you define all the layers you need to run your application stack, you just choose the operating system and the instance type to add. You can even scale the number of instances running by time of day or average CPU load. Once your stack is up and running, OpsWorks will pull the code from your repository and deploy it on your instances, and you will have a stack up and running based on the layers you defined earlier.

Using OpsWorks to automate, deploy, and manage applications saves you a lot of time. Without OpsWorks, if you needed to scale up the number of servers, you would need to manually configure everything including web framework configurations, installation scripts, initialization tasks, and database setups for each new instance. With OpsWorks, you set up and configure whatever your application needs for each layer once and let OpsWorks automatically configure all instances launched into that layer. It lets you focus on building amazing applications and services for your users without having to spend a lot of time manually configuring instances, software, and databases. It helps automate your infrastructure, gets your application to your users faster, helps you manage scale and complexity, and protects your applications from failure and downtime.

There is no additional charge for using OpsWorks. You pay for the AWS resources needed to store and run your applications.

Amazon Cognito

When you're building a mobile app, you know that your users probably have more than one device—maybe a smartphone for the work commute and a tablet for enjoying movies later. Being able to sync your user's profile information, whether that's saved game data or some other kind of information, is really important so they can have a great experience with your app whenever and wherever they're using it, regardless of which device they use. If you want to create a back end to support that kind of storage and synchronization, it is a lot of work. You have to build it, deploy it, and manage the infrastructure that it runs on. Wouldn't it be great if you could stay focused on writing your app without having to build your own back end? You just concentrate on syncing and storing users' data?

Amazon Cognito is a user identity and data synchronization service that makes it really easy for you to manage user data for your apps across multiple mobile or connected devices. You can create identities for users of your app using public login providers such as Google, Facebook, and Amazon, and through enterprise identity providers such as Microsoft Active Directory using SAML. This service also supports unauthenticated identities. Users can start off trying your app without logging in, and then when they do create a profile using one of the public logging providers, their profile data is seamlessly transferred. Amazon Cognito user pools provide a secure user directory that scales to hundreds of millions of users. User pools provide user profiles and authentication tokens for users who sign up directly and for federated users who sign in with social and enterprise identity providers. Amazon Cognito User Pools is a standards-based identity provider and supports identity and access management standards, such as OAuth 2.0, SAML 2.0, and OpenID Connect.

You can use Amazon Cognito to sync any kind of user data and key-value pairs whether that is app preferences, game state, or anything that makes sense for your app. By using Amazon Cognito, you don't have to worry about running your own back-end service and dealing with identity network storage or sync issues. You just save the user data using the Amazon Cognito API and sync. The user's data is securely synced and stored in the AWS cloud.

Amazon Cognito provides solutions to control access to AWS resources from your app. You can define roles and map users to different roles so your app can access only the resources that are authorized for each user.

It is really easy to use Amazon Cognito with your app. Instead of taking months to build a solution yourself, it just takes a few lines of code to be able to sync your users' data. if you're using other AWS services, Amazon Cognito provides you with even more benefits such as delivering temporary credentials of limited privileges that users can use to access AWS resources. Amazon Cognito lets you focus on building your app and making sure that your users have a consistent experience regardless of the device they're using without you having to worry about the heavy lifting associated with building your own back-end solution to sync user data.

Amazon Elastic MapReduce

Whatever kind of industry you are in, being able to analyze data coming from a wide variety of sources can help you to make transformational decisions. To be able to make these decisions based on data of any scale, you need to be able to access the right kind of tools to process and analyze your data. Software frameworks like Hadoop can help you store and process large amounts of data by distributing the data and processing across many computers. But at the same time, deploying, configuring, and managing Hadoop clusters can be difficult, expensive, and time-consuming. Traditionally, you had to purchase the underlying servers and storage hardware, provision the hardware, and then deploy and manage the software even before you had a chance to do anything with your data.

Wouldn't it be great if there was an easier way? Amazon Elastic MapReduce (EMR) solves this problem. Using the elastic infrastructure of Amazon EC2 and Amazon S3, Amazon EMR provides a managed Hadoop framework that distributes the computation of your data over multiple Amazon EC2 instances.

Amazon EMR is easy to use. To get started, you need to load the data into Amazon S3; then you can launch EMR clusters in minutes. Once a cluster is launched, it can start processing your data immediately, and you don't need to worry about setting up, running, or tuning clusters. Since it is a managed service, Amazon is going to take care of the heavy lifting behind the scenes. You just need to define how many nodes in the cluster you need, what types of instances you need, and what applications you want to install in the cluster. Then Amazon will provision everything for you.

Thus, you can focus on the analysis of your data. When your job is complete, you can retrieve the output from Amazon S3. You can also feed this data from S3 to a visualization tool or use it for reporting purposes. Amazon EMR monitors the job. Once the job is completed, EMR can shut down the cluster or keep it running so it is available for additional processing queries. You could easily expand or shrink your clusters to handle more or less data and to get the processing done more quickly.

In a Hadoop ecosystem, the data remains on the servers that process the data. As a result, it takes some time to add or remove a server from a cluster. In the case of EMR, the data remains decoupled between the EC2 servers and Amazon S3. EC2 only processes the data, and the actual data resides in Amazon S3. As a result, at any point in time, you can scale up or scale down. Say you are running an EMR job and you have selected only one EC2 server for running the job, and let's say the job takes 10 hours. Let's say this EC2 server costs $1 per hour, so the total cost of running this job would be $10 ($1 * 10 hours), and the amount of time it takes is 10 hours. Now instead of processing this job with one EC2 server, if you create an EMR cluster with a 10-node EC2 server, the job is going to be finished in just one hour instead of ten since you added 10 times more compute. Now price-wise, it is going to cost $10 ($1 per server * 10 servers). In this case, you are processing the same job ten times faster but paying the same amount of money to process the job.

When you store your data in Amazon S3, you can access it with multiple EMR clusters simultaneously, which means users can quickly spin off as many clusters as they need to test new ideas and can terminate clusters when they're no longer needed. This can help speed innovation and lower the cost of experimentation, and you can even optimize each cluster for a particular application.

You can have three types of nodes in an Amazon EMR cluster:

- **Master node**   This node takes care of coordinating the distribution of the job across core and task nodes.

- **Core node**   This node takes care of running the task that the master node assigns. This node also stores the data in the Hadoop Distributed File System (HDFS) on your cluster.

- **Task node**   This node runs only the task and does not store any data. The task nodes are optional and provide pure compute to your cluster.

Amazon EMR is low cost and provides a range of pricing options, including hourly on-demand pricing, the ability to reserve capacity for a lower hourly rate, or the ability to name your own price for the resources you need with spot instances. Spot instances are a great use case for Amazon EMR; you can use the spot instance for the task node since it does not store any data and is used for pure compute. You can mix and match different types of EC2 instance types for spot instances so that even if you lose a particular type of EC2 instance, the other type is not impacted when someone over-bids you.

Amazon EMR automatically configures the security groups for the cluster and makes it easy to control access. You can even launch clusters in an Amazon Virtual Private Cloud (VPC).

With Amazon EMR you can run MapReduce and a variety of powerful applications and frameworks, such as Hive, Pig, HBase, Impala, Cascading, and Spark. You can also use a variety of different programming languages. Amazon EMR supports multiple Hadoop distributions and integrates with popular third-party tools. You can also install additional software or further customize the clusters for your specific use case.

AWS CloudFormation

When you are managing infrastructure, you might use run books and scripts to create and manage everything. Version controlling and keeping track of changes can be challenging. Things get even harder when you need to replicate your entire production stack multiple times for development and testing purposes. If you want to provision infrastructure stacks directly from a collection of scripts, it is not simple. Wouldn't it be great if you could create and manage your infrastructure and application stack in a controlled and predictable way?

You can do the same seamlessly using AWS CloudFormation. CloudFormation provisions and manages stacks of AWS resources based on templates you create to model your infrastructure architecture. You can manage anything from a single Amazon EC2 instance to a complex multitier, multiregion application. CloudFormation can be used to define simple things such as an Amazon VPC subnet, as well as provision services such as AWS OpsWorks or AWS Elastic Beanstalk.

It is easy to get started with CloudFormation. You simply create a template, which is a JSON file that serves as a blueprint to define the configuration of all the AWS resources that make up your infrastructure and application stack, or you can select a sample pre-built template that CloudFormation provides for commonly used architectures such as a LAMP stack running on Amazon EC2 and an Amazon RDS. Next you just upload your template to CloudFormation. You can also select parameters such as the number of instances or instance type if necessary; then CloudFormation will provision and configure your AWS resource stack. You can update your CloudFormation stack at any time by uploading a modified template through the AWS management console, CLI, or SDK. You can also check your template into version control, so you're able to keep track of all changes made to your infrastructure and application stack. With CloudFormation you can version control your infrastructure architecture the same way you would with software code. Provisioning infrastructure is as simple as creating and uploading a template to CloudFormation. This makes replicating your infrastructure simple. You can easily and quickly spin up a replica of your production stack for development and testing with a few clicks in the AWS Management Console. You can tear down and rebuild the replica stacks whenever you want. Replicating production staff could have been time-consuming and error prone if you did it manually, but with CloudFormation you can create and manage the AWS resource stack quickly and reliably. There is no additional charge for Cloud-Formation; you pay only for the AWS resources that CloudFormation creates and your application uses. CloudFormation allows you to treat your infrastructure as just code.

To use AWS CloudFormation, you need templates and stacks. Using templates, you can describe your AWS resources and their properties. Whenever you create a stack, CloudFormation provisions the resources as per your template. A CloudFormation template is a JSON- or YAML-formatted text file. You can create a template directly from the editor available from the AWS Management Console or by using any text editor. You can save the template with an extension such as .json or .yaml.txt or .template. These templates serve as a blueprint for building all the resources. Using a template you can specify the resource that CloudFormation is going to build. For example, you can specify a specific type of an EC2 instance as a resource in your CloudFormation template. All the AWS resources collected together is called a *stack*. You can manage the stack as a single unit. For example, using a stack you can create multiple resources like an EC2 instance, VPC, or RDS database via a single CloudFormation template. You can create, update, or delete a collection of resources by creating, updating, or deleting stacks. Using AWS CloudFormation templates, you can define all the resources in a stack. Figure 7-15 shows how AWS CloudFormation works.

Whenever you have to make changes to the running resources in a stack, such as when you want to add an ELB to the existing EC2 instances, you need to update the existing stack. Before making the changes, you can generate a change set that summarizes the proposed change. Using a change set, you can foresee what is going to be the impact on your running resources if the change is being made.

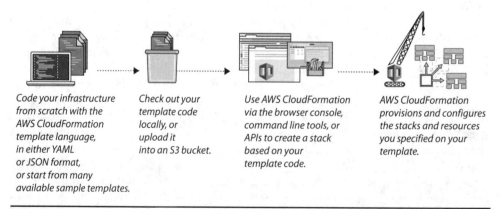

Code your infrastructure from scratch with the AWS CloudFormation template language, in either YAML or JSON format, or start from many available sample templates.

Check out your template code locally, or upload it into an S3 bucket.

Use AWS CloudFormation via the browser console, command line tools, or APIs to create a stack based on your template code.

AWS CloudFormation provisions and configures the stacks and resources you specified on your template.

Figure 7-15 How AWS CloudFormation works

Monitoring in AWS

Whenever you build or deploy your applications, you should have the capability to monitor them from end to end. By using the right monitoring tools, you will be able to find out whether the application is performing well, whether there is a security vulnerability in the application, whether the application is talking too much of your resources in terms of CPU or memory, or whether the application is constrained in terms of resources when you build or deploy your applications in AWS. In addition to these questions, you may ask some additional questions such as, How do I capture, view, and act on resource availability and state changes? How do I track the key performance indicators across AWS resources? How can API calls be logged within my AWS accounts? How do I track cost within my AWS accounts? AWS provides you with lots of tools that give you this capability. Apart from technical reasons, there are several other reasons why you should monitor your systems. Via monitoring you can find out whether your customers are getting a good experience or not, whether the changes you are making in the system are impacting overall performance, whether the same problem can be prevented in the future or not, when you need to scale, and so on.

NOTE In AWS, resources are software defined, and changes to them are tracked as API calls. The current and past states of your environment can be monitored and acted on in real time. AWS scaling allows for ubiquitous logging, which can be extended to your application logs and centralized for analysis, audit, and mitigation purposes.

In this section, we will discuss all these tools that can be used to monitor the AWS resources.

Amazon CloudWatch

Watching the cloud means monitoring all the resources deployed in the AWS cloud. Amazon CloudWatch provides capabilities to gain visibility into what's going on with your resources. You can monitor the health checks, look at the utilization, and view performance. Amazon CloudWatch monitors your AWS cloud resources and your cloud-powered applications. It tracks the metrics so that you can visualize and review them. You can also set alarms that will fire when a metric goes beyond the limit that you specify. CloudWatch gives you visibility into resource utilization, application performance, and operational health.

Let's explore what Amazon CloudWatch can do.

Metrics Collection and Tracking

Amazon CloudWatch provides metrics for all the services, and there are more than 100 types of metrics available among all the different services. You can look at these metrics for your EC2 instances (e.g., in an EC2 instance, you can look at CPU, Network In/Out, and so on), RDS, ELBs, EBS volumes, DynamoDB, and so on. Apart from the default metrics available, you can also create your own custom metrics using your application and monitor them via Amazon CloudWatch. Please login to the AWS console and browse all the metrics you can monitor via CloudWatch. You will see that you will be able to monitor almost everything via CloudWatch, but for monitoring some components you may have to write custom metrics. For example, in order to monitor the memory utilization, you have to write a custom metric. Previously (before November 2016), these metrics used to be retained for 14 days, but now the metrics are retained depending on the metric interval.

- For the one-minute data point, the retention is 15 days.
- For the five-minute data point, the retention is 63 days.
- For the one-hour data point, the retention is 15 months or 455 days.

Capture Real-Time Changes Using Amazon CloudWatch Events

Amazon CloudWatch Events helps you to detect any changes made to your AWS resource. When CloudWatch Events detects a change, it delivers a notification in almost real time to a target you choose. The target can be a Lambda function, an SNS queue, an Amazon SNS topic, or a Kinesis Stream or built-in target. You can set up your own rules and can take action whenever you detect a change. There are many ways to leverage Amazon CloudWatch Events. For example, say your company has a strict rule that whenever someone is creating an EC2 instance, they should tag it. You can create a CloudWatch event whenever an EC2 is created and send it to a Lambda function. The Lambda function will check whether the newly created instance has a tag. If it does not have a tag, it can automatically tag the instance as per the logic you define.

Monitoring and Storing Logs

You can use CloudWatch Logs to monitor and troubleshoot your systems and applications using your existing system, application, and custom log files. You can send your existing log files to CloudWatch Logs and monitor these logs in near real time. Amazon CloudWatch Logs is a managed service to collect and keep your logs. It can aggregate and centralize logs across multiple sources. Using the CloudWatch Logs Agent, you can stream the log files from an EC2 instance. The CloudWatch agent is available for both Linux and Windows. In addition to the agent, you can publish log data using the AWS CLI, the CloudWatch Logs SDK, or the CloudWatch Logs API. You can further export data to S3 for analytics and/or archival or stream to the Amazon Elasticsearch Service or third-party tools like Splunk.

CloudWatch Logs can be used to monitor your logs for specific phrases, values, or patterns. Figure 7-16 shows how you can filter a particular pattern from CloudWatch Logs.

For example, you could set an alarm on the number of errors that occur in your system logs or view graphs of web request latencies from your application logs. You can view the original log data to see the source of the problem if needed.

Set Alarms

You can create a CloudWatch alarm that sends an Amazon Simple Notification Service message when the alarm changes state. An alarm watches a single metric over a time period

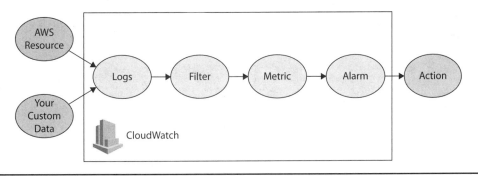

Figure 7-16   Filtering a particular pattern from Amazon CloudWatch Logs

you specify and performs one or more actions based on the value of the metric relative to a given threshold over a number of time periods. The action is a notification sent to an Amazon Simple Notification Service topic or Auto Scaling policy. Alarms invoke actions for sustained state changes only. A CloudWatch alarm will not invoke an action just because it is in a particular state; to be invoked, the state must have changed and been maintained for a specified period of time. An alarm has the following possible states:

- **OK**   This state means the metric is within the defined threshold.
- **ALARM**   This state means the metric is outside the defined threshold.
- **INSUFFICIENT_DATA**   This state means the alarm has just started, the metric is not available, or not enough data is available to determine the alarm state.

Let's look at an example to understand this. You have created an alarm to alert you when the CPU runs at or above 75 percent in an EC2 instance. Say you have set the alarm threshold to 3, which means after the third occurrence of 75 percent CPU utilization in the EC2 instance, the alarm is going to invoke the action associated with it. Say you have defined an action that says when the CPU gets to more than 75 percent, start one more EC2 instance via Auto Scaling, and after the third occurrence, Auto Scaling should add more EC2 instances for you. Figure 7-17 shows how Amazon CloudWatch metrics and CloudWatch alarms can be used together.

View Graph and Statistics

You can use Amazon CloudWatch dashboards to view different types of graphs and statistics of the resources you have deployed. You can create your own dashboard and can have a consolidated view across your resources. The Amazon CloudWatch dashboard is a single view for selected metrics to help you assess the health of your resources and applications across one or more regions. It acts as an operational playbook that provides guidance for team members during operational events about how to respond to specific incidents. It is a common view of critical resource and application measurements that can be shared by team members for faster communication flow during operational events. Figure 7-18 summarizes all the Amazon CloudWatch capabilities.

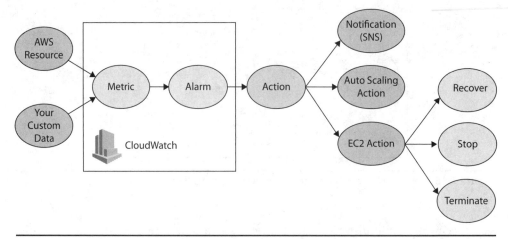

Figure 7-17   Using Amazon CloudWatch metrics and Amazon CloudWatch alarms together

AWS CloudTrail

AWS CloudTrail is a service that logs all API calls, including console activities and command-line instructions. It logs exactly who did what, when, and from where. It can tell you which resources were acted up on in the API call and where the API call was made from and to whom. That means you have full visibility into the accesses, changes, or activity within your AWS environment. You can save these logs into your S3 buckets.

CloudTrail can help you achieve many tasks. You can track changes to AWS resources (for example, VPC security groups and NACLs), comply with rules (log and understand AWS API call history), and troubleshoot operational issues (quickly identify the most recent changes to your environment). Different accounts can send their trails to a central account, and then the central account can do analytics. After that, the central account can redistribute the trails and grant access to the trails.

AWS CloudTrail shows the results of the CloudTrail event history for the current region you are viewing for the last 90 days.

You can have the CloudTrail trail going to CloudWatch Logs and Amazon Cloud-Watch Events in addition to Amazon S3. This enables you to leverage features to help

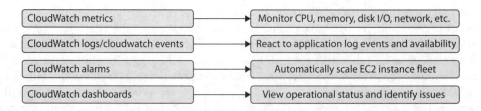

Figure 7-18   Amazon CloudWatch capabilities

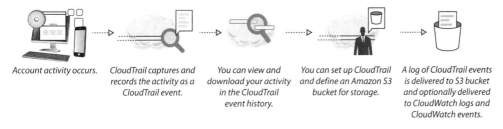

Account activity occurs.   CloudTrail captures and   You can view and   You can set up CloudTrail   A log of CloudTrail events
                            records the activity as a   download your activity   and define an Amazon S3   is delivered to S3 bucket
                            CloudTrail event.   in the CloudTrail   bucket for storage.   and optionally delivered
                                                 event history.   to CloudWatch logs and
                                                                                         CloudWatch events.

Figure 7-19 How AWS CloudTrail works

you archive, analyze, and respond to changes in your AWS resources. You can create up to five trails in an AWS region. Figure 7-19 shows how AWS CloudTrail works.

You can follow these AWS CloudTrail best practices for setting up CloudTrail:

- Enable AWS CloudTrail in all regions to get logs of API calls by setting up a trail that applies to all regions.
- Enable log file validation using industry-standard algorithms, SHA-256 for hashing and SHA-256 with RSA for digital signing.
- By default, the log files delivered by CloudTrail to your bucket are encrypted by Amazon server-side encryption with Amazon S3 managed encryption keys (SSE-S3). To provide a security layer that is directly manageable, you can instead use server-side encryption with AWS KMS managed keys (SSE-KMS) for your CloudTrail log files.
- Set up real-time monitoring of CloudTrail logs by sending them to CloudWatch logs.
- If you are using multiple AWS accounts, centralize CloudTrail logs in a single account.
- For added durability, configure cross-region replication (CRR) for S3 buckets containing CloudTrail logs.

AWS Config

AWS Config is a fully managed service that provides you with a detailed inventory of your AWS resources and their current configuration in an AWS account. It continuously records configuration changes to these resources (e.g., EC2 instance launch, ingress/egress rules of security groups, network ACL rules for VPCs, etc.). It lets you audit the resource configuration history and notifies you of resource configuration changes. Determine how a resource was configured at any point in time, and get notified via Amazon SNS when the configuration of a resource changes or when a rule becomes noncompliant.

A config rule represents desired configurations for a resource and is evaluated against configuration changes on the relevant resources, as recorded by AWS Config. The results of evaluating a rule against the configuration of a resource are available on a dashboard.

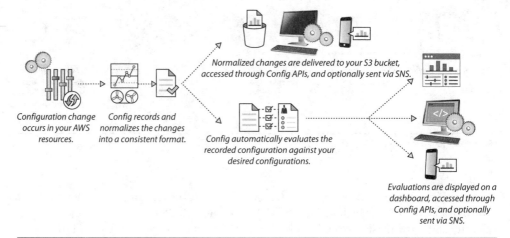

Normalized changes are delivered to your S3 bucket, accessed through Config APIs, and optionally sent via SNS.

Configuration change occurs in your AWS resources.

Config records and normalizes the changes into a consistent format.

Config automatically evaluates the recorded configuration against your desired configurations.

Evaluations are displayed on a dashboard, accessed through Config APIs, and optionally sent via SNS.

Figure 7-20   How AWS Config works

Using config rules, you can assess your overall compliance and risk status from a configuration perspective, view compliance trends over time, and pinpoint which configuration change caused a resource to drift out of compliance with a rule. Figure 7-20 shows how AWS Config works.

These are the things you can do with AWS Config:

- **Continuous monitoring**   AWS Config allows you to constantly monitor all your AWS resources and record any configuration changes in them. As a result, whenever there is a change, you can get instantly notified of it. It can make an inventory of all AWS resources and the configuration of those resources.

- **Continuous assessment**   AWS Config provides you with the ability to define rules for provisioning and configuring AWS resources, and it can continuously audit and assess the overall compliance of your AWS resource configurations with your organization's policies and guidelines. AWS Config constantly assesses your resources against standard configuration, and whenever there is a deviation, it instantly notifies you.

- **Change management**   AWS Config helps you with change management. It can track what was changed, when it happened, and how the change might affect other AWS resources. This need might arise because of an unexpected configuration change, a suspected system failure, a compliance audit, or a possible security incident. You can also track the relationships among resources and review resource dependencies prior to making changes. Once you make a change, you can look at the configuration history to find out how it looked in the past.

- **Operational troubleshooting**   Since AWS Config tracks all the changes and constantly monitors all your resources, it can be used for troubleshooting against operational issues. It helps you to find the root cause by pointing out what change is causing the issue. Since AWS Config can be integrated with AWS CloudTrail, you can correlate configuration changes to particular events in your account.

- **Compliance monitoring**   You can use AWS Config for compliance monitoring for your entire account or across multiple accounts. If a resource violates a rule, AWS Config flags the resource and the rule as noncompliant. You can dive deeper to view the status for a specific region or a specific account across regions.

Amazon VPC Flow Logs

Amazon VPC Flow Logs captures information about the IP traffic going to and from network interfaces in your VPC. The Flow Logs data is stored using Amazon Cloud-Watch Logs, which can then be integrated with additional services, such as Elasticsearch/Kibana for visualization.

The flow logs can be used to troubleshoot why specific traffic is not reaching an instance. Once enabled for a particular VPC, VPC subnet, or Elastic Network Interface (ENI), relevant network traffic will be logged to CloudWatch Logs for storage and analysis by your own applications or third-party tools.

You can create alarms that will fire if certain types of traffic are detected; you can also create metrics to help you to identify trends and patterns.

The information captured includes information about allowed and denied traffic (based on security group and network ACL rules). It also includes source and destination IP addresses, ports, the IANA protocol number, packet and byte counts, a time interval during which the flow was observed, and an action (ACCEPT or REJECT).

You can enable VPC Flow Logs at different levels.

- **VPC**   This would cover all network interfaces in that VPC.
- **Subnet**   This captures traffic on all network interfaces in that subnet.
- **Network interface**   This captures traffic specific to a single network interface.

Figure 7-21 shows VPC Flow Logs capture from different places.

You can enable VPC Flow Logs from the AWS Management Console or the AWS CLI or by making calls to the EC2 API. VPC Flow Logs does not require any agents on EC2 instances. Once you create a flow log, it takes several minutes to begin collecting data and publishing to CloudWatch Logs. Please note that it should not be used as a tool for capturing real-time log streams for network interfaces. The flow logs can capture either all flows, rejected flows, or accepted flows. VPC Flow Logs can be used both for security monitoring and for application troubleshooting. You can create CloudWatch metrics from VPC log data.

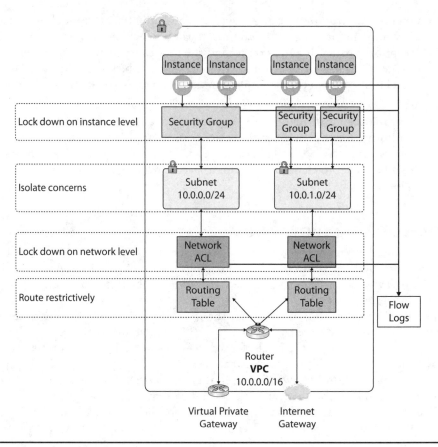

Figure 7-21   VPC Flow Logs capture

AWS Trusted Advisor

AWS Trusted Advisor provides best practices (or checks) in five categories:

- **Cost Optimization**   You can save money on AWS by eliminating unused and idle resources or making commitments to reserved capacity.
- **Security**   Helps you to improve the security of your application by closing gaps, enabling various AWS security features, and examining your permissions.
- **Fault Tolerance**   You can increase the availability and redundancy of your AWS application by taking advantage of Auto Scaling, health checks, multi-AZ, and backup capabilities.

- **Performance**   Helps you to improve the performance of your service by checking your service limits, ensuring you take advantage of provisioned throughput, and monitoring for over utilized instances.
- **Service Limits**   It checks for service usage that is more than 80 percent of the service limit. Since the values are based on a snapshot, your current usage might differ. Sometimes it may take up to 24 hours to reflect any change. For example the default service limit for EC2 instance is 20. If you have already created more than 16 instance it will be displayed on the dashboard.

The status of the check is shown by using color coding on the dashboard page.

- Red means action is recommended.
- Yellow means investigation is recommended.
- Green means no problem is detected.

Figure 7-22 shows the Trusted Advisor Dashboard screen.

These seven Trusted Advisor checks are available to all customers under various categories: Service Limits, S3 Bucket Permissions, Security Groups–Specific Ports Unrestricted, IAM Use, MFA on Root Account, EBS Public Snapshots, and RDS Public Snapshots. Customers can access the remaining checks by upgrading to a Business or Enterprise Support plan. Figures 7-23 and 7-24 show a few checks that Trusted Advisor does on the Cost Optimization and Security tabs.

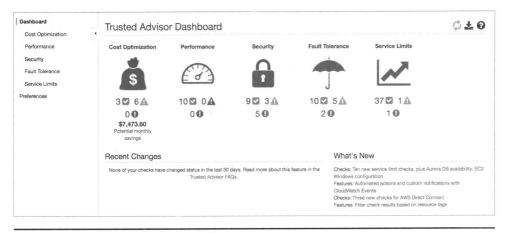

Figure 7-22   Trusted Advisor Dashboard

Figure 7-23   Checks on the Cost Optimization tab from Trusted Advisor

Figure 7-24   Checks on the Security tab from Trusted Advisor

AWS Organizations

Many AWS enterprises have found themselves managing multiple AWS accounts as they have scaled up their use of AWS for a variety of reasons. Some of these enterprises have added more accounts incrementally as individual teams and divisions make the move to the cloud.

Other enterprises use different accounts for test development and production systems or to meet strict guidelines for compliance such as HIPAA or PCI. As the number of these accounts increases, enterprises would like to set policies and manage billing across their accounts in a simple, more scalable way, without requiring custom scripts and manual processes.

Enterprises also want more efficient automated solutions for creating new accounts with the current policies applied as they create more accounts to meet the needs of their business.

AWS Organizations makes account management simple. It offers policy-based management from multiple AWS accounts. You can create groups of accounts and then apply policies to those groups that centrally control the use of AWS services down to the API level across multiple accounts. It enables you to centrally manage policies across multiple accounts, without requiring custom scripts and manual processes. For example, you can create a group of accounts that are used for production resources and then apply a policy to this group that limits which AWS service APIs those accounts can use. You can also use the organization's APIs to help automate the creation of new AWS accounts with a few simple API calls. You can create a new account programmatically and then apply the correct policies to the new account automatically. AWS Organizations' service control policies (SCPs) help you centrally control AWS service use across multiple AWS accounts in your organization.

Using AWS Organizations, you can set up a single payment method for all of these accounts through consolidated building. AWS Organizations is available to all AWS customers free of cost.

Chapter Review

In this chapter, you learned about AWS Lambda, Amazon API Gateway, and Amazon Kinesis. You also learned about Amazon CloudFront, Amazon Route 53, AWS WAF, Amazon Simple Queue Service, Amazon Simple Notification Service, AWS Step Functions, Elastic Beanstalk,AWS OpsWorks,Amazon Cognito, Amazon EMR, AWS CloudFormation,Amazon CloudWatch,CloudTrail,AWS Config,VPC Flow Logs,AWS Trusted Advisor and AWS Organizations.

With Lambda, you can run code for virtually any type of application or back-end service. Lambda runs and scales your code with high availability. Each Lambda function you create contains the code you want to execute, the configuration that defines how your code is executed, and, optionally, one or more event sources that detect events and invoke your function as they occur. AWS Lambda supports Java, Node.js, Python, and C#.

API Gateway is a fully managed service that makes it easy for developers to define, publish, deploy, maintain, monitor, and secure APIs at any scale. Clients integrate with the APIs using standard HTTPS requests. API Gateway serves as a front door (to access data, business logic, or functionality from your back-end services) to any web application running on Amazon EC2, Amazon ECS, AWS Lambda, or on-premises environment.

Amazon Kinesis Data Streams enables you to build custom applications that process or analyze streaming data for specialized needs. Kinesis Data Streams can continuously capture and store terabytes of data per hour from hundreds of thousands of sources such as web site clickstreams, financial transactions, social media feeds, IT logs, and location-tracking events.

Amazon Kinesis Data Firehose is the easiest way to load streaming data into data stores and analytics tools. It can capture, transform, and load streaming data into Amazon S3, Amazon Redshift, Amazon Elasticsearch Service, and Splunk, enabling near real-time analytics with the existing business intelligence tools and dashboards you're already using today. It is a fully managed service that automatically scales to match the throughput of your data and requires no ongoing administration. It can also batch, compress, and encrypt the data before loading it, minimizing the amount of storage used at the destination and increasing security.

Amazon Kinesis Data Analytics is the easiest way to process and analyze real-time, streaming data. With Amazon Kinesis Data Analytics, you just use standard SQL to process your data streams, so you don't have to learn any new programming languages. Simply point Kinesis Data Analytics at an incoming data stream, write your SQL queries, and specify where you want to load the results. Kinesis Data Analytics takes care of running your SQL queries continuously on data while it's in transit and sends the results to the destinations.

Amazon CloudFront is a global CDN service that allows you to distribute content with low latency and provides high data transfer speeds. Amazon CloudFront employs a global network of edge locations and regional edge caches that cache copies of your content close to your viewers.

Amazon Route 53 is the managed DNS service of Amazon. DNS translates human-readable names like www.example.com into the numeric IP addresses like 192.0.0.3 that servers/computers use to connect to each other. Route 53 is the only service that has 100 percent SLA. This service is region independent.

AWS WAF is a web application firewall that protects your web applications from various forms of attack. It helps to protect web sites and applications against attacks that could affect application availability, cause data breaches, cause downtime, compromise security, or consume excessive resources. It gives you control over which traffic to allow or block to your web applications by defining customizable web security rules.

Amazon Simple Queue Service is a fast, reliable, scalable, and fully managed queue service. Using Amazon SQS, you can quickly build message queuing applications that can run on any system. It can send, store, and receive messages between components. Like most AWS services, it's accessible through a web API, as well as SDKs in most languages.

Amazon Simple Notification Service is a web service used to send notifications from the cloud. It is easy to set up and operate and at the same time highly scalable, flexible, and cost-effective. SNS has the capacity to publish messages from an application and then immediately deliver them to subscribers. It follows the publish-subscribe mechanism.

AWS Step Functions is a fully managed service that makes it easy to coordinate the components of distributed applications and microservices using a visual workflow. It is really easy to use and scales down to little one-off shell-script equivalents and up to billions of complex multiphase tasks.

Using AWS Elastic Beanstalk, you can deploy, monitor, and scale an application on AWS quickly and easily. Elastic Beanstalk is the simplest and fastest way to deploy web applications. You just need to upload your code and Elastic Beanstalk will provision all the resources like Amazon EC2, Amazon Elastic Container Service (Amazon ECS), Auto Scaling, and Elastic Load Balancing for you behind the scenes.

AWS OpsWorks is a configuration management service that helps you deploy and operate applications of all shapes and sizes. OpsWorks provides an easy way to quickly configure, deploy, and update your applications. OpsWorks offers AWS OpsWorks for Chef Automate, AWS OpsWorks for Puppet Enterprise, and AWS OpsWorks Stacks.

Amazon Cognito is a user identity and data synchronization service that makes it really easy for you to manage user data for your apps across multiple mobile or connected devices. You can create identities for users of your app using public login providers such as Google, Facebook, Amazon, and through enterprise identity providers such as Microsoft Active Directory using SAML.

Amazon EMR provides a managed Hadoop framework that distributes computation of your data over multiple Amazon EC2 instances. It decouples the compute and storage by keeping the data in Amazon S3 and using Amazon EC2 instances for processing the data.

AWS CloudFormation provisions and manages stacks of AWS resources based on templates you create to model your infrastructure architecture. You can manage anything, from a single Amazon EC2 instance to a complex multitier, multiregion application. AWS CloudFormation allows you to treat your infrastructure as just code.

Amazon CloudWatch is a monitoring service for AWS cloud resources and the applications you run on AWS. You can use Amazon CloudWatch to gain system-wide visibility into resource utilization, application performance, and operational health. You can use these insights to react and keep your application running smoothly. Amazon CloudWatch monitors your AWS cloud resources and your cloud-powered applications. It tracks the metrics so that you can visualize and review them.

AWS CloudTrail is a service that logs all API calls, including console activities and command-line instructions. It logs exactly who did what, when, and from where. It can tell you which resources were acted up on in the API call and where the API call was made from and was made to. That means you have full visibility into and accesses, changes, or activity within your AWS environment. You can save these logs into your S3 buckets.

AWS Config is a fully managed service that provides you with a detailed inventory of your AWS resources and their current configuration in an AWS account. It continuously records configuration changes to these resources (e.g., EC2 instance launch, ingress/egress rules of security groups, network ACL rules for VPCs, etc.).

VPC Flow Logs captures information about the IP traffic going to and from network interfaces in your VPC. The flow log data is stored using Amazon CloudWatch Logs, which can then be integrated with additional services, such as Elasticsearch/Kibana for visualization.

AWS Trusted Advisor provides best practices (or checks) in five categories: cost optimization, security, fault tolerance, performance, and service limits.

AWS Organizations offers policy-based management for multiple AWS accounts. With Organizations, you can create groups of accounts and then apply policies to those groups. Organizations enables you to centrally manage policies across multiple accounts, without requiring custom scripts and manual processes.

Questions

1. What are the languages that AWS Lambda supports? (Choose two.)
   A. Perl
   B. Ruby
   C. Java
   D. Python

2. Which product is not a good fit if you want to run a job for ten hours?
   A. AWS Batch
   B. EC2
   C. Elastic Beanstalk
   D. Lambda

3. What product should you use if you want to process a lot of streaming data?
   A. Kinesis Firehouse
   B. Kinesis Data Stream
   C. Kinesis Data Analytics
   D. API Gateway

4. Which product should you choose if you want to have a solution for versioning your APIs without having the pain of managing the infrastructure?
   A. Install a version control system on EC2 servers
   B. Use Elastic Beanstalk
   C. Use API Gateway
   D. Use Kinesis Data Firehose

5. You want to transform the data while it is coming in. What is the easiest way of doing this?
   A. Use Kinesis Data Analytics
   B. Spin off an EMR cluster while the data is coming in
   C. Install Hadoop on EC2 servers to do the processing
   D. Transform the data in S3

6. Which product is not serverless?
   A. Redshift
   B. DynamoDB

    C. S3

    D. AWS Lambda

7. You have the requirement to ingest the data in real time. What product should you choose?

    A. Upload the data directly to S3

    B. Use S3 IA

    C. Use S3 reduced redundancy

    D. Use Kinesis Data Streams

8. You have a huge amount of data to be ingested. You don't have a very stringent SLA for it. Which product should you use?

    A. Kinesis Data Streams

    B. Kinesis Data Firehose

    C. Kinesis Data Analytics

    D. S3

9. What is the best way to manage RESTful APIs?

    A. API Gateway

    B. EC2 servers

    C. Lambda

    D. AWS Batch

10. To execute code in AWS Lambda, what is the size of the EC2 instance you need to provision in the back end?

    A. For code running less than one minute, use a T2 Micro.

    B. For code running between one minute and three minutes, use M2.

    C. For code running between three minutes and five minutes, use M2 large.

    D. There is no need to provision an EC2 instance on the back end.

11. What are the two configuration management services that AWS OpsWorks supports?

    A. Chef

    B. Ansible

    C. Puppet

    D. Java

12. You are designing an e-commerce order management web site where your users can order different types of goods. You want to decouple the architecture and would like to separate the ordering process from shipping. Depending on the shipping priority, you want to have a separate queue running for standard shipping versus priority shipping. Which AWS service would you consider for this?

    A. AWS CloudWatch

    B. AWS CloudWatch Events

    C. AWS API Gateway

    D. AWS SQS

13. You company has more than 20 business units, and each business unit has its own account in AWS. Which AWS service would you choose to manage the billing across all the different AWS accounts?

    A. AWS Organizations

    B. AWS Trusted Advisor

    C. AWS Cost Advisor

    D. AWS Billing Console

14. You are running a job in an EMR cluster, and the job is running for a long period of time. You want to add additional horsepower to your cluster, and at the same time you want to make sure it is cost effective. What is the best way of solving this problem?

    A. Add more on-demand EC2 instances for your task node

    B. Add more on-demand EC2 instances for your core node

    C. Add more spot instances for your task node

    D. Add more reserved instances for your task node

15. Your resources were running fine in AWS, and all of a sudden you notice that something has changed. Your cloud security team told you that some API has changed the state of your resources that were running fine earlier. How do you track who has created the mistake?

    A. By writing a Lambda function, you can find who has changed what

    B. By using AWS CloudTrail

    C. By using Amazon CloudWatch Events

    D. By using AWS Trusted Advisor

16. You are running a mission-critical three-tier application on AWS and have enabled Amazon CloudWatch metrics for a one-minute data point. How far back you can go and see the metrics?

    A. One week

    B. 24 hours

    C. One month

    D. 15 days

17. You are running all your AWS resources in the US-East region, and you are not leveraging a second region using AWS. However, you want to keep your infrastructure as code so that you should be able to fail over to a different region if

any DR happens. Which AWS service will you choose to provision the resources in a second region that looks identical to your resources in the US-East region?

   A. Amazon EC2, VPC, and RDS

   B. Elastic Beanstalk

   C. OpsWorks

   D. CloudFormation

18. What is the AWS service you are going to use to monitor the service limit of your EC2 instance?

   A. EC2 dashboard

   B. AWS Trusted Advisor

   C. AWS CloudWatch

   D. AWS Config

19. You are a developer and want to deploy your application in AWS. You don't have an infrastructure background and are not sure about how to use infrastructure within AWS. You are looking for deploying your application in such a way that the infrastructure scales on its own, and at the same time you don't have to deal with managing it. Which AWS service are you going to choose for this?

   A. AWS Config

   B. AWS Lambda

   C. AWS Elastic Beanstalk

   D. Amazon EC2 servers and Auto Scaling

20. In the past, someone made some changes to your security group, and as a result an instance is not accessible by the users for some time. This resulted in nasty downtime for the application. You are looking to find out what change has been made in the system, and you want to track it. Which AWS service are you going to use for this?

   A. AWS Config

   B. Amazon CloudWatch

   C. AWS CloudTrail

   D. AWS Trusted Advisor

Answers

1. **C, D**. Perl and Ruby are not supported by Lambda.

2. **D**. Lambda is not a good fit because the maximum execution time for code in Lambda is five minutes. Using Batch you can run your code for as long as you want. Similarly, you can run your code for as long as you want on EC2 servers or by using Elastic Beanstalk.

3. **B**. Kinesis Data Firehose is used mainly for large amounts of nonstreaming data, Kinesis Data Analytics is used for transforming data, and API Gateway is used for managing APIs.

4. **C**. EC2 servers and Elastic Beanstalk both need you to manage some infrastructure; Kinesis Data Firehose is used for ingesting data.

5. **A**. Using EC2 servers or Amazon EMR, you can transform the data, but that is not the easiest way to do it. S3 is just the data store; it does not have any transformation capabilities.

6. **A**. DynamoDB, S3, and AWS Lambda all are serverless.

7. **D**. You can use S3 for storing the data, but if the requirement is to ingest the data in real time, S3 is not the right solution.

8. **B**. Kinesis Data Streams is used for ingesting real-time data, and Kinesis Data Analytics is used for transformation. S3 is used to store the data.

9. **A**. Theoretically EC2 servers can be used for managing the APIs, but if you can do it easily through API Gateway, why would you even consider EC2 servers? Lambda and Batch are used for executing the code.

10. **D**. There is no need to provision EC2 servers since Lambda is serverless.

11. **A**, **C**. AWS OpsWorks supports Chef and Puppet.

12. **D**. Using SQS, you can decouple the ordering and shipping processes, and you can create separate queues for the ordering and shipping processes.

13. **A**. Using AWS Organizations, you can manage the billing from various AWS accounts.

14. **C**. You can add more spot instances to your task node to finish the job early. Spot instances are the cheapest in cost, so this will make sure the solution is cost effective.

15. **B**. Using AWS CloudTrail, you can find out who has changed what via API.

16. **D**. When CloudWatch is enabled for a one-minute data point, the retention is 15 days.

17. **D**. Using CloudFormation, you can keep the infrastructure as code, and you can create a CloudFormation template to mimic the setup in an existing region and can deploy the CloudFormation template in a different region to create the resources.

18. **B**. Using Trusted Advisor, you can monitor the service limits for the EC2 instance.

19. **C**. AWS Elastic Beanstalk is an easy-to-use service for deploying and scaling web applications. You can simply upload your code and Elastic Beanstalk automatically handles the deployment, from capacity provisioning, load balancing, auto-scaling to application health monitoring.

20. **A**. AWS Config maintains the configuration of the system and helps you to identify what change was made in it.

Databases on AWS

In this chapter, you will

- Learn about relational databases and Amazon Relational Database Service (RDS)
- Understand Amazon Aurora
- Learn about Amazon Redshift
- Learn about Amazon DynamoDB
- Learn about Amazon ElastiCache

RDS= Relational Database Service

Understanding Relational Databases

A *database management system* (DBMS) is the software that controls the storage, organization, and retrieval of data. A *relational database management system* (RDBMS), as defined by IBM researcher Dr. E.F. Codd, adapts to the relation model with well-defined object stores or structures. These stores and structures, commonly known as *operators* and *integrity rules,* are clearly defined actions meant to manipulate and govern operations on the data and structures of the database. All the relational databases use Structured Query Language (SQL) for querying and managing the day-to-day operations of the database.

In a relational database, the information is stored in tables in the form of rows and columns. Data in a table can be related according to common keys or concepts, and the ability to retrieve related data from a table is the basis for the term *relational database*. A DBMS handles the way data is stored, maintained, and retrieved. In the case of a relational database, the RDBMS performs these tasks. DBMS and RDBMS are often used interchangeably.

Relational databases follow certain rules to ensure data integrity and to make sure the data is always accessible. The first integrity rule states that the rows in an RDBMS table should be distinct. For most RDBMSs, a user can specify that duplicate rows are not allowed, in which case the RDBMS prevents duplicates. The second integrity rule states that column values must not have repeating groups or arrays. The third integrity rule is about the concept of a NULL value. In an RDBMS, there might be a situation where the value of a column is not known, which means the data is not available. NULL does not mean a missing value or zero.

Relational databases also have the concepts of primary keys and foreign keys. A primary key uniquely identifies a record in the table, and the unique column containing the

Employee_Number	First_Name	Last_Name	Date_of_Join	State
10001	Tim	Davis	28-Aug-01	CA
10083	Dhanraj	Pondicherry	24-Nov-03	CA
10120	Vebhhav	Singh	01-Jan-05	NY
10005	Joyjeet	Banerjee	04-Jul-02	WA
10099	Murali	Sriram	21-Dec-03	IL

Table 8-1   Employee Table

unique record is called the *primary key*. For example, in Table 8-1, there are five employees in an employee table.

This employee table is a scenario that occurs in every human resource or payroll database. In this employee table, you cannot assign the first name to the primary key because many people can have the same first name, and the same is true for the last name. Similarly, two employees can join the company on the same day; therefore, the date of join also can't be the primary key. In addition, there are always multiple employees from a state, and thus the state can't be the primary key. Only the employee number is a unique value in this table; therefore, the primary key is the Employee_Number record. The primary key can't contain any NULL value, and a table can have only one primary key, which can consist of a single field or multiple fields.

As described previously, the employee table can be maintained by the human resource department as well as the payroll department with a different set of columns. For example, the payroll table will have full details of the salary information, the tax deductions, the contributions toward retirement, and so on, whereas the employee table maintained by the human resource department may not have the columns related to tax deductions, and so on. Since both the tables contain the information related to the employee, often you need to link the tables or establish a relationship between the two tables. A *foreign key* is a field in one table that uniquely identifies rows in another table or the same table. The foreign key is defined in a second table, but it refers to the primary key or a unique key in the first table. Let's assume the name of the table that the HR department maintains is employee, and the name of the table that the payroll department maintains is employee_ details. In this case, employee_number will be a primary key for the employee table. The employee_details table will have a foreign key that references employee_number to uniquely identify the relationship between both tables.

Relational databases use SQL for all operations. There are a basic set of SQL commands that can be used across all RDBMSs. For example, all RDBMS engines use a SELECT statement to retrieve records from a database.

SQL commands are divided into categories, the two main ones being Data Manipulation Language (DML) commands and Data Definition Language (DDL) commands. The DML commands deal with the manipulation of the data such as inserting, updating, and deleting, and DDL deals with creating, altering, and dropping (deleting) the table structure.

Some common examples of DML are

- **SELECT** This command is used to query and display data from a database. Here's an example:

  ```
  SQL> SELECT First_Name, Last_Name FROM Employees WHERE State = 'CA';
  ```

- **INSERT** This command adds new rows to a table. INSERT is used to populate a newly created table or to add a new row or rows to an existing table. Here's an example:

  ```
  SQL> INSERT INTO Customers (Customer_Name, Address, City, PostalCode,
  Country) VALUES ('Tim', '55 Mowry Ave', 'berkeley', '94701', 'USA');
  ```

- **DELETE** This command removes a specified row or set of rows from a table. Here's an example:

  ```
  SQL> DELETE FROM Customers WHERE CustomerName= 'Albert Einstein';
  ```

- **UPDATE** This command changes an existing value in a column or group of columns in a table. Here's an example:

  ```
  SQL> UPDATE Customers SET  City= 'Mountain View' WHERE CustomerID = 55012;
  ```

Some common DDL commands are

- **CREATE TABLE** This command creates a table with the column names given in the CREATE TABLE syntax.
- **DROP TABLE** This command deletes all the rows and removes the table definition from the database.
- **ALTER TABLE** This command modifies the table structure. You can add or remove a column from a table using this command. You can also add or drop table constraints and alter column attributes.

The most common RDBMS software includes Oracle, MySQL, PostgreSQL, MariaDB, and so on.

Understanding the Amazon Relational Database Service

AWS provides a service for hosting and managing relational databases called Amazon Relational Database Service (RDS). Using this service, you can host the following seven RDBMS engines:

- Aurora MySQL
- Aurora PostgreSQL
- Oracle
- SQL Server

- MySQL
- PostgreSQL
- MariaDB

Before understanding RDS, let's evaluate the various ways you can host your database. The traditional method is to host the database in your data center on-premises. Using AWS, you can host the relational database either on EC2 servers or in RDS. Let's understand what it takes to host a relational database in all these scenarios.

Scenario 1: Hosting the Database in Your Data Center On-Premises

If you host the database in your own data center, you have to take care of all the steps shown in Figure 8-1. Specifically, you have to manage your data center including setting up the power, configuring the networking, configuring the server, installing the operating system, configuring the storage, installing the RDBMS, maintaining the OS, doing OS firmware upgrades, doing database software upgrades, backing up, patching, configuring high availability, configuring scalability, optimizing applications, and so on. In short, you have to take care of everything.

Scenario 2: Hosting the Database on Amazon EC2 Servers

If you host the database on EC2 servers, then you need to take care of the stuff on the left of Figure 8-2, and AWS takes care of the stuff on the right. AWS takes care of OS installation, server maintenance, racking of the servers, power, cooling, networking, and so on. You are responsible for managing the OS, OS patches installation required for RDBMS installation, database installation and maintenance, and all the other tasks related to databases and application optimization.

Scenario 3: Hosting the Database Using Amazon RDS

As shown in Figure 8-3, if you host the database using RDS, AWS does all the heavy lifting for you. From installation to maintenance of the database and patching to upgrading, everything is taken care of by AWS. Even high availability and scalability are taken

Figure 8-1
Hosting the database in your data center on-premises

App Optimization
Scaling
High Availability
Database Backups
DB Software Patches
DB Software Installs
OS Patches
OS Installation
Server Maintenance
Rack & Stack
Power, HVAC, Net

You

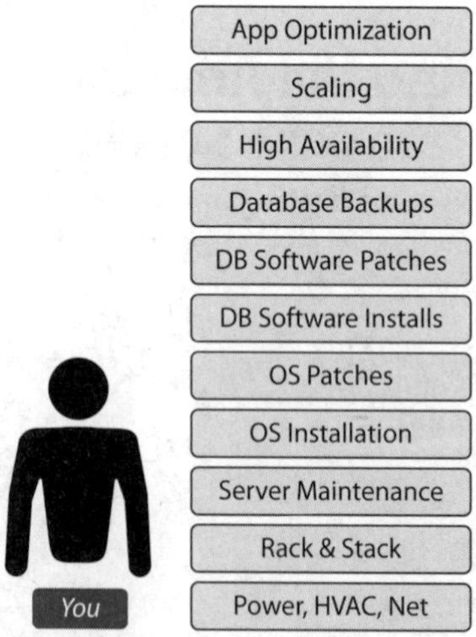

Figure 8-2
Hosting the database on Amazon EC2 servers

care of by AWS. You just need to focus on application optimization, and that's all. It is a managed database service from AWS.

The following are the benefits you get by running your database on RDS:

- **No infrastructure management**   You don't have to manage any infrastructure for the databases. As discussed previously, AWS takes care of everything.

- **Instant provisioning**   Provisioning a database on RDS is almost instant. With a few clicks, you can deploy an RDBMS of your choice in a few minutes. When you need to launch a new database, you can do it instantly, without waiting for days or weeks.

- **Scaling**   RDS is easy to scale; with a few clicks you can scale up or scale down. You can change your configuration to meet your needs when you want. You can scale compute and memory resources up or down at any point in time. I will discuss various ways of scaling a database later in this chapter.

- **Cost effective**   RDS is really cost effective. You pay only for what you use, and there are no minimum or setup fees. You are billed based on using the following database instance hours: the storage capacity you have provisioned to your database instance, the I/O requests per month, the Provisioned IOPS number per month (only if you are using this feature), backup storage, and data transfer including Internet data transfer in and out of your database instance.

charged
- instance hours
- storage capacity
- I/O Req - month
- provision IOPS
- backup storage
- data transfer

Figure 8-3
Hosting the database using Amazon RDS

- **Application compatibility**   Since RDS supports seven engines, most of the popular applications or your custom code, applications, and tools you already use today with your existing databases should work seamlessly with Amazon RDS. If you are using one of the engines that are currently supported, then there is a good chance you can get it working on RDS.
- **Highly available**   Using RDS, you can provision a database in multiple AZs. Whenever you provision the database in multiple AZs, Amazon RDS synchronously replicates your data to a standby instance in a different AZ.
- **Security**   RDS supports the encryption of data both at rest and in transit. You can encrypt the databases and manage your keys using the AWS Key Management System. With RDS encryption, the data stored at rest in the storage is encrypted. Amazon RDS also supports SSL, which is used to take care of encrypting the data in transit.

(handwritten margin note: synchronous ↓ standby)

Hosting a Database in Amazon EC2 vs. Amazon RDS

If you need to decide whether to host the database in Amazon EC2 or Amazon RDS, you should clearly understand the differences in both the offerings so you can choose the right solution for your needs. Of course, you should give RDS a try first because it eliminates a lot of routine work your DBAs have to contend with, but depending on your application and your requirements, one might be preferable over the other. RDS is a managed service, so in some cases you cannot do everything like you might do with a database running on EC2 or in your own data center. AWS does some of the administration, so there are some trade-offs. It is important for you to understand some of the limitations that exist within RDS when making a choice.

RDS fully manages the host, operating system, and database version you are running on. This takes a lot of burden off your hands, but you also don't get access to the database host operating system, you have limited ability to modify the configuration that is normally managed on the host operating system, and generally you get no access to functions that rely on the configuration from the host operating system. You also don't have superuser privilege on the database.

(handwritten margin note: no superuser on DB)

All of your storage on RDS is also managed. Once again, this takes a lot of burden off of you from an administrative standpoint, but it also means there are some limits. There are storage limits of 16TB with MySQL, SQL server, MariaDB, PostgreSQL, and Oracle; and 64TB with Aurora. Please note these numbers are as of writing this book. AWS is continuing to increase the storage limits for RDS, so please refer to the AWS documentation to find the latest information on the storage limits.

(handwritten margin note: 64TB - Aurora; 16TB - MySQL, Postgre, others)

You should choose RDS if

- You want to focus on tasks that bring value to your business
- You don't want to manage the database
- You want to focus on high-level tuning tasks and schema optimization
- You lack in-house expertise to manage databases
- You want push-button multi-AZ replication
- You want automated backup and recovery

You should choose EC2 if

- You need full control over the database instances
- You need operating system access
- You need full control over backups, replication, and clustering
- Your RDBMS engine features and options are not available in Amazon RDS
- You size and performance needs exceed the Amazon RDS offering

High Availability on Amazon RDS

Amazon RDS supports high availability (HA) architectures, so if you have a database with important data, there are many ways to configure HA. It is important to have an HA architecture in place since the database is the heart of everything. If the database goes down, everything goes down. For example, if your application has a HA but the database goes down, the application won't be usable. Let's evaluate the various architectures for RDS including the HA architectures.

Simplest Architecture: Single-AZ Deployment

If you just want to get started on Amazon RDS, do some sort of proof of concept, deploy development environments, or deploy noncritical nonproduction environments, you may not need a highly available architecture since you can live with downtime in these scenarios. Therefore, in the previously mentioned scenarios, you can launch the Amazon RDS instance in a single AZ. With this you get a single RDS instance inside a VPC with the necessary attached storage. Figure 8-4 shows this architecture.

Figure 8-4
Amazon RDS in
a single AZ

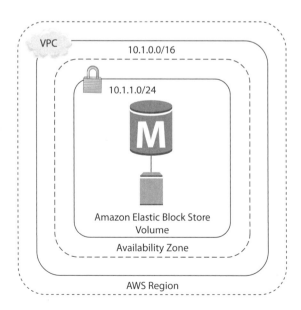

High Availability: Multiple AZs

If you are planning to run a mission-critical database, want to have an architecture where you can't afford to lose data, have a tight recovery point objective, or can't afford much downtime, you must deploy the database in a multi-AZ architecture.

When you deploy a database in a multi-AZ architecture, you can choose which availability zone you want your primary database instance to be in. RDS will then choose to have a standby instance and storage in another availability zone of the AWS region that you are operating in. The instance running in the standby will be of the same type as your master, and the storage will be of the same configuration and size as of your primary.

Figure 8-5 shows the HA architecture.

In the case of a multi-AZ architecture, the primary database, also known as the *master database*, handles all the traffic. The standby database is always kept ready and is in a state that whenever the master or the primary goes down, it takes the role of the master or primary and supports the application.

RDS takes responsibility for ensuring that your primary is healthy and that your standby is in a state that you can recover to. The standby database does not remain open when it acts as a standby database, so you can't direct the traffic to the primary and standby databases at the same time. This is like having an active/passive database. Your data on the primary database is synchronously replicated to the storage in the standby configuration. As discussed in the previous chapter, the AZs are built in such a way that provides the ability to synchronously replicate the data; hence, there is no data loss.

There can be various types of failover that RDS can handle automatically. For example, the host instance can go down, the underlying storage can fail, the network connectivity to the primary instance is lost, the AZ itself goes down, and so on.

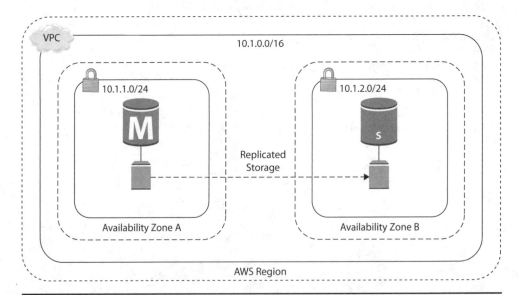

Figure 8-5 HA architecture in AWS

Figure 8-6
DNS failover
using multi-AZ
on Amazon RDS

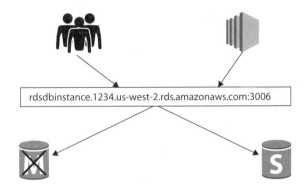

When the failover happens, the standby is automatically propagated to the master, and all the application traffic fails over to the new master. In the multi-AZ architecture of RDS, the application connects to the database server using a DNS endpoint that is mapped to the master and standby instances. As a result, you don't have to repoint the application to the new master or change anything from the application side. In the case of failover, RDS automatically does the DNS failover, which typically takes about 30 to 60 seconds. Once it happens, you are again up and running, and you do not need to do anything. Figure 8-6 shows this behavior. In this figure, users and applications are connected to the database using the endpoint `rdsdbinstance.1234` `.us-west-2.rds.amazonaws.com:3006`. (Since this is a MySQL database, the port is 3006.) Now this endpoint is mapped to both the master and the slave. When the failover happens, the users and application are reconnected to the standby that gets propagated to the master. The application and users continue to connect to the same endpoint (`rdsdbinstance.1234.us-west-2.rds.amazonaws.com:3006`). They don't have to change anything at their end.

Scaling on Amazon RDS

There are multiple ways you can scale your databases running on RDS. There could be many reasons you would like to scale up the databases running in RDS. For example, your application workload has increased, your users have grown up, you have started seeing performance degradation, or your database queries are showing a wait on the CPU or in memory. Or, when you started the application, you had no idea about the workload and now to support the business, you need to scale up. Scaling up always helps you to handle the additional workload.

Similarly, there could be reasons when you may want to scale down. For example, during the weekends, there may not be much activity in the database node, and you don't want to pay more over the weekend; you may want to scale down for the weekend.

Changing the Instance Type

The simplest way to scale up or down is to change the instance type. You can change from one class of instance to another class or move up and down between the same classes of instance. You can move up or down between any class of instance supported by Amazon RDS. It is simple to scale up or down the instance type in RDS. The steps are as follows:

1. Choose the Modify option from the Instance Actions menu of the RDS console.

2. Choose what you want your new database instance class to be.

3. Determine whether you want to apply the change immediately.

If you choose to apply the change immediately, there could be some downtime since the instance type is changed. You should make sure that the business or application can handle the small downtime. If you can't have the small outage, then don't apply the change immediately. If you do not apply the change immediately, then the change will be scheduled to occur during the preferred maintenance window that you defined when creating the database.

You can also scale up and down using the AWS CLI and AWS API. For example, if you want to scale up to a c4 large instance for your database, you can run the following command from AWS CLI and modify the instance type:

```
aws rds modify-db-instance --db-instance-identifier myrdsinstance --db-
instance-class db.c4.large --apply-immediately
```

You can even automate this by running a cron job in a cheap EC2 instance.

Since RDS is not integrated with Auto Scaling, you can't use this technology to scale up or down as you do in an EC2 instance. But you can achieve this by writing a Lambda function. For example, you can have two Lambda functions. The first one is for scaling down over the weekend, and the second one is for scaling up at the end of the weekend. The Lambda function can call the modify db instance API to either scale up or scale down.

Similarly, you can also automate the scale-up of the instance based on certain events. For example, if the CPU of your database instance goes up by 75 percent, you want to automatically increase the instance size. This can be done using a combination of Lambda, CloudWatch, and SNS notifications. For example, from the CloudWatch metrics, you can monitor the CPU utilization of the RDS instance. You can have an alarm that sends a notification to SNS when the CPU goes up by 75 percent, and you can have a Lambda function subscribed to that notification that calls the modify db instance API and triggers the job to move the database to a higher class of server.

Read Replica

A read replica is a read-only copy of your master database that is kept in sync with your master database. You can have up to 15 read replicas in RDS depending on the RDBMS engine. A read replica helps you to offload the read-only queries to it, thereby reducing the workload on the master database. There are several benefits of running a read replica:

- You can offload read-only traffic to the read replica and let the master database run critical transaction-related queries.

- If you have users from different locations, you can create a read replica in a different region and serve the read-only traffic via the read replica.

- The read replica can also be promoted to a master database when the master database goes down.

 NOTE The read replicas are kept in sync with the master database, but the replication is not synchronous. In a master-standby configuration, the replication of data is always synchronous; therefore, there is zero data loss when the standby is promoted to master. Whereas in the case of the master and read replica configuration, the replication is asynchronous; therefore, if you promote a read replica to a master, there could be some data loss depending on the scenario. If you can't afford to lose any data and you need read replicas, then go for an architecture with master, standby, and read replica. This way you will get the best of both worlds.

You can also use a read replica as a mechanism for high availability; for example, if you have a master database and a read replica and the master database goes down, the read replica can be promoted to master. The only thing you need to be careful about with this architecture is the asynchronous replication of data.

You can create the read replica in a different AZ in the same region, or you can have a read replica in a different region called a *cross-regional read replica*. A cross-regional read replica may or may not be available for all the RDBMS engines. Figure 8-7 shows a cross-regional read replica.

An *intra-region* allows you to create additional read replicas within the same AWS region, but in the same or different availability zones from your master database. This functionality is supported by MySQL, MariaDB, PostgreSQL, Aurora MySQL, and Aurora PostgreSQL.

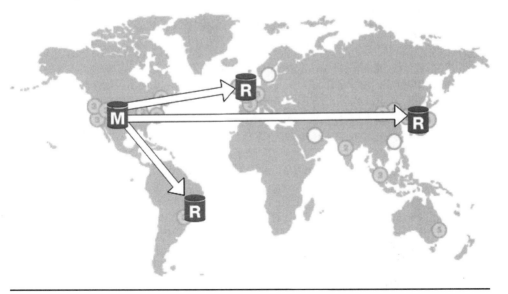

Figure 8-7 Cross-regional read replica

Cross-regional replication allows you to deploy the read replica into an AWS region that is different from the region that your master is located in. This functionality is supported by MySQL, MariaDB, PostgreSQL, Aurora MySQL, and Aurora PostgreSQL.

Currently RDS does not support read replicas for Oracle and SQL Server. However, you can still accomplish this on RDS. For Oracle you can use Oracle Golden Gate. You can also use some of the AWS partner products such as Attunity and SnapLogic to replicate data between two RDS instances of Oracle or SQL Server.

Security on Amazon RDS

There are multiple ways of securing the databases running on Amazon RDS. In this section, you will learn all the different ways of securing the database.

Amazon VPC and Amazon RDS

When you launch an Amazon RDS instance, it launches in Amazon Virtual Private Cloud (VPC). I discussed VPC in Chapter 3. Since a database always stays behind the firewall, it is recommended that you create the database in the private subnet. Of course, you may have a legitimate reason to create the database in a public subnet, but again, that could be a one-off scenario. So, with your database launched inside of VPC, you get to control which users and applications access your database and how they access it. When the database runs in the VPC, you have multiple ways of connecting to it.

- You can create a VPN connection from your corporate data center into the VPC so that you can access the database in a hybrid fashion.

- You can use Direct Connect to link your data center to an AWS region, giving you a connection with consistent performance.

- You can peer two different VPCs together, allowing applications in one VPC to access your database in your VPC.

- You can grant public access to your database by attaching an Internet gateway to your VPC.

- You can control the routing of your VPC using route tables that you attach to each of the subnets in your VPC.

You can create security groups within RDS and can control the flow of traffic using them. You have already read about security groups in Chapter 3. You can control the protocol, port range, and source of the traffic that you allow into your database. For the source, you can restrict it to a specific IP address, a particular CIDR block covering multiple IP addresses, or even another security group, meaning that your RDS instance will accept traffic only if it comes from instances in that particular security group. This gives you the flexibility to have a multitier architecture where you grant connections only from the parts of the tier that actually need to access the database.

Data Encryption on Amazon RDS

Encryption is important for many customers, and Amazon RDS provides the ability to encrypt the database. Many customers have a compliance requirement to encrypt the entire database. RDS provides you with the ability to encrypt the data at rest. RDS-encrypted instances provide an additional layer of data protection by securing your data from unauthorized access to the underlying storage. You can use Amazon RDS encryption to increase the data protection of your applications deployed in the cloud and to fulfill compliance requirements for data-at-rest encryption.

When you encrypt your RDS database with AWS-provided encryption, it takes care of encrypting the following:

- The database instance storage
- Automated backups
- Read replicas associated with the master database
- Standby databases associated with the master database
- Snapshots that you generate of the database

Thus, the entire ecosystem where the data is stored is encrypted.

If you use Oracle or Microsoft SQL Server's native encryption like Transparent Database Encryption (TDE), you can also use it in Amazon's RDS. But make sure you use only one mode of encryption (either RDS or TDE) or it will have an impact on the performance of the database.

When you choose to encrypt, the data in it uses the industry-standard AES-256 encryption algorithm to encrypt your data on the server that hosts your Amazon RDS instance. Once the data is encrypted, RDS automatically handles the decryption of the data. When you create an RDS instance and enable encryption, a default key for RDS is created in the Key Management Service (KMS) that will be used to encrypt and decrypt the data in your RDS instance. This key is tied to your account and controlled by you. KMS is a managed service that provides you with the ability to create and manage encryption keys and then encrypt and decrypt your data with those keys. All of these keys are tied to your own AWS account and are fully managed by you. KMS takes care of all the availability, scaling, security, and durability that you would normally have to deal with when implementing your own key store. When KMS is performing these management tasks, it allows you the ability to focus on using the keys and building your application.

You can also use your own key for managing the encryption. Let's take a deep dive on this. As discussed, when you are launching an RDS instance and choose to make the database encrypted, it results in an AWS managed key for RDS. This is good if you just want encryption and don't want to think about anything else related to the key. Once this key is created, it can be used only for RDS encryption and not with any other AWS service. Therefore, the scope of this key is limited to RDS. The other option is to create your own master key. If you create your own master key within KMS and then reference that key while creating your RDS instance, you have much more control over the use of that key such as when it is enabled or disabled, when the key is rotated, and what the access policies are for the key.

When RDS wants to encrypt data on the instance, it will make a call to KMS using the necessary credentials. KMS will then give RDS a data key that is actually used to encrypt the data on that instance. This data key is encrypted using the master key that was created when you launched the instance or using the key you created and specified during the instance creation. This data key is specific to that RDS instance and can't be used with another RDS instance.

Therefore, it is a two-tiered key hierarchy using encryption:

- The unique data key encrypts customer data inside the RDS.
- The AWS KMS master keys encrypt data keys.

This is depicted in Figure 8-8.

There are several benefits of using this approach. Encryption and decryption are handled transparently, so you don't have to modify your application to access your data. There are limited risks of a compromised data key. You get better performance for encrypting large data sets, and there is no performance penalty for using KMS encryption with your RDS instance. You only have to manage a few master keys and not many data keys. You get centralized access and audit of key activity via CloudTrail so that you can see every time a key is accessed and used from your KMS configuration.

Figure 8-8
Two-tiered key
hierarchy for
Amazon RDS

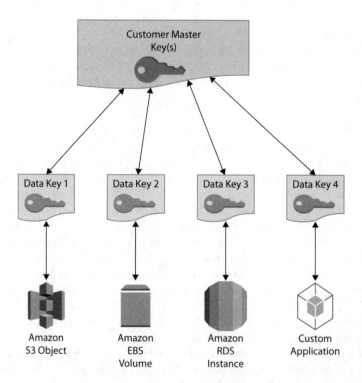

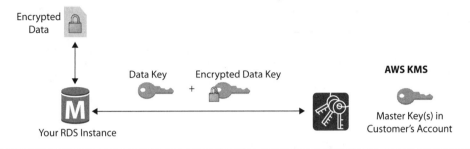

Figure 8-9   How keys are used to protect the data

Let's understand how keys are used to protect your data. This is shown in Figure 8-9.

1. The RDS instance requests an encryption key to use to encrypt data and passes a reference to the master key in the account.

2. The client requests authentication based on the permissions set on both the user and the key.

3. A unique data encryption key is created and encrypted under the KMS master key.

4. The plaintext and encrypted data key is returned to the client.

5. The plaintext data key is used to encrypt data and is then deleted when practical.

6. The encrypted data key is stored; it's sent back to the KMS when needed for data decryption.

Using RDS you can encrypt the traffic to and from your database using SSL. This takes care of encrypting the data in transit. Each of the seven RDS engines supports the ability to configure an SSL connection into your database. The steps to implement the SSL connection to the database might be different for different RDBMS engines.

Here are a couple of important things to note about encryption from the examination's point of view:

- You can encrypt only during database creation. If you already have a database that is up and running and you want to enable encryption on it, the only way to achieve this is to create a new encrypted database and copy the data from the existing database to the new one.

- Once you encrypt a database, you can't remove it. If you choose to encrypt an RDS instance, it cannot be turned off. If you no longer need the encryption, you need to create a new database instance that does not have encryption enabled and copy the data to the new database.

- The master and read replicas must be encrypted. When you create a read replica, using RDS, the data in the master and read replicas is going to be encrypted. The data needs to be encrypted with the same key. Similarly, when you have a master and standby configuration, both are going to be encrypted.

- You cannot copy those snapshots of an encrypted database to another AWS region, as you can do with normal snapshots. (You will learn about snapshots later in this chapter.) KMS is a regional service, so you currently cannot copy things encrypted with KMS to another region.

- You can migrate an encrypted database from MySQL to Aurora MySQL. You will read about Aurora later in this chapter.

Backups, Restores, and Snapshots

For all the Amazon RDS engines, except Amazon Aurora (MySQL and PostgreSQL), MySQL, PostgreSQL, MariaDB, Oracle, and SQL Server, the database backup is scheduled for every day, in other words, one backup per day. You can schedule your own backup window as per your convenience. You can also monitor the backups to make sure they are completing successfully. The backup includes the entire database, transaction logs, and change logs. By default, the backups are retained for 35 days. If you want to retain a backup for a longer period of time, you can do so by opening a support ticket. Multiple copies of the backup are kept in each availability zone where you have an instance deployed.

In the case of Aurora, you don't have to back up manually since everything is automatically backed up continuously to the S3 bucket. But you can also take a manual backup at any point in time. For Aurora, also the backups are retained for 35 days, which again can be extended by a support ticket.

When you restore a database from the backup, you create a new exact copy of the database or a clone of a database. Using RDS, it is simple to restore a database. Using backups, you can restore the database to any point in time. When you restore the database, you have the ability to restore the database to any class of server, and it doesn't have to be the same type of instance where the main database is running.

Restoring is pretty simple. You need to choose where to restore (your database instance) and when (time) to restore. While restoring a database, you define all the instance configurations just like when creating a new instance. You can choose to restore the database up to the last restorable time or do a custom restore time of your choosing. When you select both of the options, the end result is a new RDS instance with all your data in it.

Creating a snapshot is another way of backing up your database. Snapshots are not automatically scheduled, and you need to take the snapshots manually. When you take the snapshot of a database, there is a temporary I/O suspension that can last from a few seconds to a few minutes. The snapshots are created in S3, and you can also use these snapshots to restore a database. If you take the snapshot of an encrypted database and use it for a restore, the resulting database also will be an encrypted database. There are many reasons you would use database snapshots. For example, you can use a snapshot to create multiple nonproduction databases from the snapshot of the production database to test a bug, to copy the database across multiple accounts, to create a disaster recovery database, to keep the data before you delete the database, and so on.

Monitoring

Amazon provides you with multiple ways of monitoring your databases running on RDS. The basic monitoring is called *standard monitoring,* and if you want fine granular details, you can opt for advanced monitoring. RDS sends all the information for these metrics to Amazon CloudWatch, and then you are able to view the metrics in the RDS console, in the CloudWatch console, or via the CloudWatch APIs.

- **Standard monitoring**   Using standard monitoring, you can access 15 to 18 metrics depending on the RDBMS engine. The common ones are CPU utilization, storage, memory, swap usage, database connections, I/O (read and write), latency (read and write), throughput (read and write), replica lag, and so on. Figure 8-10 shows the standard monitoring. Using standard monitoring you can get the metrics at one-minute intervals.

- **Enhanced monitoring**   If you want fine granular metrics, then you can opt for enhanced monitoring. Using enhanced monitoring, you can access additional 37 more metrics in addition to standard monitoring, making a total of more than 50 metrics. You can also get the metrics as low as a one-second interval. The enhanced monitoring is also available for all the RDBMS engines that RDS supports.

- **Event notification**   Using event notifications in RDS, you can quickly get visibility into what's going on in your RDS instance. These event notifications allow you to get notifications, via Amazon SNS, when certain events occur in RDS. There are 17 different categories of events that you can choose from such as availability, backup, configuration change, creation, deletion, failure,

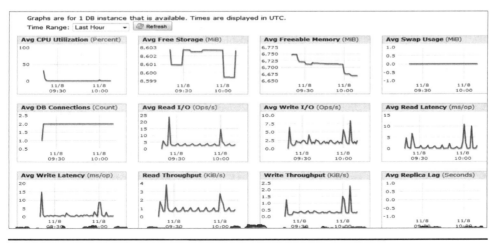

Figure 8-10   Standard monitoring

failover, maintenance, recovery, restoration, and so on. You can choose to get notified on the occurrences of those events, for example, when the database is running low on storage, when the master database is failing over to the standby database, and so on.

- **Performance Insights**   Performance Insights expands on existing Amazon RDS monitoring features to illustrate your database's performance and helps you analyze any issues that impact it. With the Performance Insights dashboard, you can visualize the database load and filter the load by waits, SQL statements, hosts, or users. Performance Insights is on by default for the Postgres-compatible edition of the Aurora database engine. If you have more than one database on the database instance, performance data for all of the databases is aggregated for the database instance. Database performance data is kept for 35 days.

The Performance Insights dashboard contains database performance information to help you analyze and troubleshoot performance issues. On the main dashboard page, you can view information about the database load and drill into details for a particular wait state, SQL query, host, or user. By default, the Performance Insights dashboard shows data for the last 15 minutes. You can modify it to display data for the last 60 minutes if desired. Figure 8-11 shows the details of SQL statements from the Performance Insights page.

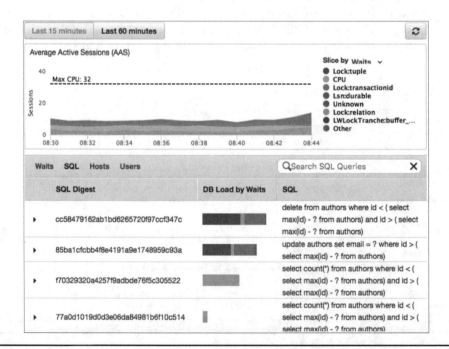

Figure 8-11   Details of SQL from the Performance Insights page

Amazon Aurora

Amazon Aurora is a cloud-optimized, MySQL- and PostgreSQL-compatible, relational database. It provides the performance and availability of commercial databases and the simplicity and cost effectiveness of open source databases. Amazon Aurora provides performance and durability by implementing a fully distributed and self-healing storage system, and it provides availability by using the elasticity and management capabilities of the AWS cloud in the most fundamental ways.

There are two flavors of Amazon Aurora; one is compatible with MySQL, and the other is compatible with PostgreSQL. For MySQL currently it is compatible with version 5.6 and 5.7 using the InnoDB storage engine, and for PostgreSQL it is compatible with the 9.6 version. This means the code, applications, drivers, and tools you already use with your MySQL or PostgreSQL databases can be used with Amazon Aurora with little or no change. And you can easily migrate from MySQL or PostgreSQL to Amazon Aurora.

With Aurora the storage is a bit different compared to regular RDS. There is a separate storage layer that is automatically replicated across six different storage nodes in three different availability zones. This is an important factor since the data is mirrored at six different places at no additional cost. All this data mirroring happens synchronously, and hence there is zero data loss. Amazon's Aurora uses a quorum system for reads and writes to ensure that your data is available in multiple storage nodes. At the same time, all the data is also continuously backed up to S3 to ensure that you have durable and available data. With Amazon Aurora, the storage volume automatically grows up to 64TB. Figure 8-12 shows the replication of Aurora storage across three different AZs.

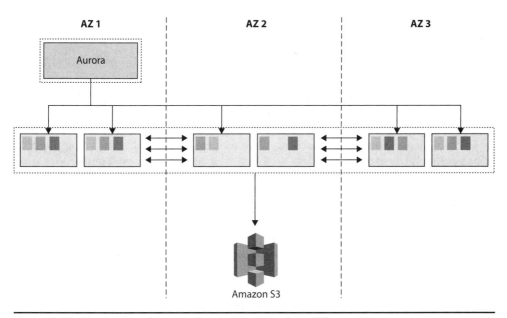

Figure 8-12   Replication of Amazon Aurora storage at three different AZs

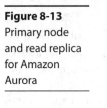

Figure 8-13
Primary node
and read replica
for Amazon
Aurora

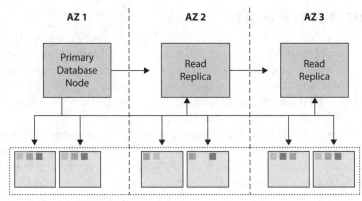

Amazon Aurora supports up to 15 copies of read replica. Please note in the case of Amazon Aurora the data replication happens at the storage level in a synchronous manner. Therefore, between the primary database node (which is also referred as *master*) and the read replica, the data replication happens in a synchronous fashion. In the case of Aurora, there is no concept of standby database, and the read replica is prompted to a master or primary database node when the primary node goes down. Figure 8-13 shows a primary node and read replica for Amazon Aurora.

On average, you get up to a five times increase in performance by running an Aurora MySQL database compared to a regular MySQL engine.

Amazon Redshift

Amazon Redshift is the managed data warehouse solution offered by Amazon Web Services. A *data warehouse* is a database designed to enable business intelligence activities; it exists to help users understand and enhance their organization's performance. It is designed for query and analysis rather than for transaction processing and usually contains historical data derived from transaction data but can include data from other sources. Data warehouses are consumers of data. They are also known as *online analytical processing* (OLAP) systems. The data for a data warehouse system can come from various sources, such as OLTP systems, enterprise resource planning (ERP) systems such as SAP, internally developed systems, purchased applications, third-party data syndicators, and more. The data may involve transactions, production, marketing, human resources, and more.

Data warehouses are distinct from OLTP systems. With a data warehouse, you separate the analytical workload from the transaction workload. Thus, data warehouses are very much read-oriented systems. They have a far higher amount of data reading versus writing and updating. This enables far better analytical performance and does not impact your transaction systems. A data warehouse system can be optimized to consolidate data from many sources to achieve a key goal. OLTP databases collect a lot of data quickly, but OLAP databases typically import large amounts of data from various source systems by using batch processes and scheduled jobs. A data warehouse environment can include an extraction, transformation, and loading (ETL) solution, as well as statistical analysis, reporting, data mining capabilities, client analysis tools, and other applications that manage the process of gathering data, transforming it into actionable information, and delivering it to business users.

Benefits of Amazon Redshift

These are the important attributes of Amazon Redshift:

- **Fast**   Since Redshift uses columnar storage, it delivers fast query performance. A query is parallelized by running it across several nodes. As a result, the query runs fast, and IO efficiency is improved.

- **Cheap**   Redshift costs less than any other data warehouse solution on the market. It is almost one-tenth the price of tools from other vendors. It starts as low as $1,000 per terabyte.

- **Good compression**   The data remains in a compressed format, which provides three to four times more compression, which allows you to save money.

- **Managed service**   Since Redshift is a managed service, Amazon takes care of all the heavy-duty work. You don't have to manage the underlying clusters, networking, or operating system. Amazon takes care of patching, upgrading, backing up, and restoring. You can also automate most of the common administrative tasks to manage, monitor, and scale your data warehouse.

- **Scalable**   Redshift uses a distributed, massively parallel architecture that scales horizontally to meet throughput requirements. The cluster size can go up and down depending on your performance and capacity needs. You can resize the cluster either via the console or by making API calls.

- **Secure**   Redshift supports the encryption of data at rest and data in transit. You can even create a cluster inside a VPC, making it isolated. You can use the AWS Key Management Service (KMS) and Hardware Security Modules (HSMs) to manage the keys.

- **Zone map functionality**   Zone maps help to minimize unnecessary IO. They track the minimum and maximum values for each block and skip over blocks that don't contain the data needed for a given query.

Amazon Redshift Architecture

An Amazon Redshift cluster consists of a leader node and compute nodes. There is only one leader node per cluster, whereas there could be several compute nodes in a cluster. Figure 8-14 shows the Redshift architecture.

The leader node performs a few roles. It acts as a SQL endpoint for the applications. It performs database functions and coordinates the parallel SQL processing. All the Postgres

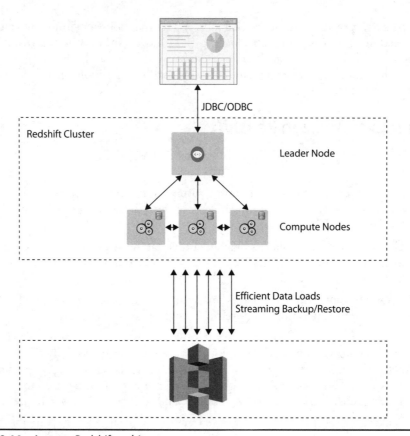

Figure 8-14 Amazon Redshift architecture

catalog tables also exist in the leader node. Since Redshift is built on Postgres, some additional metadata tables specific to Redshift also exist in the leader node. This is where you connect to your driver; you can use JDBC and ODBC. In addition to Redshift drivers that you can download from the AWS web site, you can connect with any Postgres driver. Behind the leader node are the compute nodes; you can have up to 128 of them.

The leader node communicates with the compute nodes for processing any query. The compute nodes process the actual data. The compute nodes also communicate with each other while processing a query. Let's see how a query is executed.

1. The application or SQL client submits a query.
2. The query is submitted to the leader node. The leader node parses the query and develops an execution plan.
3. The leader node also decides which compute nodes are going to do the work and then distributes the job across multiple compute nodes.

4. The compute nodes process the job and send the results to the leader node.

5. The leader node aggregates the results and sends it back to the client or the application.

The leader node does the database functions, such as encrypting the data, compressing the data, running the routing jobs like vacuum (covered later in this chapter), backing up, restoring, and so on.

All the compute nodes are connected via a high-speed interconnected network. The end client (application) can't communicate with the compute nodes directly. It has to communicate via the leader node. But the compute node can talk with services such as Amazon S3. The data is ingested directly from the S3 to the compute nodes, and Amazon constantly backs up the cluster to Amazon S3, which happens in the background.

A compute node is further divided or partitioned into multiple slices. A slice is allocated a portion of a node's CPU, memory, and storage. Depending on the size of the compute node, a node can have more or fewer slices. Figure 8-15 shows compute nodes with two slices in each one with an equal amount of compute, memory, and storage.

When the leader node distributes the job, it actually distributes it to the slices, and each slice processes the job independently. Similarly, when the data is loaded in the tables of Redshift, it is kept in the slices.

There are two types of Redshift clusters: single-node clusters and multinode clusters. In single-node clusters, there is only one node that performs the tasks of both the leader and compute nodes. There is only one node in a single-node cluster, so if the node goes down, then everything goes down, and you need to restore the cluster from the snapshot. You should not use a single-node cluster for production environments. It can be used for test/development environments.

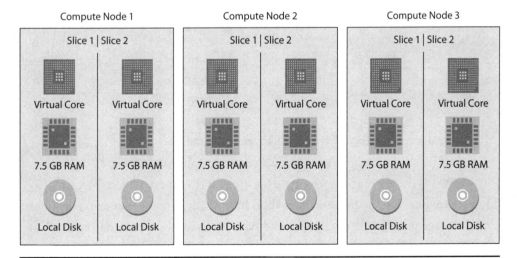

Figure 8-15 Slice in a compute node

In a multinode cluster, the leader node is separate from the compute node, and there is only one leader node per cluster. During the creation of a cluster, you can specify the number of compute nodes you need, and a multinode cluster is created with that many compute nodes. For example, if you choose three nodes during your cluster creation, then a cluster will be created with one leader node and three compute nodes. In a multinode cluster, the data is automatically replicated among the compute nodes for the data redundancy. So, even if the compute node fails, you don't have to restore it from the snapshot. When a compute node fails, it is replaced automatically, and the cluster automatically take cares of redistributing the data. This should be used for running production workloads.

There are two types of instance you can choose for Redshift clusters. One is a dense compute that has the SSD drives, and the other is dense storage, which has the magnetic hard drives. If you need faster performance and compute, then you should choose a dense compute cluster, and if you have a large workload and would like to use a magnetic hard drive, choose the dense storage cluster. The dense compute is called DC, and the dense storage type is called DS. At the time of writing this book, Amazon Redshift supports the following cluster types. Redshift uses an EC2 instance for both the cluster types.

Dense Storage Node Type							
Node Size	vCPU	ECU	RAM (GB)	Slices per Node	Storage per Node	Node Range	Total Capacity
ds2.xlarge	4	13	31	2	2 TB HDD	1–32	64 TB
ds2.8xlarge	36	119	244	16	16 TB HDD	2–128	2 PB

Dense Compute Node Types							
Node Size	vCPU	ECU	RAM (GB)	Slices per Node	Storage per Node	Node Range	Total Capacity
dc1.large	2	7	15	2	160GB SSD	1–32	5.12TB
dc1.8xlarge	32	104	244	32	2.56TB SSD	2–128	326TB
dc2.large	2	7	15.25	2	160GB NVMe-SSD	1–32	5.12TB
dc2.8xlarge	32	99	244	16	2.56TB NVMe-SSD	2–128	326TB

- vCPU is the number of virtual CPUs for each node.
- ECU is the number of Amazon EC2 compute units for each node.
- RAM is the amount of memory in gigabytes (GB) for each node.
- Slices per Node is the number of slices into which a compute node is partitioned.
- Storage per Node is the capacity and type of storage for each node.
- Node Range is the minimum and maximum number of nodes that Amazon Redshift supports for the node type and size.

Sizing Amazon Redshift Clusters

When you size an Amazon Redshift cluster, first you need to decide what type of cluster you need, dense storage or dense compute. Most of the time it depends on the business needs; if the business needs faster processing, you should go with dense compute. Then you need to decide how much data you have, including the predicted data growth. You may also want to consider compression. On average, customers get about a three to four times compression ratio. Since the compression ratio depends on the data set, you should check with your data set to see how much compression you are getting and then size accordingly.

Since the data mirroring is already included, you don't have to account for additional storage for mirroring. For example, say you have a 6TB data warehouse and you want to run that in dense compute storage. In this case, you can select three nodes of dc1.8xlarge. The capacity of each storage node is 2.56TB; therefore, with three of these nodes, you can store up to 7.68TB of data. Thus, your 6TB data warehouse is easily going to fit in the three compute nodes. The data will be mirrored as well within the three nodes, and you don't have to worry about additional storage for mirroring.

Networking for Amazon Redshift

An Amazon Redshift cluster can be run inside a VPC. If you are running a cluster using EC2-Classic (legacy), then it won't be using the VPC. A VPC is mandatory for all new cluster installations, and by using a VPC, the cluster remains isolated from other customers. You can choose a cluster subnet group (a cluster subnet group consists of one or more subnets in which Amazon Redshift can launch a cluster) for a Redshift cluster, which can be either in the private subnet or in the public subnet. You can also choose which AZ the cluster will be created in. When you choose it in the public subnet, you can either provide your own public IP address (which is EIP) or have the Redshift cluster provide an EIP for you. When you run the cluster in a private subnet, it is not accessible from the Internet. This public or private subnet is applicable only for the leader node. The compute node is created in a separate VPC, and you don't have any access to it.

A Redshift cluster provides an option called *enhanced VPC routing*. If you choose to use it, then all the traffic for commands such as COPY unload between your cluster and your data repositories are routed through your Amazon VPC. You can also use the VPC features to manage the flow of data between your Amazon Redshift cluster and other resources. If you don't choose that option, Amazon Redshift routes traffic through the Internet, including traffic to other services within the AWS network.

To recap, when you launch a Redshift cluster, either the EC2-VPC platform is available or the EC2-classic platform is available. (EC2-classic is available to certain AWS accounts, depending on the date the account was created.) You must use the EC2-VPC platform unless you need to continue using the EC2-classic platform that is available to you. You can access only the leader node. When running in EC-VPC, you can use the VPC security group to define which IP address can connect to the port in the Redshift cluster.

Encryption

Optionally you can choose to encrypt all the data running in your Redshift cluster. Encryption is not mandatory, and you should choose this option only if you have a business need. If you are going to keep sensitive data in your Redshift cluster, you must encrypt the data. You can encrypt the data both in transit and at rest. When you launch the cluster, you can enable encryption for a cluster. If the encryption is enabled in a cluster, it becomes immutable, which means you can't disable it. Similarly, if you launch a cluster without encryption, the data remains unencrypted during the life of the cluster. If at a later phase you decide to encrypt the data, then the only way is to unload your data from the existing cluster and reload it in a new cluster with the encryption setting.

You can use SSL to encrypt the connection between a client and the cluster. For the data at rest, Redshift uses AES-256 hardware-accelerated encryption keys to encrypt the data blocks and system metadata for the cluster. You can manage the encryption using the AWS KMS, using the AWS CloudHSM, or using your on-premise HSM.

 NOTE If the Redshift cluster is encrypted, all the snapshots will also be encrypted.

All Redshift cluster communications are secured by default. Redshift always uses SSL to access other AWS services (S3, DynamoDB, EMR for data load).

Security

Since Redshift is an RDBMS, just like with any other relational database, you need to create database users who will have superuser or user permissions with them. A database superuser can create a database user or another superuser. A database user can create database objects in Redshift depending on your privileges. In Redshift, a database contains one or more than one schema, and each schema in turn contains tables and other objects. The default name of a schema in a Redshift database is Public. When you create the Redshift cluster for the first time, you need to provide a master username and password for the database. This master username is the superuser in which you log in to the database. You should never delete the master user account.

To use the Redshift service, you can create IAM policies on IAM users, roles, or groups. You can use the managed policies Redshift has to grant either administrative access or read-only access to this service, or you can create your own custom policy to provide fine granular permission.

Back Up and Restore

Amazon Redshift takes automatic backups in the form of snapshots of your cluster and saves them to Amazon S3. Snapshots are incremental. The frequency of the snapshot is eight hours or 5GB of block changes. You can turn off the automated backups. Automation is available to ensure snapshots are taken to meet your recovery point objective (RPO). You can define the retention period for the automated snapshots. You can also take a manual snapshot of the cluster that can be kept as long as you want. In addition, you can configure cross-region snapshots, and by doing so, the snapshots can be automatically replicated to an alternate region. If you want to restore the Redshift cluster to a different region, the quickest way would be to enable a cross-region snapshot and restore the cluster from the snapshot.

You can restore the entire database from a snapshot. When you restore the entire database from a snapshot, it results in a new cluster of the original size and instance type. During the restore, your cluster is provisioned in about ten minutes. Data is automatically streamed from the S3 snapshot. You can also do a table-level restore from a snapshot.

Data Loading in Amazon Redshift

There can be various ways in which the data can be loaded in an Amazon Redshift cluster. You can load the data directly from Amazon S3, which is called *file-based loading*. File-based loading is the most efficient and high-performance way to load Redshift. You can load data from CSV, JSON, and AVRO files on S3.

You can load streaming data or batch data directly to Redshift using Kinesis Firehose. In addition, you can connect to the database and insert data, including doing a multi-value insert.

You can load the data either via the leader node or directly from the compute nodes. It depends on how you are going to load the data. For example, if you are going to insert the data, insert multiple values, update the data, or delete the data, you can do it by using a client from the leader node. Since Redshift supports SQL commands, you can use basic SQL statements to insert records into the table (for example, to insert into table <table_name> values), and so on. If you want to use Redshift-specific tools for loading or unloading the data or, for example, use the COPY or UNLOAD command to export the data, you can do it directly from the compute nodes. If you run CTAS (create table as select), you can run it from the compute node. The compute node also supports loading the data from Dynamo DB, from EMR, and via SSH commands.

The COPY command is the recommended method to load data into Amazon Redshift since it can be used to load the data in bulk. It appends new data to existing rows in the table.

```
COPY <TABLE_NAME> from <DATA_SOURCE>
credentials "aws_access_key_id=<access_key>; aws_secret_access_key=<secret_key>"
iam_role "arn"
format as <data_format>
parameter (argument) …
;
```

The mandatory parameters are table name, data source, and credentials. Other parameters you can specify are compression, encryption, transformation, error handling, date format, and so on.

While loading the data using the COPY command, you should use multiple input files to maximize throughput and load data in parallel. Since each slice loads one file at a time, if you use a single input file, then only one slice will ingest data. Depending on the size of the cluster, you will have a specific number of slices. If your cluster has 16 slices, you can have 16 input files and thus can have slices working in parallel so that you can maximize the throughput.

The UNLOAD command is the reverse of COPY. You can export the data out of the Redshift cluster via the UNLOAD command. It can write output only to S3. It can run in parallel on all compute nodes. This command can generate more than one file per slice for all compute nodes. The UNLOAD command supports encryption and compression.

In addition to loading and unloading the data, you need to perform some additional maintenance tasks on a regular basis. One of the tasks you would be doing often is running the command VACUUM. Whenever you load the data in the Redshift cluster using the COPY command, you need to reorganize the data and reclaim the space after the deletion. The VACUUM command take cares of that, so ideally after every COPY command, you should run the VACUUM command as well. Whenever you load new data to the Redshift cluster, it is important to update the statistics so that the optimizer can create a correct execution plan for running the query. You can run the ANALYZE command to update the statistics. Run the ANALYZE command whenever you've made a nontrivial number of changes to your data to ensure your table statistics are current.

Data Distribution in Amazon Redshift

In Amazon Redshift, you have three options to distribute data among the nodes in your cluster: EVEN, KEY, and ALL.

With the KEY distribution style, the slice is chosen based on a distribution key that is a hash of the defined column.

The ALL distribution style distributes a copy of the entire table to the first slice on each node. Though the ALL distribution helps to optimize joins, it increases the amount of storage. This means that operations such as LOAD, UPDATE, and INSERT can run slower than with the other distribution styles. The ALL distribution style can be a good choice for smaller dimension tables that are frequently joined with large fact tables in the center of your star schemas and for tables that you don't need to update frequently. Table data is placed on slice 0 of each compute node.

Use the EVEN distribution style when there is no clear choice between the KEY and ALL distribution styles. It is also recommended for small dimension tables, tables without JOIN or GROUP BY clauses, and tables that are not used in aggregate queries. Data is evenly distributed across all slices using a round-robin distribution. Figure 8-16 shows each of the three data distribution options.

When you create a table, you can define one or more of its columns as sort keys. When data is initially loaded into the empty table, the rows are stored on disk in sorted order. Information about sort key columns is passed to the query planner, and the planner uses this information to construct plans that exploit the way the data is sorted. It is used like an index for a given set of columns. It is implemented via zone maps, stored in each block header. It increases the performance of MERGE JOIN because of a much faster sort.

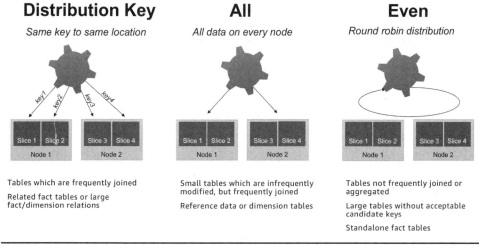

Distribution Key

Same key to same location

All

All data on every node

Even

Round robin distribution

Tables which are frequently joined

Related fact tables or large fact/dimension relations

Small tables which are infrequently modified, but frequently joined

Reference data or dimension tables

Tables not frequently joined or aggregated

Large tables without acceptable candidate keys

Standalone fact tables

Figure 8-16   Data distribution in Amazon Redshift

Amazon DynamoDB

Amazon DynamoDB is a fully managed NoSQL database service that provides fast and predictable performance with seamless scalability. NoSQL is a term used to describe high-performance, nonrelational databases. NoSQL databases use a variety of data models, including graphs, key-value pairs, and JSON documents. NoSQL databases are widely recognized for ease of development, scalable performance, high availability, and resilience.

Amazon DynamoDB supports both document and key-value data structures, giving you the flexibility to design the best architecture that is optimal for your application. Average service-side latencies are typically in single-digit milliseconds. A key-value store provides support for storing, querying, and updating collections of objects that are identified using a key and values that contain the actual content being stored, and a document store provides support for storing, querying, and updating items in a document format such as JSON, XML, and HTML.

Amazon DynamoDB is a fully managed cloud NoSQL database service. You simply create a database table, set your throughput, and let the service handle the rest. When creating a table, simply specify how much request capacity is required for the application. If your throughput requirements change, simply update your table's request capacity using the AWS Management Console or the Amazon DynamoDB APIs. Amazon DynamoDB manages all the scaling behind the scenes, and you are still able to achieve your prior throughput levels while scaling is underway.

These are some common use cases for DynamoDB. It can be used in advertising for capturing browser cookie state, in mobile applications for storing application data and session state, in gaming applications for storing user preferences and application state and for storing players' game state, in consumer "voting" applications for reality TV contests, in Super Bowl commercials, in large-scale websites for keeping session state or for personalization or access control, in application monitoring for storing application log and event data or JSON data, and in Internet of Things devices for storing sensor data and log ingestion.

Benefits of Amazon DynamoDB

These are the benefits of Amazon DynamoDB:

- **Scalable**   NoSQL databases are designed for scale, but their architectures are sophisticated, and there can be significant operational overhead in running a large NoSQL cluster. DynamoDB is scalable and can automatically scale up and down depending on your application request. Since it is integrated with Auto Scaling, Amazon take cares of scaling up or down as per throughput consumption monitored via CloudWatch alarms. Auto Scaling take cares of increasing or decreasing the throughput as per the application behavior.

- **Managed service**   Since this is a totally managed service, the complexity of running a massively scalable, distributed NoSQL database is managed by Amazon, allowing software developers to focus on building applications rather than managing infrastructure. Amazon take cares of all the heavy lifting behind the scenes such as hardware or software provisioning, software patching, firmware updates, database management, or partitioning data over multiple instances as you scale. DynamoDB also provides point-in-time recovery, backup, and restore for all your tables.

- **Fast, consistent performance**   Since DynamoDB uses SSD technologies behind the scenes, the average service-side latencies are typically in single-digit milliseconds. As your data volumes grow, DynamoDB automatically partitions your data to meet your throughput requirements and deliver low latencies at any scale.

- **Fine-grained access control**   DynamoDB is integrated with AWS Identity and Access Management (IAM), where you can provide fine-grained access control to all the users in your organization.

- **Cost-effective**   DynamoDB is cost-effective. With DynamoDB, you pay for the storage you are consuming and the IO throughput you have provisioned. When the storage and throughput requirements of an application are low, only a small amount of capacity needs to be provisioned in the DynamoDB service. As the number of users of an application grows and the required IO throughput increases, additional capacity can be provisioned on the fly, and you need to pay only for what you have provisioned.

- **Integration with other AWS services**   Amazon DynamoDB is integrated with AWS Lambda so that you can create triggers. With triggers, you can build applications that react to data modifications in DynamoDB tables. Similarly, Amazon DynamoDB can take care of automatically scaling up or down your DynamoDB tables depending on the application usage.

Amazon DynamoDB Terminology

Tables are the fundamental construct for organizing and storing data in DynamoDB. A table consists of items just like a table in a relational database is a collection of rows. Each table can have an infinite number of data items. An item is composed of a primary key that uniquely identifies it and key-value pairs called *attributes*. Amazon DynamoDB is schemaless, in that the data items in a table need not have the same attributes or even the same number of attributes. Each table must have a primary key. While an item is similar to a row in an RDBMS table, all the items in the same DynamoDB table need not share the same set of attributes in the way that all rows in a relational table share the same columns. The primary key can be a single attribute key or a "composite" attribute key that combines two attributes. The attributes you designate as a primary key must exist for every item as primary keys uniquely identify each item within the table. There is no concept of a column in a DynamoDB table. Each item in the table can be expressed as a tuple containing an arbitrary number of elements, up to a maximum size of 400KB. This data model is well suited for storing data in the formats commonly used for object serialization and messaging in distributed systems.

- **Item**   An item is composed of a primary or composite key and a flexible number of attributes. There is no explicit limitation on the number of attributes associated with an individual item, but the aggregate size of an item, including all the attribute names and attribute values, cannot exceed 400KB.

- **Attribute**   Each attribute associated with a data item is composed of an attribute name (for example, Name) and a value or set of values (for example, Tim or Jack, Bill, Harry). Individual attributes have no explicit size limit, but the total value of an item (including all attribute names and values) cannot exceed 400KB.

Tables and items are created, updated, and deleted through the DynamoDB API. There is no concept of a standard DML language like there is in the relational database world. Manipulation of data in DynamoDB is done programmatically through object-oriented code. It is possible to query data in a DynamoDB table, but this too is done programmatically through the API. Because there is no generic query language like SQL, it's important to understand your application's data access patterns well to make the most effective use of DynamoDB.

DynamoDB supports four scalar data types: Number, String, Binary, and Boolean. A scalar type represents exactly one value. DynamoDB also supports NULL values. Additionally, DynamoDB supports these collection data types: Number Set, String Set, Binary Set, heterogeneous List, and heterogeneous Map.

When you create a table, you must specify the primary key of the table. A primary key is a key in a relational database that is unique for each record. The primary key uniquely identifies each item in the table so that no two items can have the same key.

DynamoDB supports two different kinds of primary keys.

- **Partition key**   This is also known as a *simple primary key*. It consists of one attribute known as the *partition key*. The partition key of an item is also known as its *hash attribute*. The term *hash attribute* derives from the use of an internal hash function in DynamoDB that evenly distributes data items across partitions, based on their partition key values. In a table that has only a partition key, no two items can have the same partition key value.

- **Partition key and sort key** This is also known as a *composite primary key*. This type of key is composed of two attributes. The first attribute is the partition key, and the second attribute is the sort key. All items with the same partition key are stored together, in sorted order by sort key value. The sort key of an item is also known as its *range attribute*. The term *range attribute* derives from the way DynamoDB stores items with the same partition key physically close together, in sorted order by the sort key value. In a table that has a partition key and a sort key, it's possible for two items to have the same partition key value. However, those two items must have different sort key values.

A primary key can be either a single-attribute partition key or a composite partition-sort key. A composite partition-sort key is indexed as a partition key element and a sort key element. This multipart key maintains a hierarchy between the first and second element values.

Each primary key attribute must be a scalar. The only data types allowed for primary key attributes are string, number, or binary. There are no such restrictions for other, nonkey attributes.

When you create a table, the items for a table are stored across several partitions. DynamoDB looks at the partition key to figure out which item needs to be stored at which partition. All the items with the same partition key are stored in the same partition. During the table creation, you need to provide the table's desired read and write capacity. Amazon DynamoDB configures the table's partition based on that information. A unit of write capacity enables you to perform one write per second for items of up to 1KB in size. Similarly, a unit of read capacity enables you to perform one strongly consistent read per second (or two eventually consistent reads per second) of items up to 4KB in size. Larger items will require more capacity. You can calculate the number of units of read and write capacity you need by estimating the number of reads or writes you need to do per second and multiplying by the size of your items.

- Units of capacity required for writes = Number of item writes per second × Item size in 1KB blocks
- Units of capacity required for reads = Number of item reads per second × Item size in 4KB blocks

NOTE If you use eventually consistent reads, you'll get twice the throughput in terms of reads per second.

Global Secondary Index

Global secondary indexes are indexes that contain a partition or partition-sort keys that can be different from the table's primary key. For efficient access to data in a table, Amazon DynamoDB creates and maintains indexes for the primary key attributes. This allows applications to quickly retrieve data by specifying primary key values. However, many applications might benefit from having one or more secondary (or alternate) keys available to allow efficient access to data with attributes other than the primary key. To address this, you can create one or more secondary indexes on a table and issue query requests against these indexes.

Amazon DynamoDB supports two types of secondary indexes.

- A *local secondary index* is an index that has the same partition key as the table but a different sort key. A local secondary index is "local" in the sense that every partition of a local secondary index is scoped to a table partition that has the same partition key.

- A *global secondary index* is an index with a partition or a partition-sort key that can be different from those on the table. A global secondary index is considered global because queries on the index can span all items in a table, across all partitions.

Consistency Model

Amazon DynamoDB stores three geographically distributed replicas of each table to enable high availability and data durability. Read consistency represents the manner and timing in which the successful write or update of a data item is reflected in a subsequent read operation of that same item. DynamoDB exposes logic that enables you to specify the consistency characteristics you desire for each read request within your application. Amazon DynamoDB supports two consistency models. When reading data from Amazon DynamoDB, users can specify whether they want the read to be eventually consistent or strongly consistent.

- **Eventually consistent reads**   This is the default behavior. The eventual consistency option maximizes your read throughput. However, an eventually consistent read might not reflect the results of a recently completed write. Consistency across all copies of data is usually reached within a second. Repeating a read after a short time should return the updated data.

- **Strongly consistent reads**   In addition to eventual consistency, Amazon DynamoDB also gives you the flexibility and control to request a strongly consistent read if your application, or an element of your application, requires it. A strongly consistent read returns a result that reflects all writes that received a successful response prior to the read.

Global Table

Global tables build on Amazon DynamoDB's global footprint to provide you with a fully managed, multiregion, and multimaster database that provides fast, local, read, and write performance for massively scaled, global applications. Global tables replicate your DynamoDB tables automatically across your choice of AWS regions. Global tables eliminate the difficult work of replicating data between regions and resolving update conflicts, enabling you to focus on your application's business logic. In addition, global tables enable your applications to stay highly available even in the unlikely event of isolation or degradation of an entire region.

Global tables also ensure data redundancy across multiple regions and allow the database to stay available even in the event of a complete regional outage. Global tables provide cross-region replication, data access locality, and disaster recovery for business-critical database workloads. Applications can now perform low-latency reads and writes to DynamoDB around the world, with a time-ordered sequence of changes propagated efficiently to every AWS region where a table resides. With DynamoDB global tables, you get built-in support for multimaster writes, automatic resolution of concurrency conflicts, and CloudWatch monitoring. You simply select the regions where data should be replicated, and DynamoDB handles the rest.

Amazon DynamoDB Streams

Using the Amazon DynamoDB Streams APIs, developers can consume updates and receive the item-level data before and after items are changed. This can be used to build creative extensions to your applications on top of DynamoDB. For example, a developer building a global multiplayer game using DynamoDB can use the DynamoDB Streams APIs to build a multimaster topology and keep the masters in sync by consuming the DynamoDB Streams APIs for each master and replaying the updates in the remote masters. As another example, developers can use the DynamoDB Streams APIs to build mobile applications that automatically notify the mobile devices of all friends in a circle as soon as a user uploads a new selfie. Developers could also use DynamoDB Streams to keep data warehousing tools, such as Amazon Redshift, in sync with all changes to their DynamoDB table to enable real-time analytics. DynamoDB also integrates with ElasticSearch using the Amazon DynamoDB Logstash plug-in, thus enabling developers to add free-text search for DynamoDB content.

Amazon DynamoDB Accelerator

For even more performance, Amazon DynamoDB Accelerator (DAX) is a fully managed, highly available, in-memory cache for DynamoDB that delivers up to a ten times performance improvement—from milliseconds to microseconds—even at millions of requests per second. DAX does all the heavy lifting required to add in-memory acceleration to your DynamoDB tables, without requiring developers to manage cache invalidation, data population, or cluster management. Now you can focus on building great applications for your customers without worrying about performance at scale. You do not need to modify the application logic because DAX is compatible with existing DynamoDB API calls.

Encryption and Security

Amazon DynamoDB supports encryption at rest. It helps you secure your Amazon DynamoDB data by using AWS managed encryption keys stored in the AWS KMS. Encryption at rest is fully transparent to users, with all DynamoDB queries working seamlessly on encrypted data without the need to change the application code.

Amazon DynamoDB also offers VPC endpoints with which you can secure the access to DynamoDB. Amazon VPC endpoints for DynamoDB enable Amazon EC2 instances in your VPC to use their private IP addresses to access DynamoDB with no exposure to the public Internet.

Amazon ElastiCache

Amazon ElastiCache is a web service that makes it easy to deploy, operate, and scale an in-memory cache in the cloud. Amazon ElastiCache manages the work involved in setting up an in-memory service, from provisioning the AWS resources you request to installing the software. Using Amazon ElastiCache, you can add an in-memory caching layer to your application in a matter of minutes, with a few API calls. Amazon ElastiCache integrates with other Amazon web services such as Amazon Elastic Compute Cloud (Amazon EC2) and Amazon Relational Database Service (Amazon RDS), as well as deployment management solutions such as AWS CloudFormation, AWS Elastic Beanstalk, and AWS OpsWorks.

Since this is a managed service, you no longer need to perform management tasks such as hardware provisioning, software patching, setup, configuration, monitoring, failure recovery, and backups. ElastiCache continuously monitors your clusters to keep your workloads up and running so that you can focus on higher-value application development. Depending on your performance needs, it can scale out and scale in to meet the demands of your application. The memory scaling is supported with sharding. You can also create multiple replicas to provide the read scaling.

The in-memory caching provided by Amazon ElastiCache improves application performance by storing critical pieces of data in memory for fast access. You can use this caching to significantly improve latency and throughput for many read-heavy application workloads, such as social networking, gaming, media sharing, and Q&A portals. Cached information can include the results of database queries, computationally intensive calculations, or even remote API calls. In addition, compute-intensive workloads that manipulate data sets, such as recommendation engines and high-performance computing simulations, also benefit from an in-memory data layer. In these applications, large data sets must be accessed in real time across clusters of machines that can span hundreds of nodes. Manipulating this data in a disk-based store would be a significant bottleneck for these applications.

Amazon ElastiCache currently supports two different in-memory key-value engines. You can choose the engine you prefer when launching an ElastiCache cache cluster.

- **Memcached**   This is a widely adopted in-memory key store and historically the gold standard of web caching. ElastiCache is protocol-compliant with Memcached, so popular tools that you use today with existing Memcached environments will work seamlessly with the service. Memcached is also multithreaded, meaning it makes good use of larger Amazon EC2 instance sizes with multiple cores.

- **Redis**   This is an increasingly popular open source key-value store that supports more advanced data structures such as sorted sets, hashes, and lists. Unlike Memcached, Redis has disk persistence built in, meaning you can use it for long-lived data. Redis also supports replication, which can be used to achieve multi-AZ redundancy, similar to Amazon RDS.

Although both Memcached and Redis appear similar on the surface, in that they are both in-memory key stores, they are actually quite different in practice. Because of the replication and persistence features of Redis, ElastiCache manages Redis more as a relational database. Redis ElastiCache clusters are managed as stateful entities that include failover, similar to how Amazon RDS manages database failover.

When you deploy an ElastiCache Memcached cluster, it sits in your application as a separate tier alongside your database. Amazon ElastiCache does not directly communicate with your database tier or indeed have any particular knowledge of your database. You can begin with a single ElastiCache node to test your application and then scale to additional cluster nodes by modifying the ElastiCache cluster. As you add cache nodes, the EC2 application instances are able to distribute cache keys across multiple ElastiCache nodes. When you launch an ElastiCache cluster, you can choose the availability zones that the cluster lives in. For best performance, you should configure your cluster to use the same availability zones as your application servers. To launch an ElastiCache cluster in a specific availability zone, make sure to specify the Preferred Zone(s) option during cache cluster creation. The availability zones that you specify will be where ElastiCache will launch your cache nodes.

Figure 8-17 shows the architecture of an ElastiCache deployment in a multi-AZ deployment with RDS engines. Similarly, you can deploy ElastiCache with DynamoDB as well. The combination of DynamoDB and ElastiCache is popular with mobile and game companies because DynamoDB allows for higher write throughput at a lower cost than traditional relational databases.

Figure 8-17
Amazon
ElastiCache
deployment
on RDS with
multi-AZ

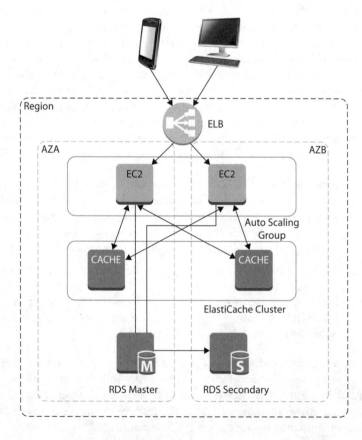

Lab 8-1: RDS: Creating an Amazon Aurora Database

In this lab, you will log in to the AWS console, spin off an Amazon Aurora database, and then connect to it.

1. Log in to the AWS Console, choose your region, and select RDS.

2. From the RDS main page or dashboard, click Launch a DB instance. Select Amazon Aurora and choose MySQL 5.6 compatible.

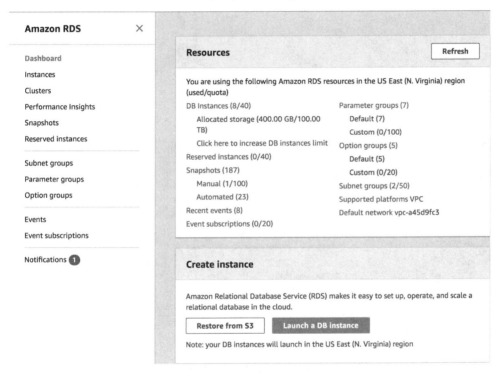

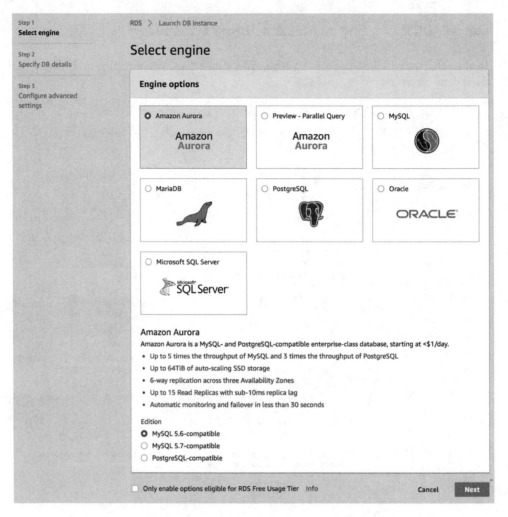

3. On the Specify DB Details screen, shown next, set the following:

   a. DB Instance Class: db.t2.small 1 vCPU, 2 GiB RAM

   b. Multi-AZ Deployment: No

   c. DB Instance Identifier: AURORA-Book

   d. Master Username: master

   e. Master Password: master123

   f. Confirm Password: master123

   g. Click Next to go to the next screen.

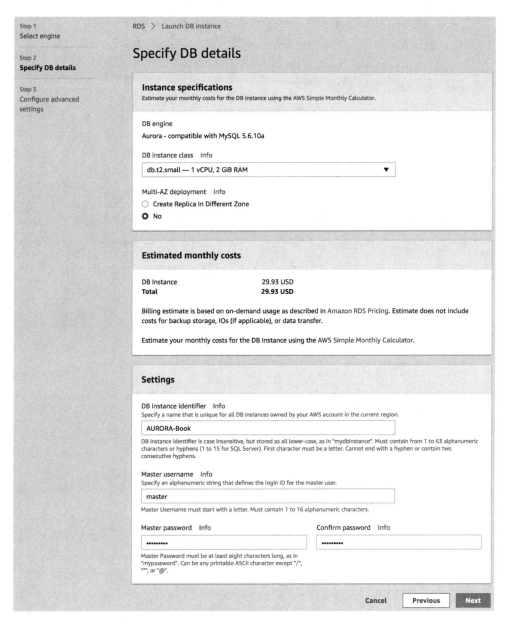

Step 1
Select engine

Step 2
Specify DB details

Step 3
Configure advanced
settings

RDS > Launch DB instance

Specify DB details

Instance specifications
Estimate your monthly costs for the DB Instance using the AWS Simple Monthly Calculator.

DB engine
Aurora - compatible with MySQL 5.6.10a

DB instance class   Info

db.t2.small — 1 vCPU, 2 GiB RAM   ▼

Multi-AZ deployment   Info
○ Create Replica in Different Zone
● No

Estimated monthly costs

DB Instance   29.93 USD
Total   **29.93 USD**

Billing estimate is based on on-demand usage as described in Amazon RDS Pricing. Estimate does not include
costs for backup storage, IOs (if applicable), or data transfer.

Estimate your monthly costs for the DB Instance using the AWS Simple Monthly Calculator.

Settings

DB instance identifier   Info
Specify a name that is unique for all DB instances owned by your AWS account in the current region.

AURORA-Book

DB instance identifier is case insensitive, but stored as all lower-case, as in "mydbinstance". Must contain from 1 to 63 alphanumeric
characters or hyphens (1 to 15 for SQL Server). First character must be a letter. Cannot end with a hyphen or contain two
consecutive hyphens.

Master username   Info
Specify an alphanumeric string that defines the login ID for the master user.

master

Master Username must start with a letter. Must contain 1 to 16 alphanumeric characters.

Master password   Info   Confirm password   Info

••••••••   ••••••••

Master Password must be at least eight characters long, as in
"mypassword". Can be any printable ASCII character except "/",
""", or "@".

Cancel   Previous   Next

4. On the Configure Advanced Settings screen, set the following:

   a. VPC: Default VPC

   b. Subnet Group: Choose the default

   c. Publicly Accessible: Yes

   d. Availability Zone: No Preference

    e. VPC Security Group(s): Create New Security Group

    f. DB Cluster Identifier: AuroraBook

    g. Database Name: AuroraDB

    h. Database Port: 3306

    i. DB Parameter Group: default.aurora5.6

    j. DB Cluster Parameter Group: default.aurora5.6

    k. Option Group: default.aurora-5-6

    l. Enable Encryption: No

    m. Please keep the default options for the rest.

5. Click Launch DB Instance.

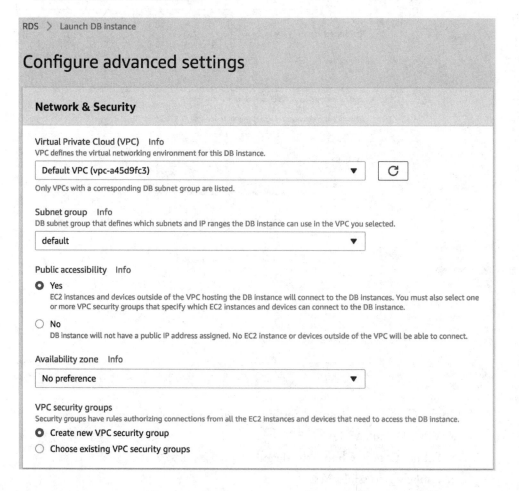

Database options

DB cluster identifier   Info

> AuroraBook

If you do not provide one, a default identifier based on the instance identifier will be used.

Database name

> AuroraDB

If you do not specify a database name, Amazon RDS does not create a database.

Database port
TCP/IP port the DB instance will use for application connections.

> 3306

DB parameter group   Info

> default.aurora5.6   ▼

DB cluster parameter group   Info

> default.aurora5.6   ▼

Option group   Info

> default:aurora-5-6   ▼

Encryption

Encryption

○ **Enable encryption** Learn more [↗]
  Select to encrypt the given instance. Master key ids and aliases appear in the list after they have been created using the Key Management Service(KMS) console.

● **Disable encryption**

Failover

Priority   Info

> No preference   ▼

Backup

Backup retention period   Info
Select the number of days that Amazon RDS should retain automatic backups of this DB instance.

> 1 day   ▼

Backtrack

Backtrack lets you quickly move an Aurora database to a prior point in time without needing to restore data from a backup.   Info

○ Enable Backtrack

● Disable Backtrack

Monitoring

Enhanced monitoring

● Enable enhanced monitoring
Enhanced monitoring metrics are useful when you want to see how different processes or threads use the CPU.

○ Disable enhanced monitoring

Monitoring Role   Granularity

| Default   ▼ | | 60 seconds   ▼ |

☑ I authorize RDS to create the IAM role rds-monitoring-role.

Log exports

Select the log types to publish to Amazon CloudWatch Logs

☐ Audit log
☐ Error log
☐ General log
☐ Slow query log

IAM role
The following service-linked role is used for publishing logs to CloudWatch Logs.

RDS Service Linked Role

ⓘ Ensure that General, Slow Query, and Audit Logs are turned on. Error logs are enabled by default.
Learn more

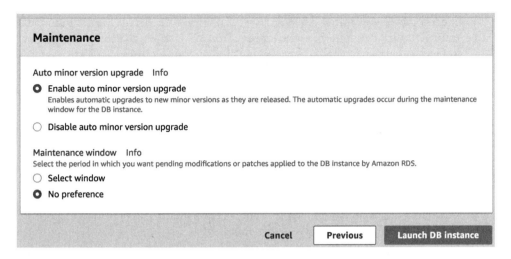

6. You will get the message "Your DB Instance is being created." Click View Your DB Instance.

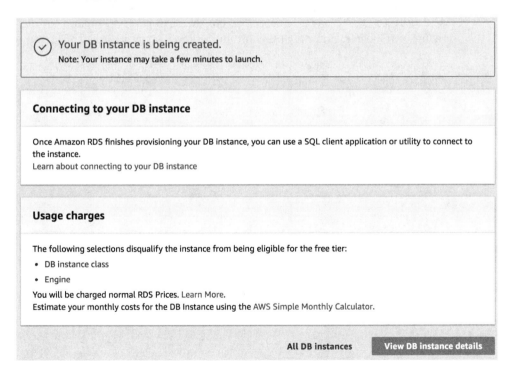

7. You will notice that when the instance is in the process of getting created, the status will show Created, and when the instance is ready, it will show Available.

8. Expand the newly created database. It will show you the details for the instance. You will notice a unique cluster endpoint. You are going to use this endpoint for connecting to the database. The endpoint for the Aurora instance in this example is `aurora-book.cluster-cnibitmu8dv8.us-east-1.rds .amazonaws.com:3306`.

Connect		
Endpoint aurora-book.cnibitmu8dv8.us-east-1.rds.amazonaws.com	**Port** 3306	**Publicly accessible** Yes

9. Download the mysqlworkbench tool from https://dev.mysql.com/downloads/workbench/ and install it on your machine.

10. Install and launch mysqlworkbench from your local machine. Click the + sign to create a new connection and enter all the details for the database. For the host, put the database endpoint excluding the port since the next prompt is for the port. Thus, the host will be similar to `aurora-book.cluster-cnibitmu8dv8 .us-east-1.rds.amazonaws.com`. For the port, enter **3306**, and for the username, put **master**. Enter the password in the keychain as **master123**.

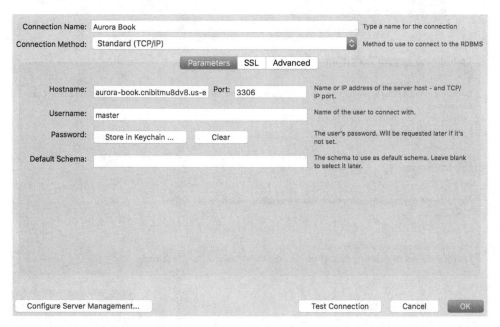

11. Once you are able to connect, you will see a success screen saying the connection to the database is successful.

Lab 8-2: Taking a Snapshot of a Database

In this lab, you will take a snapshot of the database and use that snapshot to create a new instance.

1. Expand the newly created database (step 8 from Lab 8-1). Click the Instance Actions button, and select Take Snapshot.

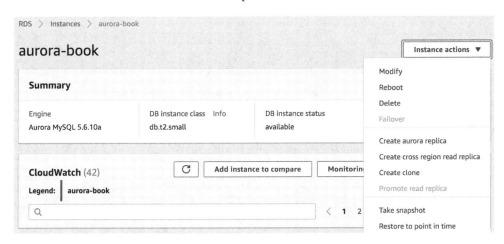

2. The system will prompt for the snapshot name. Enter **AWSBOOK** for the same and click Take Snapshot.

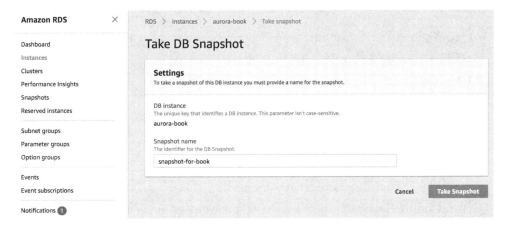

3. The console will start creating the snapshot. Once it is finished, you will be able to view it.

4. Now you will use this snapshot for restoring it and creating a new database. Select the snapshot and click Snapshot Actions; a pop-up will appear. Click Restore Snapshot.

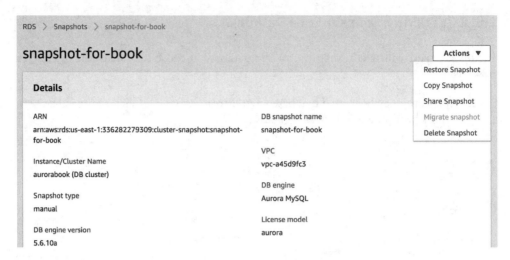

5. Now the system will ask you for details of the database as detailed in Lab 8-1, steps 3 and 5. Input all the details and click Restore DB.

Congrats, you have successfully restored a database from the snapshot!

Lab 8-3: Creating an Amazon Redshift Cluster

In this lab, you will create and launch an Amazon Redshift cluster. The goal is to get familiar with how to launch a cluster and networking involved while creating the cluster.

1. Log in to the AWS Console, choose your region, and select Redshift.

2. Click Launch Cluster.

3. On the Cluster Details screen, specify the following:

    a. Cluster Identifier: testrs

    b. Database Name: redshiftdb

    c. Database Port: 5439

    d. Master User Name: dbauser

    e. Master User Password: set any password

    f. Confirm Password: specify the same password again

4. Click Continue.

5. On the Node Configuration screen, set the following:

a. Node Type: dc2.large. In this example, I have chosen dc2.large; you can select a different one if you'd like. Once you select a instance, the screen displays all the CPU, memory, and storage details associated with that instance.

b. For Cluster Type, choose Multi Node since you are creating a multinode cluster.

c. For Number Of Compute Nodes, use 2. The system displays the maximum and minimum compute nodes you can have.

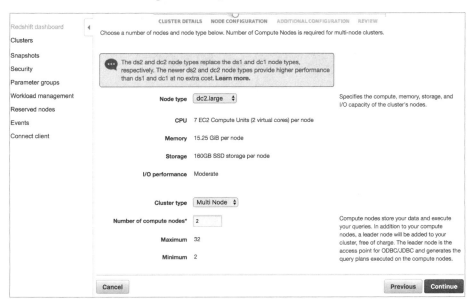

6. Click Continue.

7. In the Additional Configurations screen, set the following:

   a. Encrypt Database: None

   b. Choose A VPC: Default VPC

   c. Cluster Subnet Group: leave the default

   d. Publicly Accessible: Yes

   e. Enhanced VPC Routing: No

   f. Availability Zone: No Preference

   g. VPC Security Groups: the default security group

   h. Create CloudWatch Alarm: No

   i. The IAM role is optional, so don't select any role.

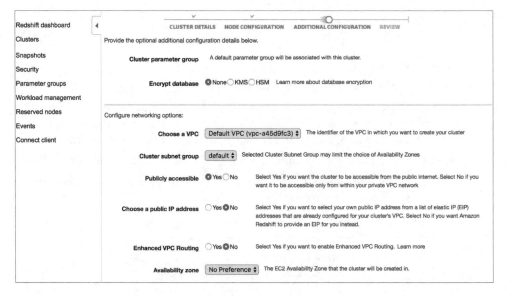

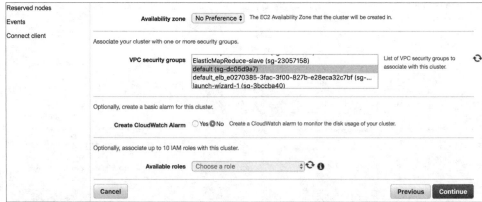

8. Click Continue.

9. The system displays all the options on the Review screen.

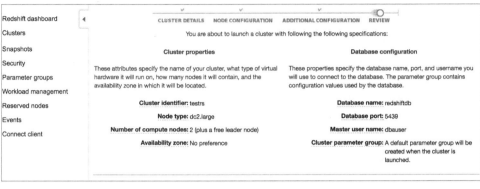

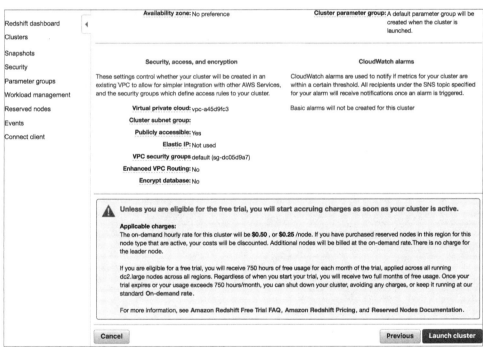

10. Click Launch Cluster to launch your cluster.

11. Congrats! You have launched the Redshift cluster. Now go to the dashboard and connect to it using a client.

Lab 8-4: Creating an Amazon DynamoDB Table

In this lab you will be creating an Amazon DynamoDB table. The goal is to get familiar with the table creation process.

1. Log in to the AWS Console, choose your region, and select DynamoDB.

2. Click Create Table.

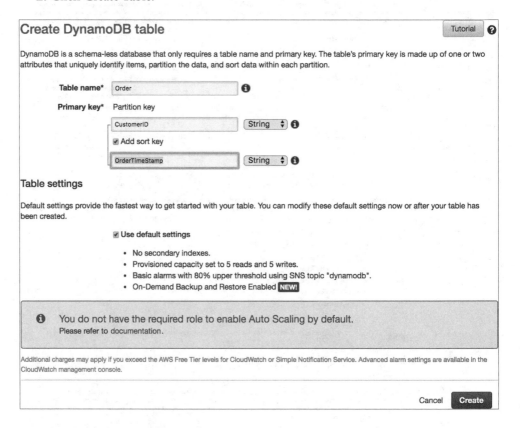

3. For Table Name, select Order.

4. For Primary Key, enter **Customer ID**.

5. Select the Add Sort Key box and enter **OrderTimeStamp** as the sort key.

6. Select Use Default Settings.

7. Click Create.

Congrats! You have created your first DynamoDB table.

8. Go to the dashboard and select the table.

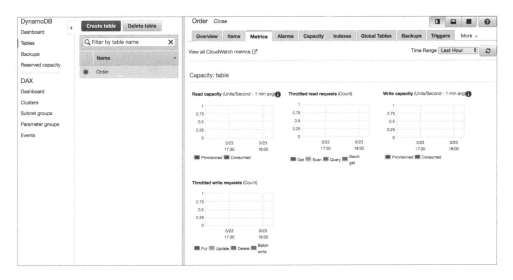

9. Look at all the options (Items, Metrics, Alarms, Capacity, Indexes, and so on) at the top.

Chapter Review

In this chapter, you learned about all the database offerings from Amazon.

Using the RDS service, you can host the following seven RDBMS engines:

- Aurora MySQL
- Aurora PostgreSQL
- Oracle
- SQL Server
- MySQL
- PostgreSQL
- MariaDB

For high availability, RDS allows you to deploy databases in multiple AZs. When you deploy a database in a multi-AZ architecture, you can choose which availability zone you want your primary database instance to be in. RDS will then choose to have a standby instance and storage in another availability zone. In the case of a multi-AZ architecture, the primary database, also known as the *master database,* handles all the traffic. The standby database is always kept ready and is in a state that whenever the master or primary goes down, it takes the role of the master or primary and supports the application.

When you host the database using RDS, AWS take cares of managing the database. From installation to maintenance of the database and from patching to upgrading, everything is taken care of by AWS. Even high availability and scalability are taken care of by AWS.

RDS allows the creation of read replica. Depending on the RDMBS engine, it can have up to 15 read replicas. This functionality is supported by MySQL, MariaDB, PostgreSQL, Aurora MySQL, and Aurora PostgreSQL.

Amazon Aurora is a cloud-optimized, MySQL- and PostgreSQL-compatible, relational database. It provides the performance and availability of commercial databases and the simplicity and cost effectiveness of open source databases. Amazon Aurora provides performance and durability by implementing a fully distributed and self-healing storage system, and it provides availability by using the elasticity and management capabilities of the AWS cloud in the most fundamental ways.

Amazon Redshift is the managed data warehouse solution offered by Amazon Web Services. A Redshift cluster consists of a leader node and compute nodes. There is only one leader node per cluster, whereas there could be several compute nodes in a cluster. The leader node acts as a SQL endpoint for the applications. It performs database functions and coordinates the parallel SQL processing. The compute node processes the actual data. All the compute nodes are connected via a high-speed interconnected network. A compute node is further divided or partitioned into multiple slices. A slice is allocated a portion of a node's CPU, memory, and storage. Depending on the size of the compute node, a node can have more or fewer slices. The leader node distributes the job across multiple compute nodes. You can create a single node or multiple-node Redshift cluster.

Amazon DynamoDB is a fully managed NoSQL database service that provides fast and predictable performance with seamless scalability. Amazon DynamoDB supports both document and key-value data structures. A key-value store provides support for storing, querying, and updating collections of objects that are identified using a key and values that contain the actual content being stored, and a document store provides support for storing, querying, and updating items in a document format such as JSON, XML, and HTML.

Amazon ElastiCache is a web service that makes it easy to deploy, operate, and scale an in-memory cache in the cloud. Amazon ElastiCache currently supports two different in-memory key-value engines: Memcached and Redis. You can choose the engine you prefer when launching an ElastiCache cache cluster.

Questions

1. You are running your MySQL database in RDS. The database is critical for you, and you can't afford to lose any data in the case of any kind of failure. What kind of architecture will you go with for RDS?

   A. Create the RDS across multiple regions using a cross-regional read replica

   B. Create the RDS across multiple AZs in master standby mode

   C. Create the RDS and create multiple read replicas in multiple AZs with the same region

   D. Create a multimaster RDS database across multiple AZs

2. Your application is I/O bound, and your application needs around 36,000 IOPS. The application you are running is critical for the business. How can you make sure the application always gets all the IOPS it requests and the database is highly available?

   A. Install the database in EC2 using an EBS-optimized instance, and choose a I/O optimized instance class with an SSD-based hard drive

   B. Install the database in RDS using SSD

   C. Install the database in RDS in multi-AZ using Provisioned IOPS and select 36,000 IOPS

   D. Install multiple copies of read replicas in RDS so all the workload gets distributed across multiple read replicas and you can cater to the I/O requirement

3. You have a legacy application that needs a file system in the database server to write application files. Where should you install the database?

   A. You can achieve this using RDS because RDS has a file system in the database server

   B. Install the database on an EC2 server to get full control

   C. Install the database in RDS, mount an EFS from the RDS server, and give the EFS mount point to the application for writing the application files

   D. Create the database using a multi-AZ architecture in RDS

4. You are running a MySQL database in RDS, and you have been tasked with creating a disaster recovery architecture. What approach is easiest for creating the DR instance in a different region?

   A. Create an EC2 server in a different region and constantly replicate the database over there.

   B. Create an RDS database in the other region and use third-party software to replicate the data across the database.

   C. While installing the database, use multiple regions. This way, your database gets installed into multiple regions directly.

   D. Use the cross-regional replication functionality of RDS. This will quickly spin off a read replica in a different region that can be used for disaster recovery.

5. If you encrypt a database running in RDS, what objects are going to be encrypted?

   A. The entire database

   B. The database backups and snapshot

   C. The database log files

   D. All of the above

6. Your company has just acquired a new company, and the number of users who are going to use the database will double. The database is running on Aurora. What things can you do to handle the additional users? (Choose two.)

   A. Scale up the database vertically by choosing a bigger box

   B. Use a combination of Aurora and EC2 to host the database

   C. Create a few read replicas to handle the additional read-only traffic

   D. Create the Aurora instance across multiple regions with a multimaster mode

7. Which RDS engine does not support read replicas?

   A. MySQL

   B. Aurora MySQL

   C. PostgreSQL

   D. Oracle

8. What are the various ways of securing a database running in RDS? (Choose two.)

   A. Create the database in a private subnet

   B. Encrypt the entire database

   C. Create the database in multiple AZs

   D. Change the IP address of the database every week

9. You're running a mission-critical application, and you are hosting the database for that application in RDS. Your IT team needs to access all the critical OS metrics every five seconds. What approach would you choose?

   A. Write a script to capture all the key metrics and schedule the script to run every five seconds using a cron job

   B. Schedule a job every five seconds to capture the OS metrics

   C. Use standard monitoring

   D. Use advanced monitoring

10. Which of the following statements are true for Amazon Aurora? (Choose three.)

   A. The storage is replicated at three different AZs.

   B. The data is copied at six different places.

   C. It uses a quorum-based system for reads and writes.

   D. Aurora supports all the commercial databases.

11. Which of the following does Amazon DynamoDB support? (Choose two.)

   A. Graph database

   B. Key-value database

   C. Document database

   D. Relational database

12. I want to store JSON objects. Which database should I choose?

    A. Amazon Aurora for MySQL

    B. Oracle hosted on EC2

    C. Amazon Aurora for PostgreSQL

    D. Amazon DynamoDB

13. I have to run my analytics, and to optimize I want to store all the data in columnar format. Which database serves my need?

    A. Amazon Aurora for MySQL

    B. Amazon Redshift

    C. Amazon DynamoDB

    D. Amazon Aurora for Postgres

14. What are the two in-memory key-value engines that Amazon ElastiCache supports? (Choose two.)

    A. Memcached

    B. Redis

    C. MySQL

    D. SQL Server

15. You want to launch a copy of a Redshift cluster to a different region. What is the easiest way to do this?

    A. Create a cluster manually in a different region and load all the data

    B. Extend the existing cluster to a different region

    C. Use third-party software like Golden Gate to replicate the data

    D. Enable a cross-region snapshot and restore the database from the snapshot to a different region

Answers

1. **B.** If you use a cross-regional replica and a read replica within the same region, the data replication happens asynchronously, so there is a chance of data loss. Multimaster is not supported in RDS. By creating the master and standby architecture, the data replication happens synchronously, so there is zero data loss.

2. **C.** You can choose to install the database in EC2, but if you can get all the same benefits by installing the database in RDS, then why not? If you install the database in SSD, you don't know if you can meet the 36,000 IOPS requirement. A read replica is going to take care of the read-only workload. The requirement does not say the division of read and write IO between 36,000 IOPS.

3. **B**. In this example, you need access to the operating system, and RDS does not give you access to the OS. You must install the database in an EC2 server to get complete control.

4. **D**. You can achieve this by creating an EC2 server in a different region and replicating, but when your primary site is running on RDS, why not use RDS for the secondary site as well? You can use third-party software for replication, but when the functionality exists out of the box in RDS, why pay extra to any third party? You can't install a database using multiple regions out of the box.

5. **D**. When you encrypted a database, everything gets encrypted including the database, backups, logs, read replicas, snapshot, and so on.

6. **A**, **C**. You can't host Aurora on a EC2 server. Multimaster is not supported in Aurora.

7. **D**. Only RDS Oracle does not support read replicas; the rest of the engines do support it.

8. **A**, **B**. Creating the database in multiple AZs is going to provide high availability and has nothing to do with security. Changing the IP address every week will be a painful activity and still won't secure the database if you don't encrypt it.

9. **D**. In RDS, you don't have access to OS, so you can't run a cron job. You can't capture the OS metrics by running a database job. Standard monitoring provides metrics for one minute.

10. **A**, **B**, **C**. Amazon Aurora supports only MySQL and PostgreSQL. It does not support commercial databases.

11. **B**, **C**. Amazon DynamoDB supports key-value and document structures. It is not a relational database. It does not support graph databases.

12. **D**. A JSON object needs to be stored in a NoSQL database. Amazon Aurora for MySQL and PostgreSQL and Oracle are relational databases.

13. **B**. Amazon Redshift stores all the data in columnar format. Amazon Aurora for MySQL and PostgreSQL store the database in row format, and Amazon DynamoDB is a NoSQL database.

14. **A**, **B**. MySQL and SQL Server are relational databases and not in-memory engines.

15. **D**. Loading the data manually will be too much work. You can't extend the cluster to a different region. A Redshift cluster is specific to a particular AZ. It can't go beyond an AZ as of writing this book. Using Golden Gate is going to cost a lot, and there is no need for it when there is an easy solution available.

AWS Well-Architected Framework and Best Practices

In this chapter, you will

- Learn how to secure your environment
- Learn how to make a reliable architecture
- Learn how to make sure the architecture is performing efficiently
- Learn how to make sure the architecture is cost effective
- Learn how to make sure the architecture is excellent in terms of operation

When you use the AWS Well-Architected Framework for building any new architecture, you get these immediate benefits:

- **Build and deploy faster**   By reducing firefighting, implementing capacity management, and using automation, you can experiment and increase value of running into cloud more often.

- **Lower or mitigate risks**   Understand where you have risks in your architecture and address them before they impact your business and distract your team.

- **Make informed decisions**   Ensure you have made active architectural decisions that highlight how they might impact your business outcomes.

- **Implement AWS best practices**   Since you will be leveraging the AWS Well-Architected Framework, the architecture you will come up with will have all the best practices inherited in it.

In this chapter, you will learn about the AWS Well-Architected Framework (WAF). (Note that WAF also refers to the AWS product Web Application Firewall, but in this chapter it means the documentation and architecture called the AWS Well-Architected Framework.) You'll also learn about AWS best practices and how to implement them. Whenever you create an architecture in AWS or deploy an application in AWS, it is important that your architecture follows all the AWS best practices. You want the architecture to be secure, efficient, scalable, reliable, and cost effective. Designing an architecture using AWS best practices can help you achieve these business goals and make your organization successful.

When you're constructing a building, if the foundation is not done properly, there a chance is that the building may collapse or end up damaged in some way over time. In the same way, wherever you are defining an architecture in AWS, you must construct the foundation carefully, which means embedding the principles of the AWS Well-Architected Framework into the design principles of the architecture. By using the AWS Well-Architected Framework, you can make sure that your architecture has all the best practices built in.

This chapter focuses on AWS WAF and the various principles behind the WAF. It also talks about the AWS best practices and what you should be doing when deploying an application to the cloud.

The AWS WAF has these five pillars:

- Operational excellence
- Security
- Performance
- Reliability
- Cost optimization

All these pillars follow a design principle followed by best practices for each pillar.

Operational Excellence

Operational excellence is measured in terms of how you are able to support the business. If you have aligned your operations team to support the business SLAs, you are in a good shape. It is important that the operations team understands the business's goals, priorities, and metrics so that it delivers according to the needs of the business.

Businesses may run several kinds of applications in the cloud. Some of those applications might be mission critical, and some of them won't be. The operations team should be able to prioritize critical applications over noncritical applications and should be able to support them accordingly.

These are the design principles for achieving operational excellence in the cloud:

- **Perform operations as code**   In the cloud, it is possible to lay down the entire infrastructure as code and update it with code. You can script most of the tasks and try to automate as much as possible. For example, you should be able to automatically trigger operating procedures in response to events; if your CPU usage goes up, Auto Scaling can automatically start a new server.

- **Document everything**   Everything should be documented for all the operations in the cloud. It does not matter if you are making small changes or big changes in the system or in the application; you should annotate the documentation.

- **Push small changes instead of big**   Instead of pushing one big change in the system, it is recommended that you push small changes that can be reversible. The damage caused by a bigger change going wrong will be much bigger compared to the damage caused by small changes. Also, if the changes are reversible, you can roll back at any point of time if it does not go well.

- **Refine operating procedures often**   The architecture keeps on evolving, and therefore you need to keep updating your operating procedures. For example, say today you are using only one web server to host an application. Whenever there is a maintenance activity, you apply the operating system bug fixes on the one server. But tomorrow if you expand the web server footprint to four servers, you need to refine your operating procedures to make sure you will apply the operating system bug fixes on four different servers and not one. Set up regular days to review and validate your operating procedures.

- **Anticipate failure**   You should not wait for an actual failure to happen. You should assume failures can happen at any point in time and proactively simulate them. For example, in a multinode fleet of web servers, shut down one or two nodes randomly and see what the impact on the application is. Is the application able to resolve the failures automatically? You should be doing all kinds of destruction testing proactively so that when a real failure happens, your application is prepared to handle it.

- **Learn from the operational failures**   You should always learn from your operational failures and make sure that the same failure does not happen twice. You should share what you have learned with other teams, as well as learn from the failures of other teams.

Operational excellence in the cloud is composed of three areas: prepare, operate, and evolve. Each one is described in the following sections.

Prepare

Your operations team should be prepared to support the business. To do so, the operations team should understand the needs of the business. Since the operations team needs to support multiple business units, the team should know what each business unit needs. The priorities for every business unit might be different. Some business units may be running mission-critical applications, and other units might be running low-priority applications. The operations team must have a baseline of performance needed by business applications, and it should be able to support it. For example, say the business needs an order management system, and it is expecting an average of 100,000 orders per day from that system. The operations team should be prepared to provide the infrastructure that not only can host the order management system but also support 100,000 orders per day. Similarly, if the business is running a report and there is a performance degradation while running that report, the operations team should be able to handle it. In addition, the operations team should be prepared to handle planned and unplanned downtime. If you want your operations team to be successful, you should anticipate failures, as described earlier. This will make sure you are prepared to handle any kind of unplanned downtime.

Operate

When you are better prepared, you can handle the operations in a much more efficient way. Operational success is measured by the outcomes and metrics you define. These metrics can be based on the baseline performance for a certain application, or they can support your business in a certain way. To operate successfully, you must constantly meet the business goals and their SLAs, and you should be able to respond to events and take actions accordingly. One of the keys for the operations team's success is to have proper communication with the business. The operations team should have a dashboard that provides a bird's-eye view of the status of all the applications' health checks. Consider the following four services when creating the dashboard:

- **Amazon CloudWatch logs**   Logs allow you to monitor and store logs from EC2 instances, AWS CloudTrail, and other sources.
- **Amazon ES**   Amazon ES makes it easy to deploy, secure, operate, and scale Elasticsearch for log analytics and application monitoring.
- **Personal Health Dashboard**   This dashboard provides alerts and remediation guidance when AWS is experiencing events that may impact you.
- **Service Health Dashboard**   This dashboard provides up-to-the-minute information on AWS service availability.

Automation can be your friend. To operate efficiently, you must automate as much as possible. If you are able to take care of automating the day-to-day operations and other pieces such as responding to certain events, you can focus on important and mission-critical activities.

Evolve

We all learn something new every day; similarly, you should always raise the operations team's efficiency by taking it to the next level. You should learn from your own experience as well as from other people's experience. You will often see that some people like to start with minimal viable products and then keep on adding more functionality on top of them. In the same way, regarding the infrastructure, they like to start small and keep evolving depending on how critical the infrastructure becomes. Thus evolve means start with small and continuously keep on adding new and new functionality or keep enhancing your architecture. An example of evolving architecture is given in the "AWS Best Practices" section of this chapter.

Security

The next pillar of the WAF is security. Needless to say, security is the heart of everything; therefore, it must be your top priority. The security pillar contains design principles, which are discussed in the following sections.

Have a Strong Identity Foundation

Use IAM to manage the accounts in AWS. Use the principle of least privilege and don't grant anyone access unless needed. There should be a central team of users responsible for granting access across the organization. This will make sure that access control is handled by only one set of people, and others won't be able to override each other. The principle of least privilege means that by default everyone should be denied access to the system. The access should be given only when someone explicitly requests it. This way, you will minimize unauthorized access to the system. In addition, you should be using either IAM users or federate users. You can use federation via SAML 2.0 or web identities. By using federation, you can leverage the existing identities, and you won't have to re-create the users in IAM. It is important to define the roles and access for each user, and employee life cycle policies should be strictly enforced. For example, the day an employee is terminated, he should lose all access to the cloud. You should also enforce a strong password policy with a combination of uppercase, lowercase, and special characters, and users should change passwords after a specified time and not be allowed to repeat any of their last ten passwords. You can even enforce MFA when IAM users log in from the console. In many cases, IAM users may require access to AWS APIs via the Command Line Interface (CLI) or Software Development Kit (SDK). In that case, sometimes federation may not work properly. In those cases, you can use an access key and secret key in addition to or in place of a username and password. In some cases, you might notice that IAM roles may not be practical. For example, when you are switching from one service to another, you should leverage AWS Security Token Service to generate the temporary credentials.

Enable Traceability

You should be able to trace, audit, monitor, and log everything happening in your environment in real time, and should have a mechanism to get an alert for any changes that are happening. You should also automate some of the actions by integrating the log and alert system with the system to automatically respond and take action in real time. It is important to enable auditing and traceability so that if anything happens, you will be able to quickly figure out who has logged in to the system and what action has been taken that has caused the issue. Make sure all the changes in the system are audited and you can account for who have made changes. You should have a strong system of control for making the changes. You can use AWS Config to track AWS resource inventory, configuration history, and configuration change notifications to enable security and governance. Without proper approvals, no change should be permissible in the system. You can also create rules that automatically check the configuration of AWS resources recorded by AWS Config using AWS Config rules. You can capture the key activities via AWS CloudTrail; it provides details about the API calls made in your account. You can also direct the CloudTrail logs to Amazon CloudWatch logs and can view whatever is happening across compute, storage, and applications under a single pane of glass.

Implement Security at All Layers

The security should be applied at all layers across the stack. Say you have EC2 servers running in both private and public subnets. In this case, you should have layers of security across the subnets by leveraging NACL, layers of security across EC2, and a load balancer by leveraging security groups, you should secure the operating system, storage, and the applications running. In short you should be able isolate every component of your infrastructure and secure each part. Let's look at an example to understand this. Say you have a three-tier architecture with a web tier, app tier, and database tier. You should have separate security groups for each tier, and only authorized users can access the web tier or app tier or database tier. You should also put the Internet-facing web tier in the public subnet and put the internal-facing database and app tiers in the private subnet. Similarly, if you want to have a firewall, you should apply on to all the layers; in other words, use a separate firewall for the database tier and a separate firewall for the application tier. Also, you can use a separate set of ACLs for a different tier. Thus, you have a security control or firewall at every virtual server, every load balancer, and every network subnet. Focus on securing all your systems. Since AWS provides the shared responsibility model, as a result half of the burden of securing the data center, physical facilities, and networking is taken care by AWS. You just need to focus on securing your application, data, and operating systems. Whenever possible, leverage the managed services since they take the burden of managing the infrastructure from you. Similarly, whenever you are designing an architecture, you should make sure that you have leveraged all the avenues for securing the design. For example, within VPC, use the public and private subnets to segregate the workload depending on who can have Internet or external access. Use a bastion host to log in to instances running on the private subnet. Always use a NAT gateway when you want to update the servers running on a private subnet, use different security groups depending on the workload, and use NACL to filter the traffic at the subnet level. Use different VPCs for different workloads. For example, create a separate VPC for the production workload, a separate VPC for the development workload, and so on.

Secure the Data

Along with security at all layers, it is equally important to protect the data. You should secure the data both at rest and in transit. Use all the different technologies to encrypt the data depending on sensitivity. When the data moves from the web tier to the app tier or from the app tier to the database tier, make sure it is encrypted. You can use SSL or TLS to encrypt the data in transit. If you are using APIs, make sure it is SSL/TLS enabled. Similarly, for all communications, you should use SSL or TLS; you can also use a VPN-based solution or Direct Connect to make sure that the communication path is also secure. For data at rest, you can use technologies such as Transparent Data Encryption (TDE) to encrypt the data at rest. When you are using AWS services, you can use Amazon S3 server-side encryption, and you can encrypt the EBS volumes. If using client-side technologies, then you can use a supported SDK or OS to make sure it meets all the standards for security. Whenever you have been given the task of securing the data, you need to think about the path of data flow and secure all the points to make sure your data is secured everywhere. One of the most common examples of data flow is from ELB to EC2 to EBS to RDS to S3. When you know your data is going to touch these components, you can secure every component plus ensure that the data in transit is secure, and thus you will have an end-to-end secured solution. If you are using keys for encryption, then you should look at the AWS Key Management Service (KMS) for creating and controlling the keys. If you are using SSL, then your content is delivered via HTTPS for which you can leverage Amazon CloudFront. Using Amazon Cloud-Front provides lots of advantages. You can use your own domain name and SSL certificates, or you can use a Server Name Indication (SNI) custom SSL (older versions of browsers do not support SNI's custom SSL), or you can use the dedicated IP custom SSL if your browser does not support SNI's custom SSL. Amazon CloudFront supports all of them.

Automate for Security

Automation can be your best friend. You can have a software-based security mechanism to securely scale more rapidly and cost effectively. You should set up alerts for all important actions so that if something goes wrong, you are immediately notified, and at the same time you should have automation so that the system can act upon it promptly. You can also set up some automated triggered responses to event-driven conditions. Also, it is important to monitor and go through the logs once in a while to make sure there are no anomalies. It is important to implement automation as a core tenant for security best practices. You can automate a lot of things to minimize risk and any errors. For example, you can install all the security patches and bug fixes into a virtual machine, save that as a gold image, and deploy this image to any server that you are going to launch. You can see by doing a small automation that you are able to implement the security fixes in all the VMs that you will be launching; it does not matter if it is hundreds of VMs or a few thousand.

Plan for Security Events

Always plan for security events well in advance. Run some simulations proactively to find gaps in your architecture and fix them before any incident can happen. Run the testing to simulate real-life attacks and learn from the outcome. Learn from other teams or different business units about how they are handling the security events. In a nutshell, your system should be ready against all kinds of attacks such as DDoS attacks and so on.

Best Practices

There are five best practices for security in the cloud: use identity and access management, use detective controls, use infrastructure protection, use data protection, and use incident response.

Use Identity and Access Management

IAM makes sure that only those who are authorized can access the system. IAM can help in protecting the AWS account credentials as well as providing fine-grained authorization. You should use this service as a best practice. You already studied this in detail in Chapter 5.

Use Detective Controls

You can use detective controls to identify a threat or incident. One type of detective control is to capture and analyze logs. If you want to do this in the on-premise world, you need to install some kind of agent on all the servers that will capture the logs and then analyze the agent. In the cloud, capturing logs is easy since assets and instances can be described without depending on the agent's health. You can also use native API-driven services to collect the logs and then analyze them directly in the AWS cloud. In AWS, you can direct AWS CloudTrail logs to Amazon CloudWatch logs or other endpoints so you can get details of all the events. For EC2 instances, you will still use traditional methods involving agents to collect and route events.

Another way to use a detective control is to integrate auditing controls with notification and workflow. A search on the logs collected can be used to discover potential events of interest, including unauthorized access or a certain change or activity. A best practice for building a mature security operations team is to deeply integrate the flow of security events and findings into a notification and workflow system such as a ticketing system, thereby allowing you to route, escalate, and manage events or findings.

These are some of the services that help you when implementing detective controls:

- **AWS Config**   This is a fully managed service that provides you with an AWS resource inventory, configuration history, and configuration change notifications to enable security and governance. With AWS Config, you can discover existing AWS resources, export a complete inventory of your AWS resources with all the configuration details, and determine how a resource was configured at any point in time. These capabilities enable compliance auditing, security analysis, resource change tracking, and troubleshooting.

- **AWS Config rule**   An AWS Config rule represents the desired configurations for a resource and is evaluated against configuration changes on the relevant resources, as recoded by AWS Config. The results of evaluating a rule against the configuration of a resource are available on a dashboard. Using AWS Config rules, you can assess your overall compliance and risk status from a configuration perspective, view compliance trends over time, and pinpoint which configuration change caused a resource to drift out of compliance with a rule.

- **AWS CloudTrail**   This is a web service that records AWS API calls for your account and delivers logs. It can be useful in answering these questions: Who made the API call? When was the API call made? What was the API call? Which resources were acted upon in the API call? Where was the API call made from, and who was it made to?

- **Amazon CloudWatch**   You can use Amazon CloudWatch to gain systemwide visibility into resource utilization, application performance, and operational health. You can use these insights to keep your application running smoothly. The Amazon CloudWatch API and AWS SDKs can be used to create custom events in your own applications and inject them into CloudWatch events for rule-based processing and routing.

- **VPC flow logs to help with network monitoring**   Once enabled for a particular VPC, VPC subnet, or Elastic Network Interface (ENI), relevant network traffic will be logged to CloudWatch logs.

- **Amazon Inspector**   This tool offers a programmatic way to find security defects or misconfigurations in your operating systems and applications. It can be easily integrated with CI/CD tools and can be automated via APIs. It has the ability to generate findings.

Use Infrastructure Protection

Infrastructure protection consists of protecting your entire infrastructure. It ensures that systems and services within your solution are protected against unintended and unauthorized access and potential vulnerabilities. You can protect network and host-level boundaries by applying appropriate configurations to your virtual private cloud, subnets, routing tables, network access control lists (NACLs), gateways, and security groups to achieve the network routing as well as host-level protection. You can protect system security configuration and maintenance by using AWS Systems Manager. This gives you visibility and control of your infrastructure on AWS. With Systems Manager, you can view detailed system configurations, operating system patch levels, software installations, application configurations, and other details about your environment through the Systems Manager dashboard. The last thing in infrastructure protection is to enforce service-level protection. The security configurations of service endpoints form the foundation of how you will maintain secure and authorized access to these endpoints. You can protect AWS service endpoints by defining policies using IAM.

Use Data Protection

The data first needs to be classified according to the level of sensitivity. Depending on the type of data, you control the level of access/protection appropriate to the data classification. Once the data has been classified, you can either encrypt it or tokenize it. Encryption is a way of transforming content in a manner that makes it unreadable without a secret key necessary to decrypt the content back into plain text. Tokenization is a process that allows you to define a token to represent an otherwise sensitive piece of information. For example, you can have a token to represent an SSN. You can define your own tokenization scheme by creating a lookup table in an encrypted Amazon Relational Database Service (Amazon RDS) database instance. The next step would be to protect the data at rest as well as in transit. Data at rest represents any data that you persist for any duration. This includes block storage, object storage, databases, archives, and any other storage medium on which data is persisted. Data in transit is any data that gets transmitted from one system to another. The encryption of data in transit can be done by using SSL or TLS, HTTPS, VPN/IPsec, or SSH, as shown in Figure 9-1.

The encryption at rest can be done at the volume level, object level, and database level; the various methods are shown in Figure 9-2. The last step in data protection is to have backups, a disaster strategy, and replication in place.

Figure 9-1

Encryption at rest and in transit

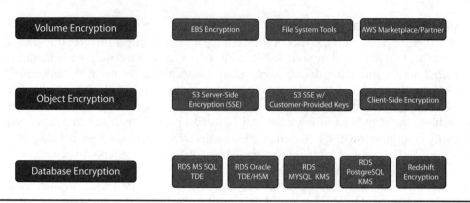

Figure 9-2 Encryption at rest

Use Incident Response

The last area of best practices for the security of the cloud is incident response. Whenever an incident happens, you should be able to respond to it quickly and act on it. Putting in place the tools and access ahead of a security incident and then routinely practicing incident response will help you ensure that your architecture can accommodate timely investigation and recovery. Products such as AWS Web Application Firewall and Shield can be leveraged to protect against SQL injection (SQLi) and cross-site scripting (XSS); prevent web site scraping, crawlers, and bots; and mitigate DDoS attacks (HTTP/HTTPS floods).

Performance

This pillar is all about the need for speed. It focuses on performance efficiency and how your business can benefit from it. In this age, every business wants to run faster, so whatever speedup you can provide will always be helpful for running the business. In this section, you will look at the design principles of this pillar and the best practices associated with it.

It has the following design principles:

- **Go global in a few clicks** AWS allows you to lay out a global infrastructure in minutes. Depending on the business needs, you should be able to design a highly scalable and available architecture, which can fail over to a different region in the case of disaster recovery. Leverage multiple AZs in your design pattern.

- **Leverage new technologies such as serverless** The biggest advantage of the cloud is that for some use cases you have the opportunity of not managing any servers but still supporting the business. Try to leverage serverless architecture as much as possible so that you don't have to manage the infrastructure.

- **Consume advanced technology**   If you are leveraging an advanced technology, you don't have to learn it or become an expert in it. Leverage the managed services and just be a consumer. For example, say on your premise you have an Oracle database and you have migrated to Aurora in AWS; you don't have to learn all the details of Aurora because it is a managed service, and all the DBA activities are taken care of by Amazon.

- **Leverage multiple technologies**   As they say, one size does not fit all when you move to the cloud. Consider a technology approach that aligns best to what you are trying to achieve. Say you have a relational database running on-premise; when you move to the cloud, evaluate how much can be offloaded to a NoSQL system, how much can go in RDS, how much can go to Redshift, and so on. Thus, instead of moving the relational database as it is in the cloud, you can choose the right technology for the right data patterns and save a lot of money.

- **Experiment more often**   The cloud gives you the opportunity to experiment more often, which can help the business to innovate faster. You can quickly deploy resources in the cloud and start executing your idea. You don't have to wait for months to procure new infrastructure. Even if your idea fails, it does not matter since you pay only for the resources used. You can quickly jump to the next idea.

Performance Efficiency

Performance efficiency in the cloud is composed of three steps: selection, review, and monitoring.

Selection

The cloud gives you a variety of choices. Choosing the right services for running your workload is the key. To select the right service, you need to have a good idea about your workload. If you know the nature of your workload, it becomes easier to choose the right solutions. Say your application needs a lot of memory; in that case, you should go with memory-intense EC2 instances. Similarly, if your application is I/O bound, you should provision PIOPS-based EBS volumes along with the EC2 server. When you are selecting a complete solution, you should focus on the following four areas:

- **Compute**   The ideal compute for an application depends on its design, usage patterns, and configuration settings. In AWS, compute is available in three forms: instances, containers, and functions. Instances are virtualized servers (EC2), and you can change their capabilities with just a few clicks or an API call. There are different types of EC2 instances available to choose from (general purpose, compute, memory, storage, GPU optimized). The key is choosing the right one for your workload. Containers are a method of operating system virtualization that allow you to run an application and its dependencies in resource-isolated processes. You can even choose containers to run your workload if you are running a microservice architecture. Functions abstract the execution environment from the code you want to execute. For example, AWS Lambda allows you to execute code without running an instance. When building new applications in the cloud, you should evaluate how you can leverage API Gateway and Lambda more instead of designing the application in the traditional way.

- **Storage**   AWS offers you various types of storage. You don't have to stick with just one kind of storage; rather, you should leverage various types of storage. Even for the same application, you don't have to use only one kind of storage. You can tier the storage as per the usage. The ideal storage solution will be based on the kind of access method (block, file, or object), patterns of access (random or sequential), frequency of access (online, offline, archival), frequency of update (WORM, dynamic), throughput required, and availability and durability constraints. This is discussed in more detail in the "Leverage Multiple Storage Options" section of this chapter.

- **Network**   The optimal network solution for a particular system will vary based on latency, throughput requirements, and so on. Physical constraints such as user or on-premises resources will drive location options, which can be offset using edge techniques or resource placement. In AWS, networking is virtualized and is available in a number of different types and configurations. This makes it easier to match your networking methods more closely with your needs. AWS provides lots of ways to optimize networks, and you should have a reworking solution that can support your business needs. For example, if you need faster networking between the EC2 instance and the EBS volume, you can use EBS-optimized instances, and Amazon EC2 provides placement groups for networking. A placement group is a logical grouping of instances within a single availability zone. Using placement groups with supported instance types enables applications to participate in a low-latency, 20Gbps network. Placement groups are recommended for applications that benefit from low network latency, high network throughput, or both. Similarly, S3 transfer acceleration and Amazon CloudFront speeds things up, Direct Connect helps quickly to move data back and forth between your data center, and Amazon VPC endpoints provide connectivity to AWS services such as Amazon S3 without requiring an Internet gateway or a Network Address Translation (NAT) instance. Latency-based routing (LBR) for Route 53 helps you improve your application's performance for a global audience.

- **Database**   Until a few years back, all data used to go to the relational database by default. Every organization used to have multiple big relational databases running with every kind of data in them. Now you don't have to put everything in the relational database. Only part can remain in a relational database, and the rest can be moved to various other types of database such as NoSQL, a data warehouse, and so on. Only the part of the data that needs relational access to datasets involving complex queries that will join and aggregate data from multiple entities can stay in a relational database, and the rest can be moved to a different type of database. If you are putting data in a relational database, you can either choose to host it in EC2 servers or use an RDS service to host it. Similarly, for NoSQL, you can use DynamoDB, and for data warehouses, you can use Redshift. In many cases, you may need to index, search, and consolidate information on a large scale. Technologies such as search engines are particularly efficient for these use cases. In these cases, you can use Elasticsearch in conjunction with Kibana and document or log aggregation with LogStash. Elasticsearch provides an easy-to-use platform that can automatically discover and index documents at a really large scale, and Kibana provides a simple solution for creating dashboards and analysis on indexed data. Elasticsearch can be deployed in EC2 instances, or you can use the Amazon Elasticsearch service, which is the managed service of AWS.

Review

Once you make the selection, it is equally important to periodically review the architecture and make continuous changes to the architecture as per the business needs. The business needs can change at any point of time, and you may have to change the underlying infrastructure. For example, the business may want to open an internal ordering tool to all its suppliers. Now all the performance metrics are going to change, and to support the business, you have to make some architecture changes. Also, AWS keeps on innovating, releasing new services, dropping the price, and adding new geographies and edge locations. You should take advantage of them since it is going to improve the performance efficiency of your architecture. To reiterate you should focus on the following from day 1.

- Define your infrastructure as code using approaches such as AWS CloudFormation templates. This enables you to apply the same practices you use to develop software to your infrastructure so you can iterate rapidly.

- Use a continuous integration/continuous deployment (CI/CD) pipeline to deploy your infrastructure. You should have well-defined metrics, both technical and business metrics, of monitoring to capture key performance indicators.

- Run benchmarks and do performance tests regularly to make sure that the performance tests have passed successfully and meet the performance metrics. During the testing, you should create a series of test scripts that can replicate or simulate the life workload so that you can compare apples to apples (load testing).

Monitoring

Once you deploy the application/workload, you should constantly monitor it so that you can remediate any issues before your customers are aware of them. You should have a way of alerting whenever there is anomaly. These alerts can be customized and should be able to automate action to work around any badly performing components. CloudWatch provides the ability to monitor and send notification alarms. You can then use these alarms to make automation work around performance issues by triggering actions through Amazon Kinesis, Amazon Simple Queue Service (Amazon SQS), and AWS Lambda.

Reliability

Using this pillar you are going design the architecture as per the service level agreements. You need to consider how the solution can recover from various failures, how much outage a business can handle, how to work backward from the RTO and RPO levels, and so on. The goal is to keep the impact of any type of failure to a minimum. By preparing your system for the worst, you can implement a variety of mitigation strategies for the different components of your infrastructure and applications. When designing the system you can think about various failure scenarios and work backward. These requirements can cause long lead times because of dependencies and therefore must be incorporated during initial planning. With AWS, most of these foundational requirements are already incorporated or may be addressed as needed. At the same time, you need to make sure that your application or workload is leveraging all the aspects of reliability. For example AWS provides multiple AZs as a foundation for high availability. If you design your application to make use of multiple AZs, your application is going to leverage HA in the context of reliability automatically.

There are five design principles for reliability in the cloud.

- **Test recovery procedures**   Simulate all the failures that you might be encountering and try to see whether you are able to recover from those failures. Try to automate as much as possible to simulate the failure. You should be doing this activity often to make sure your system can handle failures and they are always up and running.

- **Automate recovery from failure**   You should automate the recovery from failures as much as possible. You should proactively monitor the system, as well as the response to an alert. By doing this, you should always be ready to handle a failure.

- **Scale horizontally**   Instead of scaling vertically, you should try to scale horizontally and leverage multiple servers to minimize the impact. For example, instead of running the workload on a 16-core server, you can run the same workload on four different servers of four cores each. You can even run these servers across different AZs within a region to provide HA within your application.

- **Stop guessing capacity**   In the cloud, the resources are almost infinite. In an on-premise environment, the resources are always provisioned for peak loads, despite that if the resources saturate, the performance will degrade. In the cloud, there is no need to guess the right capacity. You just need to make sure you have proper automation in place that is going to spin off new resources for you as per the alerts.

- **Automate changes to the system**   All the changes to the system should be done via automation. This minimizes the chances for error.

Best Practices

There are three best practice areas for reliability in the cloud: lay the foundations, implement change management, and implement failure management.

Lay the Foundation

Before architecting any system, you must lay down the foundation. The foundation should be laid out as per the reliability needs. Find out from the business what exactly it is looking for. For example, if the business says it needs 99.99 percent availability, find out what exactly it is trying to do and then work backward. Designing applications for higher levels of availability often comes with increased costs, so it makes sense to identify the true availability needs before starting the application design. Table 9-1 shows availability and its corresponding downtime.

When you are building the foundation, you can start it right from your data center to the cloud. Do you need very large network bandwidth to your data center from the cloud? If yes, then you can start setting up Direct Connect instead of VPN. You can set up multiple Direct Connect options depending on your needs. The network topology needs to be planned well in advance, and you should also envision future growth and integration with other systems. You should keep in mind the following:

- Allow IP address space for more than one VPC per region.

- Within a VPC, keep space for multiple subnets that span multiple availability zones.

- Leave some unused CIDR block space within a VPC, which will take care of any needs for the future.

- Depending on business needs, you can have cross-account connections; in other words, each business can have their unique account and VPC that can connect back to the shared services.

- Start thinking about all the failures and work backward. Say you have Direct Connect. If that fails, then what happens? You can have a second Direct Connect. If you don't have the budget for a second Direct Connect, you can start with a VPN for failover.

Availability	Max Disruption (per Year)	Application Categories
99 percent	3 days, 15 hours	Batch processing, data extraction, transfer, and load jobs
99.9 percent	8 hours, 45 minutes	Internal tools such as knowledge management, project tracking
99.95 percent	4 hours, 22 minutes	Online commerce, point of sale
99.99 percent	52 minutes	Video delivery, broadcast systems
99.999 percent	5 minutes	ATM transactions, telecommunications systems

Table 9-1   Availability vs. Outage

There are a few areas you should focus on when designing an application for availability:

- **Fault isolation zones**   AWS has the fault isolation construct of availability zones; within a region there are two or more AZs. Whenever you are designing your workload/application, you should make sure that you are using at least two AZs. The more AZs you use in the architecture, the less chance there is of your application going down. Say you deploy your application across only one AZ. If that AZ goes down, there is 100 percent impact to your application. If you design the application using two AZs, it will have a 50 percent impact on your application if that goes down.

- **Redundant components**   One of the design principles of AWS is to avoid single points of failure in the underlying physical infrastructure. All the underlying physical infrastructure is built with redundant systems, so when you are designing the applications, you must make sure you plan for redundant components. For example, say you want to host your database on EC2 servers. Since data is the most critical part of the database, you can take multiple EBS volumes and use RAID to get HA in the storage layer.

- **Leveraging managed services**   Try to leverage managed services as much as possible because most of them come with built-in high availability. For example, RDS provides a multi-AZ architecture. If the AZ where you are hosting your database goes down, it automatically fails over to a different AZ. Similarly, if you choose to host your data in Amazon Aurora, six copies of the data are automatically written across three AZs.

Implement Change Management

Change management can make or break things. If you accidentally push the wrong code into the system, it can take down the entire system. In an on-premise environment, often the change control is a manual process and carefully coordinated with auditing to effectively control who makes changes and when they are made. In AWS, you can automate this whole part. You can also automate change management in response to key performance indicators, including fault management. When you are deploying changes in the system, you should consider these deployment patterns that minimize risk:

- **Blue-green deployments**   In this case, you have two stacks of deployment running in parallel: one stack running the old version and the other running the new version. You start with sending small traffic to the new deployment stack and watch out for failures, errors, and so on, and you send the rest of the traffic to the old stack (say 10 percent to the new stack and 90 percent to the old). If there are failures, you redirect the 10 percent traffic again to the old stack and work on fixing the issues. If things look good, you slowly keep on increasing the percentage of traffic to the new stack until you reach 100 percent.

- **Canary deployment**   This is the practice of directing a small number of your customers to the new version and scrutinizing deeply any behavior changes or errors that are generated. This is similar to blue-green deployment. If things look good, you can redirect more users to the new version until you are fully deployed, and if things keep on failing, you revert to the old version.

- **Feature toggle**   You can deploy the software with a feature turned off so that customers don't see the feature. If the deployment goes fine, you can turn on the feature so that customers can start using it. If the deployment has problems, you keep the feature turned off without rolling back till the next deployment.

Implement Failure Management

Your application should be able to handle the failure at every layer of the stack. You should evaluate every stack and think, if this stack fails or if this component goes down, how is my application going to handle it? You should ask questions like, what if the AZ fails, what if Direct Connect fails, what if the EC2 servers fails, or what if one of the hard drives goes down? Once you start thinking about all the possible scenarios, you should be able to architect your architecture in such a way that it can mitigate all types of failures. At the same time, it is important to make sure you have the proper backup and DR strategy in place. You should be regularly backing up your data and test your backup files to make sure you are able to recover from the backup. You should be running a DR simulation test to see how quickly you can spin up your infrastructure in a different region. You should be constantly shipping your data to a different region and automating the deployment of infrastructure in a different region using CloudFormation.

Cost Optimization Pillar

This pillar helps you cut down on costs and provides you with the ability to avoid or eliminate unneeded cost or suboptimal resources. You might have noticed that AWS regularly decreases the prices of its products and services and encourages its customer to optimize their resources so that they have to pay less. AWS provides lots of ways to do this, which helps a business keep its budget in check. Who does not love lower costs?

In the cloud, you can follow several principles that help you save money. If you follow cost optimization best practices, you should have a good cost comparison with on-premises, but it's always possible to reduce your costs in the cloud as your applications and environments are migrated and mature over time. Cost optimization should never end until the cost of identifying money-saving opportunities is more than the amount of money you are actually going to save.

The cost optimization pillar consists of the following design principles:

- **Choose the best consumption model**   Pay using the consumption model, which make more sense for your business. If you are going with an on-demand or pay-as-you-go pricing model, you can shut down the environments when not in use to save costs. For example, if your developers leave for home after 5 p.m. and come to the office the next day at 9 a.m., you can shut down the development environment during that time. Similarly, for production workloads, if you know that your application will need a certain number of cores for the whole year, you can go with the reserved pricing model to save money.

- **Use managed services**   Leverage managed services and serverless services as much as you can so that you don't have to deal with the infrastructure and can focus on running your business.

- **Measure the overall efficiency**   If you can measure the business output with the cost associated with it for delivery, you should be able to figure out in the long run if you are increasing costs or decreasing costs.

- **Analyze the expenditure**   The cloud provides you with all the tools to analyze the costs for running the business. You can find out which business unit is incurring which costs for running the system and can tie these back to the business owner. This way, you can find out whether you are getting enough return on investments.

- **Stop spending on a data center**   Since AWS take cares of the heavy lifting, you don't have to spend money on your data center. You can just focus on innovation and on running your business rather than on IT infrastructure.

Cost optimization in the cloud is composed of four areas: finding cost-effective resources, matching supply with demand, being aware of expenditures, and optimizing over time. The following sections describe each in detail.

Finding Cost-Effective Resources

You can do lots of things to make sure the resources you are utilizing are cost effective. You can start with minimum resources, and after running your workload for some time, you can modify your resources to scale up or down to size them correctly. If you start with minimum resources, then sometimes you may not have to scale further down. Depending on your business needs, you can choose between various purchasing options such as on-demand resources, spot instances, and reserved instances. You should choose a region that is near to your end users and that meets the business needs. For example, reduced latency can be a key factor in improving the usage of your e-commerce or other web sites. When you architect your solutions, a best practice is to seek to place computing resources closer to users to provide lower latency and strong data sovereignty. As discussed earlier, managed services or serverless services can become your best friends to avoid unnecessary IT management costs.

AWS provides a tool called Trusted Advisor, shown in Figure 9-3, that can help you control costs. Trusted Advisor looks at various AWS resources and provides guidance in terms of what you can do to get additional cost savings.

Matching Supply with Demand

In an on-premise environment, you always need to over-provision to meet the peak demand. Demand can be fixed or variable. In the cloud, you can automatically provi-

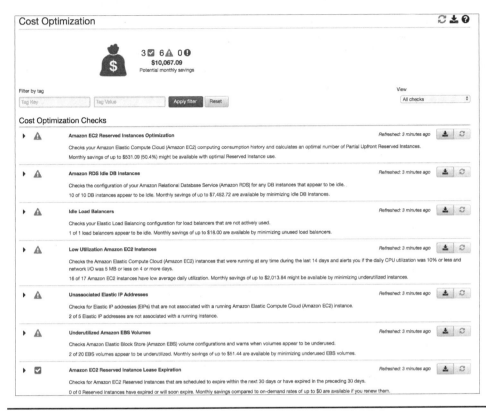

Figure 9-3 Trusted Advisor

sion resources to match the demand. For example, by leveraging Auto Scaling, you can automatically scale up or down to meet the demand. Similarly, you can start with a small instance class of RDS and move to a higher instance class when the demand goes up. Your capacity needs to match your needs but not substantially exceed what you need.

Being Aware of Expenditures

It is important that business is aware of underlying costs. This will help the business to make better decisions. If the costs of operations are higher than the revenue from the business, then it does not make sense to invest more in infrastructure. On the other hand, if the costs of operations are much lower, it makes sense to invest more infrastructure for the growth of business. While determining the cost, make sure you capture all the small details such as data transfer charges or Direct Connect charges.

Optimizing Over Time

To optimize over time, you need to constantly measure, monitor, and improve. Measure and monitor your users and applications, and combine the data you collect with data from monitoring. You can perform a gap analysis that tells you how closely aligned your system utilization is to your requirements. Say you start with an on-demand instance model. After a few months, you realize that you are using this instance 24/7, and you are going to use this instance for another year. At that time, you can switch to a reserved instance plan instead of sticking with on-demand. If you are not sure whether you might need a bigger class of instance after six months, in that case you can choose a convertible reserved instance.

AWS Best Practices

If you want to deploy applications to the cloud, there are three different ways you can do so:

- **Life and shift**   There are many applications that cannot be changed or modified. For instance, it is difficult to modify older applications. In that case, you have to "lift and shift" those applications to the cloud. Say you want to deploy Oracle ERP on the cloud; however, the application cannot be re-architected. In this case, it is important that you use the AWS core services. For example, you can use a VPC and subnets as a foundation and then use EC2 instances, EBS storage, and so on.
- **Cloud optimized**   Even if it is not possible to re-architect the application, you can still get some benefits from the cloud by optimizing the architecture for the cloud. For example, you can use native services such as RDS for provisioning the database and not EC2 servers, you can use SNS for sending the notifications, and so on.
- **Cloud native architecture**   In this case, you are starting everything from the cloud. You can leverage the full AWS portfolio and thus truly gain all the benefits of AWS in terms of security, scalability, cost, reliability, low operational cost, and so on.

Therefore, whenever you are architecting for the cloud, you should make sure that your architecture inherits all the best practices built in it. The following are the best practices you should follow for designing your architecture for the cloud.

Design for Failures

It is important that you design for failures at all layers of the stack. For the storage layer, you should mirror the data using RAID or some other technology. For the database tier, you should have high availability, and for the application tier, you should have multiple EC2 instances so that if one of them goes down, you can fail over to the other.

Let's look at a simple example to understand this. Say you have an EC2 server that is hosting the database and the application, as shown in Figure 9-4. You are also using an Elastic IP address for this server, and the end users are using Route 53 to reach the application.

If you look at Figure 9-4, do you see any problems? Yes, you have put all the components on a single EC2 server. There is no redundancy or failover. If this EC2 server goes down, what happens? Everything goes down, including your database, your applications, and everything else.

Figure 9-4
Hosting a
database and
application in an
EC2 server

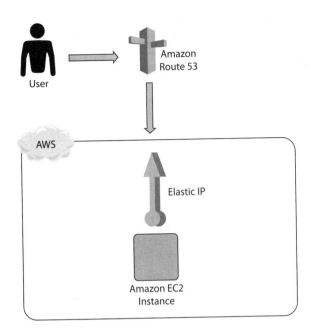

Amazon.com's CTO, Werner Vogels, has said, "Everything fails, all the time." If you design your architecture around that premise—specifically, assuming that any component will eventually fail—then your application won't fail when an individual component does.

In this case, when designing for failure, your goal is to see your application survive when the underlying physical hardware fails on one of your servers.

Let's try to work backward from this goal. In real life, you will often see that you won't be able to implement all the steps needed to make your architecture well architected in one day. Sometimes, as discussed previously, you have to evolve the design. Or you have to take small steps to reach a final architecture.

So, in this case, you can start by separating the database and the app tier. Thus, you are going to host the web tier in the EC2 server and put the database in RDS, as shown in Figure 9-5. Still, the application is vulnerable because if the database goes down, the application goes down, and if the web server goes down, the application goes down. But at least now you have segregated the database and the web tier.

In the next phase, you can address the lack of failover and redundancy in the infrastructure by adding another web tier EC2 instance and enabling the multi-AZ feature of RDS (Figure 9-6), which will give you a standby instance in a different AZ from the primary. You'll also replace your EIP with an elastic load balancer to share the load between your two web instances. Now the app has redundancy and high availability built in.

Therefore, the key takeaway from this is to avoid a single point of failure. You should always assume everything fails and design backward. Your goal should be that applications should continue to function even if the underlying physical hardware fails or is

Figure 9-5
Web server
in EC2 and
database in RDS

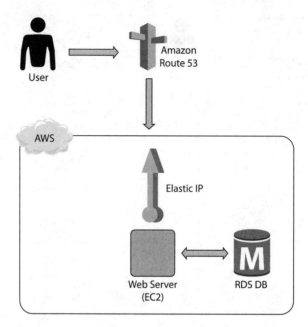

Figure 9-6
High availability
across web and
database tiers

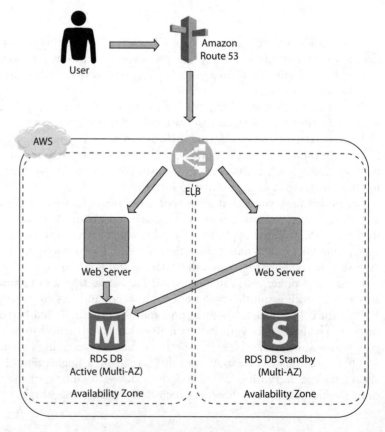

removed/replaced. If an individual component fails, the application should not have any impact. You can use the following AWS tools and technologies to do so:

- Use multiple availability zones
- Use elastic load balancing
- Use elastic IP addresses
- Do real-time monitoring with CloudWatch
- Use Simple Notification Service (SNS) for real-time alarms based on CloudWatch metrics
- Create database slaves across availability zones

Build Security in Every Layer

This was already discussed previously, but since this is such an important aspect, it is worth recapping. You should build security in every layer. For all important layers, you should encrypt data in transit and at rest. In addition, you should use the Key Management Service to create and control encryption keys used to encrypt your data. You should enforce the principle of least privilege with IAM users, groups, roles, and policies. You should use multifactor authentication to gain an additional layer of security. You should use both security groups to restrict the access to the EC2 servers and network ACLs to restrict traffic at the subnet level.

Leverage Multiple Storage Options

Since Amazon provides a wide range of storage options and size does not fit all, you should leverage multiple storage options for your application to optimize. These are the storage services provided by Amazon:

- **Amazon S3**   Large objects
- **Amazon Glacier**   Archive data
- **Amazon CloudFront**   Content distribution
- **Amazon DynamoDB**   Simple nonrelational data
- **Amazon EC2 Ephemeral Storage**   Transient data
- **Amazon EBS**   Persistent block storage with snapshots
- **Amazon RDS**   Automated, managed MySQL, PostgreSQL, Oracle, Maria DB, SQL Server
- **Amazon Aurora**   Cloud-optimized flavors of MySQL and PostgreSQL
- **Amazon Redshift**   Data warehouse workloads

Let's look at an example to understand this. Say you have built a web site on top of EC2 servers and are leveraging EBS volumes (let's say multiple EC2 servers) to host your web site. The web server is running on EC2. You are also using an RDS database instance

Figure 9-7
Web site running
on top of EC2
and RDS

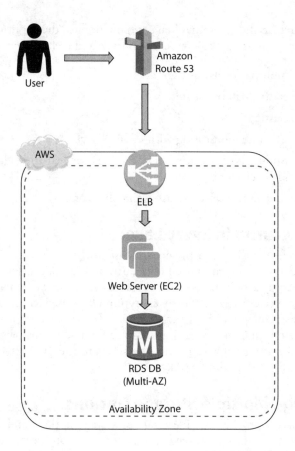

to host the database, as shown in Figure 9-7. In this example, you are only using the EBS volume to store the data. To leverage multiple storage options and optimize the architecture, you can do lots of things.

You can start by moving any static objects (images, videos, CSS, JavaScript) from the web server (EC2 servers) to S3 and then serving those objects via CloudFront. These files can be served via an S3 origin and then globally cached and distributed via CloudFront. This will take some load off your web servers and allow you to reduce your footprint in the web tier. The next thing you can do is move the session information to a NoSQL database like DynamoDB. If you do this, your session information won't be stored in the EC2 servers. Therefore, when you scale up or down the EC2 servers, you won't lose session information, and thus it won't impact the users. This is called making the tier *stateless*. You can also use ElastiCache to store some of the common database query results, which will prevent hitting the database too much. Figure 9-8 displays how you can leverage multiple storage options in this case.

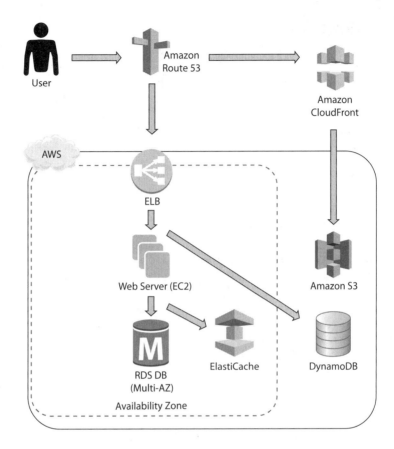

Figure 9-8
Leveraging
multiple storage
options

Implement Elasticity

Elasticity is one of the major benefits that you get by moving to the cloud. Gone are the days when you have to over-provision the hardware to meet the peak demand. With the AWS cloud, you just need to provision what is needed for now without worrying about the peak since you know that AWS provides elasticity, and you should be able to scale up and down any time to meet your demand. These are your best friends when implementing elasticity:

- **Auto Scaling**   Use Auto Scaling to automatically scale your infrastructure by adding or removing EC2 instances to your environment.
- **Elastic load balancing**   Use ELB to distribute the load across EC2 instances in multiple availability zones.
- **DynamoDB**   Use DynamoDB to maintain the user state information.

Think Parallel

AWS gives you the ability to experiment with different parallel architectures, and you should leverage all of them to make sure whatever you are doing will go quickly. Use SNS and SQS to build components that run in parallel and communicate (state, workflow, job status, and so on) by sending messages and notifications.

For example, you could publish a message to a topic every time a new image is uploaded. Independent processes, each reading from a separate SQS queue, could generate thumbnails, perform image recognition, and store metadata about the image.

- **Use multithreading and concurrent requests to the cloud service** Submitting multiple requests to cloud services shouldn't be done sequentially. Use threads to spawn simultaneous requests; a thread waiting for a response from a cloud service is not consuming CPU cycles, so you can spawn more threads than you have CPU cores to parallelize and speed up a job.

- **Run parallel MapReduce jobs** Amazon Elastic MapReduce automatically spins up a Hadoop implementation of the MapReduce framework on Amazon EC2 instances, subdividing the data in a job flow into smaller chunks so that they can be processed (the "map" function) in parallel and eventually recombining the processed data into the final solution (the "reduce" function). Amazon S3 serves as the source for the data being analyzed and as the output destination for the end results. Say you run the EMR job using just one node and that takes ten hours. Let's assume that the cost of running the EMR node is $1 per hour, so if your job runs for ten hours, you are paying $10. Now instead of running this job in one EMR node for ten hours, you can spin ten nodes in the EMR cluster. Since you have ten times more resources to process the job, your job will be finished in one hour instead of ten. You will pay $1 for each server for every hour, so that's ten servers for one hour each, making a total cost of $10. If you compare the prices, you will notice that they both cost $10, but the job took ten hours previously; with MapReduce you are able to finish the same job in just one hour. The only difference this time is you have leveraged parallelism.

- **Use elastic load balancing to distribute load** Use ELB to distribute incoming traffic across your Amazon EC2 instances in a single availability zone or multiple availability zones. Elastic load balancing automatically scales its request-handling capacity in response to incoming application traffic.

- **Use Amazon Kinesis for concurrent processing of data** Using Kinesis, you can have multiple applications process a stream of data concurrently. Have one Amazon Kinesis application running real-time analytics and the other sending data to Amazon S3 from the same Amazon Kinesis stream.

Lambda lets you run thousands of functions in parallel, and performance remains consistently high regardless of the frequency of events. Use Lambda for back-end services that perform at scale.

When uploading files in S3, you can use multipart upload and ranged gets.

Loosely Couple Your Architecture

Always design architectures with independent components; the looser they're coupled, the larger they scale. Design every component as a black box. Build separate services instead of something that is tightly interacting with something else. Use common interfaces or common APIs between the components. For example, if you are building an application for transcoding the video, you can do everything in one shot or can split the steps into multiple small processes. Don't try to do all these tasks in one step: upload the file, transcode the video, and send the user a mail notification. If the transcode fails, you need to restart from the upload. Instead of that, if you split the process into three independent steps (upload video, transcode, and send mail notification), then even if the second step fails, you won't have to start from scratch.

There Are No Constraints in the AWS Cloud

If you are coming from an on-premise ecosystem, often the resources are constrained. If your instance needs more CPU or more RAM or if your application needs a finely tuned I/O system, it takes a long time to get that. In AWS you don't really have to worry about any type of constraint. Everything is available in just a few clicks. In the cloud, since there are new technologies available, you may try something out of the box to make the best use of it. For example, in an on-premises environment, you can host your web server in a bigger box, say, of 32 cores, in the cloud. Instead of hosting your web server on one server with 32 cores, you can use four servers or eight cores each to host the web server. You can spread these web servers across different AZs to minimize the risk. You should try to use more AZs whenever possible. Here's an example to explain this:

- **First case using two AZs**   Say you have four web servers, and you have deployed two in each AZ. The probability of one of the AZs going down is 50 percent, so if one of the AZs goes down, you will immediately lose 50 percent of your resource.

- **Second case using three AZs**   If you use three AZs, then the probability of one AZ going down is 33.3 percent. When this happens, you will lose 33.3 percent of your resource, which is always better than losing 50 percent of your resource. Similarly, if you use four AZs, you will lose 25 percent of your resource, and if you use five AZs, you will lose 20 percent of your resource, respectively.

In an on-premise world, whenever there is an issue with hardware, you try to troubleshoot and fix it. For example, the memory can go bad or there might be an issue with the disk or processor. Instead of wasting valuable time and resources diagnosing problems and replacing components, favor a "rip-and-replace" approach. Simply decommission the entire component and spin up a fully functional replacement. By doing this, you don't have to spend any time troubleshooting the faulty part.

Chapter Review

In this chapter, you learned about the five pillars of the AWS Well-Architected Framework.

Operations excellence is measured in terms of how you are able to support the business. If you have aligned your operations teams to support the business SLAs, you are in good shape. The design principles for operational excellence in the cloud are to perform operations as code, document everything, push small changes instead of big, refine operating procedures often, and anticipate failure.

The security pillar makes sure that your environment is secure from all aspects. These are the design principles for security: have a strong identity foundation, enable traceability, implement security at all the layers, secure the data, automate for security, and plan for security events.

The performance pillar is all about need for speed. This pillar focuses on performance efficiency and how your business can benefit from it. It has the following design principles: go global in a few clicks, leverage new technologies such as serverless, consume advanced technology, leverage multiple technologies, and experiment more often.

The reliability pillar makes sure that the solution can recover from various failures, determines how much outage a business can handle, determines how to work backward from the RTO and RPO levels, and so on. These are the design principles for reliability in the cloud: test recovery procedures, automate recovery from failure, scale horizontally, stop guessing capacity, and automate changes to the system.

The cost optimization pillar helps you cut down on costs and provides you with the ability to avoid or eliminate unneeded costs or suboptimal resources. The cost optimization pillar consists of the following design principles: choose the best consumption model, use managed services, measure the overall efficiency, analyze the expenditure, and stop spending on a data center.

These are the best practices in the cloud:

- Design for failures.
- Build security in every layer.
- Leverage multiple storage options.
- Implement elasticity.
- Think parallel.
- Loosely couple your architecture.

There are no constraints in the AWS cloud.

Questions

1. How do you protect access to and the use of the AWS account's root user credentials? (Choose two.)

   A. Never use the root user

   B. Use Multi-Factor Authentication (MFA) along with the root user

    C. Use the root user only for important operations

    D. Lock the root user

2. What AWS service can you use to manage multiple accounts?

    A. Use QuickSight

    B. Use Organization

    C. Use IAM

    D. Use roles

3. What is an important criterion when planning your network topology in AWS?

    A. Use both IPv4 and IPv6 IP addresses.

    B. Use nonoverlapping IP addresses.

    C. You should have the same IP address that you have on-premise.

    D. Reserve as many EIP addresses as you can since IPv4 IP addresses are limited.

4. If you want to provision your infrastructure in a different region, what is the quickest way to mimic your current infrastructure in a different region?

    A. Use a CloudFormation template

    B. Make a blueprint of the current infrastructure and provision the same manually in the other region

    C. Use CodeDeploy to deploy the code to the new region

    D. Use the VPC Wizard to lay down your infrastructure in a different region

5. Amazon Glacier is designed for which of the following? (Choose two.)

    A. Active database storage

    B. Infrequently accessed data

    C. Data archives

    D. Frequently accessed data

    E. Cached session data

6. Which of the following will occur when an EC2 instance in a VPC with an associated elastic IP is stopped and started? (Choose two.)

    A. The elastic IP will be dissociated from the instance.

    B. All data on instance-store devices will be lost.

    C. All data on Elastic Block Store (EBS) devices will be lost.

    D. The Elastic Network Interface (ENI) is detached.

    E. The underlying host for the instance is changed.

7. An instance is launched into the public subnet of a VPC. Which of the following must be done for it to be accessible from the Internet?

   A. Attach an elastic IP to the instance.

   B. Nothing. The instance is accessible from the Internet.

   C. Launch a NAT gateway and route all traffic to it.

   D. Make an entry in the route table, passing all traffic going outside the VPC to the NAT instance.

8. To protect S3 data from both accidental deletion and accidental overwriting, you should:

   A. Enable S3 versioning on the bucket

   B. Access S3 data using only signed URLs

   C. Disable S3 delete using an IAM bucket policy

   D. Enable S3 reduced redundancy storage

   E. Enable multifactor authentication (MFA) protected access

9. Your web application front end consists of multiple EC2 instances behind an elastic load balancer. You configured an elastic load balancer to perform health checks on these EC2 instances. If an instance fails to pass health checks, which statement will be true?

   A. The instance is replaced automatically by the elastic load balancer.

   B. The instance gets terminated automatically by the elastic load balancer.

   C. The ELB stops sending traffic to the instance that failed its health check.

   D. The instance gets quarantined by the elastic load balancer for root-cause analysis.

10. You are building a system to distribute confidential training videos to employees. Using CloudFront, what method could be used to serve content that is stored in S3 but not publicly accessible from S3 directly?

    A. Create an origin access identity (OAI) for CloudFront and grant access to the objects in your S3 bucket to that OAI

    B. Add the CloudFront account security group called "amazon-cf/amazon-cf-sg" to the appropriate S3 bucket policy

    C. Create an Identity and Access Management (IAM) user for CloudFront and grant access to the objects in your S3 bucket to that IAM user

    D. Create an S3 bucket policy that lists the CloudFront distribution ID as the principal and the target bucket as the Amazon resource name (ARN)

Answers

1. **A, B.** It is critical to keep the root user's credentials protected, and to this end, AWS recommends attaching MFA to the root user and locking the credentials with the MFA in a physically secured location. IAM allows you to create and manage other nonroot user permissions, as well as establish access levels to resources.

2. **B**. QuickSight is used for visualization. IAM can be leveraged within accounts, and roles are also within accounts.

3. **B**. Using IPv4 or IPv6 depends on what you are trying to do. You can't have the same IP address, or when you integrate the application on-premise with the cloud, you will end up with overlapping IP addresses, and hence your application in the cloud won't be able to talk with the on-premise application. You should allocate only the number of EIPs you need. If you don't use an EIP and allocate it, you are going to incur a charge on it.

4. **A**. Creating a blueprint and working backward from there is going to be too much effort. Why you would do that when CloudFormation can do it for you? CodeDeploy is used for deploying code, and the VPC Wizard is used to create VPCs.

5. **B, C**. Amazon Glacier is used for archival storage and for archival purposes.

6. **A, D**. If you have any data in the instance store, that will also be lost, but you should not choose this option since the question is regarding elastic IP.

7. **B**. Since the instance is created in the public subnet and an Internet gateway is already attached with a public subnet, you don't have to do anything explicitly.

8. **A**. Signed URLs won't help, even if you disable the ability to delete.

9. **C**. The ELB stops sending traffic to the instance that failed its health check.

10. **A**. Create an OAI for CloudFront and grant access to the objects in your S3 bucket to that OAI.

About the Digital Content

This book comes complete with Total Tester customizable practice exam software containing 130 practice exam questions. The software is provided on the CD-ROM that accompanies the print book and is also available online for download. The Total Tester software on the CD-ROM can be installed on any Windows Vista/7/8/10 computer and must be installed to access the Total Tester practice exams. If you do not have a CD-ROM drive or wish to access an online version of the test engine, please see the "TotalTester Online" section in this appendix for instructions.

About the Total Tester

The Total Tester provides you with a simulation of the AWS Certified Solutions Architect Associate (SAA-C01) exam. Exams can be taken in Practice Mode, Exam Mode, or Custom Mode. Practice Mode provides an assistance window with hints, references to the book, explanations of the correct and incorrect answers, and the option to check your answer as you take the test. Exam Mode provides a simulation of the actual exam. The number of questions, the types of questions, and the time allowed are intended to be an accurate representation of the exam environment. Custom Mode allows you to create custom exams from selected domains or chapters, and you can further customize the number of questions and time allowed.

CD-ROM

Installing and running from the software from the CD-ROM requires Windows Vista or later and 30MB of hard disk space for full installation, in addition to a current or prior major release of Chrome, Firefox, Internet Explorer, or Safari. To run, the screen resolution must be set to 1024×768 or higher.

From the main screen of the CD-ROM menu, you may install the Total Tester by clicking the Total Tester Practice Exams button. This will begin the installation process and place an icon on your desktop and in your Start menu. To run the Total Tester, navigate to Start | (All) Programs | Total Seminars, or double-click the icon on your desktop.

To take a test, launch the program and select AWS SAA-C01 from the Installed Question Packs list. You can then select Practice Mode, Exam Mode, or Custom Mode. All exams provide an overall grade and a grade broken down by domain.

If you are unable to access the software from the CD-ROM, please see the following sections for details.

Your Total Seminars Training Hub Account

To get access to the online content, you will need to create an account on the Total Seminars Training Hub. Registration is free and you will be able to track all your online content using your account. You may also opt in if you wish to receive marketing information from McGraw-Hill Education or Total Seminars, but this is not required for you to gain access to the online content.

Privacy Notice

McGraw-Hill Education values your privacy. Please be sure to read the Privacy Notice available during registration to see how the information you have provided will be used. You may view our Corporate Customer Privacy Policy by visiting the McGraw-Hill Education Privacy Center. Visit the mheducation.com site and click on "Privacy" at the bottom of the page.

Single User License Terms and Conditions

Online access to the digital content included with this book is governed by the McGraw-Hill Education License Agreement outlined next. By using this digital content you agree to the terms of that license.

Duration of License   Access to your online content through the Total Seminars Training Hub will expire one year from the date the publisher declares the book out of print.

Your purchase of this McGraw-Hill Education product, including its access code, through a retail store is subject to the refund policy of that store.

The Content is a copyrighted work of McGraw-Hill Education and McGraw-Hill Education reserves all rights in and to the Content. The Work is © 2019 by McGraw-Hill Education, LLC.

TotalTester Online

As with the CD-ROM test engine, TotalTester Online provides you with a simulation of the AWS Certified Solutions Architect Associate (SAA-C01) exam. Exams can be taken in Practice Mode or Exam Mode. Practice Mode provides an assistance window with hints, references to the book, explanations of the correct and incorrect answers, and the option to check your answer as you take the test. Exam Mode provides a simulation of the actual exam. The number of questions, the types of questions, and the time allowed are intended to be an accurate representation of the exam environment. The option to customize your quiz allows you to create custom exams from selected domains or chapters, and you can further customize the number of questions and time allowed.

System Requirements   The current and previous major versions of the following desktop browsers are recommended and supported: Chrome, Microsoft Edge, Firefox, and Safari. These browsers update frequently and sometimes an update may cause compatibility issues with the TotalTester Online or other content hosted on the Training Hub.

If you run into a problem using one of these browsers, please try using another until the problem is resolved.

Access To access TotalTester Online, follow the instructions below to register and activate your Total Seminars Training Hub account. When you register you will be taken to the Total Seminars Training Hub. From the Training Hub Home page, select AWS-C01 from the "Study" drop-down menu at the top of the page, or from the list of "Your Topics" on the Home page. You can then select the option to customize your quiz and begin testing yourself in Practice Mode or Exam Mode. All exams provide an overall grade and a grade broken down by domain.

To register and activate your Total Seminars Training Hub account, simply follow these easy steps.

1. Go to **hub.totalsem.com/mheclaim**.

2. To register and create a new Training Hub account, enter your e-mail address, name, and password. No further information (such as credit card number) is required to create an account.

3. If you already have a Total Seminars Training Hub account, select "Log in" and enter your e-mail and password.

4. Enter your Product Key: `wq55-f74v-gq2n`

5. Click to accept the user license terms.

6. Click "Register and Claim" to create your account. You will be taken to the Training Hub and have access to the content for this book.

 NOTE Once you have registered, you may access the exam at any time by going to **hub.totalsem.com** and log in.

Technical Support

For questions regarding the Total Tester software or operation of the CD-ROM included with the print book, visit **www.totalsem.com** or e-mail **support@totalsem.com**.

For questions regarding book content, e-mail **hep_customer-service@mheducation .com**. For customers outside the United States, e-mail **international_cs@mheducation.com**.

AAAA An IPv6 address record.

ACL Access control list.

ACM AWS Certificate Manager.

AES Advanced Encryption Standard.

ALB Application load balancer.

Amazon Athena A serverless, interactive query service that enables users to easily analyze data in Amazon S3 using standard SQL.

Amazon Aurora Amazon's relational database built for the cloud. It supports two open source RDBMS engines: MySQL and PostgreSQL.

Amazon CloudFront The global content delivery network (CDN) service of AWS.

Amazon CloudSearch A fully managed web service for search solutions.

Amazon CloudWatch A monitoring service for AWS cloud resources.

Amazon Cognito A service that lets you manage users of your web and mobile apps quickly.

Amazon DynamoDB Amazon's NoSQL database.

Amazon ElastiCache A service that helps in deploying an in-memory cache or data store in the cloud.

Amazon Elasticsearch Service A fully managed web service that hosts Elasticsearch clusters in the AWS cloud.

Amazon EMR A managed hosted Hadoop framework in the cloud.

Amazon Glacier Amazon's archival storage.

Amazon Kinesis A service that allows you to ingest real-time data.

Amazon Lex A full service for building chatbots.

Amazon Lightsail A simple virtual private server (VPS) solution in the cloud.

Amazon Polly A fully managed service that converts text into lifelike speech.

Amazon Rekognition A fully managed image recognition service.

Amazon QuickSight   A managed business analytics service.

Amazon SWF   Amazon Simple Workflow Service.

Amazon VPC Flow Logs   Used to capture information about the IP traffic going to and from network interfaces in your VPC.

AMI   Amazon machine image.

API Gateway   A managed service to create, publish, maintain, monitor, and secure APIs at any scale.

archive   Where data is stored in Amazon Glacier.

ASG   Auto Scaling group.

Auto Scaling   A technology used by AWS to scale up and scale down EC2 instances.

AWS   Amazon Web Services.

AWS Batch   A service that enables users to efficiently run hundreds of thousands of batch computing jobs on AWS.

AWS CloudFormation   A tool for deploying AWS resource stacks.

AWS CloudHSM   Hardware-based key storage for regulatory compliance

AWS CloudTrail   A managed service that records AWS API calls.

AWS CodeBuild   A fully managed build service that builds and compiles source code.

AWS CodeCommit   A managed service through which you can host any private Git repository.

AWS CodeDeploy   A fully managed service that automates code deployments to any instance.

AWS CodePipeline   A fully managed continuous integration and continuous delivery service.

AWS Config   A fully managed service that helps to track configuration change.

AWS Device Farm   Service for testing mobile devices.

AWS Elastic Beanstalk   A service used for run and manage web apps

AWS Greengrass   A managed service for running IoT application in the AWS cloud.

AWS Lambda   Enables you to run code without provisioning or managing any servers or infrastructure.

AWS Marketplace   An online store where you can buy software that runs on AWS.

AWS Mobile Hub   A web service for deploying mobile applications.

AWS OpsWorks   A configuration management service that provides managed instances of Chef and Puppet.

AWS Organizations   Provides policy-based management for multiple AWS accounts

AWS Personal Health Dashboard   It provides Personalized view of AWS service health

AWS Step Functions   The visual workflow service of AWS.

AWS Systems Manager   Gives you visibility and control of your infrastructure on AWS

AWS Trusted Advisor   An online resource to help you reduce cost, increase performance, and improve security by optimizing your AWS environment.

AZ   Availability zone.

BGP   Border Gateway Protocol.

Bucket   Container for storing objects in Amazon S3.

CAA   Certification authority authorization.

CDN   Content delivery network.

CIDR   Classless Inter-Domain Routing.

CJIS   Criminal justice information services.

CLI   Command-line interface.

CNAME   Canonical name record.

CRR   Cross-regional replication.

CSA   Cloud Security Alliance.

CSM   Cloud security model.

CSV   Comma-separated values.

DBMS   Database management system.

DDL   Data Definition Language.

DDoS   Distributed denial of service.

DHCP   Dynamic Host Configuration Protocol.

DIACAP   The DoD Information Assurance Certification and Accreditation Process.

Direct Connect   Using Direct Connect you can establish private, dedicated network connectivity from your data center to AWS.

Directory Service   Directory service built on Microsoft Active Directory in the cloud.

DLQ   A dead-letter queue lets you set aside and isolate messages that can't be processed correctly to determine why their processing didn't succeed.

DML   Data Manipulation Language.

DMS   Database Migration Service.

DoD   Department of Defense.

EBS   Elastic Block Storage. It provides persistent block storage for EC2 instances.

EC2   Amazon Elastic Compute Cloud.

EC2-Classic   The original release of Amazon EC2.

ECS   EC2 Container Service.

edge location   Used to serve content to end users.

EFS   Elastic File System. Provides shared file system for EC2.

EIP   Elastic IP address.

ELB   Elastic load balancing.

ENI   Elastic Network Interface.

ERP   Enterprise resource planning.

ETL   Extract, transform, and load.

FedRAMP   Federal Risk and Authorization Management Program.

FERPA   Family Educational Rights and Privacy Act.

FIFO   First in, first out.

FIPS   Federal Information Processing Standards.

FISMA   The Federal Information Security Management Act.

fleet   A collection of EC2 servers.

GPU   Graphics processing unit.

HA   High availability.

HIPAA   Health Insurance Portability and Accountability Act.

HTML   Hypertext Markup Language.

HTTP   Hypertext Transfer Protocol.

HTTPS   HTTP Secure.

HVM   Hardware virtual machine.

IaaS   Infrastructure as a Service.

IAM   Identity and Access Management.

ICMP   Internet Control Message Protocol.

IG   Internet gateway, a component of VPC that allows your VPC to communicate with the Internet.

instance   An EC2 server is also referred to an instance.

instance store   Local storage in EC2 server.

inventory   List of Glacier archives.

IoT   Internet of Things.

IP   Internet Protocol.

ISAE   International Standard on Assurance Engagements.

ISO   International Organization for Standardization.

ITAR   International Traffic in Arms Regulations.

JDBC   Java Database Connectivity.

JSON   JavaScript Object Notation.

KMS   Key Management Service.

LAMP stack   Linux, Apache, MySQL, and PHP (LAMP) stack.

MAC   Media Access Control address.

MFA   Multifactor authentication.

MPAA   Motion Picture Association of America.

MTCS   Multi-Tier Cloud Security.

MX   Mail exchange record.

NACL   Network access control list. This acts as a firewall at the subnet level.

NAPTR   Name authority pointer record.

NAT   Network Address Translation.

NFS   Network File System.

NIST   National Institute of Standards and Technology.

NLB   Network load balancer.

NS   Name server record.

ODBC   Open Database Connectivity.

OLAP   Online analytical processing.

OLTP   Online transaction processing.

PaaS   Platform as a Service.

PCI   Payment Card Industry.

PHP   Hypertext Preprocessor.

PIOPS   Provisioned input/output operations per second.

POP   Point of presence. This is also known as an edge location.

PTR   Pointer record.

PV   Paravirtual.

Redshift   Amazon Redshift is a fully managed petabyte-scale data warehouse service.

RDBMS   Relational database management system.

RDS   Amazon's relational database service.

region   An AWS region is a unique geography in the world where AWS data centers are hosted.

REST   Representational State Transfer.

root user   Owner of the AWS account.

root volume   Instance root device contains the image that is used to boot the instance.

Route 53   Domain Name System (DNS) web service.

route table   Table consisting of routes that determine where the traffic is directed.

RPM   Revolutions per minute.

S3   Simple Shared Storage.

S3-IA   Simple Shared Storage Infrequent Access.

S3-RR   Simple Shared Storage Reduced Redundancy.

SaaS   Software as a Service.

SAML   Security Assertion Markup Language.

SDK   Software development kit.

security group   Firewall for EC2 instance.

SES   Amazon Simple Email Service.

SLA   Service level agreement. This is a commitment between a service provider and a client.

SMS   Server Migration Service.

Snowball/Snowball Edge   Amazon-owned network-attached storage (NAS) devices, used to ship customer data to AWS.

Snowmobile   Exabyte-scale data transfer service.

SNS   Simple Notification Service.

SOA   Start of authority record.

SOAP   Simple Object Access Protocol.

SOC   Service Organization Control.

SPF   Sender policy framework.

SQL   Structured Query Language.

SQLi   SQL injection.

SQS   Amazon Simple Queue Service.

SRV   Service locator.

SSAE   Standards for Attestation Engagements.

SSD   Solid-state drive.

SSH   Secure Shell.

SSL   Secure Sockets Layer.

SSO   Single sign-on.

storage gateway   A service that helps to seamlessly integrate on-premise storage with AWS cloud storage.

STS   Security Token Service.

subnet   Logical subdivision of an IP network.

TCP/IP   Transmission Control Protocol (TCP)/Internet Protocol (IP).

TDE   Transparent Database Encryption.

TLS   Transport Layer Security.

TXT   A text record.

UDP   User Datagram Protocol.

vault   Like a safe deposit box or locker in Amazon Glacier where archives are stored.

VPC   Virtual private cloud.

VPG   Virtual private gateway.

VPN   Virtual private network.

VPN CloudHub   Use to create multiple AWS hardware VPN connections.

WAF (1) Web Application Firewall. (2) Well Architected Framework.

webACL Web access control list.

WORM Write once, read many.

XML Extensible Markup Language.

XSS Cross-site scripting.

INDEX